I0890896

Contemporary Management Approaches to the Global Hospitality and Tourism Industry

Abraham Pius
Arden University, UK

Husam H. Alharahsheh
University of Wales Trinity Saint David, UK

Adenike A. Adesanmi
University of East London, UK

A volume in the Advances in Hospitality, Tourism, and the Services Industry (AHTSI) Book Series

IGI Global
DISSEMINATOR OF KNOWLEDGE

Published in the United States of America by
IGI Global
Business Science Reference (an imprint of IGI Global)
701 E. Chocolate Avenue
Hershey PA, USA 17033
Tel: 717-533-8845
Fax: 717-533-8661
E-mail: cust@igi-global.com
Web site: http://www.igi-global.com

Copyright © 2020 by IGI Global. All rights reserved. No part of this publication may be reproduced, stored or distributed in any form or by any means, electronic or mechanical, including photocopying, without written permission from the publisher.
Product or company names used in this set are for identification purposes only. Inclusion of the names of the products or companies does not indicate a claim of ownership by IGI Global of the trademark or registered trademark.

Library of Congress Cataloging-in-Publication Data

Names: Pius, Abraham, 1962- editor. | Alharahsheh, Husam H., 1992- editor. | Adesanmi, Adenike A., 1983- editor.
Title: Contemporary management approaches to the global hospitality and tourism industry / Abraham Pius, Husam H. Alharahsheh, and Adenike A. Adesanmi, editors.
Description: Hershey, PA : Business Science Reference, 2020. | Includes bibliographical references. | Summary: "This book examines new management strategies, practices, and trends in the global hospitality and tourism industry"-- Provided by publisher.
Identifiers: LCCN 2019037758 (print) | LCCN 2019037759 (ebook) | ISBN 9781799822042 (h/c) | ISBN 9781799822059 (s/c) | ISBN 9781799822066 (eISBN)
Subjects: LCSH: Hospitality industry--Management.
Classification: LCC TX911.3.M27 C655 2020 (print) | LCC TX911.3.M27 (ebook) | DDC 910.68--dc23
LC record available at https://lccn.loc.gov/2019037758
LC ebook record available at https://lccn.loc.gov/2019037759

This book is published in the IGI Global book series Advances in Hospitality, Tourism, and the Services Industry (AHTSI) (ISSN: 2475-6547; eISSN: 2475-6555)

British Cataloguing in Publication Data
A Cataloguing in Publication record for this book is available from the British Library.

All work contributed to this book is new, previously-unpublished material.
The views expressed in this book are those of the authors, but not necessarily of the publisher.

For electronic access to this publication, please contact: eresources@igi-global.com.

Advances in Hospitality, Tourism, and the Services Industry (AHTSI) Book Series

ISSN:2475-6547
EISSN:2475-6555

Editor-in-Chief: Maximiliano Korstanje, University of Palermo, Argentina

MISSION

Globally, the hospitality, travel, tourism, and services industries generate a significant percentage of revenue and represent a large portion of the business world. Even in tough economic times, these industries thrive as individuals continue to spend on leisure and recreation activities as well as services.

The Advances in Hospitality, Tourism, and the Services Industry (AHTSI) book series offers diverse publications relating to the management, promotion, and profitability of the leisure, recreation, and services industries. Highlighting current research pertaining to various topics within the realm of hospitality, travel, tourism, and services management, the titles found within the AHTSI book series are pertinent to the research and professional needs of managers, business practitioners, researchers, and upper-level students studying in the field.

COVERAGE

- Sustainable Tourism
- Destination Marketing and Management
- Leisure & Business Travel
- Customer Service Issues
- Health and Wellness Tourism
- Travel Agency Management
- Tourism and the Environment
- Service Design
- Hotel Management
- Food and Beverage Management

IGI Global is currently accepting manuscripts for publication within this series. To submit a proposal for a volume in this series, please contact our Acquisition Editors at Acquisitions@igi-global.com or visit: http://www.igi-global.com/publish/.

The Advances in Hospitality, Tourism, and the Services Industry (AHTSI) Book Series (ISSN 2475-6547) is published by IGI Global, 701 E. Chocolate Avenue, Hershey, PA 17033-1240, USA, www.igi-global.com. This series is composed of titles available for purchase individually; each title is edited to be contextually exclusive from any other title within the series. For pricing and ordering information please visit http://www.igi-global.com/book-series/advances-hospitality-tourism-services-industry/121014. Postmaster: Send all address changes to above address. Copyright © 2020 IGI Global. All rights, including translation in other languages reserved by the publisher. No part of this series may be reproduced or used in any form or by any means – graphics, electronic, or mechanical, including photocopying, recording, taping, or information and retrieval systems – without written permission from the publisher, except for non commercial, educational use, including classroom teaching purposes. The views expressed in this series are those of the authors, but not necessarily of IGI Global.

Titles in this Series

For a list of additional titles in this series, please visit:
https://www.igi-global.com/book/contemporary-management-approaches-global-hospitality/235709

Handbook of Research on the Impacts, Challenges, and Policy Responses to Oertourism
Cláudia Ribeiro de Almeida (University of Algarve, Portugal) Alfred Quintano (Independent Researcher, Malta) Moisés Simancas (University of La Laguna, Spain) Raquel Huete (University of Alicante, Spain) and Zélia Breda (University of Aveiro, Portugal)
Business Science Reference • © 2020 • 447pp • H/C (ISBN: 9781799822240) • US $285.00

Economic, Educational, and Touristic Development in Asia
Bryan Christiansen (Global Training Group, Ltd, UK) and Hakan Sezerel (Anadolu University, Turkey)
Business Science Reference • © 2020 • 400pp • H/C (ISBN: 9781799822394) • US $215.00

Industrial and Managerial Solutions for Tourism Enterprises
Atilla Akbaba (Izmir Katip Çelebi University, Turkey) and Volkan Altıntaş (Izmir Katip Celebi University, Turkey)
Business Science Reference • © 2020 • 300pp • H/C (ISBN: 9781799830306) • US $225.00

Handbook of Research on Smart Technology Applications in the Tourism Industry
Evrim Çeltek (Gaziosmanpasa University, Turkey)
Business Science Reference • © 2020 • 569pp • H/C (ISBN: 9781799819899) • US $295.00

Global Opportunities and Challenges for Rural and Mountain Tourism
Devkant Kala (University of Petroleum and Energy Studies, India) and Satish Chandra Bagri (Hemvati Nandan Bahuguna Garhwal University, India)
Business Science Reference • © 2020 • 354pp • H/C (ISBN: 9781799813026) • US $225.00

Organizational Behavior Challenges in the Tourism Industry
Şule Aydin (Nevsehir Haci Bektas Veli University, Turkey) Bekir Bora Dedeoglu (Nevsehir Haci Bektas Veli University, Turkey) and Ömer Çoban (Nevsehir Haci Bektas Veli University, Turkey)
Business Science Reference • © 2020 • 524pp • H/C (ISBN: 9781799814740) • US $225.00

IGI Global
DISSEMINATOR OF KNOWLEDGE

701 East Chocolate Avenue, Hershey, PA 17033, USA
Tel: 717-533-8845 x100 • Fax: 717-533-8661
E-Mail: cust@igi-global.com • www.igi-global.com

Editorial Advisory Board

Edwin Agwu, *Lagos Business School, Nigeria*
Nisrin Alfreahat, *BBP University, London, UK*
Batool Alharahsheh, *Kings College London, UK*
Olusoyi Richard Ashaye, *Brunel Business School, Brunel University London, UK & University of Wales Trinity St. David, London, UK*
Şule Aydin, *Nevsehir Haci Bektas Veli University, Turkey*
Zelia Breda, *University of Aveiro, Portugal*
Fátima Lampreia Carvalho, *University of Algarve, Portugal*
Mihaela Dariescu, *University of Roehampton, UK & London College of Contemporary Arts, UK*
Gorete Dinis, *Polytechnic Institute of Portalegre, Portugal*
Silvia Fernandes, *University of Algarve, Portugal*
Imad Guenane, *London College of Contemporary Arts, UK*
Eda Özgül Katlav, *Nevsehir Haci Bektas Veli University, Turkey*
Tamara Kliček, *I-Shou University, Taiwan*
Anupama S. Kotur, *Symbiosis Center for Management Studies, Symbiosis International University (Deemed), India*
Chad Manian, *Berlin School of Business and Innovation, Germany*
Mudassar Mehmood, *Nelson College London, UK*
Obioma Nwaogbe, *Federal University of Technology, Minna, Nigeria*
Dominic Owusu, *University of Cape Coast, Ghana*
Adriana Santos, *University of Aveiro, Portugal*
Natasha Saqib, *University of Kashmir, South Campus, India*

Table of Contents

Detailed Table of Contents

Wine tourism is a synthesis of elements from the wine and tourism industries that come together to form the wine tourism experience. Several elements form a part of a much larger wine tourism system and contribute directly and/or indirectly to creating and developing a wine tourism destination. Maharashtra in India has come to be popularly known as the 'wine bowl' of India, producing some of the award-winning and internationally acclaimed wines. This chapter aims to examine all those elements that have played a part in and are necessary to develop a competitive and sustainable wine tourism destination in Maharashtra. The singular objective of this research chapter is to propose a conceptual framework of the wine tourism system. The research largely relies on secondary data as well as results of previous empirical researches conducted by the author. The wider contribution of this chapter lies in developing and illustrating a model of wine tourism system. This system model can be instrumental in defining all those components that are most critical to the growth of a wine tourism destination.

This chapter is set to shed light on how the hospitality and tourism sector is to shape their assets and liquidity to either begin a new venture or expand an existing one. The first part of the chapter will give an elaborate discussion about raising financial capital in the hospitality and tourism sector. This will strengthen the points that are made under capital structure formation. Financial knowledge of budgeting is an area that deserves its place in these sectors; this is the third major highlight of the chapter. The issue of understanding financial statements, especially its use in making predictions through ratio analysis, require a thorough explanation. This is therefore the next point. The limitations and usefulness of ratio analysis will be touched upon. Finally, in this chapter, determining demand in the hospitality and tourism sector is a contemporary issue, and the review of this will give a better viewpoint.

By the end of this chapter, it is expected that one will be able to 1) establish various sources of funding that are available to a business in the hospitality industry in the international market, 2) evaluate the advantages and disadvantages of these sources of finance, 3) establish the sources that are available or unavailable for the hospitality business as compared to other industries, 4) evaluate an investment in hospitality industry using various capital budgeting techniques, 5) develop financial statement for businesses in hospitality industry, and 6) evaluate the financial performance of companies in hospitality industry using ratio analysis.

Foreword

The book has gathered national and international attention of leading practitioners and researchers in the fields of hospitality and tourism management in terms of chapters contributions. Authors of all chapters as well as the editors have reflected their long experience and research interest into their work providing a cutting-edge research and application to the field.

The book is focused on ten key subjects as the following:

1. Quality management approaches: The authors of this topic have explored key aspects of quality management, and also have provided several key activities to enable readers and educators to further apply to certain contexts. It has included variety of examples and different applications.
2. Social media use: The authors of this topic have focused on the key developments of using social media as a tool of capturing value and interaction. It has explored different communication models, and also provided further depth and application by including a trendy case study. The topic is considered as one of the most contemporary issues in the sector as it has changed the way firms and customers communicate between themselves.
3. Technology as a contemporary development in the field: The author of this topic/chapter have reflected how developments in information and communication technologies have changed the way businesses communicate. It has also discussed key advantages gained as a result, and how firms can use it as a competitive advantage tool.
4. Corporate culture: The author of this topic has discussed in details how corporate culture can further enhance the overall performance of organizations with more focus on hotels. Different sources were used to enhance the quality of the work and its applications.
5. Crisis and tourism destinations: The author of this topic has provided an interesting case study to further examine the impact of crisis event on the demand for tourism. The work is supported by different academic arguments

and contemporary applications to further deepen understanding within the discipline.

6. The use of mystery shopper programs in tourism: The authors of this topic have reflected the importance of such programs for businesses within the tourism field, and how they can be used as powerful tools to manage quality and expectations during delivery process of service.
7. Sustainable tourism: The authors of this topic have deeply discussed different aspects of sustainable tourism. Different arguments, evidences, and examples have been included to enhance application, and further understanding within this specific discipline. It is interesting to note that the aspect of sustainability is a widely discussed as one of the main challenges faced across different sectors including hospitality and tourism.
8. Profile, motivations and experiences: The authors of this topic have primarily focused on Portuguese solo female travels. The work further explores the literature on solo female travel, seeking to understand the motivations, as well as the difficulties encountered during the journey.
9. Tourism Wine system: The work developed by the author of this topic have reflected depth and application of Tourism Wine system, and how this contribute to enhancement of tourism destination. Meaningful examples and discussions were included, and followed by inclusive conclusions. This niche topic can reflect one of the new cotemporary developments in the sector.
10. Finance in hospitality and tourism: Due to the importance of financial aspects in contemporary developments within hospitality and tourism, the editors have ensured that there is more focus on these topics. Therefore, the book has two main chapters focused on finance. They provide various reflections of financial aspects ,analysis, application, as well as their usefulness to practice.

Dalvony Alkmim Savic
London College of Contemporary Arts, UK

Preface

The book is aimed to compile and reflect key contemporary trends in the sectors of hospitality and tourism. The book has gathered an international contribution and attention reflecting main developments worldwide within the fields of hospitality and tourism management. The book has eleven chapters focused on different aspects of hospitality, tourism, and service provisions in different countries. Furthermore, chapters have included several case studies and activities to enhance understanding as well as practice.

Chapter 1: Contemporary Quality Management Approaches and Practices Within the Hospitality Industry

This chapter is planned and designed to enable readers explore the concept of quality management in the hospitality sector, whilst improving efficiency and competitiveness in 21st century globalised business environment. In fact; quality is meeting or exceeding customer expectations consistently. To achieve this aim, companies should recognised all the service qualities that add to customer value and lead to satisfaction and loyalty. The readers of this chapter will be able to increase understanding of quality management systems and processes within hospitality industry and how to improve and sustain organisational performance, to gain a competitive edge in this transition period to the green economy. Also, the chapter provides readers with the relevant knowledge needed for quality assessment schemes, national/international benchmarking standards and regulatory agencies.

Chapter 2: The Use of Social Media as a Tool to Capture Customer Value and Interaction

The chapter provides in depth theoretical and conceptual explanation of social media as well as firm – customer interaction through social media highlighting several advantages and disadvantages of their uses. Furthermore, the chapter is supported using a framework relating to the development of social media channels and their uses for firms followed by inclusion of a service-based case study to further support the analysis on the communication process through social media platforms managed by the firm. Finally, the chapter highlights several challenges relevant to firms' social media activities followed by key considerations based on the analysis provided in the different sections of the chapter.

Chapter 3: Contemporary Management Approaches to the Global Hospitality and Tourism Industry – Technology as a Panacea for Sector Growth

The era of brick and mortar, hitherto called the analogue years has given way to the era of digits where everything functions with the touch of a button. From agriculture to banking, health to education, information search to manufacturing; and the hospitality and tourism sector is not left out. Information and Communication Technologies (ICT) has changed the way businesses are done in contemporary ways. The business environment and their managers have been challenged to think of how to integrate the opportunities posed by technology into their business models for competitive advantages.

Chapter 4: Corporate Culture as a Competitive Tool in Enhancing the Organisational Performance of Star-Rated Hotels in Ghana

This chapter focused on the use of corporate culture as a competitive tool to enhance the performance of organisations. however, the focus of the study was on star-rated hotels in ghana. to address this, the chapter first focused on determining the corporate culture that is dominant among the star-rated hotels operating in Ghana. secondly, it also sought to establish the influence that corporate culture has on organisational performance. out of a population of 680 star-rated hotel managers, a sample of 248 were chosen using stratified random sampling technique. self-administered questionnaires were used to solicit the views of managers of the selected hotels. in, all a total of 178 responses were retrieved and analysed using descriptive and partial least squares in structural equation modelling. findings of the study revealed that the rule-bound culture is the dominant corporate practiced by the star-rated hot hotels in ghana. the study also found that corporate culture significantly predicted organisational performance of star-rated hotels in the country.

Chapter 5: Impact of Crisis on Tourist Destination – A Case of Kashmir, India

The purpose of this chapter is to examine the impact of crisis events in Kashmir on the demand for tourism in order to establish a better understanding of changes and trends in the demand for tourism.The author has no information to assess the impact of the crisis on the brand image of Kashmir as a tourist destination. The chapter traces the evolution, growth, pattern and trends of tourism since independence (1947) in Kashmir. The historical trends in tourist arrivals in Kashmir for a period of over six decades illustrates that tourism has been highly susceptible to crises in Kashmir. The study provides a bottom-up perspective, based on observation, measurement and analysis. Provides contextualization on the tourism crisis and its impact on a tourist destination.

Chapter 6: Mystery Shopper Programs in the Tourism Sector
In today's world, there is fierce competition in the tourism sector and therefore the businesses need to improve their service qualities constantly and enhance their service processes to meet customer expectations swiftly and effectively. In recent years, tourism operators have been focusing on customer-oriented research and programs to avoid negative results that may be caused by unsatisfied customers. The service quality of tourism businesses is directly based on the performance of the employees, therefore it is very important to evaluate the performances of the employees and improve service processes to avoid potential problems. Mystery shopper programs show the true picture of the services offered to the guests by the tourism businesses. Therefore, mystery shopper programs are widely used in the world for the evaluation of employees, especially in service provider companies. The mystery shopper programs provide information on service quality, employee performance and customer satisfaction, which is used by the businesses to improve or develop their service delivery processes.

Chapter 7: Sustainable Tourism
This work compares several academic works in order to analyse if they use innovative approaches for sustainable tourism. It analyses 70 stable documents including theses, scientific papers and reports. Some goals are: assess the themes that most stand out, the contribution of academic research to the subject, and how the issues of sustainability, governance and planning relate to tourism. This contributes to approach the relationship between tourism and sustainability for development. The qualitative analysis used could discern the maturity level of research on sustainability indexes. Few works use them and, if used, most are more descriptive than quantitative. But the ones that use them have acknowledged their importance and resulting enhanced strategies, as they provide the data to decide accurately on environmental and destination matters. A challenge for the Portuguese academy is to have an ongoing role in implementing and monitoring key sustainability indexes.

Chapter 8: Profile, Motivations, and Experiences From Portuguese Solo Female Travelers
The segment of independent travelers has experienced big growth in recent years, not only worldwide but also in Portugal. This phenomenon, which is not recent, has been gaining dimension in recent times, with women playing an important role. This chapter explores the literature on solo female travel, seeking to understand the motivations, as well as the difficulties encountered during the journey. To this end,

a qualitative approach was used, with semi-structured interviews being conducted to 24 Portuguese women. The content analysis of the interviews was done with the assistance of the WebQDA software. Results show that most women traveling alone are young, single, and childless, identifying themselves mostly as adventurous, outgoing, and independent. The lack of travel companion, the freedom of choice, the experience and adventure, and the escape from the daily routine are highlighted as motivations to travel alone. The main difficulties identified are loneliness, harassment, fear of walking alone at night or being robbed.

Chapter 9: Modelling a Conceptual Framework for the Wine Tourism System
Wine tourism is a synthesis of elements from wine and tourism industries that come together to form wine tourism experience. Several elements form a part of much larger wine tourism system, contribute directly and/or indirectly in creating and developing a wine tourism destination. Maharashtra in India has come to be popularly known as the 'wine bowl' of India, producing some of the award winning and internationally acclaimed wines. This research paper aims to examine all those elements that have played a part in and are necessary to develop a competitive and sustainable wine tourism destination in Maharashtra. The singular objective of this research paper is to propose a conceptual framework of wine tourism system. The research largely relies on secondary data as well as results of previous empirical research. The wider contribution of this chapter lies in developing and illustrating a model of wine tourism system. This system model can be instrumental in defining all those components that are most critical to the growth of a wine tourism destination.

Chapter 10: Finance in the Hospitality and Tourism Sector
This chapter is set to shed light on how the hospitality and tourism sector is to shape their assets and liquidity to either begin a new venture or expand an existing one. The first part of the chapter will give an elaborate discussion about raising financial capital in the hospitality and tourism sector. This will strengthen the points that are made under capital structure formation. Financial knowledge of budgeting is an area that deserves its place in these sectors; this is the third major highlight of the chapter. The issue of understanding financial statements, especially its use in making predictions through ratio analysis require a thorough explanation. This is therefore the next point. The limitations and usefulness of ratio analysis will be touched upon. Finally, in this chapter, determining demand in the hospitality and tourism sector is a contemporary issue and the review of this will give a better viewpoint.

Chapter 11: Finance in the Hospitality Industry
By the end of this chapter, it is expected that one will be able to: 1. Establish various sources of funding that are available to a business in the hospitality industry in

the international market. 2. Evaluate the advantages and disadvantages of these sources of finance. 3. Establish the sources that are available or unavailable for the hospitality business as compared to other industries. 4. Evaluate an investment in hospitality industry using various capital budgeting techniques 5. Develop financial statement for businesses in hospitality industry 6. Evaluate the financial performance of companies in hospitality industry using ratio analysis.

The book is aimed at the following key audiences:

1. Academics within Higher education and researchers within the fields of hospitality and tourism management. However, the work is highly related as well for key sectors that depend of quality of service.
2. Higher education institutions and students focused on the fields of hospitality and tourism management.
3. Policy makers and public bodies making relevant decisions for the associated sectors of hospitality and tourism.
4. Consultants within the fields of hospitality and tourism management.
5. Readers interested to further their knowledge within the given fields of hospitality and tourism management.

The book has included key external and internal factors that influence the development of firms within the hospitality and tourism sectors. Chapters were be supported by research outcomes and have reflected several external and internal issues within the fields of hospitality and tourism management, and also explored theoretical background.

The book is sharing and disseminating research outcomes to interested readers within the given field of hospitality and tourism management at a global level, creating and developing a community of researchers reflecting global contemporary issues of the selected fields, and finally the book is sharing cutting edge research to further creativity and innovation within the fields of hospitality and tourism management at a global level.

Acknowledgment

On behalf of the book editors, we would like to deeply thank all the highly appreciated and respected academics, professionals, and researchers from different parts of the world that have contributed to the success of the book by direct chapter's contributions, peer reviews, and who provided insight and expertise that greatly assisted the development of the book.

Chapter 1
Contemporary Quality Management Approaches and Practices Within the Hospitality Industry

Abraham Pius
Arden University, UK

Husam H. Alharahsheh
https://orcid.org/0000-0002-0194-3700
University of Wales Trinity Saint David, UK

Obioma Nwaogbe
Federal University of Technology, Minna, Nigeria

Mihaela Dariescu
University of Roehampton, UK

ABSTRACT

This chapter is planned and designed to enable readers to explore the concept of quality management in the hospitality sector, while improving efficiency and competitiveness in 21st century globalised business environment. In fact, quality is meeting or exceeding customer expectations consistently. To achieve this aim, companies should recognise all the service qualities that add to customer value and lead to satisfaction and loyalty. The readers of this chapter will be able to increase understanding of quality management systems and processes within the hospitality industry and how to improve and sustain organisational performance, to gain a competitive edge in this transition period to the green economy. Also, the chapter provides readers with the relevant knowledge needed for quality assessment schemes, national/international benchmarking standards, and regulatory agencies.
DOI: 10.4018/978-1-7998-2204-2.ch001

Copyright © 2020, IGI Global. Copying or distributing in print or electronic forms without written permission of IGI Global is prohibited.

INTRODUCTION

Whatever kind of organisation you work in, whether public or private sector, production or service, and at whatever level you manage, you may find managing quality to be part of your responsibilities.

Quality as an idea is not new but its application to management strategies first in industry and then in the public sector has taken place mainly over the last 50 years. The voluntary and not for profit sector has, in turn, become involved in quality, largely because of the requirements of local authority contracts.

For many UK organisations, quality is not a nebulous concept or aspiration. It takes – to some – the seductive form of quality marks, associated frameworks and underpinning standards such as ISO 9000, Business Excellence, Investors in People and more recently Six Sigma. In UK the hospitality business can apply to quality assessment schemes such as AA, or schemes meant to assess specific operations only, such as the Food Hygiene Rating Scheme offered by the Food Standards Agency. Motives for signing up to these systems do vary, but the desire or requirement to be widely recognised as a provider of independently validated products and services tends to be near the top of the list in most operations. Even those organisations which have not adopted a formal or accredited quality system will probably be aware of their influence in the marketplace.

DEFINING QUALITY

The word 'quality' derives from the Latin 'quales' which can be translated in 'like', referring to similarities between objects. Juran (1998) defined quality as 'fitness for use' which, he said can only be determined by the customer. This makes the concept difficult for manufacturers to use because the definition of fitness for use will vary from one customer to another. He set out five quality characteristics on which fitness for use was based:

- Technological
- Psychological

Table 1.

Activity 1: What do you understand by 'quality'? How would you define it?

- Time-orientated
- Contractual
- Ethical

The quality of a manufactured product, such as a car, may be defined by reference to only two or three of these characteristics, e.g. strength (technological), beauty (psychological) or reliability (time-oriented). On the other hand, a service, such as the provision of accommodation, may involve all of those characteristics, e.g. staff customer relationship (ethical) and a guarantee of delivery (contractual).

Earlier (1974), Juran also pioneered the concept of internal customer/supplier relationships. In this idea, he envisaged that all the people who work in an organisation are providing products or services to one another. This can be applied to information flow in an office setting or to production on the shop floor. Where different workers are involved at different phases of a manufacturing process, they are dependent on one another to do a good job. Juran described this interdependence as an internal customer relationship.

The International Organisation for Standardisation (ISO) mention within the S.R. ISO 8402 – 1986 that the quality is made of a number of characteristics which make the product or the service able to satisfy the need of consumer.

Goetsch and Davis (2014, pp. 2) define the quality as "a dynamic state associated with product, services, people, processes and environments that meet customer needs and expectations and help produce superior value."

During the UNWTO Executive Council Meeting held in Malaga in May 2016, the concept of quality was referred to as "the result of a process which implies the satisfaction of all tourism product and service needs, requirements and expectations of the consumer at an acceptable price, in conformity with mutually accepted contractual conditions and the implicit underlying factors such as safety and security, hygiene, accessibility, communication, infrastructure and public amenities and services. It also involves aspects of ethics, transparency and respect towards the human, natural and cultural environment" (UNWTO, 2016)

Defining quality is not an easy task because it means different things to different people. On the one hand it is often used to mean a product or service which is out of the ordinary like Rolls Royce, while the other it might be used to signify something which is quite ordinary, like a torch battery, but always the same, i.e. it consistently meets a tight specification.

Judging the quality of a restaurant many customers will refer to a mix of elements part of the customer experience such as: service, atmosphere, food quality, unique selling points, price, cleanliness, previous experience.

Table 2.

Activity 2: Dinning out in a restaurant the customers will judge the quality of the restaurant bases on individual values and expectations. While Eating out what criteria do you use to select the restaurant? What do you mean by quality restaurant? State your points below:

In the professions such as law or health and social care services, quality might be associated with professionalism. We would recognise it because a particular profession such as a doctor makes a correct diagnosis, communicates that information sensitively to the patient and provides effective treatment promptly. Whereas with a hospitality company, quality may reside chiefly in its ability to respond quickly to customer requirements, at the standard expected. In this sense, quality is as much about internal as external perceptions. The extent to which an organisation is able to deliver a high-quality product or service will depend to a large extent on the match between internal and external perceptions. The concept of quality is the result of more components including operations from the early stage of product development (product design) as well as operations specific for the production line, leading to a product according to standards, made with minimum cost.

It is generally accepted that the quality is about identifying and meeting customer requirements, and this is a fundamental tenet of quality systems. The concepts of minimal variation, conforming to specifications or meeting standards are part of this idea. A quality product or service does what it is supposed to do and in a total quality system the product or service is said to 'consistently meet customer requirements' or 'delight the customer'.

THE DEVELOPMENT OF QUALITY MANAGEMENT

The evolution of the quality process known more phases of development. James (1996) suggests that the development of quality management has gone through four main phases:

- Pre 1914: Quality Inspection
- Post 1914: Quality Control
- 1960s on: Quality Assurance

- 1980s on: Total Quality Management

The phases set out by James are particularly relevant to the development of quality in the private sector. Engagement of the public sector with quality, according to Martinez-Lucio and Kirkpatrick (1995) came as a result of the New Right's influence on successive governments. They argue that:

'the prime objective of this strategy was to reduce the state's role in the direct provision of public services, through a combination of privatisation and the development of competitive tendering and quasi-market arrangements.'

Quality Inspection

Scientific management is generally thought to have provided the backdrop for the early development of quality management through inspection. At the time when goods were produced individually by craftsmen, they inspected their own work at every stage of production (self-evaluation) and discarded faulty items. When production increased through the development of technology, scientific management was born out of a need for standardisation rather than craftsmanship. This approach required each job to be broken down into its component tasks. Individual workers were trained to carry out these limited tasks, making craftsmen redundant in many areas of production. One result of this was a power shift away from workers and towards management.

With this change in production method, inspection of the finished product became the norm rather than inspection at every stage. This resulted in wastage because defective goods were not detected early enough in the production process. The

Table 3.

Activity 3:
Central to the development of quality management has been the evolution of four key concepts listed in the table below. The four terms are often misused or interchanged.
What is your understanding of these four terms, and can you distinguish between them?

Term	Your Understanding
Quality Inspection	
Quality Control	
Quality Assurance	
Total Quality Management	

wastage added costs which were reflected either in the price paid by the customer or in reduced profits.

As economies became more competitive, there was pressure to reduce the price to consumers which in turn required cheaper input prices and lower production costs. In many industries, emphasis was placed on automation to try to reduce the costly mistakes generated by workers. Automation led to greater standardisation, with many designs incorporating interchangeable parts. The production of arms for the 1914-18 war accelerated this process.

Therefore, in the beginning of the XX century, the quality inspection established itself as a series of measures and examinations performed as operation of production process, with the purpose of determining the standards of certain product characteristics.

Quality Control

Scientific management or Taylorism, as it became known after its originator Taylor (1911), depended on the development of tools and systems for measurement: jobs, fixtures, and gauges, which allowed inspection and quality control teams to assume greater importance in production. However, there were writers even at the time, such as Radford (1922), who signalled the need to focus on quality improvement by such means as including product designers in quality development from the beginning. At the time their ideas were largely ignored.

One of the problems with quality control through inspection of 100 percent of the completed product was that it did not necessarily guarantee that each batch would be perfect. It was also time-consuming and expensive. In addition, a lot of power was placed in the hands of inspection teams at a time when senior managers felt they could place little trust in their low-skilled workforce.

Shewhart (1930), who worked for Bell Telephone Laboratories, recognised the essentially variable nature of manufacturing and applied statistical principles to quality problems. Effectively this concept freed manufacturers from the constraints of 100 percent quality control because it accepted that variation is tolerable within certain defined limits. Shewhart distinguished between variation which was caused by chance and was therefore relatively unmanageable and variation which could be managed effectively through tackling the causes. The causes of variation were then tackled at the stage of the manufacturing process at which they occurred. This way greater control was established over the finished product through controlling variation at specific points in production. The quality control focus had therefore shifted from the end of the line to the process itself, but this was supplemented by sampling the finished product to monitor variation.

Quality control in this form was the norm in manufacturing until the early 1960s. This was a time when competition was low, most production was purchased, and few companies needed to worry about the cost of waste because they were making enough profits to cover them.

Quality Assurance

The third phase of quality management saw the development of quality systems and their application principally to the manufacturing sector. According to ISO 9000 (previously BS 5750) quality assurance is: 'those planned and systematic actions necessary to provide adequate confidence that a product or service will satisfy given requirements for quality.'

As we have seen, quality control was typically the domain of relatively few specialists in a company. Quality assurance took a broader perspective because it required the involvement of a greater number of managers and increased awareness of the implications of quality throughout the workforce. Its focus is the prevention of quality problems through planned and systematic activities in every department of an organisation. This takes place through establishing audited quality management systems. Quality audits provide evidence of the integrity of the systems which in turn ensure quality products and services. The increased attention paid to quality from the late 1960s on was directly related to the environmental impetus for greater competitiveness.

It is important to acknowledge the impact of the external environment upon the development and take-up of quality systems currently:

- Growing, and more significantly, maturing populations
- Intensifying competition for diminishing financial resources (particularly in the wake of the 1970s oil crisis)
- Proliferating media outlets and widening cultural horizons.

These converging trends contributed greatly to the demand for more, cheaper better-quality products and services, and the response from governments and businesses was reminiscent of scientific management practices: integrate functions, automate operations, standardise procedures.

Western society had the additional spur of the steady market invasion by Japanese producers. The concerted buy-in to quality assurance schemes was only one consequence of this configuration of circumstances.

Figure 1. Deming's cycle

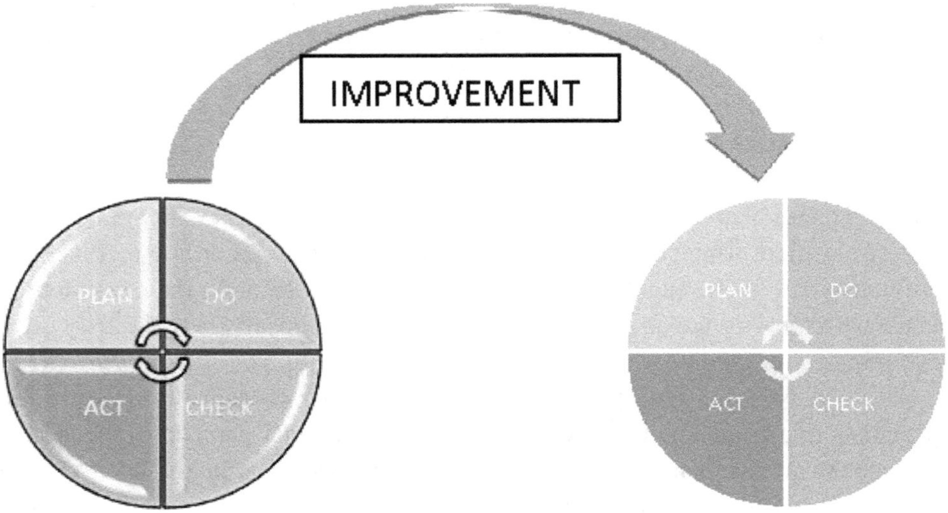

Total Quality Management

Total quality, as its name suggests involves not just managers but everyone in the organisation in a complete transformation of the prevailing culture. It means a change in the way people do things and relies on trust between managers and staff. Where it is working well, it restores the balance of power between workers and managers. TQM is applicable across all kinds of organisations, both public and private; those providing services as well as those involved in producing goods (Ajmal et al., 2016).

One of the authors contributing to the concept of TQM is Deming (1982) who proposed the PDCA wheel (see figure 1) and suggested the 'deadly diseases' which could prevent effective management practice.

The Deming wheel is used at all levels in many TQM driven organisations. Each stage can be broken down into more detailed steps to show how it works:

Plan

Identify the service or product to be improved (or an aspect of it)
Identify the internal or external customers for it
Identify those work processes or practices which can have a direct impact on it
Narrow down the quality improvement task into achievable tasks
Carry out cause and effect analysis
Develop a plan for change.

Do

Carry out the proposed change on a small-scale basis to test it.

Check

Evaluate the results of the small-scale test

Improve the proposed change

Act

Standardise the new process

Analyse customer reaction

Recognise and acknowledge success

Although Deming's wheel (based on Shewhart's cycle), has been widely adopted as a clear and practical tool to support quality implementation, it is for his statistical appreciation that he is particularly honoured.

The deadly diseases which Deming suggested could prevent effective management practice were:

- Lack of constancy of purpose, e.g. short-termism
- Emphasis on short term profits, e.g. pay-outs to shareholders which tend to weaken the companies by reducing investments of profits
- A so-called 'blame culture' and-or 'management by objectives' which can create competition and fear rather than co-operation and teamwork
- Mobility of top management. Managers may not be given enough time to learn the real problems of the job before they are moved on
- Running a company on figures alone. For example, how can you cost the effects of a dissatisfied customer?
- Excessive medical costs
- Excessive costs of warranty caused by lawyers.

Deming's 14 Point plan for success which mirrors some of the deadly diseases is as follows:

(1) Create constancy of purpose – plan for tomorrow i.e. get rid of short-termism.

(2) Adopt the new philosophy – transform the organisation through engaging everyone in the process.

(3) Cease dependence on mass inspection – use statistical evidence that quality is built into the process.

(4) End the practice of awarding business on price only – it strains relationships between organisations and their suppliers.

(5) Improve constantly the system of production and service – build quality in at the design stage.

(6) Introduce training and education in quality and its management.

(7) Generate effective leadership particularly at supervisory level.
(8) Replace the blame culture with one which seeks to solve problems and thereby drive out fear.
(9) Break down barriers within organisations which prevent people working together effectively.
(10) Eliminate unrealistic targets, slogans, and impractical goals.
(11) Remove numerical production quotas which demotivate staff.
(12) Give workers the right to have pride in their work.
(13) Provide education, training, and retraining to develop new skills and new ways of working.
(14) Ensure top management commitment to continuous quality improvement.

Another author, James (1996), explains the TQM as 'essentially about the development of an ideology, a philosophy, methods, and actions that are designed to satisfy customers completely, through their continuous improvement'. He identifies the principal objectives for an organisation which is quality orientated:

- Customer support
- Customer orientation
- Customer satisfaction
- Providing a learning environment for its staff.

Total Quality Management is not a 'quick fix' but the capacity it offers organisations (particularly, but not exclusively, those engaged in product manufacture) is characterised by James as follows:

- Meet, exceed and eventually anticipate customer needs
- Develop a whole organisation approach, breaking down the barriers between production and other traditional service elements.
- Change the application of resources from end of the line quality control to on-line inspection.
- Develop more proactive techniques for marketing, design, and manufacture in order to exactly meet customer requirements
- Ensure that marketing is an integral activity with first responsibility for establishing communication with the customer
- Make decisions using real data derived from business processes
- Benchmark internal processes, comparing both with other internal processes and best practice elsewhere.
- Provide broad-base education and training to staff.

Table 4.

Activity 4:
Using the information provided on the phases of development of quality concepts, identify the stages of development of the organization where you work.

Therefore, the total quality management is not a process that can be applied by a random middle manager and cannot be delegated but is an approach to business implemented from top to bottom, which endeavour to maximise the competitiveness of services and products by adopting a cycle of continuous improvement.

TOTAL QUALITY MANAGEMENT IN HOSPITALITY

TQM is a wide concept which applied on organisation level it enhances the competitive because it emphasises on the idea of offering the best product while applying the most efficient operation. These superlatives are reflected by the position on the market and product characteristics.

To be effective, planning for quality has to be cyclical so that the organisation becomes engaged in a continuous process of improvement. It should start from an analysis of current organisational status, which includes identifying those structures, systems, and programs which are already in place and can be built on.

It is also important that, at an early stage, the change progress should address the foundations of quality action:

- The mission and policy statements which characterise an organisation's commitment and perception of quality;
- Strategic objectives which should direct all quality action.

Quality Mission

Typically, a mission statement sets out clearly and concisely in writing for employees and customers 'how things are done here'. It makes clear to everyone the purpose of the organisation and the senior management intentions; attempts to encapsulate what it is about the organisation which makes it different from the rest.

Organisational commitment to quality should fit seamlessly within the overall strategic direction of the organisation, and ideally the overall mission statement should contain a definition of corporate aspirations in terms of quality.

Figure 2.

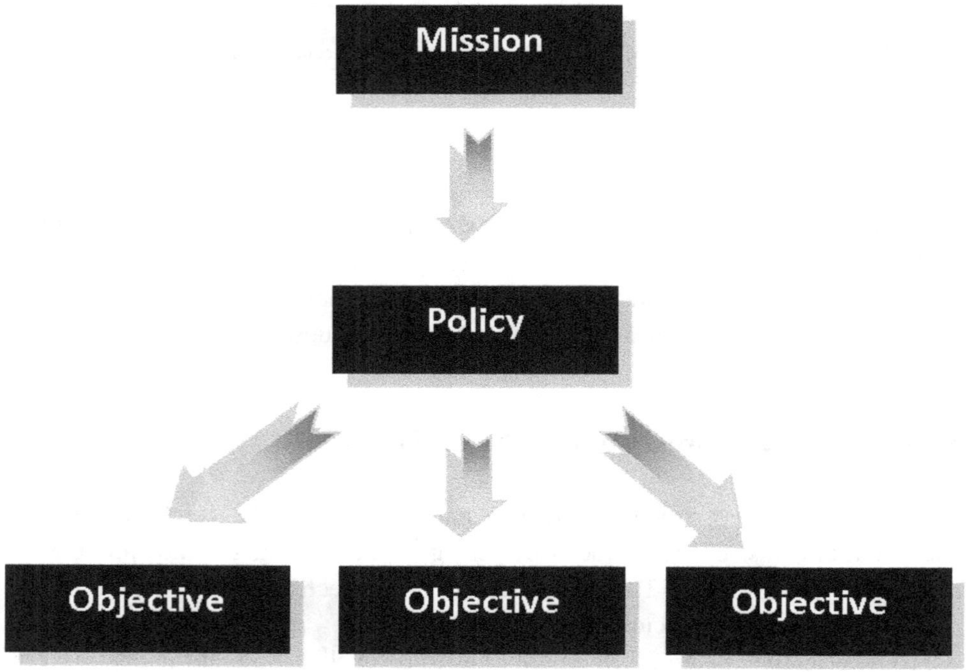

An alternative is to define a quality mission which supports the general mission, providing a framework within which the organisation operates.

Here are some examples of quality mission statements:

'Our core values make us who we are. As we change and grow, the beliefs that are most important to us stay the same—putting people first, pursuing excellence, embracing change, acting with integrity and serving our world. Being part of Marriott International means being part of a proud history and a thriving culture.' (Marriott, 2019)

To offer 'an all-day dining experience based around healthy and fresh food in a friendly, colourful and vibrant environment.' (Comptoir Libanais, 2019)

"...to be one of the world's leading producers and providers of entertainment and information. Using our portfolio of brands to differentiate our content, services and consumer products, we seek to develop the most creative, innovative and profitable entertainment experiences and related products in the world." (The Walt Disney Company, 2019)

'Our dedication to excellence and continuous improvement is demonstrated through our commitment of resources to innovation and learning. Through our Business Management System, we deliver benefits to our customer, colleagues,

Table 5.

Activity 5: What is the mission statement of the organization you work for or do business with?

business partners, owners and society by listening, building loyalty and developing mutually beneficial relationships.' (Jumeirah Group, 2019)

Quality Policy

The quality policy should stem directly from the mission statement and set out what is to be done to achieve the mission. It is a guide for all those involved in organisation, part of the quality management system and acting as a driver for continuous improvement.

A quality policy applies to the whole organisation and demonstrates to everyone top management commitment to the mission statement. The policy should set out the intention to:

- Establish systems and processes for implementation of the policy
- Identify customer needs and requirements
- Assess the organisation's ability to meet customer needs and requirements
- Ensure that suppliers meet required standards
- Establish a specified quality philosophy
- Provide focussed education and training for staff
- Review quality systems and processes regularly.
- The quality policy should be revised regularly (at least every two years) or every time there is a significant change within the business environment or business strategy.

Example of quality policy:

'Environment

Best Western Plaza Hotel has developed innovative methods to minimize environmental impact and optimise natural resource management. The last renovation project included an energy efficiency analysis and we are proud to announce that we are currently preparing our application in order to be awarded the Europen Eco – Label (known as The Flower).

All water is heated in solar boilers while a special insulation material on the roof collects the heat produced by all hotel activities and sends it back to the central hot water circulation. In cloudy days and when the water does not reach the desired temperature, extra heating is provided by new generation, efficient electric pumps instead of standard gas heaters. No fossil fuel is burnt in any stage of the procedure. All used oil from the kitchen is collected and sent to be recycled as biodiesel. Batteries are handled by a partner company specialising in battery recycling.

We have excluded from our supply chain all products with bulky packaging, especially plastics and non – recyclable materials. The water collected from the last rinse is filtered and used in the next pre – wash. We are also the first to introduce an innovative environmentally – friendly pool water cleaning technology that uses ionisation and oxidation instead of chloride and leaves a crystal – clear, safe and odour – free swimming pool to be enjoyed any hour of the day.

Services

We always try hard to offer the best quality in our services following a guest – centred approach. Our record is one of achievement as we have passed all Best Western service & facilities quality controls with a very high score. The Preferred Code of Practice of the Federation of Tour Operators is integrated and implemented in our Quality Policy and we have developed a quick response system to be in line with our guests needs.

We believe that the best way to assure that our tradition of excellence will continue is the on – going education of all hotel stuff and the flow of information. This is why we run each year a continuing education programme and we follow an open – doors policy. We strongly encourage our guests to feel free to talk to us and make any suggestions they believe could make our services even better.

Health and Safety

We have developed an integrated Health & Safety checkpoints procedure according to the HACCP protocol and we expect to obtain the official certification before the end of the summer.

Our Water Quality Management and Protection from Legionella Scheme consists of continuous on – site monitoring, regular re-systematic sampling and laboratory examinations in collaboration with certified chemical labs. We also control all stages of food preparation and kitchen hygiene and we collaborate with health advisors to assure water supply quality.

Table 6.

Activity 6: Find out whether your organization has a mission statement and policy on quality, and comment on it is makeup and effectiveness. If there is not one in place, make notes about what you think it should contain.

All our staff is being involved in our Health & Safety projects to ensure that all the procedures are well understood and implemented.' (Rhodes Plaza Hotel, 2019)

In the pursuit of continuous quality and efficiency improvement, the hospitality businesses are applying more or less comprehensive the principles of TQM, through their activities and operations as seen below:

Customer focus
- understanding customer needs
- adapting the services and products to meet customer needs
- investigating and analysing customer satisfaction level
- customer relation management (CRM)

Leadership
- business objectives
- strategic planning
- organisational structure

Employees' involvement
- team work
- emphasize on motivation
- emphasize of personal skills and abilities

Process focus
- implementing standard operation procedures (SOP)
- enhancing efficiency

System focus
- using statistics and data analysis
- planning and implementing quality cycle

Continuous improvement
- employee training
  - cyclic evaluation processes

Relationship focus
- B2B
- B2C

Figure 3.

You have seen our interpretation!

Now, what distinctions would you draw between strategic, tactical and operational planning?

Planning for Quality

Planning in many organisations takes place on an annual cycle, usually locked with budgeting. It may include:

- Reviewing the previous year's activity
- Setting objectives and targets for the coming year
- Deciding how the organisation will provide or obtain necessary resources
- Agreeing what action will be taken to meet the objectives and targets
- Specifying how the results will be assessed and/or evaluated.

There are three familiar terms often used to categorise planning activity: strategic, tactical and operational. They are different through scope, detail, timeframe and the level of the organisation at which they are applied.

- *Strategic planning* is a relatively long term and 'broad brush' method for the organisation to set out, develop and achieve goals.
- *Tactical planning* provides intermediate goals for specific departments for areas of the organisation, e.g. design, marketing, and production. It ensures that each specific area of the organisation is headed in the right direction and working on the right activities to be effective.
- *Operational planning* is relatively short term and much more focused on efficiency. It is the means through which strategic and tactical plans are translated into realistic performance measures to ensure the desired outcomes.

Figure 4. Planning for quality

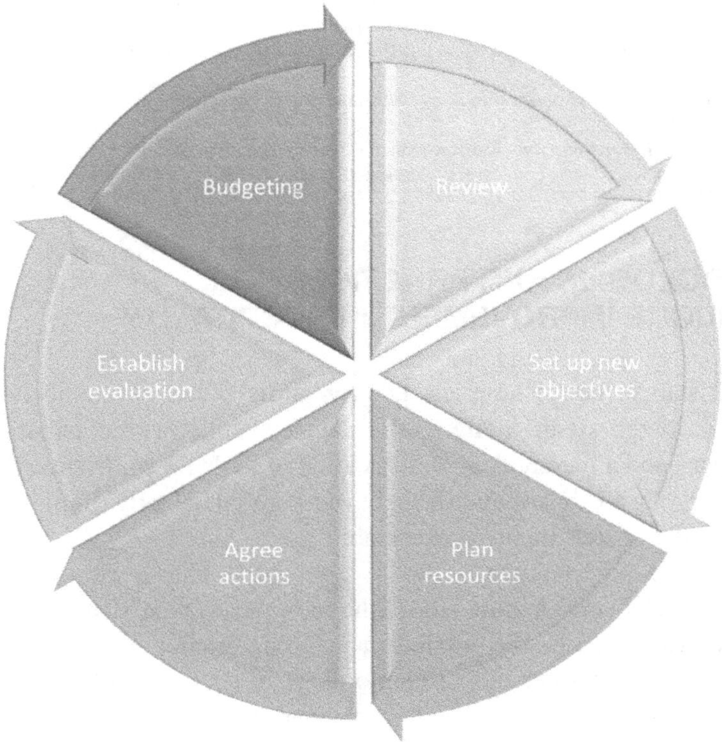

Figure 5.

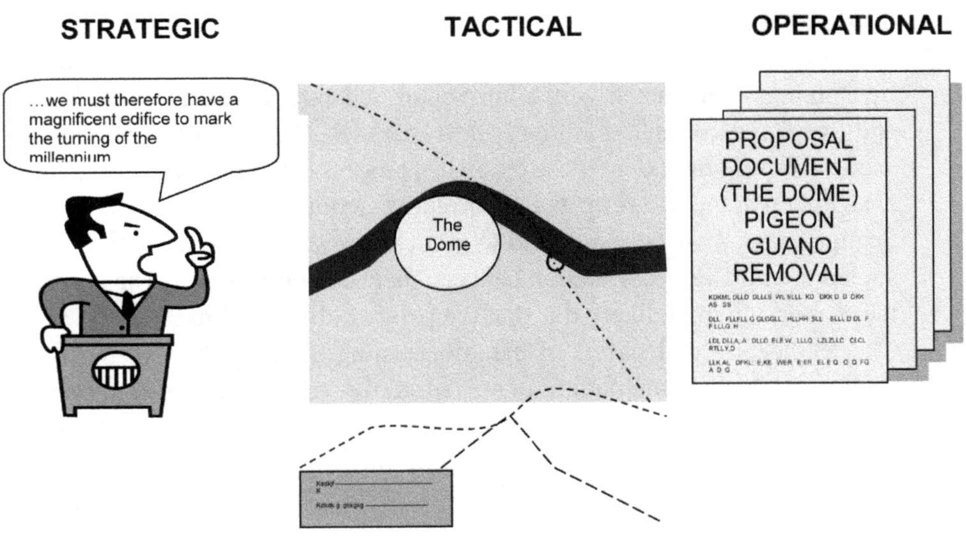

Table 7.

Activity 7: Explore the following company's website and link the elecments of organizational culture with the total quality management principles. *Jumeirah Hotels, Resorts, and Residences* http://www.jumerirah.com/en/jumeirah-groups/about-jumeiral-group/philosophy/ *Rosewood Hotels & Resorts* http://www.rosewoodhotels.com/en/about/culture *Starbucks* https://www.starbucks.com/careers/working-at-starbucks/culture-and-values

METHODOLOGIES AND PRACTICES FOR CONTINUOUS IMPROVEMENT IN HOSPITALITY

Following the influence of American quality 'gurus' in Japan, a number of Japanese writers contributed significantly to the debate. Ishikawa's contribution centred principally around a hierarchical classification of tools for statistical control.

The first group are those which he believed were sufficiently simple to be applied by a wide range of staff in any organisation:

- Cause and Effect Diagram – the Fishbone – these take a statement of a quality problem and express the possible causes diagrammatically.
- Pareto Analysis – typically a Pareto diagram is a type of bar chart arranged to show greatest frequency on the left-hand side, with decreasing frequencies the further right the eye travels.
- Histograms – visual representation of data collected, e.g. from check sheets. The shape of the histogram helps to find the most common frequency (the 'norm') and can be used to determine the breadth (standard deviation) of distribution
- Process Control Charts - these were introduced by Shewhart and later refined by Deming. Constructed with a horizontal mid-line representing the 'norm' and two standard deviation lines drawn parallel, above and below, they are used to identify the extent of variation in a process from the norm. The control is an effective tool for prioritising corrective action.
- Scatter Diagrams– these are used to plot two variables thought to be related, so that the statistical correlation between them can be assessed. The narrower the scatter, the more likely it is that the two variables are linked.
- Check Sheets – collections of data concerning the frequency of particular events which show the pattern of variation over time. These tend to be used to identify problems with a process, and the effect of any changes introduced should be visible at the end (check) part of the process.

Figure 6.

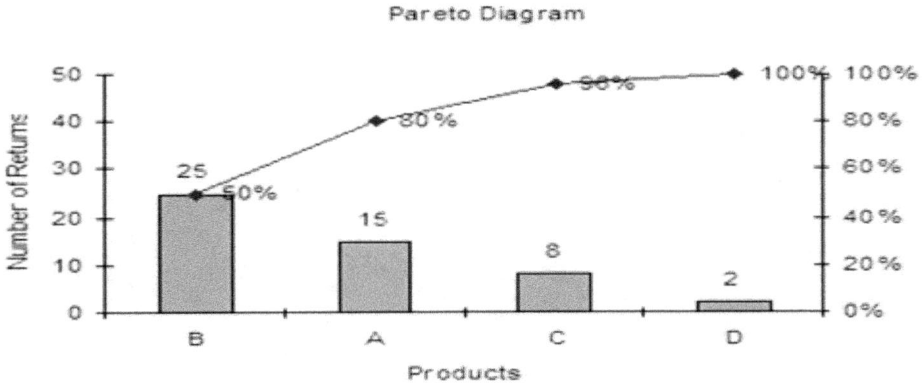

Figure 7.

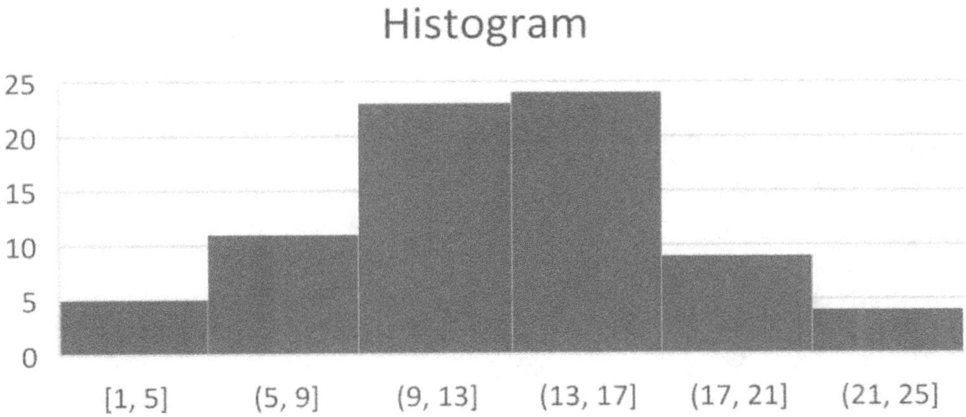

The second group of tools included hypothesis testing and sampling and were intended for use by managers and quality specialists. The last group were highly mathematical and probably suitable for use by a limited number of specialists.

Despite this apparent focus on statistical methods, Ishikawa was more people-orientated than statistical in his approach to quality. Japanese manufacturers insisted on teamwork and emphasised that all staff were equal in their contribution to the quality of the end product. He was committed to grassroots workers contributing to improvement through Quality Circle and it was supremely important to him that his statistical methods were accessible to ordinary workers.

Crosby (1967) is sometimes described as a technician rather than a philosopher, but he certainly put across the message of TQM to his audience persuasively. He

Figure 8.

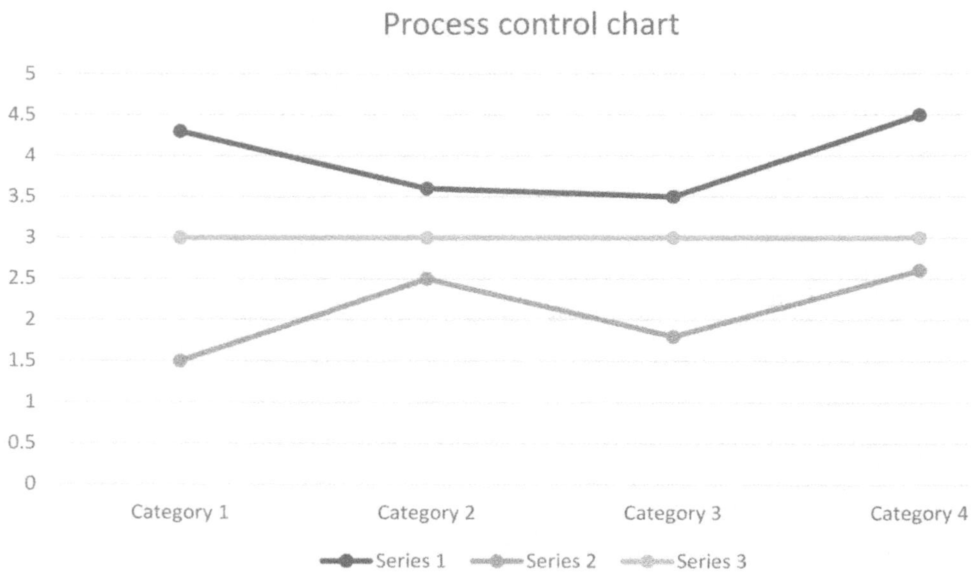

Figure 9.

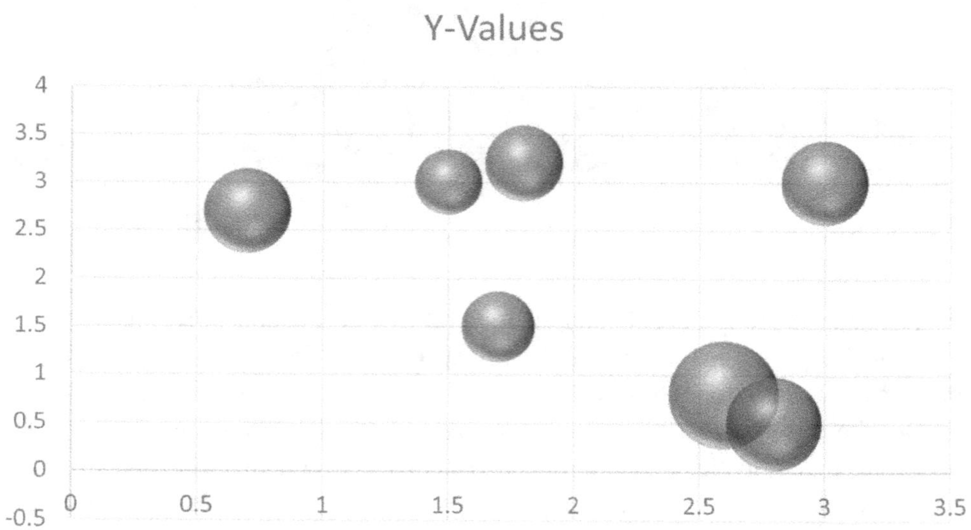

tried to distil TQM into a set of simple tools that managers could use in their concern for 'Zero Defects' and their aim of achieving excellence.

He set out fourteen points to guide the management approach and summed up with the following Crosby Absolutes:

- Quality is conformance to requirements, not goodness
- It is always cheaper to do the job right first time
- Prevention not appraisal
- The cost of quality is the only performance measurement
- Zero defects are the required performance standard.

His basic thesis is that quality is free because defects cost money.

James (1996) suggests that Crosby's fourteen-point plan for quality improvement deals mainly with implementation issues whereas Deming's fourteen points focus on management philosophy.

Crosby's fourteen-point plan is:

(1) Management commitment
(2) There should be a quality improvement team which has the responsibility of implementation
(3) Quality measurement must use accurate data and reduce waste
(4) The cost of quality is a catalyst which can generate change
(5) Awareness of quality needs to be raised across the organisation
(6) Task teams should work constantly to take corrective action to solve problems
(7) Zero defects must be planned for
(8) Supervisors need special training in quality
(9) The day when the organisation achieves zero defects should be marked as special
(10) Motivation and drive can be created through goal setting
(11) It is essential to remove the causes of systematic errors
(12) Recognition of achievement is vital, and this does not have to take the form of money
(13) The quality council, which brings together representatives of the whole organisation, has a key role to pay
(14) Continuous improvement is emphasised by the slogan – 'eliminate "do it over again"'.

Crosby's approach is top-down management of quality as he stresses that responsibility for implementation rests squarely at the top of an organisation.

According to Foundations of lodging management; Pearson Education (2011,p, 48) the aspects of quality in the hospitality sector that can be used to design and implement a quality service system as follows:

- Consider the guests being served
- Determine what the guests' desire
- Develop procedures to deliver what guests want
- Train and empower staff
- Implement revised systems
- Evaluate and modify service delivery systems.

QUALITY STANDARDS AND ACCREDITATION AGENCIES

Quality Standards

Standard setting is one of the first issues in developing a quality assurance system and increasingly organisations are relying on 'off the peg' standards rather than developing their own. Standards set out good practice and for real effect should be selected for their coverage of, and application to, quality-critical parts of an organisation's activity.

Each standard should be:

- Clearly written in language which is unambiguous
- Specific in setting out precisely what is expected
- Measurable so that the organisation can know whether or not it is being met
- Achievable, i.e. the organisation must have the resources available to meet the standard.
- They may be derived from professional standards or national codes of practice.

In relation to customer/supplier quality chains one organisation in the chain may require certain standards to be met by others in the chain. For example: where the client, a company, contracts out its marketing material to a design company it may require the design company to meet certain standards. If the design company sub-contracts to a printer then that printing company may also have to meet the standards set by the company. In turn the printer may set standards requirements for its paper supplier.

Accreditation Agencies

Documented and accredited quality systems provide reassurance for customers and stakeholders that there is a concern for quality and that certain standards are being met.

Most formal quality standards are designed to provide a framework which will ensure excellent outputs from a system where the procedural, policy and resource inputs conform to a flexible but defined quality specification. In that sense, standards like ISO 9001 and the IIP set out to determine the extent to which quality principles should be integrated within organisational policy, structure, systems and processes across the organisation.

Recent models offer an element of self-assessment followed by external verification, and this is part of a drive among quality Awarding Bodies to improve the accessibility of their standards, particularly to small businesses.

What motives might an organisation have for applying for quality accreditation?

Perhaps the most commonly cited motive among companies registering for quality awards is the need to offer a validated guarantee of quality, but it is not unusual for more virtuous aims to be expressed, such as the expectation of business benefits arising from a rigorous assessment of existing organisational practices.

Documented and accredited systems have external and internal advantages. They are a useful marketing tool, raising the profile and image of the organisation which can help, for instance, with recruitment. They may be a requirement to obtain contracts for work, but they also have internal advantages in making sure that the organisation is managed efficiently and effectively.

ISO 9000 Series

The International Standards Organisation (ISO) provides a framework by which an organisation can set up, implement and monitor quality systems in a structured way. In the United Kingdom, the British Standards Institute (BSI) distributes standards for the ISO 9000 series. The United Kingdom plays a leading role in the development of the standards and indeed ISO 9000, is still sometimes referred to as BS 5750, even though it has superseded it. Many of the series have also been adopted as European Standards and carry the prefix EN.

The aim of the ISO 9000 series is to enable organisations to demonstrate their commitment to achieving customer satisfaction by preventing problems in the products or services they produce at all stages from design to delivery. Previously there were four assessable standards:

- *ISO 9001* was appropriate for design, development, production, installation, and servicing, for example in companies such as design and build contractors, architects or solicitors where design is a key element.
- *ISO 9002* was appropriate for production, installation, and servicing, e.g. in companies such as manufacturers of relatively simple products, estate agents or financial services
- *ISO 9003* was appropriate for final inspection and testing, where the organisation only carries out such activity.
- *ISO 9004* was appropriate only for single activity operations, such as cutting timber.

The standard chosen depends on the nature of the business and there is no need to meet all three.

Today, ISO 9000 has been revised and updated to fully embrace service sector and public sector organisations, and has condensed 9001, 9002, and 9003, into a single standard: ISO9001:2000. ISO 9004:2000 still exists, but is rarely implemented as most organisations now adopt 9001 and adapt it to their activities. For example, design and development procedures are required only if a company does, in fact, engage in the creation of new products or services.

The 2000 version sought to make a radical change in thinking by actually placing the concept of process management front and center. ("Process management" is described as the monitoring and optimizing of a company's tasks and activities, instead of just inspecting the final product, as before.) The 2000 version also demands involvement by upper executives, in order to integrate quality into the business system and avoid delegation of quality functions to junior administrators. Another goal is to improve effectiveness via process performance metrics - numerical measurement of the effectiveness of tasks and activities.

The core focus is on the twin expectations of continual process improvement and tracking of customer satisfaction, which are made explicit in the current version.

ISO 9001:2000 has a structure that requires the organisation to demonstrate that it:

- Communicates with customers
- Identifies customer requirements
- Meets customer requirements
- Monitors and measures customer satisfaction
- Meets regulatory requirements
- Meets statutory requirements
- Supports internal communication
- Provides quality infrastructure
- Provides a quality work environment

- Evaluates the effectiveness of training
- Monitors and measures processes
- Evaluates the suitability of quality management system
- Evaluates the effectiveness of quality management system
- Identifies quality management system improvements

Improves Quality Management System

The emphasis is on implementing and maintaining a process approach to quality management, and expects the organisation to have the following processes in place:

- Quality Management Process
- Resource Management Process
- Regulatory Research Process
- Market Research Process
- Product Design Process
- Purchasing Process
- Production Process
- Service Provision Process
- Product Protection Process
- Customer Needs Assessment Process
- Customer Communications Process
- Internal Communications Process
- Document Control Process
- Record Keeping Process
- Planning Process
- Training Process
- Internal Audit Process
- Management Review Process
- Monitoring and Measuring Process
- Non-conformance Management Process
- Continual Improvement Process

In order to develop a quality management system that meets the new ISO 9001:2000 standard, the organisation must create or modify each of the above processes.

The organisation will need to:

- Design each process
- Document each process
- Implement each process

- Support each process
- Monitor each process
- Control each process
- Improve each process.

Previous versions of ISO9000 were criticised for being most directly applicable to manufacturing operations. As a result, it lost credibility and was ignored by many organisations, and by whole business sectors. The new version is much more acceptable to public sector, service sector, and not-for-profit organisations. Indeed, in the UK and many other developed countries, the service and public sectors are now dominant, and a credible quality assurance management system must be appropriate to their activities. ISO9001:2000 meets this requirement, and still can be applied effectively to manufacturing and production organisations, who will also benefit from the emphasis on processes and meeting customer needs.

Many companies which apply ISO 9001 do find it a useful framework for specifying and measuring good business practice. But there are still reports of dissatisfaction, even among accredited companies. The most frequent complaint against the standard is that it is bureaucratic and not practically focussed.

There is some justification in this criticism, but the fault now is likely to lie within the organisation, rather than in the ISO9001 requirements. A major weakness found in many organisations is that the system is designed and implemented in a bureaucratic and document-driven manner. This is not necessary, and in fact, is positively discouraged in the guidance accompanying the new format, but it is a style that is favoured by some management teams and by some of the more traditional, usually older, quality managers and auditors, who were initially trained and became experienced in the older versions.

Also, unlike the more recent Business Excellence Model, ISO 9001:2000 does not specifically concern itself with obtaining and retaining customers or with the quality of financial accounting practices, nor does it look beyond quality policy into the overall strategic direction of the organisation. However, it could be argued that since the system does not pretend to measure overall business success, it should be taken on for what it is: a *quality assurance management system*, chiefly aimed at producing consistent and continuously improved products or services.

ISO 9001:2008 Quality Management System, benefits for hospitality businesses:

- Improve business operations
- Improve staff morale
- Marketing advantage
- Increased efficiency and effectiveness
- Increased overall performance standards

- Continuous improvement processes are enabled
- Reducing business risks
- Increase customer confidence

Environmental Standards

ISO 14000, which mirrors ISO 9000, was developed internationally in response to concerns regarding the management of environmental pollution. The specification for environmental management was prepared in consultations between ISO and major country governments and quality organisations. It is designed to enable organisations to audit their environmental management performance against recognised international standards. It covers everyday occurrences as well as accidents and potential emergencies and can facilitate policy, planning and control activities.

ISO 14000 is now a series of internationally agreed voluntary standards and guideline reference documents, which include: Environmental Management Systems (EMS), Eco Labelling, Life Cycle Assessment, Environmental Auditing, Environmental Performance Evaluation, Environmental Aspects in Product Standards.

ISO 14001:1996 Environment Management Systems, benefits for hospitality businesses:

- Positive business image
- Finding relevant KPI for waste and energy management
- Increase competence
- Save costs on energy consumption and resources
- Minimising environmental impact

Energy Management

The Energy Management Standard, ISO 50001 provides to businesses a framework based on Deming's cycle, able to minimise the energy consumption based on systematic monitoring and improvement plans. This standard can be integrated within other quality systems.

ISO 50001 Energy Management Standard benefits for hospitality businesses:

- Enhances employees' awareness
- Helps the development and achievement of energy performance KPI
- Cut costs
- Meet customer expectations
- Promotes energy efficiency to other businesses within the supply chain

Currently, the businesses operating within the accommodation sector are conscious about energy consumption and the carbon footprint. Some of the businesses adopt international standard (ISO), but most of the businesses opt for energy saving solutions (including electricity, gas and water) offered by specialised consultants and/or property management systems. Moreover, managers concerned with energy consumption may adopt other practices such as advising the guest to ask towel and laundry change only when is required, using smart lighting systems based on motion sensors and adapting the heating system to room occupancy.

It is usual for hotels to combine the energy saving schemes with 'green' programs, embedding energy management systems with the idea of social responsibility.

Investors in People (IIP)

The Investors in People Standard was developed in 1990 by a government-convened task force which included the TUC, CBI, and Institute of Personnel and Development (IPD).

It was devised in part to address a perceived deficiency in the ISO 9000 series – the lack of a framework for human resource management. As a result, the IIP became the only people-centred quality standard.

Before general release the model was tested by various bodies including the then Training and Enterprise Councils (TECS) – they became the lead vehicle for promoting and administrating the IIP standard. IIP UK is the national Awarding Body, set up by the government as an independent organisation with a particular focus on the training and development of employees, and with responsibility for marketing the standard and validating accreditation. IIP UK is also responsible for developing the standard, and there have been two refined versions since its inception.

IIP provides a framework for accrediting an organisation's performance with regard to integrating the business strategy with an effective human resources strategy. It is relevant to organisations of all sizes and types but, in the past, has probably been seen as the most relevant to service industries, public and voluntary sectors. More recently, manufacturing and private sector service industries have begun to see its value in ensuring that strategic planning incorporates human resource planning; that business-critical information is conveyed successfully, and that line managers are managing to consistent standards.

The IIP ethos holds that people are the most valuable asset in any organisation, and that the key to business success is, therefore, effective management and development of people.

ISO9001:2000 does significantly address the human resource element of quality activity, borrowing in part from the IIP standard. However, because of its primary focus on the training, development, and empowerment of people, the IIP framework, and the approach that it promotes is one that most observers say should be implemented by every organisation, as a necessary but complementary system to ISO9001.

The IIP Standard starts from four 'principles' which are linked in a cycle similar to Deming's wheel and are:

Commit Make and maintain a commitment to your people and their learning and development
Plan Be clear about your strategy and how your people can help achieve it
Evaluate Measure and understand the impact of investing in people

Quality models evolve and IIP is no different in that respect. The current IIP Standard has 23 assessment indicators grouped under each of the four principles. These specify the performance criteria to be met.

The standard is being continuously revised. Recent revisions have placed more emphasis on *results* and *impact* rather than evidence of processes themselves. The latest version is also less prescriptive in defining what type of evidence will be acceptable and how impact should be demonstrated.

For clarification of the pertinence of the original Standard, or for more information on the new one, visit the IIP UK website at: www.investorsinpeople.co.uk

The essential point of meeting the Investors in People National Standard is to achieve the organisation's objectives of raising its level of performance and improving its competitiveness. Achieving it requires the organisation to demonstrate to a qualified, independent assessor that its training and development practices satisfy the Standard. Finally, and assuming the Standard has been achieved, the organisation will be formally recognised as an Investor in People. This, though, is by no means the end of the process.

Investors in People requires continuous effort and constant improvement against the principles and on a formal basis, no later than three years after the initial award, the organisation will be re-assessed.

The assessment process is based on:

® Evidence provided by the organisation
® The practices found to be well established in the organisation.

It will involve a thorough review of all documentary evidence and interviews with a representative sample of staff at all levels of the organisation. The time required for this will naturally depend on the size and complexity of the organisation; interviews with staff, for example, might be completed within one day for a small company but extended over several days for a large concern. And there is feedback and the opportunity to clarify matters, develop further information and generally to work with the assessment process to achieve the desired result.

Obviously, different organisations will have different approaches to business planning and management, communication with staff and to training and development. There is no single or preferred approach except, of course, in issues where current legislation needs to be met, such as health and safety, discrimination, etc. Beyond this, the assessment process respects each company's practices and the way in which it meets the Standard.

Quality Assessment Schemes

Many countries do have a quality scheme for hospitality businesses owned and managed by government (public systems), other countries rely on private quality systems managed by private organisations or associations and some countries (like USA, Egypt and United Kingdom) have a quality rating system based on both private and public model. Nevertheless, there is a general movement towards the standardisation of quality and rating schemes between countries. In Europe, it can be recognised a regional cooperation led by HOTREC (the umbrella association of hotels, restaurants and cafes in Europe) with a standard for hotel classification (Hotelstars Union, 2019) created in 2009 and adopted by 17 member countries. In other regions of the Globe, the classification of accommodation facilities is based on frameworks such as ASEAN (in South-East Asia) and ECOWAS (East Africa and West Africa).

In United Kingdom, one of the earliest quality assessment schemes for accommodation facilities, owned and managed by The Automobile Association (AA) since 1912. Today, AA provides not only star rating services for accommodation facilities, but also rosettes rating system for restaurants and pennant ratings for caravans, campsites and glamping sites. (The Automobile Association, 2019)

Later on, in 1969 it was established The British Tourism Authority known today as VisitBritain after merging with English Tourism Council in 2003. As the name suggest, its remit extends to England, Scotland, and Wales only. However, in 2009 VisitEngland, VisitScotland and VisitWales became stand-alone entities,

Table 8.

Activity 8: *Make an online investigation of hospitality businesses who applied Investors in People standards. You can start with the below websites:* https://www.hotelowner.co.ul/17095-the-landmakr-london-hotel-awarded-platinum-level-investors-in-people-award/ https://www.bbpmedia.co.uk/news/hospitality/family-run-hotel-group-strikes-gold-to-join-elite-uk-club.html

functioning as national tourist boards. As a non-departmental public body funded by the Department for Digital, Culture, Media and Sport (DCMS), VisitBritain has an important role within the development of touristic resources and activities in Great Britain. With an extensive global network, VisitBritain and the national tourist boards are not only promoting Great Britain as an excellent touristic destination through various marketing programs and campaigns, but they are also supporting hospitality and tourism businesses offering market insights, analysed data across sectors, business advisory and consultancy, policy solutions, and customer insights.

Aiming to help the businesses improve their products and meet customers' expectations, the national tourism boards developed quality grading schemes that could help hospitality businesses to strive on a global and competitive market. The quality grading schemes offered by the three boards are based on common standards, aligned as well with the standards promoted by Northern Ireland Tourism Board and AA, to enhance consistency and meet tourists' expectations.

Already running own quality assessment scheme for hospitality businesses (accommodation and F&B) since more than a century, the AA joined VisitEngland in 2017 as a partner to run the Quality Assessment Schemes (VisitBritain, 2017) for the following 3 years.

The quality scheme offers a star grading system which sums up every aspect of the business, including facilities, services and the overall quality of the customer experience. The businesses can be rated from one to five stars, where one star is considered as acceptable quality and five stars equates with excellent quality. In 2018, AA and the tourism national boards of Great Britain and Northern Ireland agreed review standards, tailored based on customer and industry feedback for accommodation products to ensure the changing customer focus from facilities to overall experience, transparency and security.

The quality assessment schemes offered either by a national tourist board or AA comes with benefits such as recognised accreditation, business advice, various awards opportunities, advantages of a wide network, rating exposure and enhanced online presence.

Table 9.

Activity 9: *Using the national tourist board websites (see below links) investigate the quality assessment schemes categories, awards, and accolades.* www.visitbritain.org/quality-assessment-your-accommodation www.visitenglandassessmentservices.com www.visitscotland.org www.visitwales.com/grading-information

In addition to the quality rating schemes and awards offered by national tourist boards and AA, the food and beverage, manufacturers, sellers and wholesalers in England, Wales and Northern Ireland benefit of the Food Hygiene Rating Scheme offered by Food Standards Agency (an independent Government department) in collaboration with the local authorities. The food and beverages facilities can receive ratings from 0 – 'urgent improvement is required' to 5 – 'hygiene standards are very good'. This scheme is set out in law, is not optional, and the standard refers to food hygiene, investigating the food handling, storage, preparation, the cleanliness of the facility and the overall management of food safety. The scheme is applied and through the local authority food safety officers which are inspecting the businesses regularly. The food safety officers are empowered to apply enforcement actions as required, considering the risk to public health. In extreme situations they could close the business until is proved to be safe again.

CONCLUSION

Quality management is a continuous quest for an organisation which is committed to achieving improved total quality standard across pertinent business functions for a sustainable growth. This involves a range of processes used to measure the quality of services according to customer expectations. It also comprises the maintenance and long-term monitoring of all of the services offered to customers, as to track developments in quality and measure the efficiency of enhancement efforts. Effective quality management and improvement can only be achieved if quality problems are clearly identified and tackled in time. Assessing the size of the gap between users' expectations and experience, organisations are delivered with actionable submissions and ideas for targeted growths, and profit from the added benefit of getting to know their target audiences better.

Furthermore, it enables organisations to identify and reduce errors and complaints from the customers. There has to be a systematic approach involving the collection and analysis of data with a feedback loop into planning. The driving force should be the customer satisfaction derived from close links between the marketing function and product/service design. In this chapter, we have outlined some of the

Table 10.

Activity 10: Using the Food Standards Agency website (www.food.gov.uk) find the food hygiene rating of your favorite restaurant.

contemporary philosophies, approaches and tools that can used for 21st century reformed hospitality sector in managing and improving quality systems. As well as, pointing out the importance of strategic managers' unswerving commitment to the process of systematic quality improvement by internalising the concept within the organisation structure and practices. Given these facts, quality management can be used as enabler of sustainable growth in the service-oriented industry "hospitality", whilst gaining a competitive advantage at the regional, national and international marketplace.

REFERENCES

Ajmal, M., Tuomi, V., Helo, P., & Sandhu, M. (2016). TQM Practices in Public Sector. *International Journal of Information Systems in the Service Sector*, *8*(1), 34–44. doi:10.4018/IJISSS.2016010103

Comptoir Libanais. (2019). *Overview.* Retrieved from https://investors.comptoirlibanais.com/

Crosby, P. (1967). Cutting the cost of quality. Industrial Education Institute.

Deming, W. E. (1982). *Quality, Productivity and Competitive Position.* Cambridge: MIT Press.

Food Standards Agency (2019). *Food Hygiene Rating Scheme.* Retrieved from https://www.food.gov.uk/safety-hygiene/food-hygiene-rating-scheme

Goetsch, D. L., & Davis, S. B. (2014). *Quality Management for Organisational Excellence* (7th ed.). USA: Pearson.

Hayes, D. K., Ninemeier, J. D., & Miller, A. A. (2012). *Foundations of Lodging Management* (2nd ed.). Pearson.

Hotelstars Union. (2019). *The System of the Hotelstars Union.* Retrieved from https://www.hotelstars.eu/system/description/

International Organisation for Standardisation. (2019). *Standards.* Retrieved from https://www.iso.org/standards.html

James, P. (1996). *Total Quality Management. An Introductory Text.* Prentice Hall.

Jumeirah Group. (2019). *Philosophy.* Retrieved from https://www.jumeirah.com/en/jumeirah-group/about-jumeirah-group/philosophy/

Juran, J. M., & Godfrey, A. B. (1998). *Juran's Quality Handbook* (5th ed.). USA: McGraw-Hill.

Marriott. (n.d.). *Core Values.* Retrieved from www.marriott.com/culture-and-values/core-values.mi#

Martinez Lucio, M., & Kirkpatrick, I. (1995). The Politics of Quality in the British Public Sector. In *The Politics of Quality and the Management of Change in the Public Sector*. Routledge.

Radford, G. S. (1922). *The Control of Quality in Manufacturing.* New York: The Ronald Press Company. Retrieved from https://archive.org/details/controlofquality00radfrich/page/n5

Rhodes Plaza Hotel. (n.d.). *Quality Policy.* Retrieved from https://www.rhodesplazahotel.com/quality-policy/

Shewhart, W. A. (1930). Economic Quality Control of Manufactured Product. *The Bell System Technical Journal, 9*(2), 2. doi:10.1002/j.1538-7305.1930.tb00373.x

Taylor, F. W. (1911). *Principles of Scientific Management.* New York: Harper The Automobile Association (2019). *Ratings and Awards.* Retrieved from http://www.theaa.com/hotel-services/ratings-and-awards

The Walt Disney Company. (2019). *About.* Retrieved from https://www.thewaltdisneycompany.com/about/

UNTWO. (2016, June 28). *Quality Management Key Competitiveness Tourism Destinations.* [Press release]. Retrieved from www.media.unwto.org/press-release/2016-06-28/quality-management-key-competitiveness-tourism-destinations

VisitBritain. (2017). *VisitEngland announces contract with the AA to run the VisitEngland Quality Assessment Schemes.* Retrieved from https://www.visitbritain.org/visitengland-announces-contract-aa-run-visitengland-quality-assessment-schemes

Chapter 2
The Use of Social Media as a Tool to Capture Customer Value and Interaction

Husam H. Alharahsheh
https://orcid.org/0000-0002-0194-3700
University of Wales Trinity Saint David, UK

Abraham Pius
Manchester Metropolitan University, UK & Arden University, UK

Imad Guenane
London College of Contemporary Art, UK

Chad Manian
https://orcid.org/0000-0002-0808-0709
Berlin School of Business and Innovation, Germany

ABSTRACT

The chapter provides in depth theoretical and conceptual explanation of social media as well as firm-customer interaction through social media, highlighting several advantages and disadvantages of their uses. Furthermore, the chapter is supported using a framework relating to the development of social media channels and their uses for firms followed by inclusion of a service-based case study to further support the analysis on the communication process through social media platforms managed by the firm. Finally, the chapter highlights several challenges relevant to firm social media activities followed by key considerations based on the analysis provided in the different sections of the chapter.

DOI: 10.4018/978-1-7998-2204-2.ch002

Copyright © 2020, IGI Global. Copying or distributing in print or electronic forms without written permission of IGI Global is prohibited.

INTRODUCTION TO THE CHAPTER

The main purpose of joining social media is for social interaction as well as increasing the sense of belonging within a community. However, over the last decade social media platforms have evolved to become platforms for other several purposes such as entertainment and shopping as well as a source of news feed offering ease of accessibility and communication at a global stage (Sarason, 1974; Zhou et al., 2001). The ease of accessibility and communication offered through social media platforms create positive influence to increase awareness and enhance reputation of firms. However, negative comments raised by customers may gain more interest and publicity widely than any other positive comments leading to a serious threat to firms as there is very limited control over the process of communication (Hu et al., 2008).

CATEGORIES OF SOCIAL MEDIA

Social media channels can be divided into two different categories (Frost, 2016):

First category: Firm's websites aiming to enhance customer community such as forums.

Second category: third party social media platforms such as Facebook, Twitter, forums accessed through third parties' websites, YouTube, and Instagram.

Firms aim to use several techniques and channels to engage customers, monitor trends, and analysis such as market intelligence leading to creation and development of offerings.

As shown in figure 1 that firms use social medial for several purposes such as marketing, sales, employee collaboration, public relations and customer services. All these purposes can be gained through development of social media enabling firms to develop as strategy on their firm – customer interaction strategy.

Interaction Between Firms and Customers

The growth of social media platforms was caused by peer and friend recommendations, and development of networks. This led to a significant increase in the importance of social media exploitation by firms as social media users had more access and connectivity to provide shared content, positive or negative reviews, and feedback (Haven, 2007). Furthermore, the use of social media includes a significant percentage of internet users, according to a study conducted by (Pew Research, 2012) that almost 70% of internet users are active on their online social media platforms providing

Figure 1. Enterprise uses of social media
Source: (Frost & Sullivan, 2016)

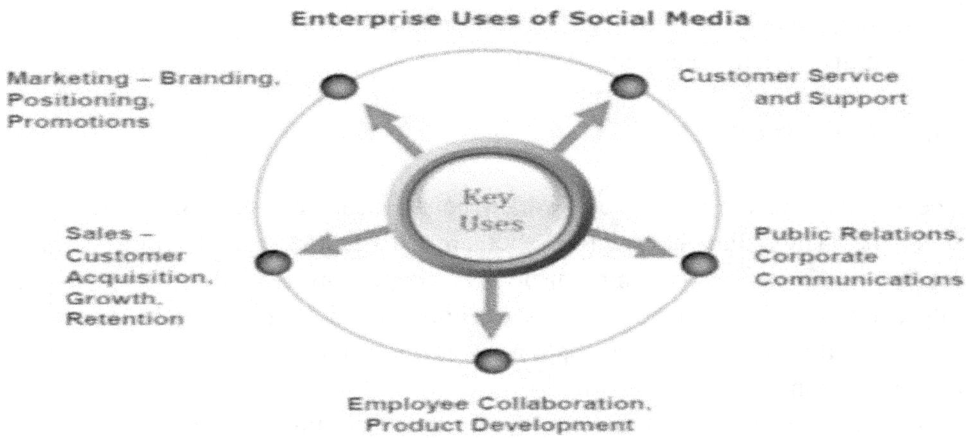

companies unimaginable opportunity to keep in touch with existing and potential customers (Shankar et al., 2011; Parent et al., 2011).

It is noted by several researchers that social media lead to more firm and customer engagement, customer satisfaction and loyalty, and increasingly became platforms for personal evaluation of company's offerings (Palmatier et al., 2006; Kumar et al., 2010; Chen et al., 2011).

Social media developed because of the rapid advancement of technology and increase of users, this provided firms unlimited opportunities to further their interaction with customers. Furthermore, several researchers highlighted the following benefits for firm – customer interaction (Mollen and Wilson, 2010; Calder et al., 2009; Cadler and Malthouse, 2005):

1. The development of social media enabled businesses to measure emotional experiences of customers.
2. Leading to greater advertising effectiveness and impact measurement.
3. Customers are further involved in determining the creation of offerings through providing product and services evaluations, and general feedback including offering related as well as emotions associated with the consumption experience.

The greater involvement in the creation and development of offerings because of firm-customer interaction can be conceptualized in steps as the following: Firstly, online content creation targeted at existing and potential customers. Secondly, content has a certain level of control from the firm side and becomes shared from the customer side. Thirdly, content shared create and enhance sense of community as it is being shared. Fourthly, comments and conversations are facilitated by firms leading to two-way communications providing valuable inputs and feedback, and leading to greater understanding of customers as well as continues offering development based on trending demands (Parent et al., 2011).

The 3M Framework

The development of the 3M Framework to enhance customer communication using social media by Gallaugher and Randsbotham (2010) provide greater understanding for firms on the process of communication and opportunities arising through the use of social media leading to development of communication strategies, the framework consists of three categories (Megaphone, Magnet, Monitor) which can be explained as the following:

Megaphone: It includes the firm's to customer communication to share firm's messages, news and updates, and to position the brand.

Magnet: It includes inbound dialog between the firm and customers such as providing access to share feedback and product evaluation leading to greater understanding of customers' needs and wants, and concerns regarding firm's offering.

Monitor: It includes firm's ability to monitor its overall social media activity and performance using several techniques such as observation of posts, and inter-customer engagement. The disadvantage of social media is that it allows competitors

Figure 2. The 3M framework
Source: Kim & Mukhopadhyay (2011) Determining Optimal CRM Implementation Strategies

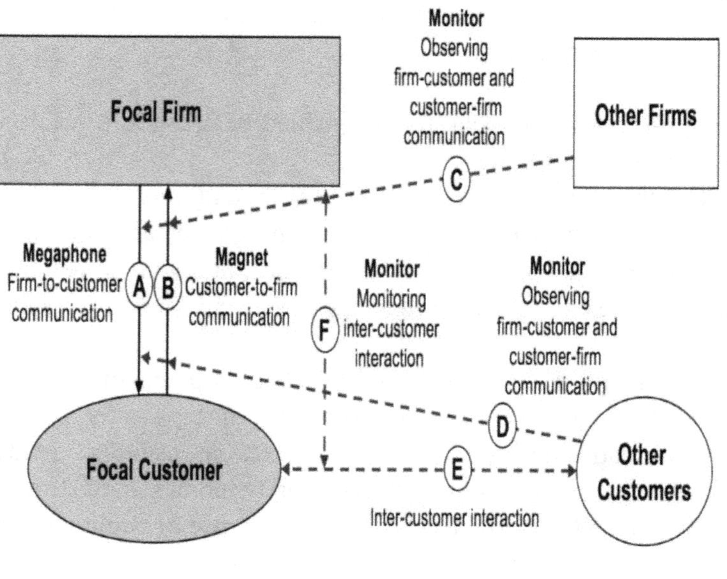

to monitor activities to determine the effectiveness of the firm's social media engagement performance (Kim and Mukhopadyay, 2011).

THE 3M FRAMEWORK AND NETFLIX

Megaphone

Netflix uses several social media platforms to communicate with customers such as Facebook, twitter, Instagram and YouTube. It is highlighted that Netflix global social media channels communicate on regular basis using the mentioned platforms to inform customers on new releases and updates, brand positing, and share of general company information.

Facebook: Netflix is considered as the main social media network as it has the highest number of followers totaling over sever million for their global page followed by over one million for their U.S. page. Netflix uses geographic segmentation for their Facebook pages by splitting their Facebook pages into several regions to provide relevant information to their targeted customers in each region.

Twitter: Similar to their Facebook pages, Netflix has several twitter accounts.

Instagram: Similar to the other social media channels, Netflix has several accounts. For example, their US and Brazil accounts have nearly 3 million followers both together.

Magnet

Netflix has a consistent communication strategy to enhance dialog between the company and customers to enhance customer relationships and engagement, as well as gaining customer feedback and evaluation.

Facebook, Twitter and Instagram: Netflix update its customers with several posts daily. However, the case varies from a regional page to another as some take longer time gaps to post. Netflix's customers highlighted the following in different reviews:

1. The company has quick response to comments/concerns raised by customers.
2. Enables feedback giving and response through ratings and offerings evaluation.
3. Fresh daily content and updates.
4. Exclusive deals offered for followers on their social media channels.

Monitor

The features provided by several social media channels enable the firm to monitor the activities within their sites as well as intervene when required. However, the firm experienced some challenges in monitoring and controlling their social media presence. For example, in 2012 Mr. Hastings, the CEO of the firm had an update in regards to one of the firm's offering commenting the following "Netflix had delivered streaming video in excess of 1 billion hours in the preceding month" despite the fact that Netflix have never announced that the CEO's social media accounts are used for stakeholders' engagement leading to some negative comments shared on social media in regards to it and required further clarification as discussed in the report by the legal consultancy firm (Simpson Thacher, 2013), this example was highlighted as a practice firms should avoid in engaging stakeholders through the use of social media.

It can be noted that the firm monitor its social media performance and activities through the use of several techniques such as:

1. Monitoring dialogue between customers on the given social media platforms.
2. Monitoring customer feedback through rating and open-ended questions providing valuable information and customer insights.

Challenges of Social Media

Based on a Harvard Business review report by (Armano, 2009) and research by (Kaplan and Haenlein, 2010) that firms face several challenges in managing their social media activities which can be summarized as the following:

1. Integration of all business departments with the new uses of social media as a new form of marketing and customer engagement.
2. Governance of social media activities such as content on the used channels as well as employees' comments shared through these platforms.
3. Human resource alignment with policies, procedures and protocols to ensure that activities on social media are legal and aligned with planed strategies.
4. Measurement and monitoring of activities as social media platforms are not only considered as a megaphone only following the 3Ms framework, but they are rather a magnet leading to high level of interactivity as well as lower levels of control.

CASE STUDY FOR DISCUSSION

Netflix

Netflix is firm operating within the entertainment industry specializing in providing video streaming services for a wide range of customers at global stage in exchange for fees charged through subscriptions. The firm is considered as one of the pioneering firms in technology utilization to provide entertainment content.

Historical Overview

The company's operations were initiated through following a classical model of renting DVDs back in 2007, then the company invested in the development of its technology and internet capabilities to introduce VoD streaming business, the company is mainly providing visual streaming through the internet. Now the company is considered as the largest company in online streaming for Movies and TV shows with millions of subscribers.

Competition

The Video on demand industry within entertainment has several major players alongside with Netflix such as Hulu. Players in the industry mainly compete on prices as well as through offering exclusive and personalized services accessible by wide range of devices. Major players within the industry used a hybrid model such as advertising revenues and complementary to other prime offerings of mega firms such as amazon (Mikhalkina, 2013).

Value Capture

The major source of revenues for the firm is gained through fees charged for subscriptions providing unlimited movies and TV shows streamed over the internet to wide range of devices. The main value proposition for the company provided to customers is the add free during the online streaming. However, this may lead to continues increases in subscription fees due to the loss of other sources of revenues such as online advertisements (Mikhalkina, 2013).

Questions for Debate and Discussions

1. What are the key challenges facing Netflix considering their current competition?

2. How can the firm enhance its value capture considering changes in the external environment such as technology developments and customer behavior trends?
3. Can successful social media strategy contribute to distinguish the current firm's offering? How?

CONCLUSION

The chapter provided an in depth theoretical and conceptual explanation on social medial and its importance for firm – customer engagement with explanation and application of the 3M framework developed by Gallaugher and Randsbotham (2010) highlighting their main advantages and disadvantages, and followed by application of the framework on Netflix's social media activities. The study also provided a list of challenges associated with firms' social media activities as well as a case study of Netflix including key questions for class debates and discussions.

It can be concluded that having a successful social media strategy could lead to a high level of engagement of customer through several social media platforms. However, some points were highlighted in different sections of the chapter such as coordination between regional activities on social media, alignment, monitoring and control, measurement and key performance indicators, and compliance.

REFERENCES

Armano, D. (2009). *Five Challenges Social Media Will Bring to Business*. Harvard Business Review. Retrieved from https://hbr.org/2009/08/a-recent-survey-conducted-by

Calder, J., & Edward, C. (2005). Managing Media and Advertising Change with Integrated Marketing. *Journal of Advertising Research*, *45*(4), 1–6.

Calder, J., Edward, C., & Ute, S. (2009). An Experimental Study of the Relationship Between Online Engagement and Advertising Effectiveness. *Journal of Interactive Marketing*, *23*(November), 321–331. doi:10.1016/j.intmar.2009.07.002

Chen, Y., Scott Fay, S., & Wang, Q. (2011). The Role of Marketing in Social Media: How Online Consumer Reviews Evolve. *Journal of Interactive Marketing*, *25*(2), 85–94. doi:10.1016/j.intmar.2011.01.003

Frost & Sullivan. (2016). Social media customer engagement. Retrieved from http://frostftp.com/JE/Events/CC/Sitel/Social_Media_Customer_Engagement.pdf

Gallaugher, J., & Ransbotham, S. (2010). Social media and customer dialog management at Starbucks. *MIS Quarterly Executive*, *9*, 1389–1404.

Haven, B. (2007). Marketing's New Key Metric: Engagement. *Forrester Research.*

Hu, N., Liu, L., & Zhang, J. (2008). Do online reviews affect product sales? The role of reviewer characteristics and temporal effects. *Information Technology Management*, *9*(3), 201–214. doi:10.100710799-008-0041-2

Kaplan, A., & Haenlein, M. (2010). Users of the world, unite! The challenges and opportunities of Social Media. *Business Horizons*, *53*(1), 59–68. doi:10.1016/j.bushor.2009.09.003

Kim, S., & Mukhopadhyay, T. (2011). Determining Optimal CRM Implementation Strategies. *Information Systems Research*, *22*(3), 624–639. doi:10.1287/isre.1100.0309

Kumar, V., Lerzan, A., Bas, D., Rajkumar, V., Thorsten, W., & Sebastian, T. (2010). Undervalued or Overvalued Customers: Capturing Total Customer Engagement Value. *Journal of Service Research*, *13*(3), 297–310. doi:10.1177/1094670510375602

Mikhalkina, T. (2013). Netflix Business Model. Retrieved from http://www.cass.city.ac.uk/__data/assets/pdf_file/0017/220517/Netflix.pdf

Mollen, A., & Hugh, W. (2010). Engagement, Telepresence, and Interactivity in Online Consumer Experience: Reconciling Scholastic and Managerial Perspectives. *Journal of Business Research*, *63*(9/10), 919–925. doi:10.1016/j.jbusres.2009.05.014

Palmatier, R., Rajiv, P., Dhruv, G., & Kenneth, R. (2006). Factors Influencing the Effectiveness of Relationship Marketing: A Meta-Analysis. *Journal of Marketing*, *70*(October), 136–153. doi:10.1509/jmkg.70.4.136

Parent, M., Kirk, P., & Anjali, B. (2011). The New WTP: Willingness to Participate. *Business Horizons*, *54*(3), 219–229. doi:10.1016/j.bushor.2011.01.003

Pew Research. (2012). *Pew Internet: Social Networking*. Retrieved from http://www.pewinternet.org/Commentary/2012/March/Pew-Internet-Social-Networking-less-detail.aspx

Sarason, S. B. (1974). *The psychological sense of community: Prospects for the community.* San Francisco: Jossey-Bass.

Shankar, J., Jeffrey I., Murali M., Eileen K., & Ross, R. (2011). Innovations in Shopper Marketing: Current Insights and Future Research Issues. *Journal of Retailing*, *87*(1), 29-42.

Stblaw.com. (2013). *Social Media and Regulation FD: SEC Uses Netflix Episode to Clarify Policy, Not Liberalize It*. Retrieved from http://www.stblaw.com/docs/default-source/cold-fusion-existing-content/publications/pub1605.pdf?sfvrsn=2

Zhou, Z., Zhang, Q., Chenting, S., & Zhou, N. (2011). How do brand communities generate brand relationships? Intermediate mechanisms. *Journal of Business Research*, 890–895.

Chapter 3
Contemporary Management Approaches to the Global Hospitality and Tourism Industry:
Technology as a Panacea for Sector Growth

Edwin Agwu
https://orcid.org/0000-0002-3384-4088
Lagos Business School, Nigeria

ABSTRACT

This chapter describes how the era of brick and mortar, hitherto called the analogue years, has given way to the era of digits where everything functions with the touch of a button. From agriculture to banking, health to education, information search to manufacturing; and the hospitality and tourism sector is not left out. Information and communication technologies (ICT) has changed the way businesses are done in contemporary ways. The business environment and their managers have been challenged to think of how to integrate the opportunities posed by technology into their business models for competitive advantages.

DOI: 10.4018/978-1-7998-2204-2.ch003

Copyright © 2020, IGI Global. Copying or distributing in print or electronic forms without written permission of IGI Global is prohibited.

INTRODUCTION

The era of brick and mortar, hitherto called the analogue years has given way to the era of digits where everything functions with the touch of a button. From agriculture to banking, health to education, information search to manufacturing; and the hospitality and tourism sector is not left out. Information and communication technologies (ICT) has changed the way businesses are done in contemporary ways. The business environment and their managers have been challenged to think of how to integrate the challenges posed by technology into their business models for competitive advantages. The technology age has led to the movement of virtually all business models to adopt the information economy which is a characteristic of digitalization. Suffice to state that ICT is a combination of different terminologies which consists of both simple and complex features. For example, cell phone applications (phone calls), internet (wireless and cable network), geographical positioning system (GPS), geographic information system (GIS), digital radio, and convergence (media, voice and data). These modern technologies have and are constantly disrupting the market space, creating a huge competition among traditional tourism experts as well investors. These disruptions have however created an avenue for new market entrants to competitively tap into the tourism sphere for opportunities exploration than ever before. Both traditional and market disrupters have agreed that ICT has aided the growth this sector by creating a global audience, available market information, conducting electronic businesses which has increased the economic efficiency, (Kayode-Adedeji and Agwu, 2015). The present business environment is classified as the fast and efficient age between tourism consumers, tourism developers and tourisms agents of distribution. The dependency on information has made the industry a pivotal and indispensable part of the economy, thereby placing at the fore in search of ICT models that will aid its effectiveness (Mason & Milne, 2002). The adoption of business to business (B2B) and business to consumers (B2C) has made the industry adoption of ICT an indispensable part of the business models, and this has shifted the traditional way in which tourism is being practised (O'Connor & Frew, 2002). For tourism suppliers, the challenge is centred on how to develop e-commerce features and products for consumers and finding ways to integrate the advantages to the tourism sector. The pivotal role of ICT is seen in different dimensions in the tourism sectors. Tourism is intangible and ICT offers the opportunities for a descriptive and better representation to consumers before they finally visit the destinations. The roles of ICT in tourism are discussed below:

Marketing

ICT has provided a channel through which information flow from end to another within seconds. These media is used to discuss and display tourism products in a specific and quantifiable way, such that the consumers will be able to relate directly with their expectations as regards what they see through the advert medium. The challenges associated with traditional tourism before the advent of ICT has always been related to conflict or disequilibrium between consumers' expectation and the site. Also, the challenges of time difference, exchange rates (in which some tourist have somewhat been stranded) are sorted out through timely provision of information as result of ICT adoption. The changing nature of tourism market distribution has been aided through the use of ICT in tourism marketing (Buhalis & Licata, 2002; Bloom, 2005; Buhalis, 2009). The marketing adopted by different tourism organizations range from collaborating with other partners to ensure consumers have better tourism experience. Typically, ICT is leveraged on to bring integration of different business owners to form a cohesive force. For example, airlines partner with tourism companies, these companies partner with hotels and these form a conglomerate aim at bringing better and informed customer experience. ICT provides a platform for timely delivery of marketing information to tourism consumers such that they can choose from the varieties of options and packages provided by the advertising firm or travel agencies. The challenge of trying to reach people living in different location is solved with the use of ICT. For example, different media are adopted and different technologies deployed as a substitute for personnel marketing which is characterised by vague interpretation of company objectives and goals. The ICT neural networks are used for market segmentation (Bloom, 2005), and the use of data analytics helps to classify customer preferences, history and choices based on their web visits, online discussions in other make a better and informed marketing choice. Consumer preferences and choices are based on their prior interaction with a brand (either online or offline). The susceptibility of consumers to online products and services are heightened because of the adoption of Internet of Things (IOT) by larger percentage of consumer population, this opportunity offers tourism organizations the opportunity to be cited first and more often by consumers, thereby, increasing their chances of being patronized by consumers (USAID, 2006). The application of statistical predictive modelling through ICT; helps marketers to determine the nature of tourism demands in future years and these helps to have a futuristic calculation of the infrastructure to put in place to meet market demands. Marketing decisions are based on numbers and statistics which are quantitatively obtained the digital footprints of potential and actual consumers. Wober (2003) supported the opinion that ICT aid information sharing in tourism which in turn help to increase consumers' base for effective profit maximization in tourism sectors. The marketing strategy adopted as a result of consumers' data analysed can help to sell the right product to the right consumer at the right time.

E-Hospitality

The tendencies for high expectations from tourism consumers are factors that pose challenges to tourism managements. Because consumers are coming from different sophisticated environment, they held on to the experiences they receive from other business sectors when going for a tour. These expectations may range from internet provisions in their rooms, virtual tour in their phones or electronic gadgets among others. Not meeting these needs implied that consumers' expectations will not be met in relation to what the tourism management offer and this may lead to customer dissatisfaction. As a result of this, the integration of ICT has helped to bring to a minimal level the effect of consumers' expectation in relation to the services offered by tourism firms.

Through ICT, consumers' preferences can be determined. They can provide enough information in relation to their budget on the website of the company in charge of their tour. These technological services can be integrated into the hospitality provisions made for the tourist, thereby, reshaping the market functioning values for better improvement of consumers' tour experiences. For example, consumers expect that their rooms are well connected with internet, well equipped with better facilities that mirror their expectations. The internet has made bookings of hotels around the tourism location easy, and transaction made during the tour are electronically done to avoid challenges (e.g. tourist robbery) associated with cash carrying. The response time associated with transaction and attendance to tourist have been minimize, in other to accommodate as many tourists as possible. The ICT enables data efficiency and control, customers' data management and relational services, which are all aimed at ensuring better services for tourists (Buhalis & Law, 2008; Aramendia-Muneta, Elena, Ollo-Lopez & Andrea, 2015).

Destination Organizations

The use of ICT has reduced the complexity associated with tourism destinations. The complicatedness associated with tourism requires that there is need for effective destination management. Destinations management organizations (DMO) help both the tourist and host communities to have a sense of what to expect. In some cases, the host communities are provided descriptive characteristics of their visitors and the tourist are also familiarized with the routes in the tourist centres through virtual simulations. This is tailored towards ensuring that residents well-being is enhanced and also to ensure that tourist are offered a satisfactory experiences, that

Figure 1. Destination Management Organization (van Hooft, 2010)

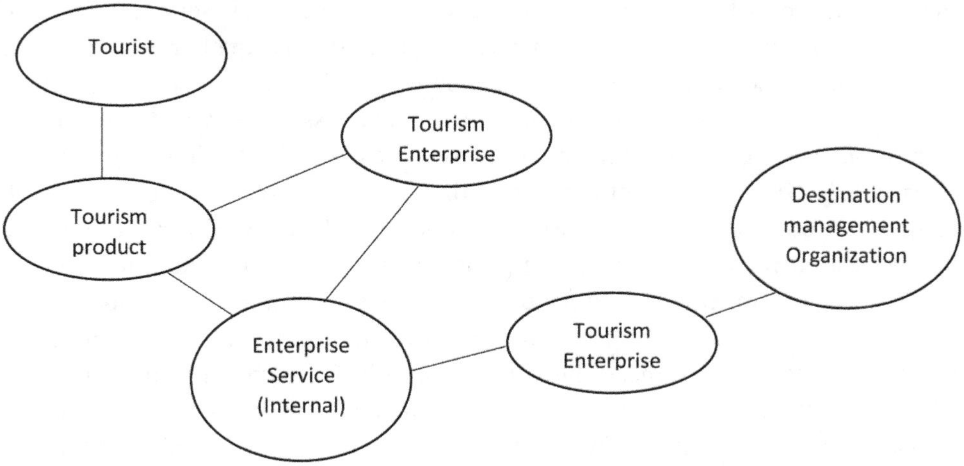

may enhance their decisions for revisiting the tourist centres in nearest future. This satisfactory experiences may be rated on a scale of minimally satisfied, moderately satisfied or/and highly satisfied (Bornhorst, Brent & Sheehan, 2010), and this can be achieved with the incorporation of ICT for effective and efficient tourism destination organizations.

Destination management organization helps to support local industries participation in the tourism industry. This collaboration is enhanced through segmentation of the local businesses within tourism environment. Every industry in the environment are classified based on their level of importance and what they have to offer to the tourist within the specified period, and they organized and presented to tourist to choose from even before they get to their tourism locations. This type of destination management enhances local businesses and brings about the development and beautification of the tourism centres due to the participation of the local communities.

Communication and Booking

Information technology (hardware and software developments) information management, system integration and intelligence applications in the tourism industry have helped improve the way booking and tourism business communication is carried out. The strategic inflow of ICT in tourism sector has aided the way booking is done. The convenience associated with the ease of engaging ICT in tourism has facilitated better consumers' outlook of the industry. The ICT engagement has provided a global reach of audience, which means that tourism industries can deliver and provide their services directly to consumers without a third party.

Tourism stakeholders (e.g. governments, hotels and lodges) are now aware of the importance of having an online presence to facilitate their services. Some of these agencies have built and are maintaining a more consumer friendly website for advertising the unique features associated with their offers, in other to promote tourists booking orders as well as promotional coupons associated with their services. The automation of payment services is also enabled by ICT. Previously, traditional tourism rely on cash payment because of the fear that payment made are not well recorded in terms of balancing consumers' order with their payment. This challenge has been eased off, as payment automation is done via online transaction and it is then verified to confirm either the authenticity of the payment or to confirm the payers' account for easy identification. ICT enables a better data processing by consumers in the tourism sector. Consumers' through the use of ICT can obtain vital information that will aid their trip planning. These vary from the security issues around the site to issues relating to number of visitors, casualties and success recorded by the site. Waghmode and Jamsandekar (2013) opined that ICT integration in the tourism sector can help tourist and tourism industries to get vital information about roads, weather condition, as well as the availability of important items (e.g. water, power, market etc.) that may needed to make tourism an interesting adventure for the tourist. The same technology can also help experts to define their boundaries, and monitor their site to wage against encroachment.

The Economic Importance of ICT in Tourism

The influx of people in the twenty-first century due to the tendencies to explore other parts of the globe has led to different advancement and innovations both in transportation and communications technologies. Most nations have begun to see the significant importance of tourism especially due to its contribution to economic activities and Gross Domestic Product (GDP) growth. The economic importance of ICT to tourism has been reported to have profound implications for job creation, environmental beautification, infrastructure development, health, education etc., (Shanker, 2008). The integration of ICT has made the transportation of information an easy one especially for job seekers and other strands of the economic pyramid. Knowledge about the tourism industries are produced, transmitted and accessed with convenience, which means that people can access information anywhere and anytime.

Job Creation

The contribution of tourism to the global economy according World Travel & Tourism Council (WTTC) (2014) was about 9.5%. The adoption of ICT within the tourism industry has significantly bolstered the number of jobs in recent times;

about 266 million jobs (8.9% of total employment) were as a result of travel and tourism. International Labour Organization (ILO, 2010) global dialogue reported that there is an expected 296 million jobs from the tourism sector in 2019, despite the global economic and social crisis, which implied that tourism is a major source of job generator. Tourism business requires that experts are engaged in line with consumers' expectations. These experts may be learned or unlearned individuals depending on their area of expertise. For example, learned individuals may involve trained professionals (accountants, robotics engineers, and industry-based professionals), while unlearned may involve local indigenes who know the different routes and taboos in the tourism locations. Kayode-Adedeji and Agwu, (2015) stressed that through the use of ICT, professionals can access to opportunities within the industry, and investors can also place their offers for any employee they want to engage. The labour intensive nature of tourism makes it a significant contributor to job generator for different hierarchy of the world's population: women, men, youth, migrants, and immigrants, etc. (Dayananda, 2014). There are developing economies that have leveraged on the economic and job creation significance of tourism to influence the number growth of their GDP. For instance, India has 25 million jobs created through tourism alone (Dayananda, 2014). Ethiopia has about 9.3% (a total of ETB 91,898.4 million) GDP contribution from tourism, and about 8.5% (2,291,500) jobs in 2014 from tourism. Blanke, Chiesa, and Herrera (2009) reported that the European Union (EU) member countries tourism report showed that governments of EU member countries (e.g. Austria, Germany, France, Spain etc.) are prioritizing the tourism sector because of its importance to their overall GDP. Accordingly, policies and efforts are directed towards ensuring that the country is well designed to suit tourist expectations, and that marketing organizations projects the country image well to international communities, thereby, making the tourism sector a key factor in European countries economy. The implication of this review is centred on the need for Nigerian tourism industries to adopt holistically the use of ICT in order to have a better patronage. Agwu, (2016) asserts that Tourism can help in the creation of more jobs through diversification of the economy within the Nigerian industries. Through the application of ICT, experts can be trained on how to navigate various areas of the tourism environments, and also different area of the economy can feel the impact of tourism activities. For example, hotels, airlines, local indigenes, government through taxation can contribute significantly to the economic growth of the country.

Environmental Management

Environmental management resulting from tourism activities has been aided in recent years through the application of technology. The natural areas which are mainly the selling points of tourism developers have been enhanced by the use of routed information from consumers' responses. To this end, planning of any area or region is tailored towards the expectation and taste of the tourism consumers. Early environmental planning during tourism landscaping has prevented negative environmental impacts proposed by different researchers (GhulamRabbany, Afrin, Rahman, Islam & Hoque, 2013), and has led to the improved environmental access which are necessary for tourism development. Early stages of tourism have witnessed the depletion of the environment due to inability to have a cleaner environment for tourism operations. These challenges are reasons provided by indigenous citizens of tourism centres for why they will be hostile to tourists. The recent application of ICT and advance technological tools has seen the mitigation against these challenges. Tourism centres now have better planned designs that give easy operation to different facilities to be used by tourists without any interruption to the daily activities of indigenous residents of the tourism environments. For example, the application of energy efficient and non-polluting materials (green building) during designs and constructions is one way that the tourism industry has enjoyed the application of ICT to the tourism sector.

Infrastructure Development

The conceptualization of smart tourism has been undoubtedly credited to the application of ICT to the tourism industry especially in the area of infrastructural development. The environmental comprehension, profit from experience, knowledge acquisition and retention, and response to the changing needs and demands of the environment significantly is fully integrated as a result of ICT adaptation to the tourism industry (Rudas & fodor, 2008). Within the tourism industry, the adoption of such characteristics enabled by ICT is one of the significant factors that help to provide necessary information that enhances better decisions, greater mobility, and tourism experiences to both consumers and service providers (Werthner, 2003; Sigala & Chalkiti, 2014). In this case, the service providers develop infrastructures based on the need and current demands in the industry, thereby informing a perceptual experience that will aid revisit by consumers. The focus on tourists' satisfaction has led to different infrastructural development from roads to physical structures such as power supplies needed for operations. From the industry perspectives, the emphasis is on the fact that these infrastructures help to build a good experience for consumers and indigenous inhabitants of the tourism centres; therefore, it is safe to say that beautifying the tourism environment is the bane of successful tourism industry. Smart tourism also considers technology as part of the infrastructures necessary for tourism industry enhancement. ICT is then not viewed as individual information systems but rather as a tourism infrastructure enabler. The ICT features like hardware, software and network technologies through integration help develop infrastructures that aid tourism industries achieve their objectives (Washburn, Sindhu, Balaouras, Dines, Hayes, & Nelson, 2010).

The Downside of Tourism On The People

Tourism has contributed to the global economy and has been cited as a means of economic development to developed and developing economies. However, the social, economic, cultural and environmental downside effects of tourism activities exist. The effects can be linked to both natural (e.g. earthquakes, and other natural disasters) and human causes (e.g. terrorism). The dangers associated with tourism are as highlighted below:

Attraction of Terrorists

Tourism activities have increased and have disrupted social orders in some closely knitted clans. Terrorism is then developed as a way of responding to this disruption (Lutz and Lutz, 2008). Tourism as a modernization tool have contributed to terrorism development by the fact that terrorist only strike those structures that disrupt what they believe to be their social or/and cultural heritage. Therefore, tourism and terrorism are incongruously connected because of their distinct characteristics. Baker (2014) proposed that the relationship between tourism and terrorism are inseparable such that they both utilize travel and communications technologies, involves citizens of different countries, and both crosses national borders. Although, the international recognition of terrorism occurred in 1972 Olympic Games in Munich, terrorist operations against tourists are still prevalent in recent times. Terrorism acts targeted at tourists in the past have been documented within the African territory. The Al Quaeda network simultaneous twin attacks in Tanzania and Kenya was a major setback for tourism in those countries (Sonmez, Yiorgos & Tarlow, 1999). These attacks result in loss of lives and properties, and massive tourism withdrawal of tourist was witnessed as a result of hotels and flight cancellations (Kelley, Redfern, Munaita, & The East African Bureau, 2002). The bombing of the Paradise Hotel in North Coast Kenya as well as the firing of the Israeli airliner which was narrowly missed are effects of tourism on the host communities of tourism activities (Agutu, 2003). In Nigeria, the security challenges are heightened in different parts of the country. Kidnapping, robbery and killings are prevalent in the south and terrorism which has led to destruction of lives and properties as well as military bases and foreign buildings are found in the North (Ndanusa, Harada & Islam, 2014). Petty

Figure 2. Number of Dead Tourist from 2006-2014 by Terrorists (Khrishna, 2015)

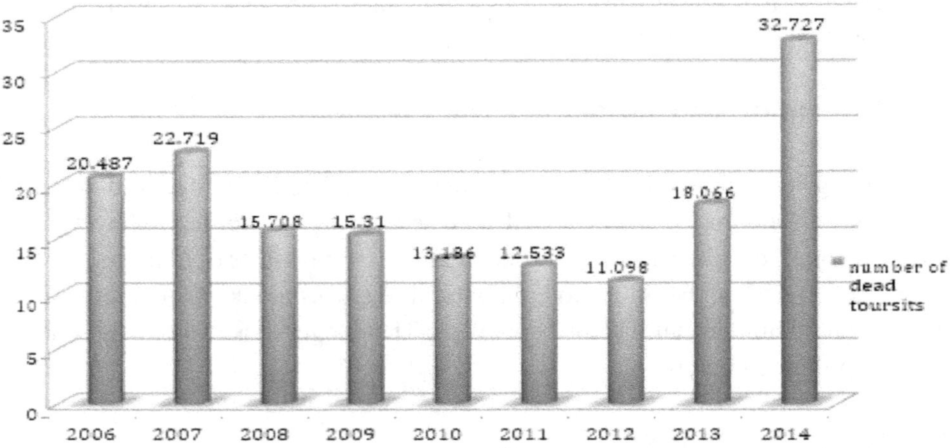

Cybercrimes

The tourism industry is largely reliant on the Internet and communication technologies for operations. This integration of ICT with tourism also poses significant threat in terms of cyber vulnerabilities. Agwu (2013) stressed that cyber-attacks have increased in recent times and major focuses of attackers have always been on foreigners because of their currency or their security vulnerabilities. Cyber-attacks are launched by criminals and criminal organizations with the sole aim of obtaining financial gain from online visitors' activities (Grimes, 2005; Deloitte, 2006, Olding, & Turner, 2007). The current malicious cyber environment poses greater risks for tourism industry; as a result, there will be panic withdrawal or loss of interest from potential tourist due to inability to trust organizations handling their classified personal information and the creation of spurious websites used in defrauding tourist within the tourism industries (Olding, & Turner, 2007).

Based on the above, it is evident that technology in all its facets can effectively and efficiently play a vital role in cubing various social vices while promoting the sector. The internet and websites can be used to showcase tourist attractions in various forms.

REFERENCES

Agwu, E. M. (2013, April-June). Cyber criminals on the internet super highways: A technical investigation of different shades and colours within the Nigerian cyber space. *International Journal of Online Marketing*, *3*(2), 56–74. doi:10.4018/ijom.2013040104

Agwu, M. E. (2016). ICT Diffusion, Adoption and Strategic importance in Nigerian SMEs. *International Journal of Research in Management. Science & Technology*, *4*(3), 64–75.

Aramendia-Muneta, M.E. & Ollo-Lopez, A. (2015). ICT impact on tourism industry. Retrieved from https://www.researchgate.net/publication/268563002_ICT_impact_on_tourism_industry

Baker, D. M. A. (2014). The effects of terrorism on the travel and tourism industry. *International Journal of Religious Tourism and Pilgrimage*, *2*(1), 9.

Blanke, J., Chiesa, T., & Herrera, E. T. (2009). The travel and tourism competitiveness index 2009: measuring sectoral drivers in a downturn. In J. Blanke, & T. Chiesa (Eds.), *The travel and tourism competitive report 2009* (pp. 3-38). Geneva, Switzerland: World Economic Forum.

Bloom, J. Z. Market Segmentation. (. (2005). A Neural Network Application. *Annals of Tourism Research*, *32*(1), 93–111. doi:10.1016/j.annals.2004.05.001

Bornhorst, T., Brent, R. J. R., & Sheehan, L. (2010). Determinants of tourism success for DMOs & destinations: An empirical examination of stakeholders' perspectives. *Tourism Management*, *31*(5), 572–589. doi:10.1016/j.tourman.2009.06.008

Buhalis, D. (1998). Strategic use of information technologies in the tourism industry. [online]. *Tourism Management*, *19*(5), 409–421. doi:10.1016/S0261-5177(98)00038-7

Buhalis, D., & Law, R. (2008). Progress in information technology and tourism management: 20 years on and 10 years after the Internet—The state of eTourism research. *Tourism Management*, *29*(4), 609–623. doi:10.1016/j.tourman.2008.01.005

Buhalis, D., & Licata, C. (2002). The future eTourism intermediaries. *Tourism Management*, *23*(3), 207–220. doi:10.1016/S0261-5177(01)00085-1

Dayananda, K. (2014). Tourism and Employment: Opportunities and Challenges in Karnataka - Special Reference to Kodagu District. *IOSR Journal of Humanities and Social Science,* 19, 11.

GhulamRabbany, M., Afrin, S., Rahman, A., Islam, F., & Hoque, F., (2013). Environmental effects of tourism. *American Journal of Environment, Energy and Power Research, 1*(7), 117-130

International labour organization. (2010). *Development and Challenges in Tourism and Hospitality Sector.*

Kayode-Adedeji, T. K. & Agwu, M.E. (2015). Application of ICT to agriculture as a panacea to unemployment in Nigeria. *International Journals of Multidisciplinary Research Academy, 3*(4), 26-48.

Kelly, K. J., Redfern, P., & Munaita, P. (2002). How Western security failure led to bombing. The East African weekly. Retrieved from http://www.nationaudio.com

Khrisna, R. (2015). Effects of terrorism in tourism industry. A case study of 9/11 terrorist attacks in world trade centre. Unpublished Bachelor's thesis, Centria University of Applied Sciences. Retrieved from https://www.theseus.fi/bitstream/handle/10024/103202/krishna.pdf?sequence=1

Lutz, J. M., & Lutz, B. J. (2008). *Global Terrorism.* Oxford: Oxford University Press. doi:10.4324/9780203895030

Mason, D., & Milne, S. (2002). E-Commerce and Community Tourism. In P. C. Palvia, S. C. Palvia & E. M. Roche (Eds.), Global Information Technology and Electronic Commerce: issues for the New Millennium (pp. 294–310). Marietta, Gerogia: Ivy League Publishing Ltd.

Ndanusa, M. M., Harada, Y., & Islam, M. (2014). Challenges to Growth in Tourism Industry of a Developing Country: The Case of Nigeria. *Asian Social Science, 10*(19), 282–290. doi:10.5539/ass.v10n19p282

O'Connor, P., & Frew, A. J. (2002). The future of hotel electronic distribution: Expert and industry perspectives. *The Cornell Hotel and Restaurant Administration Quarterly, 43*(3), 33–45. doi:10.1016/S0010-8804(02)80016-7

Olding, A., & Turner, P. (2007). Cyber vulnerabilities and the tourism industry: developing a conceptual framework. In *ACIS 2007 Proceedings.* Academic Press.

Rudas, I. J., & Fodor, J. (2008). Intelligent systems. *International Journal of Computers, Communications & Control, III*(Suppl.), 132–138.

Shanker, D. (2008). ICT and tourism: Challenges and opportunities. *Paper presented at Conference on Tourism in India – Challenges Ahead.* Academic Press.

Sigala, M., & Chalkiti, K. (2014). Investigating the exploitation of web 2.0 for knowledge management in the Greek tourism industry: An utilisation–importance analysis. *Computers in Human Behavior*, *30*, 800–812. doi:10.1016/j.chb.2013.05.032

Sonmez, S. F., Yiorgos, A., & Tarlow, P. (1999). Tourism in crisis: Managing the effects of terrorism. *Journal of Travel Research*, *38*(6), 3.

USAID. (2006). Information Communication Technologies (ICT) and Tourism. Presentation hold in Arusha, Tanzania. Retrieved from www.usaid.gov/our_work/agriculture/landmanagement/tourism/sidebar/ict.pdf

Van Hooft, S.J.C. (2010). Towards an ICT framework for sustainable tourism (Masters Dissertation). Retrieved from https://webcache.googleusercontent.com/search?q=cache:crsritxHRTUJ:https://www.ru.n /publish/pages/769526/towards_an_ict_framework_for_sustainable_tourism__sander_van_hooft.pdf+&cd=1&hl=en&ct=clnk&gl=ng

Waghmode, M. L., & Jamsandekar, P. P. (2013). Role of ICT in tourism. *International E-journal of ongoing research in management and IT*.

Washburn, D., Sindhu, U., Balaouras, S., Dines, R. A., Hayes, N., & Nelson, L. E. (2010). Helping CIOs Understand "Smart City" Initiatives. UWForum. Retrieved from http://www.uwforum.org/upload/board/forrester_help_cios_smart_city.pdf

Werthner, H. (2003). Intelligent Systems in Travel and Tourism. In *Proceedings of International Joint Conference on Artificial Intelligence (IJCAI 2003)* (pp. 1620-1625). Retrieved from http://ijcai.org/Past%20Proceedings/IJCAI-2003/PDF/286.pdf

Wöber, K. W. (2003). Information supply in tourism management by marketing decision support systems. *Tourism Management*, *24*(3), 241–255. doi:10.1016/S0261-5177(02)00071-7

WTTC. (2014). *Travel and Tourism Economic Impact*.

Chapter 4
Corporate Culture as a Competitive Tool in Enhancing the Organisational Performance of Star-Rated Hotels in Ghana

Dominic Owusu
Department of Marketing and Supply Chain Management, School of Business & College of Humanities and Legal Studies University of Cape Coast, Ghana

ABSTRACT

This chapter focuses on the use of corporate culture as a competitive tool to enhance the performance of organisations. However, the focus of the study was on star-rated hotels in Ghana. To address this, the chapter first focused on determining the corporate culture that is dominant among the star-rated hotels operating in Ghana. Secondly, it also sought to establish the influence that corporate culture has on organisational performance. Out of a population of 680 star-rated hotel managers, a sample of 248 were chosen using stratified random sampling technique. Self-administered questionnaires were used to solicit the views of managers of the selected hotels. In all, a total of 178 responses were retrieved and analysed using descriptive and partial least squares in structural equation modelling. Findings of the study revealed that the rule-bound culture is the dominant corporate practiced by the star-rated hot hotels in Ghana. The study also found that corporate culture significantly predicted organisational performance of star-rated hotels in the country.

DOI: 10.4018/978-1-7998-2204-2.ch004

Copyright © 2020, IGI Global. Copying or distributing in print or electronic forms without written permission of IGI Global is prohibited.

INTRODUCTION

One of the critical issues in business today is for businesses to identify key areas of the business that the business is doing better compared to competitors. Such areas determine the competitive advantage of the firm. Competitive advantage of the firm is meaningless if it cannot enhance the performance outcomes of businesses. In order to address this chapter focuses on corporate culture as one of the key areas of businesses that can be used as a competitive tool to enhance performance of businesses. One of the key areas which businesses can use to enhance their competitive advantage and also drive organizational performance is the culture of the organisation (Joseph & Francis, 2015; Yaprak, Tasoluk & Kocas, 2015). Organizational culture refers to the values and norms that are shared by members of the organisation that also define the way things are done in the organisation (Desphande & Farley, 2004). Han and Verna (2012) defined organisational culture based on the anthropological concepts such as symbolism, myth and rituals. The authors explained that the structure of an organisation can therefore be analysed based on these anthropological concepts.

The oil find in Ghana and the political stability of the country has made Ghana one of the attractive countries in the sub-region for businesses. This has contributed to rising number of multinational hotels in Ghana over the past five years. These developments in the hotel industry of Ghana have resulted in intense competition. As the number of tourist arrivals in the country continue to rise, the demand for hotel accommodation in the country continues to increase. The oil-find, the influx of Chinese nationals in search of business opportunities have also contributed to the increased number of hotels including Kempinski, Movenpick, Ambassador hotel and Tang palace.

As competition in the hotel industry of Ghana continue to intensify as a result of the influx of new hotels, the hotels in Ghana should be able to identify and adopt the right culture which sets the hotels apart from their competitors and also enable the hotels to achieve higher performance. As established in the study of Kim, Lee and Yu (2004) a strong culture which is shared by a majority of employees is a predictor of the overall performance of an organisation. Organisational performance is the sum of accomplishments achieved by the various departments of an organisation. These accomplishments are measured within a given period of time (Lee & Huang, 2012). Despite the link between culture and organisational performance, little research has focused directly on how hospitality businesses in general and hotels in particular can maximize performance by adopting a particular corporate culture which can be used as a competitive tool in driving performance (Han & Verma 2012).

Though studies have indicated that organizational culture predicts performance (Han & Verma, 2012, Jogaratnam, 2017) most of the studies were not based on the global hospitality and tourism industry of which the hotel sector feature prominently

(Han & Verma, 2012). Furthermore, though many studies have investigated the relationship between corporate culture and firm performance, results have been inconsistent (Han & Verna, 2012). For example, whereas studies by Doran, Haddad and Chow (2003), Jogaratnam (2017) and Nikpour (2017) lend support to the direct effect of corporate culture on performance, the findings by Kim, Lee and Yu (2004) prove otherwise.

It is against this background that this chapter focuses identifying the dominant culture that characterizes the operations of star-rated hotels in Ghana and further assess the effect that corporate culture has on organisational performance of star-rated hotels in Ghana. The results of the study would identify the corporate culture type that hotels should adopt in order to enhance their competitiveness and maximize performance. Furthermore, the findings of the study will also contribute to the academic discourse on how hotels can use corporate culture to develop competitive advantages that will enhance their performance.

LITERATURE REVIEW

Corporate Culture

Although the concept of organizational culture was popularized in the early 1980s. According to Hudrea (2006) its roots can be traced back to the early human relations view of organizations that originated in the 1940s. Research on organisational culture shifted focus to its more measurable aspects, particularly employee attitudes and perceptions and/or observable organizational conditions thought to correspond to employee perceptions (Cameron & Quinn, 1999).

There is a multiplicity of typologies of corporate culture. Lund (2003) explains that the difficulty in measuring or identifying a typology of corporate culture is because the shared assumptions and understandings lie beneath the conscious level of individuals. Cameron and Freeman (1991) identified a useful framework of corporate culture types by integrating the works of several researchers (Campbell, Bommer & Yeo, 1993, Mason & Mitroff, 1973, Mitroff & Kilmann, 1975, Quinn, 1988; Smircich, 1983; Wilkins & Ouchi, 1983 among others).

The resulting culture types are clan, adhocracy, hierarchy and market. Each culture type is also characterized by a particular set of shared beliefs, style of leadership, set of shared values that act as a bond or glue for members. These constructs have been used and validated in several studies on corporate culture. While validating the usefulness of the above typology of cultures, Desphande, Farley and Webster (1993) emphasize that these culture types are modal or dominant rather than mutually exclusive. Conceivably, most firms can and do have elements of several types of cultures. It also follows that organisations are dominated by one type or have attributes of several types. Similarly, in the study of Han and Verma (2012) the same typology of culture were used in measuring corporate culture. The current study utilizes the framework of organizational cultures typology and analysis by Cameron and Freeman (1991).

Organizational Performance

Cui and Hu (2012) posit that measurement of corporate performance has always been the unique question which researchers are trying to answer. Wadongo, Odhuno, Kambona, and Othuon (2010) explain that performance of an organization has traditionally been measured by looking at the revenues or the profits made at the end of the year, or using key financial ratios. Despite the development of performance measurement systems in the hospitality industry, various researchers (Brander-Brown & McDonnell, 1995; Atkinson & Brander-Brown, 2001; Harris & Mongiello, 2001) have pointed to the reluctance of the hospitality industry to use balanced measures and rely solely on financial measures. However, Orgaad, Larsen and Marnburg (2008) are of the view that no single indicator will give a comprehensive picture of the performance of a firm. This therefore calls for the use of different performance measures.

Several constructs have been used to measure financial performance of firms often referred to as the accounting measurement of performance. These measurements according to Hermalin and Weisbach (1991) and Barney (1986) include profit rate, return on assets (ROA), long-term profitability and sales growth rate. Calori and Sarnin (1991) also used the return on investment ratio, the return on sales ratio and the annual variation of the net turnover which a non-financial variable in measuring performance of a firm. What is common to researchers in the field of organizational performance is the use of accounting measurement of performance.

Other studies have also indicated that non-financial indexes such as employee satisfaction, customer satisfaction, turnover rate, quality of products/services and some other variables in the organizational aspects should be used in measuring performance (Cui & Hu, 2012). Besides these indexes Kaplan and Norton (2007) developed the balance score card to emphasize the importance of customer, internal business processes, learning and growth. Bagozzi Verbeke and Gavino (2003) also divided corporate performance into in-role performance and extra-role performance.

The in-role performance includes sales volume, communication effectiveness and relationship building while the extra-role performance is made up of courtesy, helping, sportsmanship and civic virtue. Researchers have argued that the non-financial variable is the new trend for performance appraisal and related research such as the development of the employee behaviour and the consciousness of social responsibilities, these variables are of equal importance as the accounting variables (Calori & Sarnin, 1991).

Corporate Culture and Organizational Performance

According to Doran, Haddad and Chow (2003) findings on the relationship between corporate culture and performance have been highly consistent. For example, the extent to which an organization clearly communicates its goals, makes fair and rational decisions, encourages cooperative communication among subunits and encourages individual initiative are positively correlated to organizational performance in terms of profitability, financial strength, morale and public goodwill (Gordon & DiTomaso, 1992). There is also empirical evidence to the effect that corporate culture differs systematically across industries (Chatman & Jehn, 1994; Gordon & Christensen, 1993; Spender, 1989). The demands of activities that businesses within an industry are supposed to undertake differs and may also require different approaches and styles in dealing with such demands.

In a study by Sorensen (2002) entitled, strength of corporate culture and the reliability of firm performance. It concluded that firms perceived to have strong corporate cultures exhibit superior and more reliable performance. This therefore suggest that in these environments, the consensus surrounding organizational goals and values which is characteristic of strong-culture firms enhances their ability to exploit established competencies. Though the study was able to establish a link between corporate culture and firm performance, respondents did not assess the culture of their respective firms but were asked to assess the strength of the corporate culture in each of the other sampled firms that were in the same industry as their own firm. This mode of assessing could lead to bias on the part of the respondents which may not be a true reflection the assessed organisations.

Lund (2003) in a study involving marketing professionals in America, also established linkages between organizational culture and performance. However, performance in this study was based on the extent to which employees were satisfied with their jobs. Armstrong and Overton (1977) also found out that satisfaction of employees varied across corporate cultural typologies. The study established that clan and adhocracy cultures were positively related to job satisfaction of employees whereas market and hierarchy cultures showed a negative relationship with job satisfaction.

However, in a study by Kim, Lee and Yu (2004) which sought to validate the culture construct and also assessed how culture affects organizational performance, two contrasting results for the relationship between corporate culture and performance. On one hand, the study was able to establish a strong relationship between corporate culture and performance of firms within the manufacturing sector. However, it also established that no relationship existed between corporate culture and performance of firms within the service industry such as hospitals and insurance companies.

Shahzad, Luqman, Khan and Shabbir (2012) also established in their study entitled the impact of organizational culture on organizational performance that when employees share the same norms and values, performance of that organisation increases toward realizing the overall goals of the organisation. Mushaq, Fayyaz and Tanveer (2013) in a study on organizational culture in the hotel industry of India also established that organizational culture either in the form of values or practices had a significant influence on the performance and long-term effectiveness of organisations. However, the study established that resort operators who performed poorly lacked good culture.

Jogaratnam (2017) also found out that corporate cultures such as innovative and supportive cultures are better predictors of performance. Similarly, Nikpour (2017) also found out that organizational culture impacted positively on organizational performance. Pantiyasa and Michelle (2017) concluded in his study entitled organizational culture and its impact on performance of hotel employees that there is a correlation between organizational culture and employees' performance. Nazarian, Atkinson and Faroudi (2017) in a study entitled influence of national culture and balanced organizational culture on the hotel industry's performance established that national culture of hotel employees influences balanced organizational culture which in turn influences performances. Though extant literature exists to describe the relationship between corporate culture and organizational performance, most of the studies were undertaken outside Ghana. On the basis of the literature reviewed, it is hypothesized that

H_0: corporate culture has no significant effect on organizational performance

MATERIALS AND METHODS

Measurement of Variables

Corporate Culture

Corporate culture was measured based on the scale developed by Cameron and Freeman (1991). Four culture types were identified based on the framework. These are clan, adhocracy, hierarchy and market cultures. The items in Cameron and Freeman (1991) were expanded to make it easy for respondents to understand and respond to the issues in order to separate those items that were multi-dimensional.

In all 36 items were used to measure the four culture types based on the shared beliefs, leadership, bonding and strategic emphasis.

Organisational Performance

With respect to the measurement of organizational performance, both financial and non-financial indicators were used. The financial indicators relied on subjective approaches to measuring financial performance. Justifications provided for the use of subjective measurement of performance are: owners/managers are unwilling to disclose actual figures of their performance for fear of being taxed or for being targeted by the government (Zulkiffli & Perera, 2011).

The use of non-financial measures was also informed by Kaplan and Norton (1992). Twelve items were used to measure both financial and non-financial organizational performance namely profitability, return on investment, growth in profitability, daily sales, increment in volume of sales, retaining customers, supplier relations, quality of service delivery, occupancy rate, size of customers and productivity of our employees compared to industry average.

Sample Size And Sampling Procedure

Based on the total population of 680 managers of star-rated hotels, a sample of 248 hotel managers were chosen based on the table developed by Krejcie and Morgan (1970). The respondents were then selected using the stratified random sampling technique. The population was divided into Five (5) strata. The groups were managers and supervisors of five star-rated hotels, four star-rated hotels, three star-rated hotels, two star-rated hotels and one star-rated hotels. A proportion of each stratum was calculated to get the number of respondents for each stratum based on the sample size of 248. Next, respondents were randomly selected until the sample for each stratum was obtained.

Instrument

Questionnaire was the main data collection instrument used for the study. The questionnaire comprised three sections; Section A, B and C. Section A collected data on the corporate culture orientations of the star-rated hotels, Section B focused on organizational performance and Section C also focused on demographic characteristics of the respondents. In all 36 items were used to measure corporate culture, 12 items were used to measure both financial and non-financial organizational performance. Five items were used to collect data on the demographic characteristics of respondents.

Out of the 248 questionnaires distributed, 178 were received and used for the analysis representing 71.72% response rate.

Data Analysis

Data preparation was in two stages. Firstly, the raw data collected through the questionnaire were edited, coded and converted into the actual variables of interest. Upon receipt, each questionnaire was checked carefully for incompleteness and inconsistencies. Out of a total of 248 distributed questionnaires, 178 of the received questionnaire were considered valid for data analysis after screening and doing away with uncompleted questionnaires.

Next, processed data were analyzed using partial least squares in structural equation modeling. PLS-SEM is widely recognized for its remarkable advantages in behavioural studies (Hair, Ringle, & Sarstedt, 2011), as it helps researchers to understand the relationship among sets of observed variables (Hair, Hult, Ringle, & Sarstedt, 2016).

RESULTS AND DISCUSSION

Demographic Characteristics of Respondents

A preliminary analysis was carried out to examine the demographic information of the respondents. The results are depicted in Table 1.

Table 1 presents the demographic characteristics of respondents. Out of a total of 178 respondents, 99 were males and 79 were females representing 55.62% and 44.38% respectively. Concerning the age distribution of respondents, 31 were aged between 18-24. Seventy-four were also aged between 25-31 representing 41.57%. Forty-nine of the respondents were also aged between 32-38 representing 27.53%. Thirteen were aged between 39-44, six were also aged between 45-51 representing 7.30% and 3.37% respectively.

Five of the respondents were also aged above 51 representing 2.81 percent. Table 1 shows that more than 50% of the respondents were aged between 18-38. This means that most of the respondents were youthful. According to Jogaratnam (2017) the hotel business, like many other services, is people intensive and requires for direct person-to-person interactions and people who are energetic to meet the variety of customer needs.

In terms of academic qualification, most of the respondents had various qualifications ranging from Higher National Diploma, First Degree to Post Graduate Degree. Fifty-six of the respondents had completed HND representing 31.5%, 61 had

Table 1. Demographic characteristics of respondents

Item	Frequency	Percentage (%)
Gender		
Male	99	55.62
Female	79	44.38
Age		
18-24	31	17.42
25-31	74	41.57
32-38	49	27.53
39-44	13	7.30
45-51	6	3.37
52 and above	5	2.81
Level of Education		
Senior high school or lower	40	22.5
Higher National Diploma (HND)	56	31.5
First Degree	61	34.3
Postgraduate Degree	21	11.8
Work experience		
1-5 years	97	54.49
6-10 years	54	30.34
11-15 years	11	6.18
16 years and above	16	8.99
Position		
Assistant manager	25	14.05
Manager	47	26.41
Senior manager	11	6.18
Supervisor	95	53.37

Source: Field survey, Owusu (2018)

completed first degrees representing 34.3% and 21 were having post graduate degrees representing 11.8%. Forty of the respondents had completed secondary education representing 22.5%. This indicates that the respondents were educated and could understand and respond to the issues of corporate culture, strategic orientation and performance of the hotels they managed. To buttress this point, respondents also held positions ranging from supervisor to manager which made them well placed to understand the culture of their respective hotels. Ninety-five of the respondents were supervisors representing 53.37%. Forty-seven of the respondents were managers representing 26.41%. Twenty-five of the respondents were also assistant managers representing 14.05 whiles 11 of them were also senior managers, also representing 6.18%.

Dominant Corporate Culture of Star-Rated Hotels in Urban Cites of Ghana

The study sought to determine the dominant corporate culture exhibited by the star-rated hotels in Ghana. To achieve this, each respondent was presented with four questions, each assessing the organization's general culture characteristics, leadership style, institutional bonding and strategic emphasis. Each respondent's four culture scores were ascertained by putting all the values for clan, adhocracy, hierarchy and market together. Table 2 presents the summary of respondent's mean scores and standard deviations for the four culture types they perceived in their respective hotels.

From Table 2, the category mean scores indicate that respondents perceived the hierarchy culture as the dominant culture (Mean = 4.0000, SD = 0.82339). Adhocracy was identified as the second dominant culture with a mean score of 3.9434. Market culture was also identified as the third dominant culture with a grand mean of 3.9307. The last culture identified based on the category mean scores is clan culture with a score of 3. 9003.

The mean scores presented also indicate that the individual hotels exhibit elements of all the four culture types with category mean scores of 3.9003, 3.9434, 4.0048 and 3.9307 representing clan, adhocracy, hierarchy and market cultures respectively. This finding is therefore consistent with past studies that have reported multiple subcultures in a firm to be the norm (Deshpande et al., 1993; Van Maamen & Barley (1984). Gregory, Harris, Armenakis and Shook (2009) also support the view that organizational culture must have a balance of all the four cultural types if is to be flexible in thinking and also if it is to propel the organization into achieving higher performance outcomes. This therefore supports the control theory that indicates that people behave according to their basic needs and when the needs of an employee align with organisational demands, the desired behaviour is achieved (Luria, 2008). This explains the reasons for the multiplicity of cultures exhibited by hotels.

Within the context under which the current study was undertaken, the respondents were managers of hotels and are therefore required to perform a number of activities in order to keep their jobs, keep staff well committed and motivated to perform their responsibilities and above all keep current customers and attract new ones. A combination of cultures is therefore required to be able to perform these varied tasks.

Table 2. Mean and standard deviation scores for the four culture types

Item	Mean	Std. Deviation
Clan culture		
Kind of organization		
My hotel promotes interpersonal relationships	4.1966	0.83062
Like an extended family	3.4270	1.22024
Has people who share a lot of themselves	3.6629	0.94413
Leadership		
The head of my hotel is considered to be a mentor	4.1854	0.89847
Sage	3.4551	1.01997
Father	3.8933	0.99425
Bonding		
Loyalty	4.1461	0.89000
Tradition	3.7416	0.98035
Commitment	4.1685	0.79881
Strategic emphasis		
Human resources	4.0281	0.89840
Cohesion	3.7753	0.94782
Morale	4.1236	2.35456
Category mean	**3.9003**	
Adhocracy		
Kind of organization		
A dynamic place	4.0112	0.70502
An entrepreneurial place	3.9663	0.84972
Has people who are willing to stick their necks out	3.7135	1.04256
Leadership		
Risk taker	3.9607	0.85939
Bonding		
Innovation and development	4.0449	0.93168
Emphasis on being the first	3.9775	0.90169
Strategic emphasis		
Growth	4.0562	0.85515
Acquisition of resources	3.8708	1.06306
Meeting new challenges	3.8933	0.95955
Category mean	**3.9434**	

continued on following page

Table 2 continued

Item	Mean	Std. Deviation
Hierarchy		
Kind of organization		
A formalized and structured place	4.0000	0.82339
Has established procedures to govern what people do	3.9888	0.93874
Leadership		
An organizer	3.9213	0.91719
Bonding		
Formal rules and policies	3.9382	0.98669
Strategic emphasis		
Permanence and stability	4.0393	1.01047
Efficiency	4.1742	0.87528
Category mean	**4.0048**	
Market culture		
Kind of organization		
Is production oriented	3.9719	0.85984
Work is done without personal involvement	3.5955	1.18578
Leadership		
A technician	3.5000	1.11106
A producer	3.9326	0.94836
A hard-driver	3.9663	1.01346
Bonding		
Tasks and goal accomplishment	4.1180	0.85873
Production	3.8258	0.93760
Strategic emphasis		
Achievement	4.3202	0.72388
Measurable goals	4.1461	0.95729
Category mean	**3.9307**	

Source: Field survey, Owusu (2018)

Corporate Culture and Performance Of Star-Rated Hotels In Urban Cities Of Ghana

To find out whether corporate culture is a predictor of performance of star-rated hotels, a model was developed to illustrate the linkage. Before analyzing the model, reliability and validity of the model was evaluated and established using composite

Table 3. Quality criteria and discriminant validity for measuring model one

Items	Corporate culture	Performance
Items	B 30 - B 65	C 66 – C 76
Cronbach's Alpha	0.9238	0.7207
Composite reliability	0.9342	0.8132
Average variance extracted (AVE)	0.5060	0.5250
R^2		0.3247
Adjusted R^2		0.3209
Loadings Min – Max	0.584 – 0.820	0.603 – 0.820
Path coefficient		
Corporate culture		0.5699
Performance		
F^2 (effect size)		
Corporate culture		0.4809
Performance		
Discriminant validity		
Fornell-Larcker criterion		
Corporate culture	0.7113	
Performance	0.5699	0.7246

Notes: Loadings between 0.4 and 0.7 are acceptable. >0.7 is high. Cronbach's $\alpha > 0.7$ is acceptable and high. Composite reliability should be 0.7 or higher. AVE should be 0.5 or higher. R^2 of 0.75 is substantial, 0.50 is moderate, and 0.25 is weak.

reliability scores, average variance extracted and discriminant validity. Table 3 and Figure 1 illustrates the evaluation criteria for the model.

An examination of the outer loadings of the latent variables (corporate culture and organizational performance) indicate that loadings are between 0.584 and 0.820 for corporate culture and 0.659 and 0.820 for organisational performance. However, as removing indicators below 0.7 does not change overall reliability, these indicators remained in the model. Composite reliability scores and the AVE indicate good reliability and validity. Discriminant validity was determined according to the Fornell and Lacker (1981) criterion. The off-diagonal values in the matrix in Table 3 specify the correlations between the latent constructs. Thus, the outcomes specify there is discriminant validity between all the constructs based on the cross loadings. The numbers within the circles illustrated in Figure 1 showed how much variance of organizational performance is being explained by corporate culture. In this study as indicated in Figure 1, the coefficient of determination, which is used to explain

Figure 1. Model depicting the influence of corporate culture on organizational Performance
Source: Field survey, Owusu (2018)

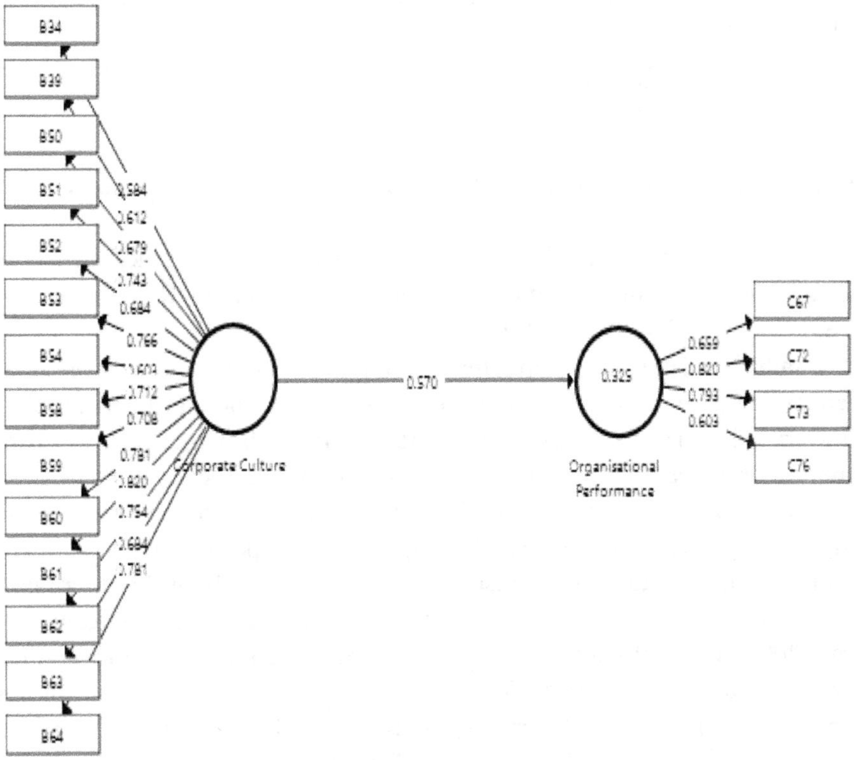

the variance is the (R^2) with a score of 0.3247. This means that corporate culture explains 32.47% of the variance in organizational performance.

Numbers on the arrow which are called path coefficients displayed how strong the effect of one variable is on the other variable. The weight of each path coefficients allow researchers to rank variables according to their statistical importance. Based on the finding as presented in Figure 1, corporate culture has a strong effect on performance (0.570). To check if the path coefficients of the inner model are significant or not, bootstrapping procedure was run. Using a two-tailed *t*-test with a significance level of 5%, the path coefficient should be significant if the T-statistics is larger than 1.96. The findings presented in Table 4 showed that the linkage between corporate culture and organizational performance is significant (T-value 13.1804, sig. 0.0000) which confirms the study findings that corporate culture is a predictor of organizational performance. The hypothesis that corporate culture has no significant effect on organizational performance is therefore rejected as the

Table 4. Bootstrapping results and t-statistics for path coefficients (inner model)

Variables	Original Sample (O)	Sample Mean (M)	Standard Deviation (STDEV)	T Statistics (|O/STDEV|)	P Values
Corporate Culture -> Performance	0.5699	0.5876	0.0432	13.1804	0.0000

Source: Field Survey, Owusu, 2018.

study findings indicates that corporate culture significantly predicts organizational performance.

In addition, the model's effect size (f^2), which showed how much an exogenous latent variable contributes to an endogenous latent variable's R^2 value, highlights large effect size of 0.4809 (see Table 3).

The findings of the study imply that the way things are done in an organization influences the level of organizational performance of the star-rated hotels. This finding is consistent with several studies who established linkages between corporate culture and organizational performance. For example, in the study of Gordon and Di Tomaso (1992), it was found out that how an organization communicates with its employees is positively correlated to organizational performance.

Similarly, in the study of Sorenson (2002) it was found out that there is a link between corporate culture and organizational performance. Furthermore, in the study of Lund (2003), it was also found out that there are linkages between corporate culture and organizational performance. The study is also consistent with the findings of Shahzad et al. (2012), Han and Verman (2012), Odhiambo et al. (2015), Wang (2015), Wahjudi et al. (2016), Michelle et al., (2016); Jogaratnam (2017) and Pantiyasa and Michelle (2017) who in their respective studies found out that corporate culture influences the level of performance of firms.

As posited in the study of Chatman et al. (1994), the demands that businesses within an industry are supposed to undertake differs and therefore requires different approach and style in dealing with such demands. This therefore suggest that the kind of industry one operates demands for certain cultural attributes in order for one to succeed and remain competitive in that industry. This is confirmed in the study of Kim et al. (2004) who studied the effect of corporate culture on organizational performance using the manufacturing and the service industry and found no relationship between corporate culture and organisational performance of firms within the service industry.

CONCLUSION

The following conclusion was drawn based on the findings of the study. It is concluded that the rule bound hierarchy culture dominates the cultural orientations of star-rated hotels in Ghana. However, all the other cultural types could also be found to be practiced in the star-rated hotels. The study concludes that how the star-rated hotels adapt and positions themselves in responding to their business environment influenced the level of organizational performance.

On theory, the result of the study that the hotels do not exhibit a single culture is supported by the control theory. The theory indicates that people behave according to their basic needs and when such needs are aligned with organizational needs, the desired behaviour is achieved. The different culture types exhibited by the hotels therefore explain the varied needs of employees hence the different corporate culture types exhibited by the star-rated hotels. Furthermore, the result of the study contributes to the resource-based view theory. The corporate culture exhibited by hotels thus constitute part of the intangible assets that hotels can use to develop competitive advantages which would propel the hotels to achieve a certain level of performance. Based on the findings, the study therefore recommends for the adoption of market, hierarchy and adhocracy cultures in order to enhance organisational performance of star-rated hotels in Ghana.

REFERENCES

Armstrong, J. S., & Overton, T. S. (1977). Estimating nonresponse bias in mail surveys. *JMR, Journal of Marketing Research, 14*(3), 396–402. doi:10.1177/002224377701400320

Atkinson, H., & Brander Brown, J. (2001). Rethinking performance measures: Assessing progress in UK hotels. *International Journal of Contemporary Hospitality Management, 13*(3), 128–136. doi:10.1108/09596110110388918

auMushtaq, A. L., Ahmad Fayyaz, S., & Tanveer, A. (2013). Organizational Culture in Hotel Industry: Perceptions and Preferences among Staff. *Advances In Management, 6*(5).

Bagozzi, R. P., Verbeke, W., & Gavino, J. C. Jr. (2003). Culture moderates the self-regulation of shame and its effects on performance: The case of salespersons in The Netherlands and the Philippines. *The Journal of Applied Psychology, 88*(2), 219–233. doi:10.1037/0021-9010.88.2.219 PMID:12731706

Brander Brown, J., & McDonnell, B. (1995). The balanced score-card: Short-term guest or long-term resident? *International Journal of Contemporary Hospitality Management*, *7*(2/3), 7–11. doi:10.1108/09596119510146751

Calori, R., & Sarnin, P. (1991). Corporate culture and economic performance: A French study. *Organization studies, 12*(1), 049-74.

Cameron, K. S., & Freeman, S. J. (1991). Cultural congruence, strength, and type: Relationships to effectiveness. *Research in Organizational Change and Development*, *5*, 23–58.

Cameron, K. S., & Quinn, R. E. (1999). *Diagnosing and changing organisational culture*. Reading: Addison-Wesley.

Campbell, D. J., Bommer, W., & Yeo, E. (1993). Perceptions of appropriate leadership style: Participation versus consultation across two cultures. *Asia Pacific Journal of Management*, *10*(1), 1–19. doi:10.1007/BF01732221

Chatman, J. A., & Jehn, K. A. (1994). Assessing the relationship between industry characteristics and organizational culture: How different can you be? *Academy of Management Journal*, *37*(3), 522–553. doi:10.5465/256699

Cui, X., & Hu, J. (2012). A literature review on organization culture and corporate performance. *International Journal of Business Administration*, *3*(2), 28. doi:10.5430/ijba.v3n2p28

Deshpandé, R., Farley, J. U., & Webster, F. E. Jr. (1993). Corporate culture, customer orientation, and innovativeness in Japanese firms: A quadrad analysis. *Journal of Marketing*, *57*(1), 23–37. doi:10.1177/002224299305700102

Doran, M., Haddad, K., & Chow, C. (2003). The Relationship between Corporate Culture and Performance in Bahrain Hotels. *International Journal of Hospitality & Tourism Administration*, *4*(3), 3. doi:10.1300/J149v04n03_04

Gordon, G., & Christensen, E. (1993). Industry influences on the relationships between management culture and performance. In *annual meeting of the Academy of Management, Atlanta, GA*.

Gordon, G. G., & DiTomaso, N. (1992). Predicting corporate performance from organizational culture. *Journal of Management Studies*, *29*(6), 783–798. doi:10.1111/j.1467-6486.1992.tb00689.x

Hair, J. F. Jr, Hult, G. T. M., Ringle, C., & Sarstedt, M. (2016). *A primer on partial least squares structural equation modeling (PLS-SEM)*. Sage Publications.

Hair, J. F., Ringle, C. M., & Sarstedt, M. (2011). PLS-SEM: Indeed a silver bullet. *Journal of Marketing Theory and Practice, 19*(2), 139–152. doi:10.2753/MTP1069-6679190202

Han, H., & Verma, R. (2012). The Effect of Corporate Culture and Strategic Orientation on Financial Performance: An analysis of the South Korean Upscale and Luxury Hotels. *Cornell Hospitality Report, 12*(4), 6–14.

Harris, P. J., & Mongiello, M. (2001). Key performance indicators in European hotel properties: General managers' choices and company profiles. *International Journal of Contemporary Hospitality Management, 13*(3), 120–128. doi:10.1108/09596110110388909

Hermalin, B. E., & Weisbach, M. S. (1991). The effects of board composition and direct incentives on firm performance. *Financial Management, 20*(4), 101–112. doi:10.2307/3665716

Hudrea, A. (2006). Organizational Culture. *Transylvanian Review of Administrative Sciences, 2*(16), 47–56.

Jogaratnam, G. (2017). How organizational culture influences market orientation and business performance in the restaurant industry. *Journal of Hospitality and Tourism Management, 31*, 211–219. doi:10.1016/j.jhtm.2017.03.002

Joseph, O. O., & Francis, K. (2015). The influence of organizational culture and market orientation on performance of microfinance institutions in Kenya. *International Journal of Business and Management, 10*(8), 204. doi:10.5539/ijbm.v10n8p204

Kaplan, R. S., & Norton, D. P. (2007). Using the balanced scorecard as a strategic management system. *Harvard Business Review, 85*(7/8), 150.

Kim Jean Lee, S., & Yu, K. (2004). Corporate culture and organizational performance. *Journal of Managerial Psychology, 19*(4), 340–359. doi:10.1108/02683940410537927

Krejcie, R. V., & Morgan, D. W. (1970). Determining sample size for research activities. *Educational and Psychological Measurement, 30*(3), 607–610. doi:10.1177/001316447003000308

Lund, D. B. (2003). Organizational culture and job satisfaction. *Journal of Business and Industrial Marketing, 18*(3), 219–236. doi:10.1108/0885862031047313

Mason, R. O., & Mitroff, I. I. (1973). A program for research on management information systems. *Management Science, 19*(5), 475–487. doi:10.1287/mnsc.19.5.475

Nazarian, A., Atkinson, P., & Foroudi, P. (2017). Influence of national culture and balanced organizational culture on the hotel industry's performance. *International Journal of Hospitality Management*, *63*, 22–32. doi:10.1016/j.ijhm.2017.01.003

Nikpour, A. (2017). The impact of organizational culture on organizational performance: The mediating role of employee's organizational commitment. *International Journal of Organizational Leadership*, *6*(1), 65–72. doi:10.33844/ijol.2017.60432

Orgaad, T., Marnburg, E., & Larsen, S. (2008). Perception of organizational structure in the hospitality industry: Consequences for commitment, job satisfaction and perceived performance. *Tourism Management*, *29*(4), 661–671. doi:10.1016/j.tourman.2007.07.006

Ouchi, W. G., & Wilkins, A. L. (1985). Organizational culture. *Annual Review of Sociology*, *11*(1), 457–483. doi:10.1146/annurev.so.11.080185.002325

Pantiyasa, I. W., & Michelle, M. (2017). Organization culture impact to performance of hotel employees (case study: Hotel Legian Resort–Bali). *Journal of Business on Hospitality and Tourism*, *2*(1), 330–346. doi:10.22334/jbhost.v2i1.68

Quinn, R. E. (1988). *Beyond rational management: Mastering the paradoxes and competing demands of high performance*. Jossey-Bass.

Shahzad, F., Luqman, R. A., Khan, A. R., & Shabbir, L. (2012). Impact of organizational culture on organizational performance: An overview. *Interdisciplinary Journal of Contemporary Research in Business*, *3*(9), 975–985.

Smircich, L. (1983). Concepts of culture and organizational analysis. *Administrative Science Quarterly*, *28*(3), 339–358. doi:10.2307/2392246

Sørensen, J. B. (2002). The strength of corporate culture and the reliability of firm performance. *Administrative Science Quarterly*, *47*(1), 70–91. doi:10.2307/3094891

Spender, J. C. (1989). Industry recipes: The nature and sources of managerial judgment. *Oxford, UK: Basic Blackwell.(1994)," Knowing, Managing and Learning. Management Learning*, *25*(3), 387–412. doi:10.1177/135050769402500302

Wadongo, B., Odhuno, E., Kambona, O., & Othuon, L. (2010). Key performance indicators in the Kenyan hospitality industry: A managerial perspective. *Benchmarking. International Journal (Toronto, Ont.)*, *17*(6), 858–875.

Wilkins, A. L., & Ouchi, W. G. (1983). Efficient cultures: Exploring the relationship between culture and organizational performance. *Administrative Science Quarterly*, *28*(3), 468–481. doi:10.2307/2392253

Yaprak, A., Tasoluk, B., & Kocas, C. (2015). Market orientation, managerial perceptions, and corporate culture in an emerging market: Evidence from Turkey. *International Business Review*, *24*(3), 443–456. doi:10.1016/j.ibusrev.2014.10.003

Zulkiffli, S. N. A., & Perera, N. (2011). A Literature Analysis on Business Performance For SMEs: Subjective or Objective Measures?

Chapter 5
Impact of Crisis on Tourist Destination:
A Case of Kashmir, India

Natasha Saqib
University of Kashmir, South Campus, India

ABSTRACT

The purpose of this chapter is to examine the impact of crisis events in Kashmir on the demand for tourism in order to establish a better understanding of changes and trends in the demand for tourism. The author has no information to assess the impact of the crisis on the brand image of Kashmir as a tourist destination. The study limits itself to what is a first step in this assessment and assumes that periods of low demand for destination Kashmir are linked in some way to the tourism crisis. The article traces the evolution, growth, pattern, and trends of tourism since independence (1947) of Kashmir. The historical trends in tourist arrivals in Kashmir for a period of over six decades illustrates that tourism has been highly susceptible to crises in Kashmir. The study provides a bottom-up perspective, based on observation, measurement and analysis. Also provided is a contextualization of the tourism crisis and its impact on a tourist destination.

DOI: 10.4018/978-1-7998-2204-2.ch005

Copyright © 2020, IGI Global. Copying or distributing in print or electronic forms without written permission of IGI Global is prohibited.

INTRODUCTION

A crisis may be defined as the perception of an unpredictable event that threatens important expectancies of stakeholders and can seriously impact an organization's performance and generate negative outcomes (Coombs, 2012). Crisis is also seen as a disruption that physically affects a system as a whole and threatens its basic assumptions, its subjective sense of self, and its existential core (Pauchant and Mitroff, 1992). The notion of a crisis in tourism can be understood in the context of the difficulties that tourists face in travelling or even with respect to the problems facing businesses (Ross, 2005). Or more specifically Hai, (2011) states that tourism crisis means undesired events that influence the confidence of the tourists about a destination and affects the abilities of organization or countries to operate normally. Tourism crisis is an event which can be threat for the normal operations and conduct of tourism related businesses, spoil a tourist destination's image for safety, attractiveness, and comfort by negatively influencing tourists perceptions of that destination and disrupt the business operations of the local tourism industry by reducing tourist arrivals and damages the destination image for safety and attractiveness (Sonmez et al., 1999) According to Hall (2010) there are different types of tourism crises (financial, economic, environmental, ecological, biodiversity, energy, oil, political and water) that impact the demand for tourism.

Tourism Crisis has received much attention lately in the tourism and hospitality management fields due to recent unexpected events and developments such as the Asian financial crisis, the occurrence of foot and mouth disease in the UK, the terrorist attacks on America on September 11, 2001, the bombing in Bali, the outbreak of SARS, Tsunami in India and the war on Iraq. And as such there have been a substantial number of publications that have looked at tourism crisis and its impact. However, the majority of research in tourism on crisis concentrates on economic and financial crises. And research in some areas of crisis in tourism is significantly influenced by particular periods of recession or by crisis events such as 9/11 or sudden oil shocks. There are surprisingly few papers that explicitly focus on political crisis and crisis due to natural disasters. Moreover, these papers have studied regions that faced an unexpected one-time crisis such as a terrorist attack or a natural disaster (e.g., Mansfeld and Pizam, 2006; Ritchie, 2009; Walters and Mair, 2012). There has been less attention to the study of regions with a prolonged negative image caused by long-lasting problems, such as political crisis.

In the light of this, we deem it essential to examine the impact of crisis events on the demand for tourism in a region with a prolonged negative image, in order to establish a better understanding of changes and trends in the demand for tourism in Kashmir. From 1989 to 2016, the Kashmir tourism industry experienced three major crisis events, including the 1989 political unrest, 2014 floods and 2016 political unrest. To accomplish the objective proposed in this work the author compiled tourism statistics from 1947 t0 2016 with a goal of finding no of domestic and foreign tourist visits to Kashmirfor this period. The following databases were searched - Ministry of Tourism, Government of India; Department of Tourism, Jammu and Kashmir and Indian statistics website.

LITERATURE REVIEW

Few of the studies discusses tourism crisis specifically crises related to political and natural disasters. Arana and Leon (2008) examined the short-run impacts of the September 11 attacks in New York on tourist preferences for competing destinations in the Mediterranean and the Canary Islands and found that the attacks caused a shock to tourists' utility, and a change in the image profile of destinations.

Chu (2008) used the September 11 attacks as examples of economic and political blows, and analyzed the accuracy of using a fractionally integrated ARMA model to predict tourism and make comparisons. Goodrich (2001) also studied the September 11 attack and analyzed its immediate impact on tourism in the US and the subsequent industry response. Blake and Sinclai (2003) analyzed the downturn in the United States following September 11 using a computable general equilibrium model of the US and also examined potential and actual policy responses to the crisis. Pizam and Fleischer (2002) showed that, between May 1991 and May 2001, tourism demand in Israel was highly dependent upon the frequency of terrorist activities. Terrorist attacks resulted in a drastic reduction of international tourists arriving in Israel. Ender and Sandler (1991) and Enders, Sandler and Parise (1992) used monthly data and time series analysis to prove a significant negative impact of terrorism on tourism revenues in Spain and other European countries, and to support substitution effects between countries as a result of the tourists' goal of minimizing the risk of facing a terror attack. Athanasopoulos and Hyndman (2008) examined the influence of the Sydney 2000 Olympics and the bomb blast in Bali in 2000 on domestic tourism demand in Australia, and found that Sydney 2000 promoted an immediate demand in business travel, whereas the number of visitors meeting friends and relatives increased significantly after the blast in Bali.

Huang and Min (2002) examined the impact of the 21st September 1999 earthquake in Taiwan, and found that the recovery period exceeded 11 months, with restricted growth of inbound tourist arrival. The earthquakes in Turkey in August 1999 and in Japan in January 1995 have resulted in similar setbacks in the respective regional tourism. Turkey tourism suffered when a catastrophic quake hit the area near Istanbul, with tourist arrivals cut sharply in the succeeding months. (Goetzl & Healy, 2000). Min 2008 adopted an intervention model to estimate the impacts of two disasters, the 9-21 Earthquake and SARS on the tourism industry in Taiwan and found during and after these events the island's economy was greatly impacted, with the worst damage to inbound tourism where tourist numbers were drastically reduced.

Tourism demand is subject to the effects of natural disasters, such as floods, hurricanes, volcano eruptions, earthquakes, tsunamis, and epidemics, and man-made disasters, such as terrorism, political turmoil, war, and international conflict. Therefore, demand can fluctuate drastically, and economic losses are inevitable (Wang, 2009). The reports that have investigated the impact of political crisis and natural disasters on tourism have determined that they do significantly affect the tourism industry.

Tourism Destination: Kashmir

The combination of individual tourist attractions at a particular place makes a tourist destination. Tourist destination is a particular place which attracts the tourists for a temporary or long-term stay. It includes city, village, country, region or a specific purpose-built resort (Baker & Crompton, 2008). According to Buhalis (2000) destinations are places towards which people travel and where they choose to stay for a while in order to experience certain features or characteristics a perceived attraction of some sort. Tourist destinations are amalgamations of tourism products, which give assimilated experience to the visitors. A tourist destination is perceived as a single entity, which comprises of several stakeholder groups like tourists, business entities operating in the tourism sector, the public sector, the host population and representatives of non-governmental organizations. The main components of tourist product are destination attractions, environment, destination facilities and services, accessibility to the destination, image of the destination and price to the consumer (Middleton & Clarke, 2001)

Kashmir is one of the most important and famous tourist destinations of the state of Jammu and Kashmir because of its strategic location and uniqueness. Kashmir is spread over an area of 105 sq. km. Located approximately 1730 m above the sea level; the south of Kashmir is bordered by Punjab, while on the south-west it has Himachal Pradesh. The Valley of Kashmir covers an area of about 7.2 per cent (15,948 sq. km) out of the total area of Jammu and Kashmir State. Kashmir lies between the 32° 22' to 34° 43' N latitudes and in between 73° 52' to 75° 42'E longitude. It lies beyond the upper bounds of the tropical zone and the lowest latitude coincides with 32° 17' N. The spindle shaped valley has a basin of about 85 miles (104 km) long and 25 miles (40 km) wide. Kashmir is bounded by mountains in at an average height of 6000 feet above the sea level. The mountain range rising to a height of 18000 feet on the north-east, dip down to something 9,000 feet in the South. As far as the geography of Kashmir is concerned, the valley has river Jhelum flowing through it, along with its tributaries. The river Jhelum mainly drains the Kashmir valley. The main source of the Jhelum is a spring at Verinag. Some of the other important drainage basins are Lidder, Bringi, Sindh. Vaishav, Madhumati and many small others The display of natural boundaries, the physical location, the compatible seasonal division, the richness of flora &luscious fruits and tempting vegetables have attracted every body's imagination to the valley of Kashmir and as such it is rightly called "Paradise on Earth", its evidence traces back to over 1000 B.C.

The valley of Kashmir with its copious side valleys is a perfect resort for leisure tourism. From ancient times, Kashmir has been frequently visited by travellers who desired to gain knowledge as it has been a place of great learning, thus attracted scholars, sages and philosophers from all parts of India and neighbouring countries. In the Buddhist period, even people from Greece and Egypt took long journeys for the same purpose. The tourist industry of Kashmir also flourished due to the writings of various travellers since time immemorial. Huientsang, the well-known Chinese Pilgrim, who travelled through India and Central Asia for 16 years in the 7th century A.D, was captivated by the lovely valley of Kashmir and he spent two years in Kashmir. There is also reference to Kashmir in the travels dairy of Marcopolo, his remarks about Kashmir were "The men are brown and clean, but the women taking them as brunettes, are very beautiful. The clime is finely tempered, but neither very hot nor very cold". As per German Baron, Charles Hugel, "The most wonderful objects in the world were the Taj Mahal and Kashmir." Similarly Thomas More in his book titled *"LallaRookh"* in the middle of the 19th century provoked the curiosity of many travellers about Kashmir. The foreign authors have played a great role in highlighting the Kashmir as a tourist spot. In view of appreciable influence through their writings a large number of tourists were attracted to the valley of Kashmir. No wonder that Kashmir is referred as the "Switzerland of India". Hence the vast geography and cultural diversity of Kashmir provides it with a bounty of attractions to draw both domestic and international tourists.

Tourist Attractions in Kashmir

Tourism and tourist attractions are interconnected with each other. According to Lew (1987), "Without tourist attractions, there would be no tourism and without tourism, there would be no tourist attractions." This argument clearly shows the importance of attractions in tourism industry. Tourist attractions are the rudimentary origins on which the tourism is developed (Lew, 1987). According to him any phenomenon could be a tourist attraction if it has three characteristic - a tourist, a site which can be visited and an image which makes that particular site considerable. According to this generalized definition, an attraction would not only restricted to historical buildings, amusement parks and sceneries but also includes services and facilities which gratify tourists to meet their everyday needs (Lew, 1987). Kashmir possesses numerous tourist attractions varied in type and appealing to a wide range of interests. The attractions include historical, cultural, archaeological, scenic, climatic, and adventure resources .Such a unique combination of attractions within a single state has no match in the Asian continent, or rarely anywhere else does. Kashmir offers a myriad of options for tourists in terms of natural recreational settings available. But the management of the tourism resources has been such that only a handful of tourist centres are known to the visitors coming from outside. For the management and administrative purposes the tourist centres in the region have been divided into different development authorities. Currently there are thirteen development authorities which take care of the tourism development of the respective areas.

Tourism Industry in Kashmir Region

Tourism is one of the largest and fastest growing economic sectors in the world. The growth of the Travel & Tourism sector in 2017 (4.6%) outpaced that of the global economy. The sector is shown to account for 10.4% of global GDP and 9.9% of total employment, in 2017. The WTTC has identified India as one of the world's foremost tourist growth centres in the coming decade. India earned US$ 27.31 billion in foreign exchange earnings from tourism receipts in 2017. The tourism industry in India has come a long way from just 15,000 tourists in 1950 to 1679.38 million in 2017. Most of the states like Tamil Nadu, Uttar Pradesh, and Andhra Pradesh, Karnataka, Maharashtra, Tripura, Madhya Pradesh West Bengal, Gujarat, Rajasthan in India are having good demand for tourism. But, despite Kashmir being the most beautiful tourist destination in India, the share of Kashmir in Indian tourism was less than one per cent and ranked 17th in India in terms of number of tourists visiting the region in the year 2017.

Kashmir has a long history as a tourist destination, even at a time when relatively few people travelled to the Kashmir for leisure – from 1950's through the 1980's Kashmir was promoted as an iconic holiday location. Indeed, for those with the money and any inclination to travel Kashmir was the favoured destination. Tourism sector in Kashmir flourished after 1947 but there are wide fluctuations in the trend during the different phases. The tourism cycle in Kashmir can be divided into four phases

i. Pre Crisis Phase (Before 1987)
ii. Crisis Phase (1987-1996)
iii. Post Crisis Phase (1997-2013)
iv. Crisis phase 2 (2014 onwards)

Pre-Crisis Phase (Before 1987)

Table –1 show historical trends in tourist arrivals in Kashmir for a period of over four decades (1951-1989) i.e. before the crisis started in 1989. It illustrates a number of features and episodes of Kashmir tourism industry. As can be seen from the *Figure-1* the number of tourists during the 1951 -1959 period registered a positive growth, from 10579 in 1951 to 71220 in 1959 except in 1957, because of the major flood when entire valley was submerged, the number of tourist arrivals declined by 33.15% in relation to 1956. However, the inflows of tourist improved again due to the various schemes undertaken for the development of tourism, such as construction of Tourist Reception Centre at Srinagar and improvement of Mughal Gardens besides the publicity it received from print and electronic media across the continental levels. Also Shakti Samant released his film 'Kashmir Ki Kali' in 1956, which overnight brought the knowledge of the beautiful landscape and territory to the knowledge of urban population of the various states of India.

The rising trend continued in 1960 – 1962 but during the period from 1963-1965 the valley witnessed negative growth in the tourist traffic there were many reasons responsible for this setback, like Chinese attack in 1962, seventeen day Indo-Pakistani war in 1965 and also socio-political disturbance in the valley .After the end of Indo-China war in 1962 and Indo-Pakistan war of 1965. The valley again witnessed increase in tourist arrivals from1966-1968. The Indian government established Indian Tourism Development Corporation to develop infrastructure all

Table 1. Total Tourist Visits to Kashmir from 1951-1989

Year 1950's	Total Tourist Visits	Year 1960's	Total Tourist Visits	Year 1970's	Total Tourist Visits	Year 1980's	Total Tourist Visits
1950	-	1960	74560	1970	121153	1980	594517
1951	10579	1961	92455	1971	94852	1981	642300
1952	13100	1962	93615	1972	108445	1982	603834
1953	21381	1963	83687	1973	175829	1983	439529
1954	34645	1964	56720	1974	167619	1984	229142
1955	51025	1965	45541	1975	184790	1985	503614
1956	64354	1966	119276	1976	324490	1986	589716
1957	43018	1967	146081	1977	442040	1987	721654
1958	60557	1968	140696	1978	582665	1988	722035
1959	71220	1969	106959	1979	582600	-	-

Source: Author's Compilation based on secondary data Ministry of Tourism, Govt. of India; Department of Tourism, Jammu and Kashmir, Indian statistics website.

Figure 1. Total Tourist Visits to Kashmir during Pre -Crisis Phase (1950-1988)
Source: Author's Compilation based on secondary data from Ministry of Tourism, Govt. of India; Department of Tourism, Jammu and Kashmir, Indian statistics website.

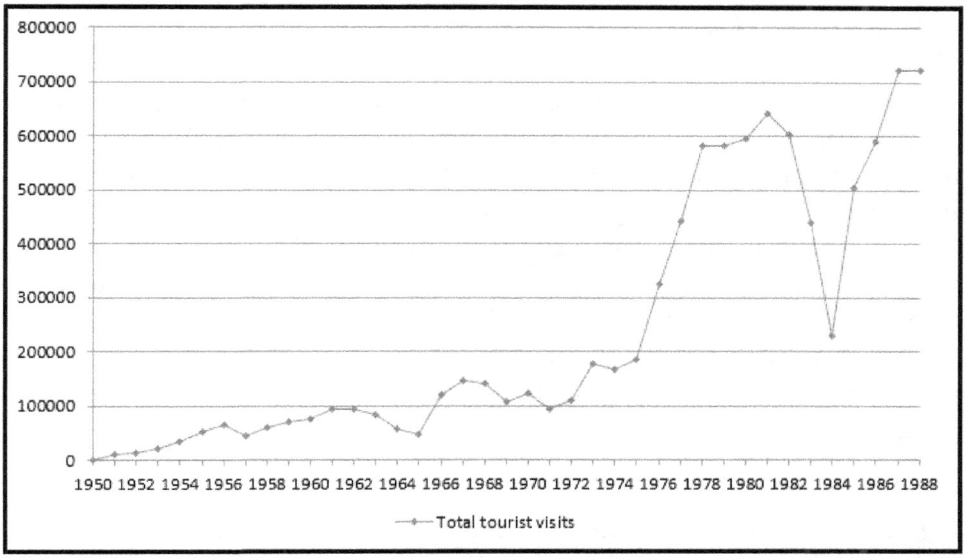

over the country and to promote adventure tourism winter sports was also started at Gulmarg but there was again decrease in tourist flow in 1969

The 70's era started with an increase in the tourist flow. It was in 1970 that the Jammu and Kashmir Tourist Development Corporation (JKTDC) was established to monitor and supervise the industry and direct public investment into accommodation and transport. In 1971 there was substantial decrease of tourists arrivals compared to1970. The reason for this downfall in tourist number was the "Bangladeshi-Pakistani war", which resulted in one more Indo-Pak war. After Indo-Pak war the tourist flow increased again in 1972 and 1973 and in 1974 there was again decrease in tourist arrivals. From 1975 onwards the tourist flow shows constant increase and reached to the number of 5.8 lakh in the year 1978 as compared to 1.6 lakh in1974. The main reasons for the increase in the tourist inflow was return of peace and tranquillity in the valley and the government paid a lot of attention towards the promotion of this industry. The 1970's decade can be considered as a relatively prosperous period in the early history of Kashmir valley.

The domestic tourist flow to the valley shows an Increasing order up to 1981 and after 1981 recorded signs of decline up to 1984. The number of tourist arrivals declined from to 6.4 lakh in 1981 to 2.2 lakh in 1984. The reason for this de-accelerated growth during the period 1980-1984 was due to political disturbances widespread in the valley and militancy at its peak in the neighbouring state of Punjab. The tourist flow to Kashmir after 1984 has increased up to 1988. The flow reached to7.2 lakh in 1988 from 5 lakh in 1985.But the depression again started from 1989 (Itoo, 2013).

Crisis Phase (1989-1996)

Unfortunately, the first tourism boom ended with the eruption of insurgency in 1989. In 1989 everyday life in the valley was transformed when the conflict took a violent turn. During the period 1990 to 1996 tourist influxes registered a negative growth rate because of the insurgency in the valley (See Table 2). Turmoil and disturbance in Kashmir laid a terrible impact on the tourist places of the valley. The previous two years 1988 and 1987, before the turmoil started in 1989 had respectively recorded an overwhelming number of 721650 and 722031 tourists. This number came down to 557980 in 1989; and in the year 1990, it substantially came down to a dismal figure of 10722. The abysmal decrease in the tourist flow from 1989-1996 is depicted in the *Figure*-2.

Figure 2. Total Tourist Visits to Kashmir during Crisis Phase (1989-1996)
Source: Author's Compilation based on secondary data from Ministry of Tourism, Govt. of India; Department of Tourism, Jammu and Kashmir, Indian statistics website.

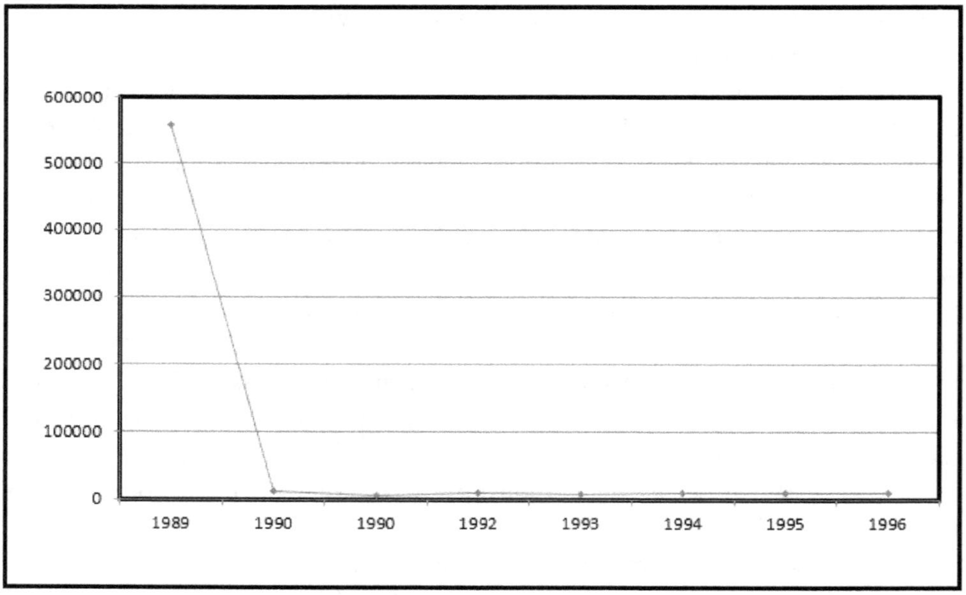

Table 2. No of Domestic and Foreign Tourist Visits to Kashmir 1989-2016

Year	No of Domestic Tourist Visits(DTV's) to Kashmir	No Of Foreign Tourist Visits(FTV's) to Kashmir	Total Tourist Visits To Kashmir
1989	490215	67762	557977
1990	5095	4627	10722
1991	1400	4887	6287
1992	1175	9149	10324
1993	0	8026	8026
1994	500	9314	9814
1995	320	8198	8518
1996	370	9592	9962
1997	7027	9111	16131
1998	99636	10247	109883
1999	200162	15990	217292
2000	104337	7575	111912
2001	66732	5859	72591
2002	24670	2686	27356
2003	182205	8959	191164
2004	358095	18634	376729
2005	585702	19680	605382
2006	412879	20002	432888
2007	417264	24576	441840
2008	551041	21588	572629
2009	577348	23904	601252
2010	710504	25984	736488
2011	1282360	32110	1314470
2012	1274674	37166	1311840
2013	1142865	29143	1172008
2014	1140446	27172	1167618
2015	898861	28954	927815
2016	600945	22987	623932
2017	708883	25684	734567
2018	800000	50000	850000

Source: Author's Compilation based on secondary data from Ministry of Tourism, Govt. of India; Department of Tourism, Jammu and Kashmir.

Post Crisis Phase (1997-2013)

Since elected government was established in the state after a gap of six years in 1997 the socio-political conditions in Kashmir became better as compared to the past years and tourism in Kashmir bounced back. The total tourist flow increased from 16131 in 1997 to 2.1 lakh in 1999. But unfortunately, the effect of Kargil war of 1999, cataclysmic events of the September 2001 terrorist attacks on the world trade centre buildings and the pentagon in the U.S.A followed by the terrorist attacks on the Jammu and Kashmir legislative assembly in October 2001 and on the parliament on 13th December, 2001 was evident in the decreased tourist flow from 2000-2003 .However the peace process initiated by Prime Minister Vajpayee during April 2003 helped tourism gaining momentum. A substantial increase over the past one and half decade was seen in 2005 when the number of tourists visiting Kashmir rose to 6 lakh, the number would have been more promising if in October Kashmir wouldn't have witnessed earthquake .In July 2006 the attacks on two buses of tourists from west Bengal dampened the tourism growth and tourist inflow again decreased to 4.3lakh.

During the (2007-2012) period the sector emerged in modern sense and can be considered as a relatively prosperous period in the history of Kashmir tourism. 2008 was a difficult year because of the 61 days Amaranth land row agitation tourism pilgrimage tourism was affected to a great extent. But Global recession (2009) failed to affect Kashmir tourism industry more and more tourists thronged the valley as many domestic tourists cancelled their tours to European countries and visited to Kashmir valley. It took 21 years for Kashmir to recover its position of 1988 in tourist flow and cross the mark of 7 lakhs in 2010 though the number would have been more promising if Kashmir wouldn't have been engulfed in June 2010 unrest .Despite fears about security Kashmir in 2011 became one of the famous tourist destinations of India with 13 lakh tourists visiting to Kashmir that is believed to be highest number of tourist arrivals in valleys tourism history. Likewise, Kashmir witnessed a huge tourist flow in 2012. However, the number of tourists visiting the Kashmir from the year 2013 has reflected a negative trend (Figure 3).

Crisis Phase 2: (2014 onwards)

During 2014 – 2018 Kashmir tourism faced worst crisis in last two decades. In 2014 Kashmir suffered disastrous floods across many of its districts and tourism sector witnessed negative growth of -0.2 when tourist visits decreased to 11.6 lakh. Since Kashmir was still battling the aftereffects of the floods the winter tourism in 2015 was dead and because of this the tourist flow in 2015 decreased to 9.2 lakh. Though Kashmir tourism sector got off to a good start in 2016, turmoil precariously

Figure 3. Total tourist visits to Kashmir during Post -Crisis phase (1997-2013)
Source: Author's Compilation based on secondary data from Ministry of Tourism, Govt. of India; Department of Tourism, Jammu and Kashmir.

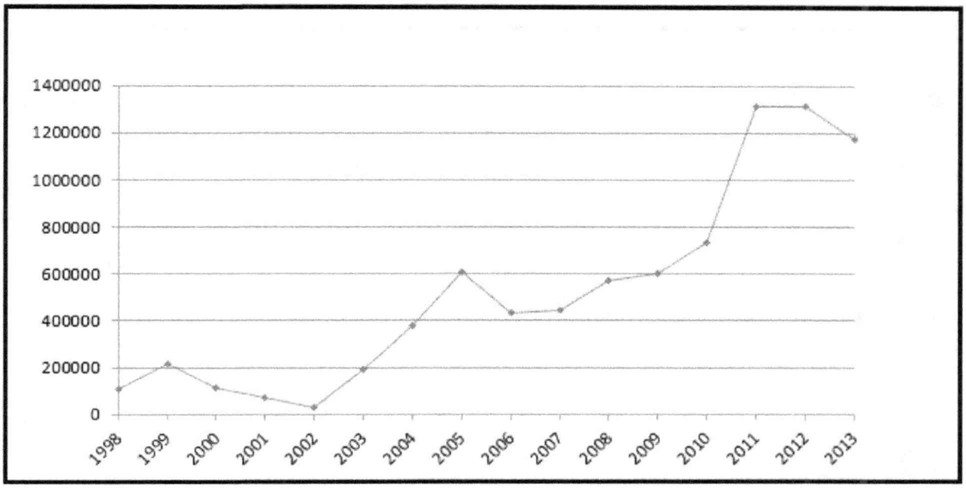

engulfed the Kashmir and resulted in loss of tourist season, 64% of the tourist and working season was lost and only 6.2 lakh tourist visited Kashmir in 2016. The effect of 2016 unrest was ubiquitous in the year 2017 only 7.3 lakh tourists visited Kashmir. In 2018 also Kashmir witnessed lowest ever tourist footfall in 6 years, mere 8.5 lakh tourists visited Kashmir as compared to 13 lakh tourists in 2012. It means a decline of over 4.5 lakh tourists meaning a 35 percent dip in tourist arrivals in 6 years keeping 2012 as base year (*Figure-4*).

DISCUSSION AND CONCLUSION

The foregoing analysis of the tourism industry in Kashmir shows that although the industry has registered an all-round development in the valley during the last six decades. One of the biggest impediments to tourism industry in Kashmir is Crisis (*Figure 5*). Kashmir has been challenged by political unrest, turmoil wars and natural disasters over the decades. The tourism in Kashmir after 1947 was first hard hit in 1962 Chinese attack and 1965 Indo-Pak war. The tourism sector again got blow in 1971 Indo-Pak war. But the 1989 insurgency was one of the major setbacks to tourism industry in Kashmir and there was an abysmal decrease in the tourist flow from 1990-1996. Further the effect of Kargil War in 1999 was prevalent in early 2000's to tourism sector in Kashmir when tourism sector again witnessed negative growth. 2008 and 2010 unrest in Kashmir also affected the tourism sector to some extent.

Figure 4. Total tourist visits to Kashmir during Crisis Phase 2 (2014-2018)
Source: Author's Compilation based on secondary data from Ministry of Tourism, Govt. of India; Department of Tourism, Jammu and Kashmir, Indian statistics website.

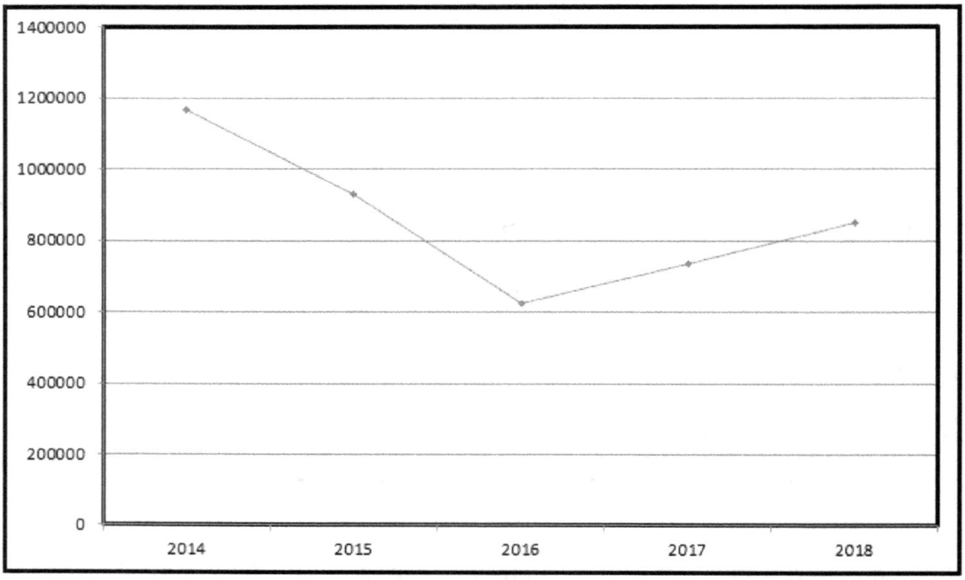

Figure 5. Total tourist visits to Kashmir (1950-2018)
Source: Author's Compilation based on secondary data from Ministry of Tourism, Govt. of India; Department of Tourism, Jammu and Kashmir and Indian statisitics Website.

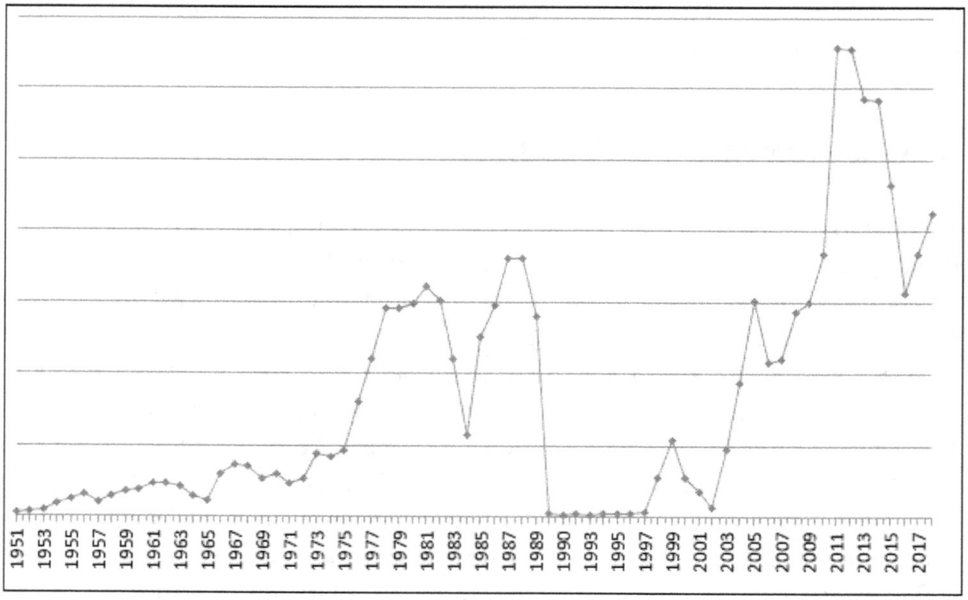

Most recent is the 2016 unrest when 90 per cent tourists left the Valley onset of the turmoil. According to the State Economic Survey (2016). Tourism sector suffered a loss of around 13,291 crore due to the unrest and only 4.03lakh tourists visited Kashmir in 2016. The impact of natural disasters has also been more profound in Kashmir. 1957 and 1959 floods, 2005 earthquake and recent 2014 floods (5th most deadly disaster worldwide in 2014.). Although the impact of earthquake was not so significant, tourism sector in Kashmir was hard hit by 1957 and 2014 floods.

Consequently, the risks involved in visiting one the world's top tourism destinations, Kashmir, have increased. According to Beirman (2003) long lasting series of crises poses almost a significant threat to the destinations public image and its ability to attract tourists (especially if it is dramatised or distorted through rumours (Ritchie et al., 2002) and when it comes to choosing vacation destinations, tourists often avoid sites of terrorism and seek places with stable political situations that ensure their safety (Wang, 2009.) The crisis in the region has resulted to the negative image of Kashmir in the minds of tourists and has challenged the regions' competitiveness and share in world tourism as a top tourist destination.

REFERENCES

About Jammu and Kashmir: Information on Tourism, Industries, Economy & Geography. (2017). Retrieved from http://www.ibef.org/download/Jammu-Kashmir-August-2017.pdf

About Jammu and Kashmir: Information on Tourism, Industries, Economy & Geography. (2018). Retrieved from http://www.ibef.org/download/Jammu-Kashmir-January-2018.pdf

Annual Report 2017-18. (n.d.). Ministry of Tourism Government of India. Retrieved from http://tourism.gov.in/sites/default/files/annualreports/MoT%20Annual%20Report%20201617_English.pdf

Arana, J. E., & León, C. J. (2008). The impact of terrorism on tourism demand. *Annals of Tourism Research*, *35*(2), 299–315. doi:10.1016/j.annals.2007.08.003

Athanasopoulos, G., & Hyndman, R. J. (2008). Modelling and forecasting Australian domestic tourism. *Tourism Management*, *29*(1), 19–31. doi:10.1016/j.tourman.2007.04.009

Baker, D. A., & Crompton, J. L. (2000). Quality, Satisfaction and Behavioural Intentions. *Annals of Tourism Research*, *27*(3), 785–80. doi:10.1016/S0160-7383(99)00108-5

Blake, A., & Sinclair, M. T. (2003). Tourism crisis management - US response to September 11. *Annals of Tourism Research*, *30*(4), 813–832. doi:10.1016/S0160-7383(03)00056-2

Buhalis, D. (2000). Marketing the Competitive Destination of the Future. *Tourism Management*, *21*(1), 97–116. doi:10.1016/S0261-5177(99)00095-3

Chu, F. L. (2008). A fractionally integrated autoregressive moving average approach to forecasting tourism demand. *Tourism Management*, *29*(1), 79–88. doi:10.1016/j.tourman.2007.04.003

Coombs, W. T. (2012). *Ongoing crisis communication: planning, managing, and responding* (3rd ed.). Thousand Oaks, CA: Sage.

Domestic Tourist Arrival in Kashmir. (n.d.) Retrieved from http://www.Jammuandkashmirstat.com/tourism/29/stats.aspx

Enders, W. & Sandler, T. (1991). Causality between Transnational Terrorism and Tourism: The Case of Spain. *Terrorism, 14*(January), 49–58.

Enders, W., Sandler, T., & Parise, G. (1992). An Econometric Analysis of the Impact of Terrorism on Tourism. *Kylos, 45*(4), 531–554. doi:10.1111/j.1467-6435.1992.tb02758.x

Goetzl, D., & Healy, B. (2000). Turkey lures visitors with historical appeal. *Advertising Age, 71*(26), 50–51.

Goodrich, J. N. (2001). September 11, 2001 attack on America: A record of the immediate impacts and reactions in the USA travel and tourism industry. *Tourism Management, 23*(6), 573–580. doi:10.1016/S0261-5177(02)00029-8

Hai. A.M, Chik.R.A (2011) Political stability: country image for tourism industry in Bangladesh.

Huang, J. H., & Min, J. C. H. (2002). Earthquake devastation and recovery in tourism: The Taiwan case. *Tourism Management, 23*(2), 145–154. doi:10.1016/S0261-5177(01)00051-6

India Tourism Statistics. (2015). Retrieved from http://tourism.gov.in/market-research-and-statistics

India Tourism Statistics. (2017). Retrieved from http://tourism.gov.in/market-research-and-statistics

India Tourism Statistics. (2018). Retrieved from http://tourism.gov.in/market-research-and-statistics

Itoo, M.A. (2013). Tourism industry of Kashmir (1947-1989). *International journal of management and sustainability, 2*(4), 63-71.

Jammu and Kashmir State Economic survey. (2016). Retrieved from https://openbudgetsindia.org/dataset/jk-economic-survey-2016-2017-18/resource/7f67ef5f-222c-4bd3-80e8-fba10e61578d

Lew, A. A. (1987). A framework of tourist attraction research. *Annals of Tourism Research, 14*(4), 553–557. doi:10.1016/0160-7383(87)90071-5

Mansfeld, Y., & Pizam, A. (2006). *Tourism, Security, and Safety: From Theory to Practice*. Burlington, MA: Elsevier Butterworth-Heinemann.

Michael, H. C. (2010). Crisis events in tourism: Subjects of crisis in tourism. *Current Issues in Tourism, 13*(5), 401–417. doi:10.1080/13683500.2010.491900

Middleton, V. T. C., & Clark, J. (2004). *Marketing in Travel and Tourism* (3rd ed.). Cornwall: Elsevier: Butterworth-Heinemann.

Min, J. C. H. (2008). Forecasting Japanese tourism demand in Taiwan using an intervention analysis. *International Journal of Culture, Tourism and Hospitality Research, 2*(3), 197–216. doi:10.1108/17506180810891582

Parikshat, S. M. (2012). Sustainable and responsible tourism: Trends practices and cases. PHI learning.

Pauchant, T., & Mitroff, I. (1992). *Transforming the Crisis Prone Organization.* San Francisco, CA: Jossey-Bass Publishers.

Pizam, A., & Fleischer, A. (2002). Severity Versus Frequency of Acts of Terrorism: Which Has a Larger Impact on Tourism Demand? *Journal of Travel Research, 40*(3), 337–339. doi:10.1177/004728750204000301 1

Ritchie, B. W. (2009). *Crisis and disaster management for tourism.* Bristol, UK: Channel View. doi:10.21832/9781845411077

Ritchie, B.W., Dorrell, H., Miller, D., & Miller, G. (2002). Crisis Communication and recovery for the tourism industry: Lessons from the 2001 Foot and Mouth Disease Outbreak in the United Kingdom.

Ross, G. F. (2005). Tourism industry employee workstress – a present and future crisis. *Journal of Travel & Tourism Marketing, 19*(2/3), 133–147. doi:10.1300/J073v19n02_11

Sonmez, S. F., Apostolopoulos, Y., & Peter, E. T. (1999). Tourism in crisis: Managing the effects of terrorism. *Journal of Travel Research, 38*(1), 13–21. doi:10.1177/004728759903800104

State-wise Number of Domestic Tourist Visits in India. (n.d.). India stat. Retrieved from http://www.indiastat.com/tourism/29/stats.aspx

Survey on Domestic Tourism. (n.d.). Retrieved from http://www.jammuandkashmirstat.com/tourism/29/stats.aspx

Walters, G. A., Mair, J. A., & Ritchie, B. (2012). *The Australian Tourism Market's Response to the 2011 Queensland Floods.* Australia: University of Queensland.

Wang, Y. S. (2009). The impact of crisis events and macroeconomic activity on Taiwan's international inbound tourism demand. *Tourism Management*, *30*(1), 75–82. doi:10.1016/j.tourman.2008.04.010

World Trade and Tourism Council Report. (2018). Travel & Tourism Economic Impact 2018. Retrieved from Https://Www.Wttc.Org//Media/Files/Reports/Economic%20 impact%20research/Regions%202016/World2018.Pdf

Chapter 6
Mystery Shopper Programs in the Tourism Sector

Eda Özgül Katlav
https://orcid.org/0000-0002-4168-909X
Nevsehir Haci Bektas Veli University, Turkey

Şule Aydin
https://orcid.org/0000-0002-8760-643X
Nevsehir Haci Bektas Veli University, Turkey

ABSTRACT

In today's world, there is fierce competition in the tourism sector, and therefore, the businesses need to improve their service qualities constantly and enhance their service processes to meet customer expectations swiftly and effectively. In recent years, tourism operators have been focusing on customer-oriented research and programs to avoid negative results that may be caused by unsatisfied customers. The service quality of tourism businesses is directly based on the performance of the employees; therefore, it is very important to evaluate the performances of the employees and improve service processes to avoid potential problems. Mystery shopper programs show the true picture of the services offered to the guests by the tourism businesses. Therefore, mystery shopper programs are widely used in the world for the evaluation of employees, especially in service-provider companies. The mystery shopper programs provide information on service quality, employee performance, and customer satisfaction, which is used by the businesses to improve or develop their service delivery processes.

DOI: 10.4018/978-1-7998-2204-2.ch006

Copyright © 2020, IGI Global. Copying or distributing in print or electronic forms without written permission of IGI Global is prohibited.

INTRODUCTION

In today's world, there is fierce competition in the tourism sector and therefore the businesses need to improve their service qualities constantly and enhance their service processes to meet customer expectations swiftly and effectively. In recent years, tourism operators have been focusing on customer-oriented research and programs to avoid negative results that may be caused by the unsatisfied customers (Kotler, 2000). The service quality of the tourism businesses is directly based on the performance of the employees, therefore it is very important to evaluate the performances of the employees and improve service processes to avoid potential problems.

In the hospitality industry, the businesses are required to provide quality products or services and offer them to their customers at expected standards consistently. Providing quality service is one of the biggest challenges that tourism managers will face in the next years; because it is an essential condition for success in intensely competitive, global hospitality markets. There are several tools to measure and improve service quality, as well as the quality recognition mechanisms in the tourism sector (Kapiki, 2012: 53). In terms of tourism businesses, mystery shopper programs are an effective way to measure and improve the performances of the employees. Mystery shopper program is a good tool for the depth analysis of the perceptions of the employees.

Today, the businesses identify their weaknesses by looking through the eyes of their customers and use mystery shopper programs to find solutions to the problems and increase customer satisfaction. For this reason, mystery shoppers operate at the markets, banks, hospitals, restaurants, hotels -in short, everywhere where service is provided- in order to inspect the service of the business. Although, the mystery shopper programs are used in many sectors, they are more widely used in restaurants, banks and retail sectors.

Mystery shopper programs show the true picture of the services offered to the guests by the tourism businesses. In addition to the customer satisfaction surveys and customer complaints, the mystery shopper programs help businesses to identify and solve problems in their services and improve existing service standards. Therefore, mystery shopper programs are widely used in the world for the evaluation of employees, especially in service provider companies. The mystery shopper programs provide information on service quality, employee performance and customer satisfaction, which is used by the businesses to improve or develop their service delivery processes. In this section, the concept of the mystery shopper, mystery shopper programs, process of mystery shopper programs, mystery shopper programs in tourism sector, the advantages and disadvantages of mystery shopper program and problems caused in terms of ethics have been explained and then, the examples of tourism sector have been described.

Mystery Shopper Programs

Mystery Shopper Programs are accepted to be in line with the business purposes such as providing service to meet the needs and expectations of the customers, delivering complete and accurate service and ensuring customer satisfaction (Murat & Çelik, 2017). According to Tavmergen (2002), the businesses should conduct market research before, during and after the service, identify needs and expectations of the customers and monitor any changes in order to provide successful quality services.

It is important to measure the quality of service offered in the service sector. Because, when the service quality is measured, it cause businesses to evaluate its services from the eyes of the customers and the information obtained from this activity helps them to improve their service quality and to increase their competitiveness. While quality and performance indicators are easy to identify and measure in manufacture sectors, these measurements are more difficult to be determined in service sectors. Because, it is hard to identify the benefit of the services with quantitative criteria. Therefore, generally, the scales are developed to measure the level of perception of the customers. The most widely used measurement tool is SERVQUAL/SERVPERF scale, which is developed by Parasuraman, Zeithaml & Berry to measure service quality (Eleren & Kilic, 2007).

Another practice that is used to measure service quality is quality awards. Quality awards are seen as a guideline for reaching and exceeding standard service quality. The Ritz Carlton Hotel implements quality awards and has a system that starts with identifying certain service targets and developing strategies of quality with the participation of employees. The quality system created by Ritz Carlton has been managed very well and it is the only service provider that received the Malcolm Baldrige National Quality Award (MBNQA) twice (Torres, 2012).

Another quality assessment tool is the mystery shopper program. The mystery shopper program is an application that aims to evaluate the quality of the products and employees and is conducted by trained and anonymous shoppers (MSPS 2017, www.mysteryshop.org) Although mystery shopper programs have been widely implemented by the businesses for almost a hundred year (Manolica & Roman, 2012), they were originally used by the kings or sultans at earlier times (PamInca, 2009: 3). The kings used to conceal their identities, dress like someone from the public, mix with the community and learn what was said about the king and kingdoms (Öter, Ayaz Olay & Kömürcü, 2015).

The first mystery shopper programs were seen in the banking sector in the United States at the beginning of the 1900s, and implemented to prevent bank employees to take some money or run a scam. In the 1940s, the mystery shopper programs were started to be used for measuring quality standards in the service sector (Zikmund, Babin, Carr, & Griffin, 2009: 17). In the 1970s and 1980s, mystery shopper programs became popular under the name 'Shop'n Chek'. In the 1990s, with the widespread use of the internet, mystery shopper programs grew rapidly and expanded to other fields (Ramesh, 2010). Today, mystery shopper programs are widely used by the enterprises as an evaluation and monitoring tool (Zikmund, Babin, Carr, & Griffin, 2009).

In the hospitality industry, mystery shoppers are widely used to evaluate customer service experiences (Beck, Lalopa & Hall, 2004). Mystery shopper program focus on the service delivery process rather than the result of the service provided. The service delivery process is important to ensure customer satisfaction, similar to the result of the service or the benefit gained from it (Wilson, 2001). The mystery shopper program has become a method which is used for evaluating the performance of employees working in the hospitality industry, for monitoring the service delivery process and its results, and comparing it with competitors (Rood & Dziadkowiec, 2010). A mystery shopper provides neutral assessments and allow businesses to see their services through the eyes of a guest (Stefanelli, 1994). The Mystery Shopping Providers Association (MSPA) defines Mystery Shopper Program as follows (www.gizlimüşterionline.com): Mystery Shopper Program is an act of individuals, who received training before the activity, who pretend to be a real or prospective customer and experience and evaluate service processes and report their experience in an impartial manner.

The fact that mystery shopping programs have become a frequent practice of the businesses to increase their quality of service has led to the emerge of a world-wide mystery shopper service providers. Mystery Shopper Providers Association (MSPA) has more than 150 members worldwide and embody market research companies, private research companies, and training organization companies and conducts research to measure service quality through mystery shoppers (MSPA 2017, www.mysteryshop.org). Many agencies offer mystery shopping service under the roof of 'Mystery Shopper Providers Association'. According to a report prepared by the association in 2005, the market has reached a volume of 1 billion dollars and it is growing by 11.1% per annum (Yıldırgan, Met & Batman, 2016).

Mystery shopper program has become a method to assess the performance of employees, to monitor the service delivery process and its results in the hospitality industry. Mystery shopper program provides an neutral perspective to the businesses in tourism sector. In the practice of mystery shoppers, employees do not know the who the mystery shopper is during service delivery and they serve and behave as if they do to any other customer. However, the employees are aware that each shopper can be a potential mystery shopper and they may be evaluated. This information motivates the employees to work better (MSPA 2017, www.mysteryshop.org). In the broadest sense, mystery shopper program in service sector is a "tool for evaluating and improving customer service". It is used as a performance measurement method for the pre-determined quality standards in service sector (Erstad, 1998, Wilson, 1998).

According to the official guidelines established by MSPA (2011), the businesses should pay attention to the following technical criteria when conducting their mystery shopper program (www.mspa-es.org, 2017):

- Mystery shopper program make a neutral record of the service delivery of a real customer receives. For this reason, a mystery shopper program should include various conditions that best reflect the true shopper experience in practice.
- Appropriate shopping scenarios should be designed so that service, sales or operational behaviour can be tested in the framework of mystery shopper program. The designed scenarios should represent realistic and natural consumer behaviours.
- Scenarios used in mystery shopper programs should not contain anything that could be illegal or risky or that would force employees to disclose any personal information unwillingly, or that lead mystery shoppers to get access to staff records of the employees for the propose of monitoring.
- The businesses which are planning to implement mystery shoppers program should inform their employees that they can be inspected by mystery shoppers.
- The objectives and the results of this program should be explained to the employees.
- The names of the employees can be disclosed by in videos, tapes, etc., but only if the employees were informed about it in advance.
- If bonus, incentive pay or awards will be given as a result of employee performances are based entirely or partly on mystery shopper program, this should be explained to the employees.

It is possible to define mystery shopper program as a participatory observation method that used by researchers to measure service quality and by allowing service staff to think that they are serving to real customers (Wilson, 2001). Mystery shopper programs aim to test the consistency and appropriateness of the processes and procedures used for service delivery at pre-determined standards. It is aimed to measure service quality by deceiving service personnel in order to see service delivery from the eyes of customers during mystery shopper program (Tükeltürk, 2008). When conducting the mystery shopper program, it is important to protect the confidentiality of both the mystery shopper and the employee, to inform the employees about this program, to develop appropriate scenarios and to conduct it with trained individuals.

Hereby, the service providers seek to monitor the suitability and consistency of the processes and procedures used in service delivery according to their pre-determined standards by conducting mystery shopper programs. In service businesses, these processes and standards are determined by managerial staff and line managers. However, implementation of the processes and providing standards are depends on the employees who come face to face with the customers and serve them directly. For this reason, the businesses should monitor the performance of the employees and examine the quality of service they provide (Tükeltürk, 2008). Furthermore, the mystery shopper program assist businesses to identify their strengths and weaknesses, compare them with the competitors and specify necessary training activities and policy improvements (Leeds, 1996).

Definition of Mystery Shopper

The most important element of the mystery shopper program is to choose the right mystery shopper to conduct the survey. The mystery shopper assist the business in various ways, including measuring quality of service, identifying critical failure points, specifying necessary training requirements and comparing it with its competitors (Van Der Wiele, Hasselink, & Van Iwaarden, 2005).

The mystery shopper is the person who acts as a real customer and who is trained about the processes of the program, the evaluation methods and measurement of quality of the customer experiences (Calvert, 2005; Tükeltürk, Perçin & Göksu, 2008). Mystery shoppers are the researchers who gets the service offered by the business as real shoppers (Akt, Allison, Severt, Dikson, 2010). In the mystery shoppers program, trained individuals make observations according to an assessment scale and evaluate the service delivery of the employees through the eyes of the customers. Mystery shoppers are trained people who evaluates the service quality based on predetermined criteria. Mystery shopper focuses on events and procedures that occur or do not occur, rather than gathering ideas about the service experience.

Mattila (2008) states that mystery shoppers should possess the following abilities (Akt Manolica & Roman, 2012):

- must be well organized in order to plan visits and deliver reports according to the timeline specified.
- must be a good observer to be able to conduct evaluation criteria accurately.
- must be a good narrator to tell about his/her visit.
- could summarize the situation, avoid meaningless details.

- could stay neutral (the report should only contain the visit, should not mention his/her own thoughts).

In addition, although anyone trained in the field can become a mystery shopper, he/she should be reliable, honest, harmonious, calm, objective, give attention to detail, have a strong memory and good perception, be capable of acting well, can transmit accurate information, write good reports by using the language well, can work at flexible time (www.gizlimusterionline.com, 2017).

According to the Mystery Shopper Occupational Standards accepted by MSPA and adopted by mystery shopper research companies, all mystery shoppers are required to act honestly and ethically, to perform in accordance with the procedures and regulations adopted by the MSPA members, and they agree to follow the principles and inform the public about the reliability of mystery shopper surveys (www.mspa-es.org, 2017). In addition, the mystery shoppers should be well trained about the rules and regulations and briefed about necessary situations.

In the light of this information, the mystery shoppers can be defined as the people who act like real shoppers, who are trained about the processes and programs used in service delivery, who have reliable personality, who have good acting abilities, who can stay neutral and who can focus on details. When mystery shoppers performing their tasks, they should not act in suspicious way indicating they are mystery shoppers, nor they insist on seeing the names of employees or observing a specific area. The mystery shopper should submit a written report in neutral manner at the end of the task, but it should not include unnecessary details and should present information like a photography shot.

The Purpose and the Importance of Mystery Shopper Programs

It is important to be able to ensure customer satisfaction for tourism businesses in hospitality industry where competing conditions are fierce. But, the satisfied customers are more likely to purchase more and become loyal customers. A satisfied customer usually purchases additional products and services and disseminate information about the service they received with word of mouth. The business can pay less attention to the advertisements of the competitors and it gives attention to the ideas and suggestions and most importantly, a satisfied customer cost less to the business (Hesselink, Iwardeen & Wiele, 2004).

For these reasons, service providers make every afford to provide quality services and to measure it. Businesses often use mystery shopper program in order to ensure the service standards and to solve problems emerging from the employees during service delivery. Mystery shopper program is a method often used to determine how the problems occur at each stage of the service, to see how the customers are treated through the eyes of the customers. According to MPSA, the purpose of the mystery shopper program is to gain information on quality of service in order to develop appropriate training activities and to make service improvements, and to ensure customer satisfaction, and to hold customer loyalty and commitment. However, mystery shoppers reports should not be used as the sole reason to punish and / or dismiss employees (http://www.mspa-ea.org, 2017).

In tourism sector, the service delivery and consumption is a simultaneous matter, therefore customer-employee interaction is one of the most important factors in determining service quality. The quality of the physical spaces becomes more evident if the employees are skilled and had good manners and if they enjoy their jobs and perform well (Yıldırgan, Met & Batman, 2016). Therefore, evaluating employees through the eyes of the customers is an important factor for the businesses to reach their targets.

Mystery shopper programs serve the purpose of many businesses. Because, mystery shopper program test if the quality of the service promised to the customers were provided in real- time or not. With this program, the businesses can also determine how successful they are in achieving their strategies and tactics in regard to the quality service delivery. Businesses can detect the problems that occur during service delivery and develop solution proposals. Another aim of this program is to measure the performances of the employees during the service delivery. After the completion of mystery shopping program, the problems of service delivery and employee performances can be identified and appropriate training programs can be established according to the needs of the employees in line with the pre-determined standards.

In service enterprises, business blindness may occur after some time. Business blindness is the problem of not identifying the malfunctions of the methods or procedures, or not recognizing possible future opportunities or the risks. The business blindness can arise as a results of the situation that the same people do the same job with the same team members and have increasing the ties to routine and habits (Altınay, Mercan, Akyansar & Sert, 2012). The businesses in service sector set quality standards for their services and seek to improve them constantly but the business blindness can make it even difficult to solve even very easy problems according to the customers. Mystery shopper program helps businesses to solve problems, such as business blindness (myopathy), by evaluating the services offered with an external eye (Öter, Ayaz Olay & Kömürcü, 2015).

The fact that the mystery shopper programs make many contributions to the businesses, encourage them to implement mystery shopper programs even more, especially in service sector. However, the businesses should obtain necessary information about how to implement mystery shopper programs and have an administration plan.

Mystery Shopper Program Implementation Process and Important Factors to Consider

The use of mystery shopper programs in many sectors in the world has brought up the need for the research about how the program should be processed and what factors should be considered into the agenda. Therefore, the researchers tried to explain the mystery shopper program in several steps. Erstad (1998) mentioned six basic steps in mystery shopper programs. These steps are: determination of targets, preparation of the evaluation form, selection and training of the mystery shoppers, evaluation, conducting analysis and realization of the necessary activities. These steps are briefly described at below:

- **Determination of targets**

Businesses must identify their targets before starting the mystery shopper program. These targets should be prepared based on the service processes and should especially focus on the problems in the process. For example, they should be based on previous shopper complaints or issues that enhance shopper satisfaction. The views of business executives and employees should be consulted when setting targets for service problems. Apart from business problems, it is also used for controlling or improving the operation processes and service standards, observing customer relations to evaluate employee performances (Erstad, 1998, Wilson, 2001, Tükeltürk, 2008).

- **Preparation of Evaluation Form**

At this stage, it is necessary to prepare an evaluation form which is clear, understandable, easy to analyse and has sufficient perspective to reach the predetermined targets. It is important to take the opinion of everyone in operation from the top management to the employees while preparing an evaluation form in order to achieve targets. A problem that may arise at this stage may cause problems and affect the quality of the research results (Erstad, 1998, Tükeltürk, 2008).

- **Mystery Shopper Selection and Training**

A mystery shopper is a well-trained person who acts like a normal customer and fully observes what's going on and what can be improved during the service delivery. In addition, mystery shoppers must be independent, objective, critical, and anonymous. When choosing a mystery shopper, it is necessary to choose from the potential shoppers who match the profile of the business. In addition, demographic characteristics such as social status, income levels and living standards of mystery shoppers should be taken into consideration. Furthermore, people with an aggressive or defensive personalities should not be preferred (Wilson, 1998: 417; Hesselink, Iwardeen & Wiele, 2004).

Another important decision in the selection of mystery shopper is whether he/she will be recruited from internal sources or external sources. Providing from internal sources seems less costly, but if the business will be conducting this program for the first time, it will be more effective if an expert carries out the task. The training of the mystery shopper can sometimes be more costly than recruiting from external sources. In addition, the efforts can be wasted because the mystery shopper selected from internal sources are more likely to be identified and recognised (Calvert, 2005; Erstad, 1998).

Before the implementation of the program, the mystery shoppers should be trained well. They should be provided with the information about business and services and should also be briefed about the matters which may help them to collect data. The mystery shoppers are subjected to memory tests as they have to make post-event assessments and training is given to strengthen their memory. In addition, mystery shoppers are provided with information about the scenarios they will use during the evaluation. They are subjected to several tests to understand if they can act naturally at the moment of implementation and if they are credible (Wilson, 2001; Tükeltürk, 2008).

- **Evaluation**

After completing training sessions, the shoppers go to the businesses where they will act like a normal customers according to the pre-determined scenario and prepare an evaluation. Mystery shoppers make some requests in line with the pre-determined scenario and try to assess the service process and the performance of the employees. It is necessary for mystery shoppers to behave naturally, not to insist much and not to draw attention during evaluation process. It is important not to insist to learn the names of the employees who provide services, in order not to disclose their identity as mystery shopper (Hudson, Snait, Miller & Hudson, 2001). The second step of the evaluation process is completed when the evaluation form was filled. It is important t to fill the evaluation form with neutral manner and the expressions are stated in a clear and understandable manner.

- **Analysis**

After the information obtained by the mystery shoppers and the evaluation form was completed, the data will be analysed. It is important that the results of the analysis is shared with senior management without any delay. Furthermore, it is also important that further information to be collected from other sources and analysed in order to obtain more beneficial results (Erstad, 1998).

- **Implementation of the Necessary Activities**

The last step of the process is to take actions according to factors determined in the analysis of the data. The aim of the mystery shopper program is to determine the problems of the service delivery and make necessary improvements. In addition, mystery shopper program allow businesses to evaluate performances of employees, who can be recognised and awarded as a result of the positive outcome of the mystery shopper program (Wilson, 1998; Erstad, 1998).

Hesselink and Wiele (2003) describe the mystery shopper procedure as design (purpose, frequency and feedback), data collection, mystery shopper and reporting. It can be said that his definition of the process is a shorter version of the procedures described by Erstad (1998). The first step of the procedure is design. Same as the previous procedure, the objective of the mystery shopper program should be defined. In this step, the identified targets should be made transparent and a checklist should be prepared to measure these targets. When creating a checklist, service delivery should be taken into consideration and attention should be paid to any previous customer surveys and failures results in customer complaints. Certain issues concerning the quality of service should be formulated and they should be related to the strategic positioning of the business on the market. The second step of the process is collecting data. This step should be in line with the strategy of the organization. The checklist for the collection of the data should reflect the key performance indicators of the mission and vision of the business and should cover the dimensions of quality of service (Hesselink & Wiele, 2003).

The third step is a mystery shopper practice, in which the mystery shopper conducts activities according to the checklist prepared in line with the business objectives. In this step, a mystery shopper should be selected. It is necessary that the mystery shopper should follow a route to reach a reliable picture of the service provided to the guests. It is also important that although the employees should know that mystery shoppers will visit the business, they should not know the date/time of this visit. Furthermore, mystery shoppers should be trained about general characteristics of the businesses and the special circumstances they may face. The last step of the process is to prepare a report. In this step, the mystery shopper prepares a report based on the evaluation criteria and present it to the management as soon as possible. It is important that he/she should stay as impartial as possible when writing the report (Hesselink & Wiele, 2003; Tükeltürk, 2008).

Two researchers propose two different procedures for the implementing of mystery shopper program. However, when we examine the both procedures, it is seen that they are very similar to each other. In both methods, firstly, it is stated that it is necessary to determine what the business is targeting by mystery shopper program. Then, the checklists and scenarios need to be prepared in this direction. Both methods focus on the selection and training of mystery shoppers and emphasize its importance. In the first procedure,, the evaluation, analysis and the post-activities are presented with more detail, but these stages were only mentioned slightly in the second procedure. However, whichever procedure is used during the mystery shopper program, it will be a successful implementation.

Advantages and Disadvantages of Mystery Shopper Program

Although the mystery shopper programs are frequently used in service sector for the evaluation of service quality, there are some advantages and disadvantages. Mystery shoppers provide some advantages to businesses as they focus on evaluation of the process and the assessment is carried out at the exact moment of service delivery. It may be a motivating factor for the employees as the program also evaluates the service performance (Öter, Ayaz Olay & Kömürcü, 2015).

The disadvantages of mystery shopper program can be listed as follows (Ramesh, 2010: 39); mystery shopper program can be seen as an disturbing element by the employees. Also, the employees, who know that a mystery shopper will visit the business, may not do their job in fully when the times they think he/she will not visit. In addition, there may have been day-specific problems with the service provided by the business. Therefore, the frequency of the mystery shoppers is very important. Furthermore, the mystery shoppers write their reports at a later time, not at the moment of their visits. For this reason, they might show the situation better or worse than actual conditions.

In addition, the ethical dimension of mystery shopper program is also discussed by researchers. Some researchers (Dawson & Hillier, 1995; Ng Kwet Shing &Spence, 2002; Wilson, 2001) find the deceiving employees as an unethical act and criticize it for that reason. According to Jorgensen (1989), the right to privacy is not broken by the mystery shoppers, therefore it is considered to be an ethical act (Akt. Öter, Ayaz Olay & Kömürcü, 2015). Mystery shopper program is also criticized for its validity and reliability. The problems may arise because of the perception of the mystery shopper and may affect the reliability and validity of the reports (Morrison, Colman & Preston, 1997, Boon & Davies, 1993, Allison, 2009).

Mystery Shopper Programs in Tourism Sector

One of the sectors widely use mystery shopper programs is tourism. Travel agencies, tourism bureaus, hotels, food and beverage businesses, car rental companies, airports and the transport companies all use mystery shopper programs (Wilson, 1998). Many tourism companies want to inspect the service of their employees in order to gain or sustain competitive advantage and increase the level of preference by the customers. It is also a method frequently used by businesses to meet customer requests and expectations, deal with complaints and to measure the service performance of employees. The largest tourism companies of the world, such as Four Seasons, Royal Caribbean International, Fox Restaurant Concepts, Small Luxury Hotels of the World, Hyatt, Marriott, Wolfgang Puck Catering, Holiday Inn, Crowne Plaza and Turkish Airlines, all benefit from mystery shopper programs. (www.coylehospitality.com; www.bdrc-continental.com; www.cnnturk.com). For example, Michelin, the world-known guide for restaurant and culinary evaluation, uses mystery shopper method to measure the quality of service of the restaurants and hotels, by the inspectors (mystery shoppers) in the preparation of the guide (Mcmullen & Akesson, 2011: 8). Similarly, Starbucks, a world-renowned coffee brand, uses mystery shoppers to measure service performances (www.amazonaws.com/academia.edu, 2017).

In the tourism sector, mystery shopper programs are widely used in hotel business. Beck & Miao (2003) stated that their study show that information provided by mystery shoppers in hotels, can be used for evaluation of service quality, evaluation of official hotel ratings, to control of cash handling practices of various departments, department managers and employees. For mystery shopper programs to be productive in hotel businesses, the employees should possess necessary training to carry out continuous improvements, which were determined as a result of the feedback obtained from mystery shopper program. However, there should not be penalty system based on the mystery shopper program which is used to measure service performance.

Mystery shopper programs also help hotel managers follow the criteria based on specific standards. Tourism enterprises use mystery shopper programs to improve their service quality. In order to solve problems, they can prepare training programs for the workforce and educate them in the subjects they need training (Mallet, 2008).

Tourism businesses can find and train mystery shoppers from their internal sources, but also can get support from a specialized companies in this field. There are some worldwide organizations who award internationally recognized certification to the tourism businesses in order to increase the quality of services and standardize the service delivery. These organizations use mystery shopper programs to evaluate the service provided by the tourism businesses before issuing any documents. For example, Hotelcert International, a service standard organisation for the tourism sector, makes a classifications according to the service quality of the accommodation enterprises. The star system used in the accommodation sector based on the rating system of the facilities/equipment provided by the business, but there is no rating provided for the service quality.

Star rating of accommodation businesses differs from one country to another. The accommodation businesses get this certificate to show that their service quality is evaluated according to the internationally accepted criteria and to assure their customers. Businesses seeking to obtain Hotelcert International certification are inspected under mystery shopper program. After inspection, the tourism businesses receive feedback about their strong and weak points and inappropriate situations if there is any. Based on these results, training programs are prepared and continuous improvements are carried out in business processes (www.turizmdunyasi.com.tr, 2017).

For example, Hotelcert carries out the evaluation of the service standard of the accommodation enterprises by the mystery shopper and the procedures are as follows: Firstly, all the questions for the mystery shoppers are prepared by the certificate issuer organisation. Then the accommodation enterprise checks this list, and add additional criteria if necessary. Later, if a mystery shopper makes a reservation by himself/herself. At this stage, the mystery shopper inspect and report the reservation unit. The mystery shopper checks in the hotel like a normal customer and completes the inspection by monitoring the processes and completing checklist. The next day he introduces himself during the check-out and completes his inspection together with hotel management, entering the areas she/he could not have access and asking randomly selected rooms to be open. The investigator should then submit an evaluation report within 5 working days. If the result of the inspection is positive, the tourism business is awarded with Hotelcert International Certificate (www.turizmdunyasi.com.tr, 2017).

CONCLUSION AND RECOMMENDATIONS

Mystery shopper programs are used all over the world to measure service quality and performance evaluation, especially in service sectors. Although physical elements that tourism businesses offer to customers are easily imitated by their competitors, it is difficult to imitate service offered. For this reason, tourism operators want to evaluate their service, to increase the standards and quality of their services and also to motivate employees to increase their service performance. Although there are many different methods to measure the quality of service, mystery shopper programs provide evaluations of pre-service, during-service and post-service activities through the eyes of the customers and therefore it is highly preferred.

In order for the mystery shopper program to be successful, the businesses first should decide if they use internal mystery shopper or recruit from an external company. Michelin, who wants to determine the quality of service of the restaurants, uses its own inspectors as mystery shoppers to evaluate the businesses in accordance with their star criteria. However, the world famous chain hotels receive service by specialized firms. After deciding how to conduct their mystery shopper program, the tourism businesses should then decide what targets they want to achieve. After deciding how to conduct the mystery shopper program, the tourism businesses should determine their targets. Another important factor is that tourism businesses should know the process quite well and administer it accordingly and use the results of the survey to make necessary improvements. Business management should keep the identity of the mystery shoppers confidential and take every precautions to prevent it from disclosure during the visit. The other important factors for the mystery shopper program are the selection and training of mystery shoppers, protecting their identity, how many visits are needed for effective results and how many mystery shoppers are required, and the cost.

The employees know that they can be inspected by the mystery shoppers at any time during the program. However, they do not have any idea when the mystery shopper will come and who will be. This can cause some problems as some researchers criticize mystery shopper programs and argue that this situation is not ethical because it involves deception and cheating of employees. Another problem of the mystery shopper program is that the employees may guess the time of the mystery shopper's arrival and may behave differently to other shoppers apart from these times. For example, if they think that mystery shoppers will come in the morning or in the evening, towards the end of the business hours, they may behave differently to the customers outside those hours. Another problem in this practice is that a well-functioning employee may not be having a good day on this specific date and it may not be appropriate to assess whole of her/his service delivery. Furthermore, the frequency and duration of mystery shopper visits are also important. However, these problems can be solved by making several visits at certain periods.

One of the starting points of mystery shopper programs is to evaluate the performances of the employees and solve problems in service delivery. Therefore, it is important that employees should feel that they will not be harmed by these practice. It would also be appropriate to explain the purpose of this program to the employees and show them how the results will be used. Furthermore, more healthy results can be obtained, if mystery shopper program is combined with other performance assessment methods and all the data is compared (Tükeltürk, 2008).

Many sectors and businesses around the world use mystery shopper programs to provide better service. However, there is a problems at this point. Businesses that is willing to conduct mystery shopper programs are mostly assisted by an expert agencies in this field but it is not known that how the data obtained as a results of the mystery shopper programs were used by the agencies. Also, there is no conclusive result that the methods used in the mystery shopper program can accurately measure the service quality. When the literature in this field was examined, it is noticed that it is very difficult to reach to clear information about how mystery shopper programs were carried out and which measurement tools were used.

When the scientific studies related to the mystery shopper programs are examined, it is seen that mainly the reliability of the program and the ethical matters were discussed. The mystery shopper program was compared with other measurement tools of service quality and it is debated whether it is reliable or not. In addition, the ethicality of this method are also being discussed as it involve deception of employees. Since there is not sufficient number of studies in this field, the arguments stayed as unanswered. However, the method is widely used by many successful businesses and it is an evidence of its being beneficial.

As a result, the mystery shopper programs evaluate and compare the services offered and determines the strengths and weaknesses of the businesses. In addition, this program assist businesses to obtain data for market research purposes and examine pricing policies. After the implementation of the program, information obtained can be used to improve services which is possible do in a short period of time. With this program, the performances of the employees are evaluated. As a result, the employees had to behave honestly and changes in corporate culture increase the service awareness of employees. As a result of the program, training needs are determined and training programs are prepared for the necessary topics. Mystery shopper program help business to provide quality products, encourages the establishment of good relations with the customers and offers solutions to increase customer loyalty and sales.

Case Study: Turkish Airlines Mystery Shopper Program "The Limit of Our Service Quality is the Sky"

According to the research conducted by Skytrax in 2017, Turkish Airlines (THY) is listed as the Best Airline of Europe and it is one of the best airlines in the world (https://p.turkishairlines.com/tr-tr/haberler-ve-basin-bultenleri/index.html). THY wants to be in the top in the aviation sector and it is conducting many activities to improve standards of service continuously. In 2007, they started "mystery shopper" and "honorary observer" programs for the first time in order to increase the quality of service provided (www.cnnturk.com).

THY declared the year 2007 as a quality year and aims to learn how its services through the eyes of the customers at pre-service, during service and post-service stages by using mystery shopper program and predefined scenarios. Under the project

Figure 1.

with a slogan of "The limit of our service quality is the sky", the trained staff of independent research company evaluates each process related to the flights with various shopper roles. On the other hand, honorary observers are the THY passengers voluntarily share their flight related evaluations. Honorary observers submit their evaluations after each flight to THY and within the scope of these evaluations, relevant departments determines the problems in the service process and carry out the necessary improvements (www.turkishairlines.com ; www.cnnturk.com).

Head of THY Business Development Department Dr. Haşmet Gökırmak gave information about mystery shopper and voluntary observer program and stated that customer satisfaction is always their first priority. Dr. Gökırmak also added that they are open to all kind of channels that can help them to communicate with their passengers in order to increase customer satisfaction and loyalty. They have created a platform where the passengers can share experiences of their journey and communicate with THY for 7/24, through call centre and internet pages. They have supported mystery shopper and honorary observer programs to provide better service and to evaluate and improve service performances of employees (www.turkishairlines.com ; www.cnnturk.com).

Figure 2.

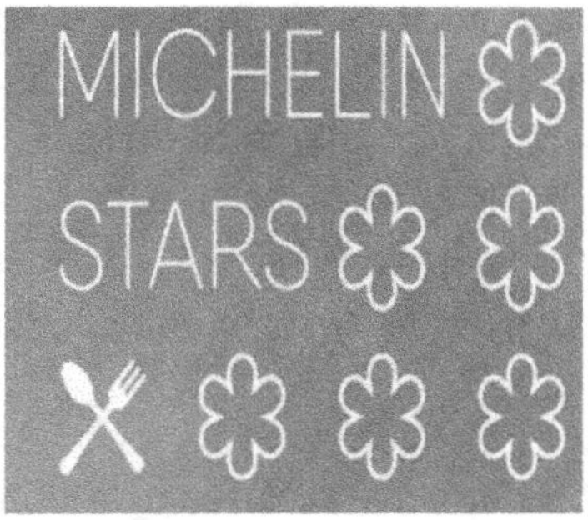

Case Study: Restaurants with Michelin Stars are evaluated by mystery shoppers.

The emergence of Michelin's guide is to encourage more drivers to drive vehicles. The Michelin Star begins with a guide published by Andre and Edoard Michelin in 1900 for motorcycle and car drivers. This guide included information which may be useful for motorists and car drivers, such as maps, tire repair stations. Later, in 1926, Michelin began to give stars to restaurants. Stars given to restaurants are as follows; 1 Michelin Star restaurants are classified as best in their category, 2 Michelin Star restaurants are excellent in culinary services and it is worth to change your route, 3 Michelin Star restaurants offer exceptional culinary service and it is worth to travel there just for this restaurant (https://guide.michelin.com/us/chicago/about-us, 2017; https://tr.linkedin.com, 2017).

As it is important to get stars for the restaurants, it is also very important to inspect them accurately. Therefore, the restaurants that receive the Michelin Stars are inspected by mystery shoppers before and after receiving the star. Michelin restaurants mystery shopper program is implemented as follows (www.hotellerie-restauration.ac, 2017); Michelin chose its inspectors from frequent travellers, who had worked at hotel and restaurant industry, expert in this field and they are paid by Michelin. Their task is to search, select and update the addresses and price categories of the best hotels and restaurants. When choosing a restaurant or a hotel, inspectors compare one establishment to the other based on exact and homogeneous criteria in all countries, with an emphasis on the gastronomic characteristics of the country (tapas bar, agro tourism, gastronomic bars ...).

In this framework, mystery shoppers make a reservation in different name, they make selections without asking the suggestion of the employees and receive services from the establishment. They leave after making the necessary payment. A mystery shopper writes the report for each visit in accordance with pre-determined criteria. Every Michelin inspector travels to France and Europe within the scope of mystery shopper program and perform evaluations of the 240 restaurants and 130 hotels each year, on average. They can also conduct face-to-face interviews with 800 people during the inspection of restaurants. Starred enterprises are visited every eighteen months on average. However, some businesses can be visited by mystery shoppers even twelve times a year. The requests, comments of the readers, the need for assessment of the stability of businesses can be a reason for a new visit (www.hotellerie-restauration.ac, 2017).

Case Study: Starbucks Mystery Shopper Case Study

Starbucks is one of the leading international coffee brands in the world and operates mystery shopper program to inspect service performance. An inspection that Starbucks has conducted under the mystery shopper program is narrated in an article of Capital Magazine (2008) (https://www.capital.com.tr, 2017).

It is 9 o'clock in the morning ... A customer goes in the Starbucks cafe. As soon as he is inside, he looks around to check if the tables are clean enough. Then, he checks how the baristas (trained people who make coffee) are serving to the customers. He also checks if the place they make coffee is hygienic- without being noticed-, and orders a big cappuccino.

He's takes out his debit card to make the payment but a problem arise during the payment process. The mystery shopper starts to run the chronometer in his bag. He secretly make a note of the time spend for the solving the problem and the preparation time of the coffee. During this time, he examines the changes in the face expressions of the barista. As soon as the problem with the card has been solved, he asks, "What new drinks do you have? ". After taking note of baristas exact answer to this question, he leaves Starbucks with his coffee and disappears from the eyes.

This story is an example of self-evaluation of Starbucks, which is one of the most successful brands in the world, using "mystery shoppers". Today, not just Starbucks, but also many successful brands and companies use "mystery shoppers" for different purposes.

REFERENCES

Allison, P., Severt, D., & Dickson, D. (2010). A conceptual model for mystery shopping motivations. *Journal of Hospitality Marketing & Management, 19*(6), 629–657. doi:10.1080/19368623.2010.493077

Allison, P. B. (2009). *Mystery shopper motivations and the presence of motivation crowding*. University of Central Florida.

Altinay, A., Mercan, N., Aksanyar, Y., & Sert, S. (2012). Işletme körlüğü, silo sendromu ve çözüm önerisi olarak örgütsel zekâ. *Organizasyon ve Yönetim Bilimleri Dergisi, 4*(1).

Beck, J., Lalopa, J., & Hall, J. (2004). Insuring quality service: Training mystery shoppers. *Journal of Human Resources in Hospitality & Tourism, 2*(2), 41–56. doi:10.1300/J171v02n02_03

Beck, J., Lalopa, J., & Hall, J. (2004). Insuring Quality Service. *Journal of Human Resources in Hospitality & Tourism, 2*(2), 41–56. doi:10.1300/J171v02n02_03

Beck, J., & Miao, L. (2003). Mystery shopping in lodging properties as a measurement of service quality. *Journal of Quality Assurance in Hospitality & Tourism, 4*(1-2), 1–21. doi:10.1300/J162v04n01_01

Calvert, P. (2005). It's a mystery: Mystery shopping in New Zealand's public libraries. *Library Review, 54*(1), 24–35. doi:10.1108/00242530510574138

Dawson, J., & Hillier, J. (1995). Competitor mystery shopping: Methodological considerations and implications for the MRS code of conduct. *Journal of the Market Research Society, 37*(4), 417–428. doi:10.1177/147078539503700406

Eleren, A., & Kılıç, B. (2007). Turizm sektöründe SERVQUAL analizi ile hizmet kalitesinin ölçülmesi ve bir termal otelde uygulama. *Afyon Kocatepe Üniversitesi, İİ BF Dergisi, IX-1*, 235–263.

Erstad, M. (1998). Mystery shopping programmes and human resource management. *International Journal of Contemporary Hospitality Management, 10*(1), 34–38. doi:10.1108/09596119810199318

Hesselink, M., van der Wiele, T., & Shopping, M. (2003). *In-Depth Measurement of Shopper Satisfaction*. ERIM Report Series Reference No. ERS-2003-020-ORG. Available at SSRN: https://ssrn.com/abstract=411653

Hesselink, M., van Iwaarden, J., & van der Wiele, T. (2004). Mystery shopping: A tool to develop insight into shopper service provision. *ERIM Report Series Research in Management, 9*(3).

Hudson, S., Snaith, T., Miller, G. A., & Hudson, P. (2001). Distribution channels in the travel industry: Using mystery shoppers to understand the influence of travel agency recommendations. *Journal of Travel Research, 40*(2), 148–154. doi:10.1177/004728750104000205

Kapiki, S. T. (2012). *Quality management in tourism and hospitality: An exploratory study among tourism stakeholders.*

Kotler, P. (2000). *Pazarlama Yöntemi*. İstanbul: Beta Pub.

Leeds, B. (1995). Mystery shopping: From novelty to necessity. *Bank Marketing, 27*, 17–17.

Mallett, M. (2008). Pair training with mystery shopping. *Restaurant Hospitality, 92*(4), 20.

Manolică, A., & Roman, T. (2012). Globalisation–advantages and disadvantages from the perspective of the manufacturer. Editorial Board, 747.

Mcmullen, R., & Åkesson, E. (2011). *Mystery Shopping: En mätning av kvaliteten på Connect Hotels* (Master's thesis). Örebro Universistet Restaurang- och Hotellhögskolan Grythytte Academy.

Morrison, L. J., Colman, A. M., & Preston, C. C. (1997). Mystery shopper research: Cognitive processes affecting accuracy. *Journal of the Market Research Society, 39*(2), 349–361. doi:10.1177/147078539703900203

Mystery Shopping Providers Web Site. (n.d.). Retrieved from http://www.mysteryshop.org/

Ng Kwet Shing, M., & Spence, L. J. (2002). Investigating the limits of competitive intelligence gathering: Is mystery shopping ethical? *Business Ethics, 11*(4), 343–353. doi:10.1111/1467-8608.00294

Öter, Z., Ayaz Olay, N., & Kömürcü, S. (2015). *Gizli Müşteri Uygulamaları. In Turizm Pazarlamasında Güncel Yaklaşımlar*. İstanbul: Beta Yayıncılık.

PamInCa. (2009). The Essential Guide to Mystery Shopping. Silicon Valley. *Happy About, 2009*, 119.

Rood, A. S., & Dziadkowiec, J. (2010). Why use importance performance analysis in mystery shopping? A USA–Poland comparative answer. *Journal of Quality Assurance in Hospitality & Tourism*, *11*(1), 1–16. doi:10.1080/15280080903520592

Rood, S., & Dziadkowiec, J. (2010). Why Use Importance Performance Analysis in Mystery Shopping? A USA–Poland Comparative Answer. *Journal of Quality Assurance in Hospitality & Tourism*, *11*(1), 1–16. doi:10.1080/15280080903520592

Stefanelli, J. M. (1994). Using mystery shoppers to maintain hospitality company service standards. *Hospitality & Tourism Educator*, *6*(1), 17–18. doi:10.1080/23298758.1994.10685540

Stefanelli, J. M. (1994). Using mystery shoppers to maintain hospitality company service standards. *Hospitality & Tourism Educator*, *6*(1), 17–18. doi:10.1080/23298758.1994.10685540

Tavmergen, İ. P. (2002). *Turizm Sektöründe Kalite Yönetimi*. Seçkin Pub.

Torres, E. N. (2012). *Hotel general managers' use of consumer, expert, and internal feedback to improve service quality*(Doctoral dissertation). Purdue University.

Tükeltürk Aydın, Ş. (2008). *Hizmet İşletmelerinde Gizli Müşteri Uygulamalarının İnsan Kaynakları Yönetimi Açısından Değerlendirilmesi*. Ekim-Kasım-Aralık.

Wiele, T. V. D., Hesselink, M., & Iwaarden, J. V. (2005). Mystery shopping: A tool to develop insight into shopper service provision. *Total Quality Management & Business Excellence*, *16*(4), 529–541. doi:10.1080/14783360500078433

Wilson, A. M. (1998). The use of mystery shopping in the measurement of service delivery. *Service Industries Journal*, *18*(3), 148–163. doi:10.1080/02642069800000037

Wilson, A. M. (2001). Mystery shopping: Using deception to measure service performance. *Psychology and Marketing*, *18*(7), 721–734. doi:10.1002/mar.1027

Yıldırgan, Ö. G. R., Met, Ö. L., & Batman, O. (2016). Müşteri İlişkileri Yönetimi Kapsamında Gizli Müşteri Alışverişi: Zincir Otel Örneği. *Journal of Travel and Hospitality Management*, *13*(3), 56–67.

Zikmund, W. G., Babin, B. J., Carr, J. C., & Griffin, M. (2013). *Business research methods*. Cengage Learning. Retrieved from http://bdrc-continental.com/solutions/mystery-shopping/

Chapter 7
Sustainable Tourism:
What Trends Does Academic Production Reveal?

Fátima Lampreia Carvalho
University of Algarve, Portugal

Silvia Fernandes
https://orcid.org/0000-0002-1699-5415
University of Algarve, Portugal

ABSTRACT

This chapter compares several academic works in order to analyse if they use innovative approaches for sustainable tourism. It analyses 70 stable documents including theses, scientific papers, and reports. Some goals are assess the themes that most stand out, the contribution of academic research to the subject, and how the issues of sustainability governance and planning relate to tourism. This contributes to approach the relationship between tourism and sustainability for development. The qualitative analysis used could discern the maturity level of research on sustainability indexes. Few works use them, and, if used, most are more descriptive than quantitative. But the ones that use them have acknowledged their importance and resulting enhanced strategies, as they provide the data to decide accurately on environmental and destination matters. A challenge for the Portuguese academy is to have an ongoing role in implementing and monitoring key sustainability indices.

DOI: 10.4018/978-1-7998-2204-2.ch007

Copyright © 2020, IGI Global. Copying or distributing in print or electronic forms without written permission of IGI Global is prohibited.

INTRODUCTION

Given the close relationship between natural resources and a very large segment of the tourism industry, a lack of progress on fostering sustainability will reduce tourism development opportunities. Besides environment, also cultural and socio-economic issues become involved in this equation of tourism sustainability. Many works discuss this subject, revealing its increasing importance for today's global and local decisions about tourism development (Cordeiro, 2008).

This research aims to establish what proportion of academic works, listed in the scientific repository of open access RCAAP, has proposed innovative strategies for sustainable tourism. Among those, which portion has used approaches grounded on international/national sustainability indexes. RCAAP promotes access and diffusion of the results of academic production in Portugal and Brazil. This is interesting to compare because Brazil is a good reference in tourism and Portuguese universities have been receiving more and more Brazilian students. Academic research on sustainable tourism not always refers to international indexes, such as the Travel & Tourism Environmental Sustainability Index and the Global Destination Sustainability Index. This might be due to different factors such as lack of funding, complexity of data collection and lack of statistical training in tourism schools (Dias, 2016; GDS Sustainability Index, 2017).

This analysis initially looked at 164 theses and other scientific works containing the keywords: sustainable tourism, sustainability index, and governance. However, the final selection retained 70 stable documents which were downloadable and according to the criteria considered.

CONTEXT AND OBJECTIVES

In 2017 the World Travel & Tourism Council (WTTC) estimated that tourism contributed with 10% of the world's GDP and accounted for just under 10% of its total employment. However, Gossling et al. (2013) show that the contribution from tourism sector to global climate change was approximately 5% of carbon emissions. Some economies can be considerably more carbon-intense than others, thus supporting the need to monitor their growth and sustainability in the coming years. According to the environmental footprint, Portugal (with a population of 10,291,027) is one of the countries that make a difference in setting a goal of achieving carbon neutrality in 2050. Its carbon footprint is now under the European average.

Brazil, with a population of 208,862,818 (IBGE, 2015) has experienced success in slowing rain forest destruction, resulting in vast reductions of carbon emissions. The case of Brazil shows that it is possible to promote sustainability while still growing the economy. The country has reduced deforestation by 70% and kept 3.2 billion tons of CO2 out of the atmosphere, because forests use carbon as they grow. That makes it the biggest reduction in greenhouse gas emissions of any country in the world. It became the first major developing country to pledge an absolute reduction in greenhouse gas emissions ahead of Paris climate talks. Other affected dimensions, besides environment, are of culture, social and human nature. Nevertheless, climate and community issues are more approached when discussing sustainability matters.

The main objective of this research is to investigate in what ways academic works, especially doctoral theses, papers and reports in Portugal and Brazil, respond to the growing pressure that tourism is placing on the environment and society. Thus, the overall goal is to analyse the academic works on sustainable tourism produced in Portuguese and Brazilian higher education from 2004 to 2017. Key aspects to be assessed are: 1) which contents are most salient; 2) what differences exist between Brazil and Portugal in this matter; and 3) how topics such as sustainability, governance, planning and regulation relate to tourism sustainability indexes.

Tourism in Higher Education

In the period 2006-2017, the number of academic works written in Portugal and Brazil at the end of tourism graduations and post graduations increased in 2012, with 24 works produced that year. Then they decreased considerably, and increased again in 2015. There was a higher productivity of theses by students enrolled in courses such as Tourism (80), Tourism Leisure and Culture (20) and the Development of Products of Cultural Tourism (19).

In Portugal, the University of Aveiro issued the largest number of doctoral theses in Tourism, with more than 40 theses written on the topic, followed by the Faculty of Economics of the Algarve's University with 18 theses. This last is followed by the Institute of Geography of the Lisbon's University, with 12 theses. The themes of the theses developed at the University of Aveiro are more related to: rural tourism, destination competitiveness, tourists' behaviour, and factors of investment in the tourism sector. Only three directly discussed the issues of tourism planning and tourism sustainability (in 2008, 2010 and 2012). And the theses from the Faculty of Economics of the Algarve's University are mainly related to: destination's image, welfare, and economic evaluation. Only two of these works discussed tourism planning and sustainability (in 2009). Finally, the theses developed at the Institute of Geography of the Lisbon's University are mostly related to tourism management and cultural tourism, and just one of those discussed tourism planning and governance (in 2011).

More than 160 dissertations and theses were found in tourism and sustainability at the OASISBr portal in the period considered (2004-2017). This Brazilian portal of open access scientific publications is a multi-disciplinary search engine that allows free access to the scientific production of authors linked to Brazilian universities and research institutes. Through OASISBr, you can also search for Portuguese sources of information.

Of the Brazilian works deposited, 24 approached directly the theme of sustainability in tourism being 7 of PhD and 17 masters. Directly related to indicators are 8, being 3 PhD and 5 masters. It should be noted that there is a growing trend in addressing indicators, because of these 8 works 4 are 2016. And joining them to work on sustainability in tourism, are more than 10 in the recent period of 2015-2017. The other work focuses on other areas of tourism, such as: environmental concerns (17); Local communities (10); Rural tourism (8); Creative Cities and Clusters (5); Behaviors (2), among other sub-areas (hospitality, restoration, economic evaluation, etc.).

Given that the scope of sustainable development is seen as a way for the current society to meet its needs without compromising the survival of future generations, it is necessary to use indicators for this control to be effective. Due to globalization, mobility and competitiveness tourism often overloads or affects locals. Tourism activities should increasingly meet the principles of sustainability, which boil down to maintaining balance and equity between social, environmental and economic dimensions without neglecting the social actors involved.

Focusing on the collection of RCAAP, the present study inspected the academic production of Portuguese and Brazilian higher education, with the expression of research "sustainable tourism". A sample of 70 works was considered and it includes: 33 Master's dissertations, 9 theses of PhD, 18 scientific papers and 7 reports. The other 3 works are undergraduate course projects. In this sample, regarding the work in Portuguese institutions and addressing sustainable tourism, one could observe a growing trend to address sustainability and governance (for example, in recent works from 2015 to 2017). This academic production relates this area especially to stakeholders and environment. In 2012 there was a higher production of academic works in tourism, with works closely related to growth in tourism, local development, and economic evaluation. In particular, 6 works of the sample at hand addressed sustainability indexes (Stilwell, 2011). A type of work that mostly addresses the issue of indexes is the international reports, promoting certain innovative measures based on them.

Importance of International Reports

World tourism organisations and other international institutions are the most relevant bases of leadership on the subject for sustainability indicators whereas it is understandable that allusions to sustainability indicators are minor in PhD, MA theses and journal articles. Governmental, non-governmental and supra-national organisations' reports and guidebooks such as the WTO Indicators of Sustainable Development for Tourism Destinations refer to different types of indicators, each with a different utility to decision-makers (WTO, 2004).

Table 1 gives prevalence to eight national and international reports containing explanations of sustainability measures. The objective here is to compare the sustainability indexes regarding their targets, proposals and custodian agency.

Table 1. Tourism sustainability indicators in main international reports

Report	Indicators	Objectives/targets
National strategy for the Sustainable development ENDS 2005-2015 (Mota et al., 2005)	Sustainable Development Indicators (SDI) for monitoring the National Strategy for Sustainable Development	Qualification of Portuguese towards knowledge society; productivity growth with strong investment in sectors of marketable goods; model of development integrating environmental protection; better articulation of policies and territorial planning instruments; withstand the shock of ageing of population; international cooperation
Atlantic axis of the Northwest Peninsular (2011) Sustainability of the Euro-region Galicia-north of Portugal by Eixoecologia	Agenda 21's urban and sustainable transport indicators	Social demographic components; sustainable production and consumption; climate changes and clean energy; mobility; conservation and management of natural resources and planning of the territory
Global Destination Sustainability (GDS) Index Report (2017)	The Global Destination Sustainability (GDS) Index	Measure environmental performance; social performance; supplier performance; sustainability policy and communication
Sustainable tourism index: Enhancing the global travel environment (2017)	The Sustainable tourism index	Political and regulatory environment; environmental sustainability; socio-cultural sustainability; economic sustainability; travel and tourism industry
Travel and Tourism Competitiveness Report 2017 UNWTO and World Travel & Tourism Council	Travel and Tourism Competitiveness Index (TTCI)	Focus on ensuring the industry's sustained growth in an uncertain security environment while preserving the natural environment and local communities
Sustainable Development Goals (Portugal, Agenda 2030)	Sustainable Development Indicators for Portugal, Agenda 2030	Policies to promote sustainable tourism (jobs, local culture and products); achieve higher levels of economic productivity (diversification, innovation, high-value added); achieve universal and equitable access to safe water
Sustainability Report 2016 by Tourism Portugal	Tourism Sustainability Indicators for Portugal	Monitoring indicators of sustainability in tourism; constitution of an observatory of sustainability; definition of desired positioning of tourism sustainability of Portugal and underlying implementation strategy
Indicators of Sustainable Development for Brazil (IBGE 2015)	Indicators of Sustainable Development	Focus on the environmental dimension - pressure and impact factors related to the preservation of the environment, fundamental for quality of life of generations

The most directly useful indexes may be those that help to predict problems. Several other types of indicators are: early warning indicators (e.g., decline in number of tourists who intend to return); indicators of stresses (e.g. water shortages, or crime indices); measures of the current state of industry (e.g. occupancy rate, tourist satisfaction); measures of the impact of tourism development on the biophysical and socio-economic environments (e.g. level of deforestation, changes in consumption patterns, income levels in local communities); measures of management effort (e.g. clean-up cost for coastal contamination); and measures of management results or performance (e.g. changed pollution levels, greater number of returning tourists) (WTO, 2004).

Next section introduces our methodological tools, with focus on the emerging topics in the previous academic background, to discern tendencies and lessons to learn according to the objectives proposed.

Research Framework

The main objectives are to study academic production on sustainable tourism produced in Portuguese and Brazilian higher education institutions from 2004 to 2017. Key aspects to be analyzed are: what contents are more salient; what differences exist between academic production in Brazil and Portugal; and how topics such as sustainability, governance, planning and regulation relate to tourism sustainability. One of the concerns to be addressed is the perception that academic outputs in tourism studies not always refer to international indexes.

The main database used in this work is RCAAP, the Scientific Open Access Repository of Portugal. It promotes, facilitates and supports the adoption of the open access movement in scientific knowledge across Portugal. Documents as theses, reports and academic articles were collected. The aim is to identify what kind of innovative strategies for sustainable tourism has been discussed in academic works submitted in Portugal's higher education institutions. These works can be authored by Portuguese or Brazilian students.

An implication of this study is to assess how the incorporation of sustainability indexes in academic projects collaborates to the creation of new strategic proposals for sustainable tourism. The methodology used to analyze the multiple documents is content analysis assisted by Nvivo12, a software used to produce a systematic qualitative analysis of content. This analysis helped to establish what proportion of works discussed innovative governance strategies with basis on existent or new sustainability indicators. Figure 1 illustrates the underlying areas emerged, whose content Nvivo analyzed.

Figure 1. Guiding framework for the proposed case study

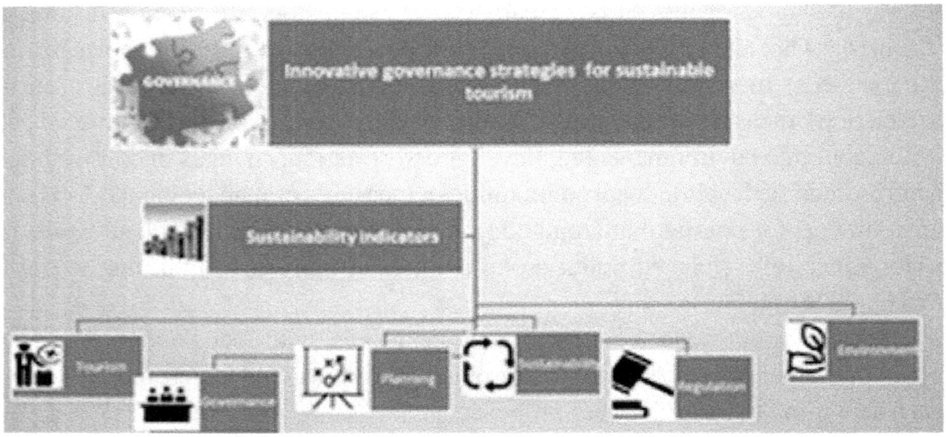

The six thematic areas - tourism, governance, planning, sustainability, regulation, environment - which emerged through a first reading of the academic production selected, are now used as key themes (nodes) for a content analysis. Next section presents a theoretical approach to the central linking theme of this guiding map (or central node): 'sustainability indicators'. The reason for this is that sustainability indicators are the central tools used by policy makers, governments and non-governmental organisations to monitor and stir effective policies to foster sustainable tourism.

Content Analysis Applied

The objectives proposed, according to the related literature, require a qualitative approach. Qualitative researches intend to evaluate, interpret or explain social, cultural or economic phenomena. Related works analyse data like interviews, surveys, web pages, audio visual material, theses and journal articles. The software Nvivo, for qualitative analyses, can help to explore and find patterns in data. It does not favour a particular methodology as it is designed to facilitate common qualitative techniques, no matter what method is used. Nvivo version 12 was used to organise the 70 documents on sustainable tourism, collected from RCAAP, amongst the categories of theses, journal articles, master dissertations and international reports.

Having in mind our key objectives, outputs derived in Nvivo can answer to these research issues. In order to obtain them, we need to describe the cases and nodes prepared.

Coding Cases

In Nvivo, coding is one of the several techniques for making sense of our data. The way to handle coding depends on our methodology and research design. According to Nvivo's functioning and to the content obtained, used in the development of our guiding framework (figure 1), the cases here correspond to the categories or types of the academic works collected from our search in RCAAP. These works or cases will be gathered into nodes which are the themes derived, according to the guiding framework. Nodes are the structures that allow gather related material so that we can look for emerging patterns and ideas.

Coding Nodes

Coding the sample's content by topics or themes will constitute the nodes. This is fundamental in most qualitative projects as it organizes our material into broad topic areas. This tends to be a cumulative rather than a one-stage process, as the node for each topic can be explored toward more detailed coding.

When we open a node in Nvivo, it shows all its content which can be text, audio, video, pictures (that have been coded at that node). The node can be linked to a memo to describe the analytical insights or coded on to other topics. Regarding the guiding framework for this research, the nodes derived were: tourism, governance, planning, sustainability, regulation, environment, and as a central node the topic of Sustainability indicators.

Questioning the data/content from the works collected, a first query was the word frequency. This first exploratory analysis - word cloud (figure 2) - shows that, when taking all sources into account, the central term in the selected academic works is 'tourism'. The word cloud also illustrates a more close connection of tourism to the term 'development' than to the terms 'sustainable' and 'sustainability'. There is an even lower relevance of the term 'indicators', due to its low frequency in the cloud. This corroborates the limited number of works with focus on indexes of sustainability.

Regarding the two sides of the term 'tourism', the top side ('development') appears more related with terms such as environment, economy, impacts, policies, sector, strategy, tourists, growth. The underside ('sustainable') appears more related with terms such as destinations, community, resources, governance, quality, planning, residents, indicators.

Handling qualitative data is not usually a step-by-step process. Instead, it tends to be an iterative process to explore, code, memo, code some more, query, etc. According to another output of Nvivo12, the Project map, the themes 'Tourism', 'Regulation' and 'Environment' appear at the centre of it. Nodes such as 'Planning', 'Sustainable tourism', 'Indicators' and 'Governance' appear at the middle left of the map.

Figure 2. Word cloud

DISCUSSION OF RESULTS

Researchers working in methodologies such as phenomenology and discourse analysis may get straight into detailed coding and then, later on, combine and group the nodes into related categories. The process of coding brings us closer to data in order to ask questions such as: 'How do the data help answer the research questions/ objectives?', etc. Coding facilitates the use of queries and visualizations allowing us to look for connections between topics and test our understanding. Queries and maps support the iterative nature of qualitative research and help to investigate hunches as we progress through a project. They can help us focus on the questions we want to ask and prompt us to code accordingly. They also help to determine whether we need to gather additional files of data or re-frame the questions asked before.

In Nvivo, the techniques of re-coding and querying contribute to integrate results to better compare and discuss them. Thus, from a query based on cluster analysis of the nodes derived, figure 3 illustrates two main clusters or groups: 1) one that reflects the use of sustainability indicators for regulation matters; and the other 2) where governance relates to sustainable tourism and planning.

Figure 3. Cluster analysis of the nodes derived

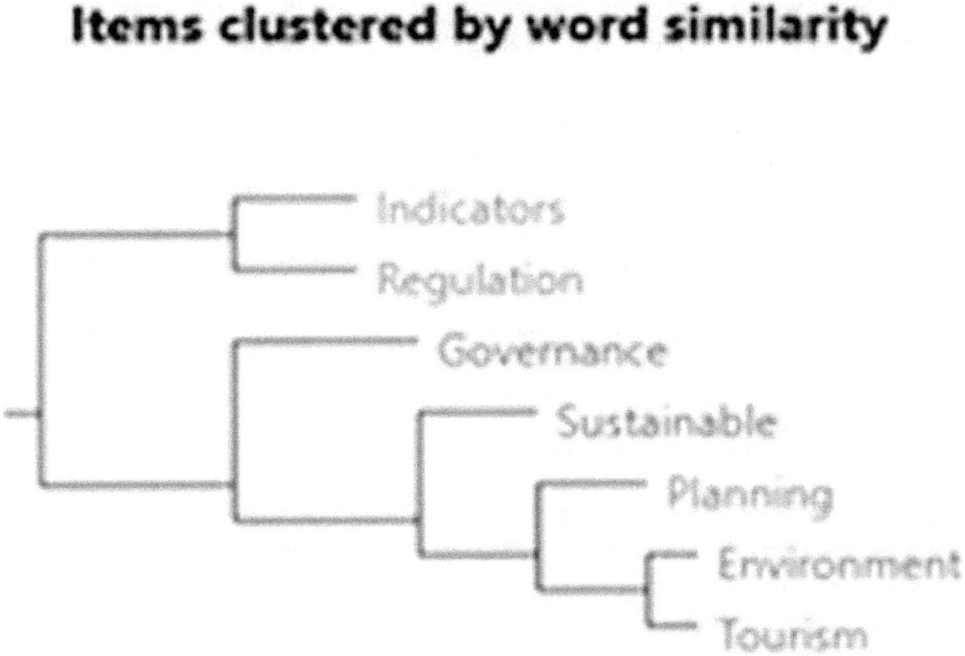

This scenario suggests an increasing concern with governance and regulation, and that sustainability indicators are addressed especially for regulatory issues. Thus, there is a growing awareness of the importance of regulation and the need for effective and lasting policy measures. However, from this research, we acknowledge that quantitative indexes for governance and planning are still minimally approached (Simão and Partidário, 2012).

There is only one international report and two scientific articles that play appropriately on the theme of using sustainability indices to support tourism governance. The other works that mention these issues are more descriptive.

Doing deeper clustering in Nvivo12, to better compare the sample between Portugal and Brazil, the Portuguese focus on themes more related to territorial planning, stakeholders involved, natural destinations, governance, rural tourism, eco-tourism and resources evaluation (PENT, 2015). The Brazilian focus on themes more related to environmental education, redefinition of local power, participation, tourism consequences, ecological footprint and ethical issues (Mota and Almeida, 2016).

Thus, Portuguese investigation on sustainable tourism has been focusing on resources/ stakeholders and Brazilian research on local power/community. This latter is due to a focus of the Brazilian academic works on local policies, of the regions where the universities are placed, which facilitate data collection. Getting resources in Brazil is a more complex issue, passing through the scrutiny of economists and technocrats.

This is in line with Brazilian context, mainly the hope that the public power, local community and companies can join forces to structure a tourism development plan, considering the balance ratio of the dimensions of sustainability. Also, we acknowledge that in the Brazilian case there is more diversity of themes, which is in line with the educational policies in Brazil that have sought to provide the conditions for new initiatives for the diversity of educational projects in higher education, in order to meet the diversified demands in the different regions of the country.

CONCLUSION

The key for sustainable tourism development is an integrated approach to management, supported by the right indicators. As WTO (2013) suggested, indicators are tools that provide accurate information for decision-making, leading to the implementation of solutions, better planning and management. They are not an end in themselves, but rather signals of important trends and changes; catalysts for discussion on plans, risks and impacts to the destinations. They can also serve as performance measures for progress towards sustainability. Indicators are not a one-time procedure, they are most useful when measured repeatedly and consistently through long-term monitoring programs. Only when information is available over time, on a regular basis, can the most effective use of indicators occur, providing context for the understanding of changes and their importance to policy priorities.

In the present work, based on selected academic research from RCAAP, quantitative indexes for governance and planning are still weakly approached. Only two scientific articles and one international report appropriately approach the application of sustainability indices to support tourism governance and regulation. The other works that touch these issues are more descriptive.

The aim of indicators development is not solely the measurement of factors, production of tables or publication of reports, but better decision-making for the sustainable development of the destination. Indicators, therefore, should be an integral part of planning and monitoring processes. The information generated by government authorities, at different levels, by different private and civil sector organizations or through research, can be all important for sustainable tourism indicators. Also, indicators at local levels can be building blocks for applications at regional and national levels. Making indexes accessible and sharable is the only route to informed decision making and involvement of all stakeholders in the decision process. Measures can empower destinations, providing the information needed to negotiate future investments, development standards, joint ventures, and the sharing of benefits. They also support approaches to consensus on what is important to sustain and how to achieve it, such as the limits to acceptable change.

Many indicators begin as measurements done through scientific research. The academic community has been important in initiating indicator studies, developing methodological tools and generating information. Too often, however, academic studies have been one time initiatives. There is the initial study of a problem and the establishment of baseline information, but without follow up through linear studies and monitoring. A challenge for the academic community is to obtain sufficient resources to support an ongoing role in implementation of key indicators, as well as applied research on their validation and evaluation of their impact.

Another need is for academic institutions to transform information generated through scientific research into forms where it can be easily understood and used in policy making by practitioners. Finally, in order for future tourism professionals to be familiar with the need of indicators and their monitoring, academic institutions should include, in tourism studies, cases and methodologies for development and use of indexes.

ACKNOWLEDGMENT

This paper is financed by National Funds provided by FCT- Foundation for Science and Technology through project UID/SOC/04020/2013.

REFERENCES

Cordeiro, I. (2008). *Instrumentos de avaliação da sustentabilidade do turismo: Uma análise crítica*. Dissertação de Mestrado, Universidade Nova de Lisboa.

Dias, J. (2016). Environmental sustainability measurement in the Travel & Tourism Competitiveness Index: An empirical analysis of its reliability. *Ecological Indicators*, *73*, 589–596. doi:10.1016/j.ecolind.2016.10.008

Gössling, S., Scott, D., & Hall, C. (2013). Challenges of tourism in a low-carbon economy. *WIREs Clim Change*, *4*(6), 525–538. doi:10.1002/wcc.243

IBGE – Instituto Brasileiro de Geografia e Estatística. (2015). *Estatísticas – população*. Available at: https://www.ibge.gov.br/estatisticas-novoportal/sociais/populacao.html

Mota, I., Pinto, M., Sá, J., Marques, V., & Ribeiro, J. (2005). *Estratégia Nacional para o Desenvolvimento Sustentável ENDS 2005-2015*. Available at: https://infoeuropa.eurocid.pt/files/database/000015001-000020000/000019537.pdf

Mota, K., & Almeida, J. (2016). Educação superior em turismo, hospitalidade e lazer no Brasil: Análise do panorama de cursos ofertados frente ao contexto contemporâneo. *Revista Turismo & Desenvolvimento*, *26*, 65–77.

PENT - Plano Estratégico Nacional do Turismo. (2015). *Ministério da Economia e do Emprego*. Available at: https://www.portugal.gov.pt/media/820185/20130111%20consulta%20publica%20pent.pdf

Simão, J., & Partidário, M. (2012). How does tourism planning contribute to sustainable development? *Sustainable Development*, *20*(6), 372–385. doi:10.1002d.495

Stilwell, D. (2011). *Indicadores de sustentabilidade aplicados ao contexto do desenvolvimento turístico português. Dissertação de Mestrado*. Faculty of Sciences, University of Lisbon.

Sustainability Index, G. D. S. (2017). *Sustainable destination management trends and insights: A path to a brighter future*. Available at: http://www.100carbonneutral.com/assets/sustainable-destination-management-trends-and-insights--a-path-to-a-brighter-future.pdf

WTO - World Tourism Organisation. (2004). Indicators of sustainable development for tourism destinations. A guidebook. Author.

WTO - World Tourism Organisation (2013). *Sustainable Tourism for Development*. Author.

Chapter 8
Profile, Motivations, and Experiences From Portuguese Solo Female Travelers

Zelia Breda
https://orcid.org/0000-0002-5882-063X
GOVCOPP, University of Aveiro, Portugal

Adriana Santos
University of Aveiro, Portugal

Tamara Kliček
I-Shou University, Taiwan

Gorete Dinis
GOVCOPP, Polytechnic Institute of Portalegre, Portugal

ABSTRACT

The segment of independent travelers has experienced big growth in recent years, not only worldwide but also in Portugal. This phenomenon, which is not recent, has been gaining momentum in recent times, with women playing an important role. This chapter explores the literature on solo female travel, seeking to understand the motivations, as well as the difficulties encountered during the journey. To this end, a qualitative approach was used, with semi-structured interviews being conducted to 24 Portuguese women. The content analysis of the interviews was done with the assistance of the WebQDA software. Results show that most women traveling alone are young, single, and childless, identifying themselves mostly as adventurous, outgoing, and independent. The lack of travel companion, the freedom of choice, the experience and adventure, and the escape from the daily routine are highlighted as motivations to travel alone. The main difficulties identified are loneliness, harassment, fear of walking alone at night or being robbed.

DOI: 10.4018/978-1-7998-2204-2.ch008

Copyright © 2020, IGI Global. Copying or distributing in print or electronic forms without written permission of IGI Global is prohibited.

INTRODUCTION

Although men have always had a prominent role as travellers, women have also played a part, whether they travelled alone or accompanied (Kroller, 1990; Warner-Smith, 2013; Wilson & Little, 2005). Perhaps this is not the most widely publicized idea, since reports have always described men as discoverers and adventurers, who sought new destinations and extended territories (Warner-Smith, 2013; Wilson & Little, 2005). But this idea seems to be changing as there is a growing number of women who travel, with a greater percentage of them doing it individually (Marzuki, Chin, & Razak, 2012; McNamara & Prideaux, 2010; Wilson & Little, 2005). Nevertheless, this is not a recent phenomenon. The literature refers to cases of women of the Victorian era who travelled the world alone, avoiding rules and obligations (Kroller, 1990).

Nowadays, the number of women travelling alone is exponentially higher than in the past (Wilson & Little, 2005). With the increase of this phenomenon, blogs dedicated to solo female travel began to appear in recent years, being run by women who have been solo travellers themselves, and approaching diverse topics, from where to go, what to worry about and how to have the courage to do so. The stories that address the decision-making process of travelling alone and the freedom that derives from it have increased exponentially on the Internet (Amandanoventa, 2015; Antunes, 2015; McCulley, 2015), with the Press also paying attention to the phenomenon, by publishing articles on the subject (Ross, 2015).

Notwithstanding the recent interest on solo female travel, it is still far from being explored. In fact, studies on the topic are still scarce (Marzuki et al., 2012), and there has been little concern in studying gender differences in tourism, since studies have been focusing essentially on men (Meng & Uysal, 2008). From the studies on the subject, two divergent lines of though can be highlighted. The first one relates to the fact that leisure habits of men and women are different, and there is a need to create niche markets (Collins & Tisdell, 2002; Jucan & Jucan, 2013; Marzuki et al., 2012; Small, 1999). However, the other line of thought questions whether these differences are so marked and if men and women do not engage in similar activities in their free time and during their holidays (Carr, 2000; Meng & Uysal, 2008). The prevailing view is that women choose leisure and tourism activities differently from men. Therefore, the literature has focused on the perception of what should be improved in the tourism sector to facilitate travel and make it more enjoyable for women. Studies on what is valued by women in hotels (Marzuki et al., 2012) or even in airlines (Westwood, Pritchard, & Morgan, 2000) have shown that, even though activities are similar, the needs are quite different.

The rise of solo female travel is related to sociodemographic changes, with women increasingly marrying at a later stage in life, also delaying the decision to have children. Their economic situation has also improved substantially as they have fixed and fairly well-paid jobs. In other words, independence is greater and women in their 30s and 40s see themselves with all the possibilities to travel (Chiang & Jogaratnam, 2006; Jucan & Jucan, 2013; Laesser, Beritelli, & Bieger, 2009; Wilson & Little, 2005).

Although women are increasingly adventurous, the truth is that travelling alone is not always easy, with obstacles existing due to different factors. It often happens that women are afraid, which might be associated with themselves, with the destination they have chosen, or the fact that, for some reason, they feel unprotected. This is one of the most common obstacles identified in the literature (Carvalho, Baptista, & Costa, 2015; Wilson & Little, 2008). They might also feel uneasy due to cultural or even physical differences. Being women also makes them the target of many prying eyes, which leaves them more insecure (Carvalho et al., 2015, Wilson & Little, 2005). Although this phenomenon is becoming more frequent, there are still some people who do not support the decision of sole female travellers, considering them inconsequential. Therefore, they try to convince them not to travel or to find companion (Wilson & Little, 2005).

This chapter aims to explore the literature on solo female travel, seeking to understand the motivations, as well as the difficulties encountered during the journey. To this end, a qualitative approach was used, with semi-structured interviews being conducted to 24 Portuguese women. The content analysis of the interviews was done with the assistance of the WebQDA software. The paper is organized as follows: first, the literature on solo female travel is reviewed, namely in what concerns the profile of women that travel alone and the preferred destinations and services, following which travel motivations and barriers are addressed. Subsequently, the methodology used for the empirical study is described in more detail. Finally, research findings are reported and discussed, and their implications for further research are highlighted.

LITERATURE REVIEW

Profile of Solo Travellers

Studies that occurred until the early 1990s showed that the travel decision-making power was in the hands of men (Collins & Tisdell, 2002). However, studies now point to the opposite. Meng and Uysal (2008) concluded that the decision within the family on where to go on vacation is done together. However, analysing the decision making in stages, women end up playing a dominant role. This idea is shared by

Marzuki et al. (2012) and Jucan and Jucan (2013), who defend that this is because women have a greater control over how the family budget is used. Marzuki et al. (2012) go further, stating that women can have the decision-making power of other people's vacations, such as employers or employees.

The segment of solo travellers has experienced big growth in recent years, with women also playing an important role. A solo traveller is someone who arrives alone at a particular location (Laesser, Beritelli, & Bieger, 2009). As this definition only refers to arrival, McNamara and Prideaux (2010) have further developed it by considering that a solo traveller cannot travel as part of a package or group.

In Australia, since the 1950s, there has been a significant increase in the number of women who travel alone abroad, especially young people, between the ages of 20 and 24 (Warner-Smith, 2013). As far as inbound tourism is concerned, an estimated 200,000 women travel alone to Australia each year, representing around 15% of all visitors (McNamara & Prideaux, 2010). In the United States of America, it was estimated that by the turn of the century about 35% of people would travel alone, almost half of whom were women (Chiang & Jogaratnam, 2006). In Portugal, there is no information on the percentage of women who choose to travel alone, however, data from the National Statistics Institute unveils that women are traveling more than men. Although it is not possible to know if they travel accompanied or alone, it is an interesting indicator of the demand growth trend.

Although there are a few studies that report that men and women have more similarities than differences while traveling (Carr, 2000; Meng & Uysal, 2008), and both spend substantially the same money on vacation (Jucan & Jucan, 2013), Collins and Tisdell (2002) identified different types of travel patterns. According to them, women seek culture and travel, above all, for fun, with work travel not playing a preponderant role. Men travel more for business reasons and, when traveling in leisure, seek adventure. Wilson and Little (2005) disagree, noting that women seek more adventure tourism than men. Women travel more for business reasons when they are young. This is associated with late marriage and maternity, from which they are no longer available for this type of travel. However, in leisure and vacations, women dominate, traveling more than men (Collins & Tisdell, 2002; Marzuki et al., 2012).

As a large proportion of women marry in their early 30s, having children a short time later, middle-aged women who travel alone are few in number and are considered atypical, being looked at reprovingly, associated with the stigma of lonely losers (Heimtun, 2012). However, in the West, there is a paradigm shift, with women of this age group starting to venture on their own (Heimtun, 2012).

According to McNamara and Prideaux (2010), there are different studies that identify the traveller in two different ways: for some it is a woman who is afraid, for others an adventurer. For these authors, and contrary to what one might suppose, women who travel alone are not lonely. Although some travel because they do not have companion, most of the time it is by their own choice, because they like it (Heimtun, 2012). In this study, the authors characterize these travellers as bold, adventurous, and confident women, who travel when they want, regardless of whether they have someone to accompany them or not. These women like to travel during the high season (April to September), and many of them are backpackers and stay in hostels or with relatives. Not many choose a hotel as their accommodation. In conclusion, women who travel alone are financially independent, willing to leave their normal day-to-day environment. They are, above all, adventurers. Feeling safe, they engage in the same activities as men. They admit that without travel they would not be able to work at the same pace or with the same vitality (Pennington-Gray & Kerstetter, 2001).

Travel Motivations

It is true that the role of women as tourists has been evolving. Formerly they travelled mostly in family, with rare exceptions. But now, traveling alone is part of the routine and begins to be an increasingly cross-cultural reality. It is, therefore, important to identify the reasons that allowed the increase of women traveling alone. One of the main aspects mentioned by many authors is a paradigm shift. Until recently, a single woman aged 30 years old and over was regarded as lonely and noncompliant with normal behavioural patterns (Heimtun, 2012). However, this idea has begun to change. Today, it is common for women to reach this age single and childless, by choice, thus having more leisure time and freedom to travel (Collins & Tisdell, 2002; Jucan & Jucan, 2013; Laesser et al., 2009). For Stone and Nichol (1999), the increase of single people is an interesting phenomenon. According to their study, in 2016, the percentage of single people in Britain would be 36%[1]. This percentage is explained by the fact that the pressure to marry and have children has decreased substantially in recent years, making responsibilities different (Wilson & Little, 2005). In addition, staying single becomes an option for life (Jucan & Jucan, 2013). When traveling, women enjoy their independence and feel in control over what they do and where they go (Heimtun, 2012).

In addition to the fact that there are more single women and less pressure to have children, for solo female travel to be possible it was necessary for women to conquer their financial independence as well. Their presence in the labour market has been increasing (Collins & Tisdell, 2002). Jucan and Jucan (2013) emphasize the fact that women occupy about half of existing jobs. In this way they have the financial autonomy to be able to invest in what they want, often opting for travelling. And the paradigm shift allowed women to travel alone. However, it remains to identify what motivates them to do so.

Women travel alone for a variety of reasons; however, one of the main reasons is related to confidence boost. They want to be sure that they can stand up for themselves and be self-reliant. When they challenge themselves to be alone, in another city or even in a different country, they are testing their limits. In this way they end up leaving their comfort zone, proving that they are capable and showing that they can enjoy their freedom (Chiang & Jogaratnam, 2006; Wilson & Little, 2008).

Chiang and Jogaratnam (2006) developed a study on what motivate women to travel alone, identifying four different reasons. It was mentioned by the interviewees that they like to travel because it allows them to "explore new experiences, gain new knowledge and understand different ways of seeing the world and thinking" (Chiang & Jogaratnam, 2006, p. 61). The four dimensions identified were experience, escape, relaxation and socialization. Self-esteem was also identified, although with less importance, and was not included in the main motivations. The experience is an important element of traveling alone, that is, the experience related to knowing something new without the security of being accompanied. Since women are on the labour market in large numbers, being able to relax and escape from daily life pressures become important and a way of dealing with the routine. Lastly, socializing is also a strong motivation. When traveling, women are more open-minded and get to know places and travellers that otherwise would not happen. The authors conclude, then, that campaigns that appeal to escapism and new experiences are more appealing to this market segment.

Barriers

Traveling involves some difficulties, whether accompanied or alone. When travelling to other countries people face obstacles, either caused by cultural differences or even from time and currency constraints. When we are talking about solo female travel, the difficulties are compounded.

Fear is something present at the time of traveling alone (Carr, 2000; Carvalho et al., 2015, Wilson & Little, 2008), but this fear, rather than being a result of past experiences, is acquired culturally and socially (Wilson & Little, 2008). It begins to emerge through external stimuli, such as other people's stories, informal channels, and pre-conceived images. This means that women are afraid because they are taught that they should be. In addition, it is instilled in them that alone, in an unfamiliar country, they take risks and are not safe (Carr, 2000). These images of fear are often induced by relatives and friends who, finding unsafe the idea of traveling alone, alarm potential female solo travellers with stories and opinions. They often make these women feel irresponsible when traveling without companion. Destinations' official websites themselves feed off stigma, with warnings about how to travel alone so they do not take so many risks (Wilson & Little, 2008).

There is also the idea that during the day is always safe and that the night is always a source of insecurity. Thus, according to Carr (2000), there are places travellers consider safe during the day, but refuse to visit after the sun goes down. This fear is often the result of a preconceived image that the night is not safe, much less for a woman alone. The same author also concluded that this fear is easily surpassed when women begin to become familiar with the place. As they get to know it, they begin to feel at ease and end up losing this preconceived idea, which is replaced by their own idea.

With so many warnings, alerts, and preconceived ideas, women begin to self-restrict themselves. They avoid places and feel that whatever bad happens to them can be caused by their behaviour or actions (Wilson & Little, 2008). For example, the fear of being harassed is constant for many women who are in an unknown environment (Wilson & Little, 2008). For this reason, they often feel the need to nullify themselves, using simpler clothes and discreet makeup to avoid risks (Carvalho et al., 2015), They feel that it is their responsibility to avoid putting themselves in situations that may cause problem.

Another difficulty encountered relates to the fact that, when travelling to different countries, they might be physically different, because of the skin/hair colour or physical structure. This makes them feel looked sideways by the locals. Being Caucasian or Western can be a disadvantage (Carvalho et al., 2015, Wilson & Little, 2008). Carvalho et al. (2015) concluded that younger women suffer harassment in foreign countries, especially Brazilian, which lead them to feel vulnerable and in need to be in constant alert. Some women stop traveling because of their fears. In parallel, a new generation of travellers are emerging who are more courageous and are not afraid of having a spatial behaviour similar to that of men (Carr, 2000).

Fear is what makes travelling more difficult and what raises more questions, not only before the travel but also during the journey, determining the route and the activities to be carried out. In addition, tourism destinations were designed in the image of men, not being adapted to women's way of seeing and living the world (Wilson & Little, 2008).

One point mentioned by many independent travellers, identified by Heimtum (2012), is that they feel alone during their solo travel, especially at meals. This activity, seen as something done in the company of others, when done in isolation makes them feel lonely, as if everyone was watching, analyzing and judging. One of the interviewees said that while dining outside she felt alone and isolated, and it was so disturbing that she just wanted to cry. This activity, apparently innocuous, generated a sense of social exclusion in travellers, being stressful for them.

Wilson and Little (2005) identified four types of constraints to travel:

(i) practical – these are common to both genders and are not related to traveling alone or accompanied. This restriction has to do with the fact that sometimes there is no time, or even money, to travel. According to the authors, this is a common problem for those who have a stable life and bills to pay.

(ii) sociocultural – these are already directly linked to the role of women in society, or at least to what is believed to be their role. This restriction happens when women are questioned about their decision to travel alone or when, while travelling, they suffer some type of discrimination because of their gender.

(iii) personal – these are directly linked to the fear and insecurity felt before traveling and during the journey.

(iv) spatial – these are related to all obstacles to the free movement of women. For example, it has been pointed out that they cannot travel to certain destinations, either because they are banned or because they feel they are not welcome and seen as intrusive.

What we can conclude is that, even though women have apparent freedom to travel, there are restrictions that arise and sometimes make travel difficult or, in some cases, impossible.

Destinations and Services

The image of modern women is associated with being independent, having a greater economic capacity for not having a family and for starting to have access to better jobs, with higher remunerations (Chiang & Jogaratnam, 2006; Marzuki et al., 2012). The truth is that more and more women are traveling alone, and with their economic power the tourism market should start to pay more attention to them. They are an important segment (Marzuki et al., 2012) and seek many travel opportunities (Collins & Tisdell, 2002).

Although almost all destinations are within their reach, they are beginning to identify some destinations of choice, namely European cities (Carvalho et al., 2015; Heimtun, 2012; Warner-Smith, 2013). This trend exists since the 1950s, when Australian women began to travel more alone (McNamara & Prideaux, 2010). Heimtun (2012) points out resorts on the Mediterranean coast as attractive destinations for women traveling alone. Finally, McNamara and Prideaux (2010) point to Australia as a country that receives many foreign women traveling alone. All these destinations have a common feature: they are perceived as relatively safe.

There is no consensus in the literature as to whether or not this reality is taken into account by the tourism industry. If, on the one hand, there are some authors who argue that travel agents have come to value the female segment (Chiang & Jogaratnam, 2006; Small, 1999), on the other hand, there are many more who think that there is discrimination (Heimtun, 2012; Jucan & Jucan, 2013; Marzuki et al., 2012; Stone & Nichol, 1999). Heimtun (2012) argues that most tourism promotional campaigns are focused on the image of the family or the heterosexual segment. In particular, he points out that the industry does not see middle-aged women as possible clients of individual trips, being seen only as mothers or wives and, therefore, the promotion focuses on this idea.

Jucan and Jucan (2013) justify that gender is part of people's basic identity, however, it is often a source of discrimination, a fact that is true even in the tourism sector. This can be seen when trying to find a product adapted to women – something rare, but necessary –, since the segment has particular needs. This idea is shared by Marzuki et al. (2012), who consider that, when designing the product, marketeers do not take into account gender differences. Customers and their needs must be considered, i.e. the needs of women traveling alone who are looking for packages that offer flexibility and freedom, as well as being pre-programmed and well organized (Laesser et al., 2009). In a search for travel tailored to their needs, women traveling alone can hardly find packages that meet these needs. Due to the lack of knowledge on the potential of this segment, travel agencies focus on the classic segment – families –, neglecting others in growth (Stone & Nichol, 1999).

Marzuki et al. (2012), who focused their study on what women seek at the accommodation level, found that security is a key issue. Women value places with security 24 hours a day, which respond to one of their biggest constraints when travelling alone – fear (Carr, 2000; Wilson & Little, 2008). They also value comfort, design, cleanliness and ease of check-in and check-out. Details such as skirt hangers or the type of magazines that are available in the lobby can make all the difference at the time of choice (Marzuki et al., 2012). Hotels that do not take into account these needs end up losing customers.

Westwood et al. (2000) conducted a study on the fact that airlines do not take gender into account when preparing their airplanes and waiting spaces, being gender-blind. When interviewing marketing departments of 15 companies, only three showed paying attention to women, especially those traveling on business, the focus of the study. These companies have stated that what does not leave women satisfied is not so much the experience of the flight, but the lack of spaces adapted to their needs during the waiting time. For them, cleanliness, especially in the bathrooms, is important, since they need these places to get ready when they are about to reach the destination. The public spaces are also dominated by men, which does not make them comfortable and, if the waiting room is relatively empty leaves them unsafe.

The company's treatment is differentiated, as they often ignore women who travel for business and make upgrades difficult.

Although the tourism industry begins to give some attention to solo female travellers, it is still not responding to their expectations and needs. It is necessary to create better products for this segment and adapt the old ones, since the segment is increasing considerably.

Methodology

Qualitative research has been widely used in studies on gender issues in tourism (Pritchard, Morgan, Ateljevic, & Harris, 2007; Wilson, 2004; Wilson & Little, 2008). Similarly, this study used a qualitative approach. The semi-structured interview was selected as the data collection technique. The construction of the interview script was based on the literature, focusing on the sociodemographic profile of the interviewees, and their travel patterns.

In order to draw up the sociodemographic profile of the interviewees, the most basic questions were asked: age, marital status, academic qualifications, profession, if they have children, and, if so, how many and their age. In this way, it was assured that the interviewees had the profile described in the literature (Collins & Tisdell, 2002; Heimtun, 2012; Jucan & Jucan, 2013; Laesser et al., 2009; Wilson & Little, 2005). They were also asked how they describe themselves (McNamara & Prideaux, 2010).

In order to understand their travel habits, it was asked if they had travelled accompanied before, and, if so, for which destinations and with whom. Regarding the solo travel, it was aimed to know when these women had started traveling alone, the destinations they chose (Carvalho et al., 2015; Heimtun, 2012; McNamara & Prideaux, 2010; Warner-Smith, 2013) and the preferred type of accommodation (McNamara & Prideaux, 2010). More importantly, the focus was on understanding what are the motivations for traveling solo (Chiang & Jogaratnam, 2006; Collins & Tisdell, 2002; Jucan & Jucan, 2013; Laesser et al., 2009; Wilson & Little, 2008) and the difficulties and defence mechanisms (Carr, 2000; Carvalho et al., 2015; Heimtun, 2012; Wilson & Little, 2005, 2008).

In the qualitative method, large samples, representative of a given population, are not used, as in the quantitative method (Corbetta, 2003; Gentles, Charles, & Ploeg, 2015; Jupp, 2006). Perhaps because of this, authors such as Flick (2007) believe that one should not even talk about sampling in qualitative research. When using this method, one should look for cases that will best respond to the problem in question. Before starting the interviews there was no sample size in mind. This is because the number of interviewees was defined when new information ceased to appear, that is, when saturation was reached (Gentles et al., 2006; Guest, Bunce, & Johnson, 2006). Saturation usually refers to reaching a point of information redundancy, where additional data collection contributes little or nothing new to the study (Gentles et al., 2015). In total, 24 interviews were made.

For the selection of the interviewees, some characteristics were defined, namely having travelled at least once alone, having 18 years old or over, and being Portuguese. To reach women with these characteristics, non-probabilistic sampling was used (snowball). The interviews were conducted by telephone, during the month of August and September of 2016, and lasted on average about 25 minutes (the shortest interview lasted 11 minutes and the longest 56 minutes). They were recorded and later transcribed.

The content analysis of the interviews was done with the help of the WebQDA software, which allows categorizing the content of the interviews into tree codes. Altogether, more than 150 tree codes have been identified. In addition to analysing each case individually in the light of the literature, cross-case analysis was also performed.

ANALYSIS AND DISCUSSION OF RESULTS

Sociodemographic Profile

Of the 24 interviewees, only nine (37.5%) were over 35 years old, which is in line with the literature, since a large proportion of solo female travellers are young women (Collins & Tisdell, 2002; Marzuki et al., 2012). The vast majority were single, with only five exceptions (20.8%): three divorced, one widow and one married. In addition, except for three interviewees, they do not have children, and those who have they are already adults.

As mentioned in a number of publications, solo female travellers are usually young, with rare exceptions of women over 35 years old who choose to travel alone (Chiang & Jogaratnam, 2006; Heitmtun, 2012; Jesse & Laucher, 2013, Laesser et al., 2009; Wilson & Little, 2005). In addition, there are few solo travellers who have younger children or are married, thus having all the independence to travel without companion.

According to Chiang and Jogaratnam (2006) and Mazuki et al. (2012), women nowadays have a more favourable economic situation, since they have access to education and, consequently, to better jobs. This was also verified in our study. Out of the 24 interviewees, only four (16.7%) did not have a higher education degree. The educational level ultimately reflects on their jobs. The vast majority were "specialists in intellectual and scientific activities" (58.3%), one was a student (4.2%) and two were unemployed (8.3%). In addition to having jobs that give them economic independence, four solo travellers were self-employed (16.7%), taking full control of their time.

McNamara and Prideaux (2010) report that independent female travellers are often confident and adventurous. In fact, there were eleven women (45.8%) who characterized themselves in such way. Other mentioned characteristics are "independent" (45.8%), "extroverted" (45.8%), and being "sociable" (33.3%). The adjective "timid" was mentioned by five different women (20.8%), "introverted" and "antisocial" have only been identified once, however, this shows that not all independent travellers are adventurous and outgoing.

Solo Travel

Previous Travel Experience

All the interviewees have had the experience of traveling with companion before they travelled alone, being Europe the most frequently mentioned destination. Within Europe, Portugal is the main destination (45.8%). Other visited destinations were South and Central America (20.8%), Asia and Africa (12.5% each) and North America (8.3%). They usually travelled with family members (79.2%), friends (62.5%), or teachers and colleagues (16.7%), in the case of study trips. Few women reported having travelled with a partner (25%).

No reference in the literature has been found about the age in which women usually start travelling alone. This question turned out to show that there is a high likelihood of starting out at a relatively young age. Of the total, fifteen (62.5%) began traveling alone before reaching the age of 30, with one interviewee starting before age 18. Seven of the interviewees (29.2%) began solo travelling between the ages of 30 and 40, with one starting later, at age 52. It is interesting to note that although there is a predominance of women who started traveling before the age of 30, this is not so high. Thus, it can be concluded that, contrary to Heimtun's (2012) work, older women feel no less capable of traveling alone nor do they fail to do so for the stigma that may exist.

Traveling Alone

Destinations

In the literature it was found that there are two destinations that women seem to enjoy visiting: Australia and Europe, and within Europe the resorts of the Mediterranean coast (Carvalho at al., 2015; Heimtun, 2012; McNamara & Prideaux, 2010; Warner-Smith, 2013). This study confirms the predominance of trips within Europe, although only one interviewee mentioned the Mediterranean coast. The most visited countries are France, England and Spain. Following today's trends, eight women

(33.3%) reported having been to Asia alone, namely to Vietnam, Nepal, Japan and Philippines. America (16.7%) and Africa (20.8%) were also mentioned. Although McNamara and Prideaux (2010) state that Australia is a destination of choice for solo travellers, none of the interviewees mentioned having been there.

Preferential Time for Travel And Duration Of The Trip

McNamara and Prideaux (2010) also state that usually solo travellers choose to travel during the high season. This is confirmed in our study, as 42.1% of the interviewees mentioned that they prefer to travel in the summer. Nevertheless, three interviewees (15.8%) prefer the low season, associating their preference with work, since it is when they have more freedom to travel. Six women (31.6%) admit that they do not have an ideal time to travel, depending on the availability of money and time.

Regarding the duration of the travel, the vast majority (70%) say that they travel for short periods, less than two weeks. Women who travel longer are in a smaller number (22%), but usually stay away for one month. Two interviewees seem to have no preference over the duration of the trip, doing both short and long duration trips.

Relating the duration of the travel with the time of year, it has been noticed that the interviewees who make longer trips usually choose the high season. On the other hand, women who take shorter trips do not have a standard for the time of year. Only one usually travels in low season, with four traveling in high season and five saying that it is indifferent.

Type of Accommodation

According to the literature, solo travellers usually stay in hostels or with relatives and friends, and few people choose to stay in a hotel (McNamara & Prideaux, 2010). Our study shows that there are a significant number of women who like to stay in hotels (37.5%) for several reasons, namely safety and comfort. Usually, women who stay in hotels never stay in hostels, and vice versa. Hostels are the most commonly used means of accommodation, having been referenced ten times (41.7%). Some of the interviewees also take into consideration other alternatives, such as home or room rental, camping or Couchsurfing. Staying with friends or relatives is also popular, being referenced by nine of the interviewees (37.5%).

There is a pre-made idea that usually hostels are targeting younger people, while hotels are usually sought by older people with greater economic availability. This seems to be confirmed by our study. The age group that mostly use hostels is from 20 to 30, and to a lesser extent from 30 to 40. Of the seven women over 40, only one stay in hostels, the hotel being the preferred type of accommodation.

Motivations for Traveling Alone

Motivations is one of the subjects that many authors approach when studying solo travellers (e.g. Chiang & Jogaratnam, 2006; Jucan & Jucan, 2013; Wilson & Little, 2008). Therefore, it was important to understand what motivates these women to travel solo. Nineteen women (79%) admitted that they travel alone because they are not able to get a travel companion, mostly because the people they could travel with had financial restrictions. Another reason is the lack of time availability of friends and relatives to accompany them. It is interesting to note that, except for one interviewee, these women have already made more than one trip alone. That is, although lack of travel companion is often one of the factors to become solo travellers, this does not prevent them from traveling and enjoying doing so.

Apart from the lack of companion, another relevant motivation for traveling alone is to have more freedom (45.8%), with no one to limit or influence the choices of places to visit or the schedules. It is interesting to note that, for example, one interviewee tried to travel with friends, yet she could not adapt to the way they travelled. Therefore, between choosing to travel alone or not going, she chose to go alone. In this way, she was able to visit the sites of her choice and at her own pace, to wake up when she wanted, and to stop wasting time shopping.

Chiang and Jogaratnam (2006) have identified four motivations for solo female travel: experience, escape, relaxation and socialization. According to these categories, nd, in fact, these were some of the reasons pointed out by the interviewees. Nine of these women travelled alone for the experience (37.5%). They believe that, by travelling alone, they immerse themselves in the local culture, and have better and more authentic experiences. They also seek some adventure, which often is not be possible if travelling accompanied. Solo travellers also admit that they frequently travel alone to be with themselves, to escape from the stress of everyday life (25%). Escape have different facets for different travellers: to be able to read, reflect, get away from work, be in silence, or distance themselves from the problems of everyday life. Although Chiang and Jogaratnam (2006) refer to socialization as a driver to solo travel, one thing that came to light during the interviews is that socialization, rather than motivating travel, turns out to be considered an advantage of traveling alone. Few interviewees travel only to socialize. Similarly, relaxation is also not very mentioned by the interviewees. Only one woman mentioned that she travels alone to be able to relax (4.7%). Other motivations identified in the literature are self-reliance and independence (Chiang & Jogaratnam, 2006; Wilson & Little, 2008). Four women travel to prove their value and that they do not need a companion to be able to travel (16.7%).

Barriers to Solo Travel

When traveling, some difficulties might be encountered due to different languages and culture, or unforeseen circumstances that arise when one is out of the usual environment. However, when women are traveling alone, these difficulties are greater and very specific (Carr, 2000; Carvalho et al., 2015; Heimtun, 2012; Wilson & Little, 2005, 2008). The interviewees identified several difficulties they encountered while traveling, all of them in accordance to what is being referred in the literature.

The most mentioned difficulty is loneliness. Eleven women (45.8%) reported having felt alone at some point in their travels. Loneliness came at different times and for different reasons, for example having no one to share their experiences with, taking a photograph, or eating at a restaurant, something that Heimtun (2012) says is common. This sensation often causes them to strategize their meals to feel less lonely, such as eating on the move or with someone they met while traveling. Loneliness can make the trip difficult psychologically and emotionally. But it is interesting to see how each person feels loneliness differently and even at different times. In this group, loneliness seems to be age-related. That is, women who reported having felt lonely are between 20 and 40 years old. Although we cannot draw conclusions, younger women might suffer more from loneliness.

Harassment and fear are also very common difficulties. Six of them (25%) admitted having suffered harassment during their travels. Virtually every interviewee reported having been afraid, in one way or another. Some were simply afraid to be alone, or to walk without a companion who they could turn to in a more distressed moment, especially at night, which is regarded as more dangerous, as Carr (2000) points out. The fear of being robbed was also reported by five women, although it is very common for people, even if traveling accompanied, to fear being robbed and being left without money or identification. One interviewee also reported a general fear acquired by information released by Portuguese official entities, which did not recommend travelling to the destination of her choice. She mentioned being afraid before reaching the destination, however upon arrival she realized that it was not as depicted by the entities.

According to Carvalho et al. (2015), being different is often a difficulty experienced by women. For example, Caucasian women when travelling in Middle and Far East stand out and are seen as a target. This happened with two women, who travelled to India and Africa.

One interviewee pointed out something that is not widely mentioned by other women. She feels that traveling alone is more expensive and requires a greater economic effort, which is acknowledged by Rosenbloom (2015).

It is also interesting to notice that there are interviewees who said they felt no difficulty. Four women (16.7%) reported that they had no difficulty at all and, in fact, throughout the interview, did not mention any episode that indicated they had experienced something less good during their travels.

The difficulties faced by most of these women lead them to create defence mechanisms. In all, eight different methods were identified by the interviewees. The most common one is the search for companion to do certain activities (37.5%). Often, there are points of interest that are not advised to go alone. The fear of going unaccompanied to these places require them to take certain care. And while there are interviewees who prefer to find someone to go with them in order not to miss these points of interest, there are others who prefer not to take risks and fail to visit these places considered unsafe for solo travel (29.2%). The fear of the night is very common among solo travellers, therefore, the best way to defend themselves when they are alone is to avoid going out after sunset (29.2%).

Searching for companion, not going out at night and avoiding certain areas are the three most commonly mentioned defence mechanisms. Other strategies have also been mentioned by a few respondents, namely adjusting the clothing they wear to the destination (16.7%). This happens for two reasons: not to stand out and also not to go against the local culture. Being always connected through smartphones, tablets and computers, information and communication technology is one of the methods used to make them feel safer and not so lonely when traveling (12.5%).

There are countries where solo female travel is frowned upon (Wilson & Little, 2005). Therefore, some interviewees mentioned that they felt the need to lie in order to be safe during the trips, saying that they were married or had friends waiting for them. In this way, they managed to prevent locals from interfering in their way (16.7%). To make their story the most credible, two respondents use fake wedding rings.

Finally, two other methods have been identified, but with less expression. One woman reported that one of her most common defence methods is to always respond to any unwelcome comment or harassment she may suffer. Another respondent mentioned to do her best to get in touch with local residents to better understand the culture and identify places to avoid.

CONCLUSION

The segment of independent travellers has experienced growth in recent years, not only in the world but also in Portugal. This phenomenon, which is not recent, has been gaining strength in recent times. Women start to travel alone early in their lives and keep this practice for several years, age not being a very relevant factor. On the other hand, the existence of children and marital status play a more significant role in solo travel, with the number of solo travellers with children or married being much lower than the single and childless.

Results show that most women traveling alone are young, single and childless. There are few solo travellers who have young children or who are married, thus having more independence to travel. The vast majority have at least a bachelor's degree and their educational level ends up reflecting their jobs, which allow them a favourable economic situation. These independent travellers identify themselves mostly as adventurous, outgoing and independent women.

All women who participated in the study have had the experience of traveling accompanied before their first solo travel. Portugal and other European countries are the most mentioned destinations, having been accompanied by relatives, friends, or teachers and colleagues, in the case of some study visits.

There is a predominance of women who have started traveling alone before the age of 30. However, there are cases of older women, who feel no less able to travel alone, nor do not do so for the stigma that may exist. In relation to destinations for solo travel, Portugal stands out. Other destinations in Europe are also quite mentioned, namely France, England and Spain. The share of other continents is still relatively small, with the predominance of Asian destinations.

Most women prefer to travel in the high season, however, there are cases where time and financial availability dictates the time of year in which they decide to travel. Short trips, with less than two weeks, are the most common. Hostels are the most widely used type of accommodation. The age group that uses them the most is from 20 to 30 years. For those over 40 years, the hotel is the preferred accommodation.

Regarding the motivations to travel alone, the lack of time or financial availability of friends and relatives to accompany them, the freedom of choice on the places to visit or the schedules, the experience and adventure that this type of travel provides, and the escape from the routine of everyday life are highlighted. Relaxation and socialization are not much mentioned *per se*. Sometimes, it is not just one reason that makes them travel alone, it is a combination of several reasons.

The main difficulties identified are loneliness, harassment, fear of walking alone at night or being robbed. Once they encounter various difficulties, solo travellers feel the need to create defence mechanisms. Looking for a companion, not going out at night and avoiding certain areas are the three most mentioned strategies. Adapting the clothing to the visited place and the use of technologies are also methods used to overcome some of the travel difficulties.

REFERENCES

Amandanoventa. (2015). Mulheres que viajam sozinhas são mais autoconfiantes. Retrieved October 20, 2015, from http://viagem.estadao.com.br/blogs/amanda-viaja/mulheres-que-viajam-sozinhas-sao-mais-autoconfiantes/

Antunes, L. (2015). 7 Relatos de mulheres para te inspirar a viajar sozinha. Retrieved October 21, 2015, from http://www.360meridianos.com/2015/01/relatos-de-mulheres-que-vao-te-inspirar-a-viajar-sozinha.html

Carr, N. (2000). An exploratory study of young women's use of leisure spaces and times: Constrained, negotiated, or unconstrained behaviour? *World Leisure Journal*, *42*(3), 25–32. doi:10.1080/04419057.2000.9674193

Carvalho, G., Baptista, M. M., & Costa, C. (2015). Brazilian women's perception of risk when travelling alone. In Risk in travel and tourism: Geographies, behaviours and strategies (pp. 22–25). Lisbon: ATLAS: Association for Tourism and Leisure Education and Research.

Chiang, C.-Y., & Jogaratnam, G. (2006). Why do women travel solo for purposes of leisure? *Journal of Vacation Marketing*, *12*(1), 59–70. doi:10.1177/1356766706059041

Collins, D., & Tisdell, C. (2002). Gender and differences in travel life cycles. *Journal of Travel Research*, *41*(2), 133–143. doi:10.1177/004728702237413

Corbetta, P. (2003). Social research: Theory, methods and techniques. London: SAGE Publications; doi:10.4135/9781849209922.

Flick, U. (2007). Designing qualitative research. London: SAGE Publications; doi:10.4135/9781849208826.

Gentles, S. J., Charles, C., & Ploeg, J. (2015). Sampling in qualitative research. The SAGE Encyclopedia of Social Science Research Methods, 20(11), 1772–1789. doi:10.4135/9781412950589.n885

Guest, G., Bunce, A., & Johnson, L. (2006). How many interviews are enough? An experiment with data saturation and variability. *Field Methods*, *18*(1), 59–82. doi:10.1177/1525822X05279903

Heimtun, B. (2012). The friend, the loner and the independent traveller: Norwegian midlife single women's social identities when on holiday. *Gender, Place and Culture*, *19*(1), 83–101. doi:10.1080/0966369X.2011.617881

Jucan, M. S., & Jucan, C. N. (2013). Gender trends in tourism destination. *Procedia: Social and Behavioral Sciences*, *92*, 437–444. doi:10.1016/j.sbspro.2013.08.698

Jupp, V. (2006). The SAGE Dictionary of social research methods. London: SAGE Publications; doi:10.4135/9780857020116.

Kroller, E.-M. (1990). First impressions: Rhetorical strategies in travel writing Victorian Women. A Review of International English Literature, 21(4), 87–99.

Laesser, C., Beritelli, P., & Bieger, T. (2009). Solo travel: Explorative insights from a mature market (Switzerland). *Journal of Vacation Marketing, 15*(3), 217–227. doi:10.1177/1356766709104268

Laesser, C., Beritelli, P., & Bieger, T. (2009). Solo travel: Explorative insights from a mature market (Switzerland). *Journal of Vacation Marketing, 15*(3), 217–227. doi:10.1177/1356766709104268

Marzuki, A., Chin, T. L., & Razak, A. A. (2012). What women want: Hotel characteristics preferences of women travellers. In M. Kasimoglu (Ed.), Strategies for tourism industry: Micro and macro perspectives (pp. 143–164). Rijeka: InTech; doi:10.5772/37101.

McCulley, K. (2015). Adventurous Kate's solo female travel blog. Retrieved October 21, 2015, from http://www.adventurouskate.com/blog/

McNamara, K. E., & Prideaux, B. (2010). A typology of solo independent women travellers. *International Journal of Tourism Research, 12*(3), 253–264. doi:10.1002/jtr.751

Meng, F., & Uysal, M. (2008). Effects of gender differences on perceptions of destination attributes, motivations, and travel values: An examination of a nature-based resort destination. *Journal of Sustainable Tourism, 16*(4), 445–466. doi:10.1080/09669580802154231

Office for National Statistics. (2018). Population estimates by marital status and living arrangements, England and Wales: 2002 to 2017. Retrieved on July 23, 2019 from https://www.ons.gov.uk/peoplepopulationandcommunity/populationandmigration/populationestimates/bulletins/populationestimatesbymaritalstatusandlivingarrangements/2002to2017#an-increasing-proportion-of-50-to-64-year-olds-are-single-never-married-and-cohabitation-for-this-group-is-becoming-more-common

Pennington-Gray, L. A., & Kerstetter, D. L. (2001). What do university-educated women want from their pleasure travel experiences? *Journal of Travel Research, 40*(1), 49–56. doi:10.1177/004728750104000107

Pritchard, A., Morgan, N., Ateljevic, I., & Harris, C. (Eds.). (2007). Tourism and gender: Embodiment, sensuality and experience. Oxfordshire, UK: CABI; doi:10.1079/9781845932718.0000.

Ross, A. (2015). Why every woman should travel alone. Retrieved October 20, 2015, from http://time.com/3708374/women-travel-alone/

Small, J. (1999). Memory-work: A method for researching women's tourist experiences. *Tourism Management*, *20*(1), 25–35. doi:10.1016/S0261-5177(98)00091-0

Stone, G. J., & Nichol, S. (1999). Older, single female holidaymakers in the United Kingdom: Who needs them? *Journal of Vacation Marketing*, *5*(1), 7–17. doi:10.1177/135676679900500102

Warner-Smith, P. (2013). Travel, young women and "The Weekly", 1959-1968. *Annals of Leisure Research*, *3*(1), 33–46. doi:10.1080/11745398.2000.10600884

Westwood, S., Pritchard, A., & Morgan, N. J. (2000). Gender-blind marketing: Businesswomen's perceptions of airline services. *Tourism Management*, *21*(4), 353–362. doi:10.1016/S0261-5177(99)00069-2

Wilson, E. (2004). A "Journey of her own"? The impact of constraints on women's solo travel (PhD Thesis). Griffith University.

Wilson, E., & Little, D. E. (2005). A "relative escape"? The impact of constraints on women who travel solo. *Tourism Review International*, *9*(2), 155–175. doi:10.3727/154427205774791672

Wilson, E., & Little, D. E. (2008). The solo female travel experience: Exploring the "geography of women's fear". *Current Issues in Tourism*, *11*(2), 167–186. doi:10.2167/cit342.0

ENDNOTE

1 In 2017, 34.4% of the population aged 16 years and over in England and Wales were single, and an estimated 12.9% of those aged between 50 and 64 years had a marital status of single, a steady increase from 6.1% in 2002 (Office for National Statistics, 2018).

Chapter 9
Modelling a Conceptual Framework for the Wine Tourism System:
A Case Study of the Wine Tourism Industry in India

Anupama S. Kotur
https://orcid.org/0000-0003-4202-4716
Symbiosis Center for Management Studies, Symbiosis International University (Deemed), India

ABSTRACT

Wine tourism is a synthesis of elements from the wine and tourism industries that come together to form the wine tourism experience. Several elements form a part of a much larger wine tourism system and contribute directly and/or indirectly to creating and developing a wine tourism destination. Maharashtra in India has come to be popularly known as the 'wine bowl' of India, producing some of the award-winning and internationally acclaimed wines. This chapter aims to examine all those elements that have played a part in and are necessary to develop a competitive and sustainable wine tourism destination in Maharashtra. The singular objective of this research chapter is to propose a conceptual framework of the wine tourism system. The research largely relies on secondary data as well as results of previous empirical researches conducted by the author. The wider contribution of this chapter lies in developing and illustrating a model of wine tourism system. This system model can be instrumental in defining all those components that are most critical to the growth of a wine tourism destination.

DOI: 10.4018/978-1-7998-2204-2.ch009

Copyright © 2020, IGI Global. Copying or distributing in print or electronic forms without written permission of IGI Global is prohibited.

INTRODUCTION

Maharashtra, in India has been a pioneer and frontrunner in wine tourism the country has witnessed since early 2000s. Maharashtra is home to largest numbers of vineyards in India that offer a wide range of wine tourism products and services such as vineyard resorts, vineyard restaurants, wine festivals, vineyard-based events and wine tours clubbed with various vineyard based activities for wine tourists. Wine tourism, as a form of special interest tourism is witnessing small but significant level of growth in the recent years. While the wine industry has demonstrated phenomenal success wine tourism remains to experience a similar high growth rate. Almost two decades after organised wine tourism began in early 2000 in Maharashtra; the quantum of growth has been rather sluggish. Some of the larger wineries, however, have successfully ventured and succeeded in turning wine tourism initiatives into profitable ventures, many a smaller vineyards are yet to undertake wine tourism development within their vineyards fervently.

Indian Wine Industry

The Indian wine industry experienced a steady growth starting from the year 2000 and wine culture has gradually become a part of urban life style as an alternate to traditionally preferred hard liquor. Indian wines are making their presence felt in the global wine markets with some of their unique varietals. 'With a young population, increasing urbanisation and the position of wine as a 'status choice', India has parallels with other Asian markets where there is a growing acceptance and preference for wine among the upper and middle classes' (Morley, NA). For the year 2017-18 Indian wine industry clocked 'a CAGR of about 20 per cent'. In India, grapes are cultivated in 'an area of 111.4 thousand ha with a total production 1,234.9 thousand tons' (APEDA, 2018). Of the total grapes produced in the country around 1.2% is processed into wine. Wineries in India have also expanding their export portfolio into major countries like, France, Italy, Germany, USA, UK, Singapore, Belgium, etc. The export of wine is expected to grow at 9% per annum. With opportunities, so immense, wine tourism in the country is but a natural beneficiary. 'Growing interest in wines, constant demand for novel tourism experiences and increasing disposition to spend in order to meet those demands among the *au courant* Indian travellers are the crucial factors for the growth of wine tourism in India' (Kaddi, 2013). At this juncture, it becomes imperative to study the overall business eco system the wineries operate in that support the inclusion and development of wine tourism facilities within their wine business framework. While globally there are many studies pertaining to wine tourism systems and wine tourism experience models, very little or none exist in an Indian context. This lacuna presented an opportunity to the author for carrying out research in this area.

This study was undertaken with a singular objective of proposing a conceptual framework for wine tourism system that demonstrates and illustrates all those factors forming a part of the overall eco system of wine tourism industry in Maharashtra. The theoretical construct attempts to illustrate all factors that contribute – directly or indirectly – to the development and growth of wine tourism product. The research largely relies on secondary data as well as results from previous empirical research conducted by the author in the field of wine tourism motivation and wine tourism infrastructure. The wide-ranging contribution of this paper lies in modelling a general yet definitive framework for wine tourism system with specific reference to Maharashtra. The framework can be particularly useful to policy makers and strategic decision makers in areas relating to wine tourism product development in Maharashtra and India in general.

Literature Review

There are several models and conceptual frameworks that illustrate a wine tourism system broadly describing wine tourism experience and wine tourism motivational studies. In this literature review, some of the widely accepted and referred models of wine tourism system have been discussed with their important contributions and shortcomings. The literature review also explores the suitability of these models for Maharashtra. This critical evaluation is further aimed at forming the basis for developing an integrated wine tourism system with specific reference to wine tourism in Maharashtra.

One of the earliest and most notable models that described wine tourism system was put forth by Gronroos (1987). This concept was extensively used by Morris & King (1998) in their study on wine tourism in Margaret River, Australia. According to Morris & King (1998) the model intended 'to reflect a total image and positioning not only of the wine but of the entire wine tourism product' (Alonso, 2005). Shaped in the form of a multi-layered flower, this model is divided into three dimensions representing the various levels of tourism products and services that can be added to enhance the visitor experience at wineries / vineyards.

The flower of wine tourism explained how wineries can change their focus from wine to wine tourism by expanding their product offerings. This model of wine tourism experience brings out the salient points as discussed below:

i. In the first dimension, the wineries introduce basic services beyond making and selling wines such as the Cellar door tasting rooms, restaurants & cafe; local produce shops & souvenirs and gallery.

ii. In the second dimension, wineries introduce elements that purely serve the demands of wine tourists such as guided wine tours, overnight stay facilities, tourist information centres and other entertainment facilities.
iii. Finally, in the third dimension, all other service elements that integrate the total wine tourism experience are added such as customer service resources, responsiveness, empathy, physical appearance & ambience, internal and external communication.

This model successfully illustrated the progression in development of wine tourism offering from a *wine centred* product to a *wine tourism centred* product. While the core of the product remained firmly rooted in wine production and sales, by adding tourism products and services eventually to the mainstream wine business, wineries can not only create a parallel source of income but also further enhance the image of the winery. While this model highlights the natural progression of wine tourism development of winery, external factors of demand and supply were entirely outside the purview of this model. Also, the elements within dimensions may be chosen to be added in the preceding dimensions given the demand, marketing, revenue objectives of the winery. For instance, Sula vineyards in Nashik, Maharashtra introduced wine tours as their primary offering even before vineyard restaurants were introduced.

Another most important and widely referred wine tourism system models was proposed by Donald Getz in his paper *Wine tourism: Global Overview and Perspectives on its Development* (1998). The author proposed that a winery, besides having basic resources, must also integrate other tourism products and services in order to be able to develop wine tourism. These can also be termed as the 'core elements' (Getz, 1998) required to develop wine tourism in the wine region. Getz suggests that 'apart from the more basic requirements, such as producing grapes, making wine, and providing visitor services, there is the need for additional attributes "to augment the basic product"' (Getz, 1998, p. 25), and to contribute to wine tourism's success. These attributes include 'tours to and within the region, festivals, and special events with a wine theme' (Getz, 1998)'.

Getz's system of wine tourism, divides the model into three distinct parts. First part comprises of elements that tourists seek from their wine tourism experience which can be categorised as the demand side of wine tourism. The second part on the right hand side comprises of the supply side of wine tourism system made up of principle suppliers such as transport, accommodation, catering, retail and other service providers. The third part of the model highlights the interaction between the demand and supply aspects of wine tourism which leads to various destination functions and developments. Such an interaction leads developments in the destination where many additional services are provided to ensure that the demand of the tourists is met by suppliers of wine tourism services satisfactorily. These include developmental initiatives, marketing and promotional initiatives. These initiatives can be undertaken either by government agencies or wineries themselves. In some cases, both government and wineries have also come together to create these initiatives.

Getz's model was the first one that introduced interaction of demand and supply elements as a part of the wine tourism system. However, wine tourists' motivational aspect that typically leads to such a demand are not within the purview of this study. Alonso (2005) observed that 'one of the critical issues associated with winery visitation regards motivational factors influencing individuals to travel to wineries'. Further, the wine tourism model may be well applicable for larger and evolved wineries. Smaller and developing wine regions with limited resources may not have or be willing to invest in tourism infrastructure given the limited and varying numbers in winery footfalls.

Yet another notable and widely acclaimed model on wine tourism experience was presented by Mitchell, Hall & McIntosh (2000) indicating its various aspects that make up the wine tourism product. According to the authors 'firstly, the model illustrates the winery attributes, such as the setting and wine tasting on-site. Secondly, it illustrates the region, including regional wineries, regional population, regional cuisine, and accommodation. Thirdly, emphasis is placed on the experience of the outside region, represented by restaurants, festivals, and wine shows. The final dimension represents the individual, or visitors' personal characteristics; these characteristics emphasise, among other elements, previous experience, and personality' (Mitchell, 2000). These four categories or dimensions make up for the most important aspects of a wine tourism experience. This model created a clear distinction between four most important aspects that encompass the wine tourism experience.

1. Inherent characteristics of a winery / vineyard,
2. Regional attributes of the area where the winery / vineyard is located,
3. Experience outside the wine region,
4. Characteristics of the visitors themselves.

However, Alonso (2005) argues that this model of winery experience 'although useful in explaining potentially significant elements surrounding the winery experience, the meanings of some elements in this model seem broad, even ambiguous. For example, other attractions, scenery, accommodation, staff empowerment, entertainment, empathy, and personality could not only be related to winery visitors' experience, but also apply to tourists looking for any attraction, particularly while travelling in rural areas.' Although, this model was considered as ambiguous on some accounts, it is one of the first models that brought out the characteristic features of wine tourism experience. This model highlights the four distinct aspects of wine tourism and how these four aspects are interrelated and interlinked to create an overall wine tourism experience.

Hall, Sharples, Cambourne & Macionis (2000) in their book *Wine Tourism around the World* introduced yet another, much comprehensive concept of wine tourism system. 'The model attempts to integrate the demand and supply of the wine tourism experience. The focal point of the model is the wine tourism experience' (C. Michael Hall, 2009). The model comprises of two important parts viz.,

a) Demand related aspects of wine tourism (Culture, Wine tourist expectations, Motivation, and Destination Image)
b) Supply related aspects of wine tourism (Wine Industry, Tourism Industry, Human Resources and regional attributes of the wine region etc.).

Further explaining the demand related aspects of wine tourism; the authors described the importance of motivation and perception in the wine tourism experience. 'The perceptions of the traveller comprise three different elements: past experience, preferences and information. The choice of destinations and visits to attractions will be affected by previous experiences and their relative enjoyment' (C. Michael Hall, 2009). The supply side of wine tourism comprises of all the service providers from wine industry, tourism industry and other related enterprises. 'The supply side of wine tourism includes all the resources utilized by tourists for the purpose of wine tourism and the businesses and institutions which transform those resources into a wine tourism product' (C. Michael Hall, 2009).

This model, in many respects, may be considered as one of the most comprehensive models. The model shows wine tourism experience as a result of interaction between wine tourists' demand related elements and wine tourism industries supply related elements. Wine tourism demand is a result of tourist expectations from wine tourism activities, perception related to wine and wine related activities, motivating factors leading to selection of a particular winery or wine region and together with past experiences. Further, the supply side of wine tourism comprises of an entire range of attractions such as winery, vineyard, *terroir* among other wine centric attractions and non-wine centric attractions such as landscape, culture, cuisine, souvenirs among other attractions. The model highlights the importance of human resource in both wine and tourism industries. Wine maker, wine cellar staff, tour guides and managers at the wineries and owners together contribute the creation and development of wine tourism experience. Legal aspects related to wine and tourism industry have also been highlighted as a part of the wine tourism system. Although, they may have no significant bearing on the wine tourism experience as such, the authors have highlighted their importance as a part of the overall wine tourism system. One of the limitations of the model, however, is that it does not describe the role of National

Tourism Organisations as a part of the wine tourism system. NTOs are integral to the development of wine tourism destinations and their marketing.

Erica Croce & Giovanni Perri (2017) in their book *Food and Wine Tourism* explained the intertwining between wine tourism and other forms of tourism using an integrated model of food and wine tourism. According to them 'one of the most positive aspects of food and wine tourism is that it integrates so easily with other types of tourism. Food and Wine tourism shares many of the same features as cultural tourism' (Erica Croce, 2017). 'It is plain to see that there is a very strong link between the two types of tourism: a holiday that is based around offering a gastronomic experience will necessarily include one or more components of cultural tourism' (Erica Croce, 2017).

This may be considered as one of the most comprehensive models describing many facets of wine tourism, primarily focussing on supply side of it. The model does not indicate the interaction between the elements and also the role of NTOs in the process of product creation and development is excluded from the purview of this wine tourism system model. Some of the other similar research works referred to were:

a. The wine tourism service-profit chain. Based on Heskett, Jones, Loveman, Sasser and Schlesinger (1994, in Morris & King, 1998)
b. The wine tourism value chain (Source: Getz, 1998)
c. Antecedents and outcomes of winery tourism. Source: Dodd (2000).
d. The experiences model, featuring four different consumer experiences by Ali-Knight and Pitt (2001)
e. The wine tourist - a three dimensional analysis. Source: Charters and Ali-Knight (2002).
f. Conceptual framework for terroir tourism by Mitchell and Hall (2006)

Research Gap

While there are many studies that have highlighted aspects that are pivotal to a wine tourism system, there seem to be other factors that are integral to wine tourism development and growth as well. Also interaction between elements of the wine tourism system is yet another area that requires further exploration and research. This research paper tries to bridge this gap by constructing a conceptual framework for an integrated wine tourism system. Further, the applicability of these models for an emerging wine tourism destination such as Maharashtra needs to be elucidated.

Approach Used to Develop the Conceptual Framework

A twofold approach was adopted for the purpose of this paper. Extensive literature review forms the foundation of this qualitative synthesis. Published research articles, books and other academic works on the subject were reviewed followed by a descriptive evaluation of wine tourism systems, models and conceptual frameworks. The basis on which the wine tourism experience models and systems were selected by the author is enumerated as below:

a) Models / systems describing or associated with visitor experience at wineries;
b) Models / systems describing motivational aspects / dimensions of wine tourists / characteristics of winery visitors;
c) Models that have been proposed or developed between 1990 and 2019, allowing an examination of evolution of such models / systems;
d) Further, general relevance with the research objectives.

The suggested framework borrows relevant and applicable elements from the existing models and consolidates into a single framework. Secondly, field visits undertaken by the author and interviews with important stakeholders (winery owners, wine tourism service providers and wine tourism operators) were also instrumental in lending inputs to the conceptual framework.

FINDINGS AND SUGGESTION

Wine tourism is essentially a synthesis of various elements from wine and tourism industries that come together to form a wine tourism experience. The review of various perspectives in wine tourism systems is especially useful in understanding the multi-dimensionality of wine tourism. Wine tourism, a niche form of food and drink tourism is a part of much larger cultural tourism. Several aspects of cultural tourism may be amalgamated to create a unique blend of tourism activities to suit tourists with varied interests and preferences.

The wine tourism system model, as proposed by the author, amalgamates all the aspects that integrate to create a wine tourism destination experience. The model takes insights from the various wine tourism system models discussed above and attempts to contribute a conceptual framework of wine tourism system by integrating of contemporary elements observed through extensive field study and research. The proposed conceptual framework of tourism system is divided into three distinct dimensions namely the demand side, supply side and finally the resulting tourism

Figure 1. Conceptual Framework of Integrated Wine Tourism System

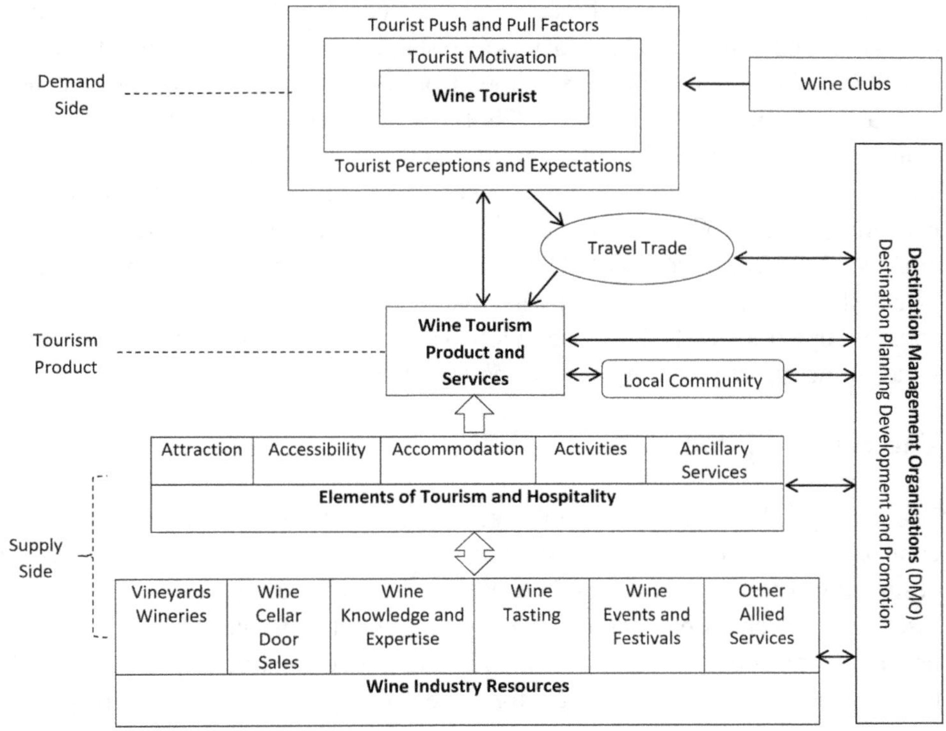

product. The demand side takes insights from Wine Tourism Experience model by Hall, Sharples, Cambourne & Macionis (2000).

The Demand Dimension

The demand side of the system comprises of wine tourist whose demand for wine tourism products and services is influenced by various forces. Travel motivators are central to wine tourist's choice of destination and activities at the destination. The travel motivators of tourists are the *raison d'être* why they undertake to travel to a particular destination or choose a particular travel experience. These motivators may be rest and relaxation, seeking wine knowledge and experience or experiencing regional wine and cuisine. The motivators also, to a great extent, determine the type of activities tourists choose to undertake at the destination. Push and pull factors along with wine tourists' perceptions and expectations also have a bearing on the wine tourists' demand for wine tourism products and services.

Push factors may include intrinsic factors such as need for learning, rest and relaxation etc., while the pull factors may include brand of the vineyard, current travel fads and publicity. These factors also shape tourists' perception of the chosen travel destination and their expectations from the tourism services they intend to avail at the destination and the overall holiday experience. All these factors together constitute the demand side of wine tourism system. Wine clubs comprising of wine aficionados also, to a great extent, shape the demand for wine tourism by way educating wine enthusiasts in wine nuances and etiquettes. In Maharashtra, wine clubs such as The GrapeWine Oenophiles, The Nagpur Wine Lovers Club, The Wine Club are among the active wine clubs promoting wine culture in the region and country. Wine clubs have been globally recognised for their role in promoting wine culture greatly and thereby promoting wine tourism.

The Supply Dimension

The supply side of wine tourism system is divided into two parts that together constitute to make the tourism product. Pivotal elements that contribute in creating a destination experience are the tourism resources that a place has to offer. These tourism resources may either be - natural or manmade; tangible or intangible; temporary or permanent resources - which enable in creating a destination experience. In wine tourism, elements of wine industry form the primary resources for creating a wine tourism product. When these resources are combined with elements from tourism and hospitality, the wine tourism product is created. Wine industry's resources include vineyards, wineries, wine cellars, wine knowledge and expertise, wine tasting facility, wine events and festivals at the vineyard or elsewhere hosted by the vineyards. Table 1 below lists the various wine themed festivals that take place in Maharashtra.

The basic constituents of tourism industry include attraction, accessibility, accommodation, activities and ancillary services or amenities. When wine industry resources are combined with elements from the tourism and hospitality such as guided wine tours, vineyard restaurants, vineyard resorts, souvenir shops, conferencing facilities etc. wine tourism product is created to deliver a complete wine tourism experience. Figure 2 illustrates the supply side of wine tourism experience.

Most vineyards in India and elsewhere are typically located in the rural settings. Local community or host community at the wine tourism destinations are many-a-times a part of the wine tourism experience. For instance, Farmstays or homestays at the vineyards, experiencing local cuisine made using local produce, dance shows, performances and activities highlighting local culture and way of life are a part of wine tourism experiences in many parts of the world. Local communities also contribute to developing wine tourism experience by way of participating in allied

Table 1. List of Wine Festivals and Events in Maharashtra

Name of the Wine Festival / Wine Event	Hosted By	City	Time of the year	Nature of the Event
SulaFest	Sula Vineyards	Nashik	February	Annual Music and Wine Cantered Event
Sanskruti	Sula Vineyards	Nashik	October	Annual Cultural and Wine Event
The Great Grover Stomp	Grover Zampa Vineyards	Nashik	January / February	Annual Grape Harvest Festival
York LIVE	York Vineyards	Nashik	January / February	Music and Wine Cantered Event
The Grape Harvest Festival	All India Wine Producers Association and India Grape Processing Board	Nashik	February	Annual Music and Wine Cantered Event
Kala Ghoda Wine Festival	Terrier One (Mumbai Chapter of the Delhi Wine Club), Indian Wine Academy and All India Wine Producers Association	Mumbai	February	Annual Wine Festival
Nagpur Wine Festival	Nagpur Wine Lovers' Club	Nagpur	March	Annual Wine Festival

Figure 2. The Supply Dimension of Wine Tourism

businesses such as highway restaurants, pit shops, souvenir stores, and farmers markets etc. making them a much essential part of wine tourism system.

Travel trade refers to travel intermediaries such as travel agents, tour operators and event mangers who are a crucial channel in the tourism distribution system. The travel intermediaries package and distribute wine tourism products and services thereby reaching out to various tourist markets. Sales and distribution in wine tourism may happen either through the intermediaries or in many cases sold directly by the wineries themselves.

Destination Management Organisations (DMOs) are essential to the overall organisation and success of a wine tourism destination. DMOs can be instrumental in facilitating an organised and structured development of the tourism destination on the whole. DMOs, although important, can be considered peripheral to the creation and development of wine tourism product. Nashik, Maharashtra has seen some of the standalone wineries promoting wine tourism for the entire wine region with limited assistance from the local DMO, Maharashtra Tourism Development Corporation (MTDC) a body of the Government of Maharashtra. DMOs can either be in the form of an initiative or undertaking by the local government or can also be in the form of a consortium of local wineries, wine tourism service providers and other stakeholders. Destination Management Organisations are typically responsible for tourism planning, development and promotion of the destinations. The nature, structure and functions of DMOs often vary from one country to another. For instance, *Movimento Turismo del Vino* of Italy focuses mainly of promotion of wineries that offer wine tourism, Napa Valley Conference and Visitors Bureau (NVCVB) focusses on marketing of wine tourism globally and Wines of South Africa (WOSA) participates in not only in wine tourism promotion but also in promoting South African wines globally. And, in the case of Maharashtra, All India Wine Producers Association (AIWPA), a consortium of wine producers in the country, have, in addition to MTDC, undertaken to promote wine tourism. DMOs can contribute at various levels such as creation and development of the wine tourism products and services, marketing and promotion of wineries and wines of the region, by way of providing information and also by providing a platform for sales and distribution of wine tourism services.

CONCLUSION

The review and analysis of various wine tourism systems bring out many dimensions of this multi-faceted special interest tourism. Wine tourism, much a part of cultural tourism, presents scope for amalgamation with other forms of cultural tourism activities making it an ever evolving leisure activity. Authors and researchers, in their study of wine tourism systems have chosen to highlight various perspectives that make up the wine tourism experience. Each system with its own unique contribution to the study of wine tourism paves way for newer concepts to emerge from it. This proposed conceptual framework may be useful to researchers in the field of wine tourism in developing /adapting/ building upon the existing wine tourism system model. Further, this framework is specific to a developing destination and this framework can help in drawing parallels between Maharashtra and other developing destinations globally.

The author, in the future, intends to test the conceptual framework to empirically verify its validity. Future areas of study in this area can be case studies on role of DMOs in development of wine tourism products, role of local community in creation and enhancing wine tourism experiences, role of intermediaries in creation and supply of wine tourism experiences, role of wine clubs in promoting wine culture and tourism.

REFERENCES

Alonso, A. D. (2005). *Wine Tourism Experience in New Zealand: An Exploratory Study*. Lincoln University. Retrieved from https://core.ac.uk/download/pdf/35460457.pdf

APEDA. (2018). *Grapes*. Retrieved from www.agriexchange.apeda.gov.in: http://agriexchange.apeda.gov.in/Market%20Profile/MOA/Product/GRAPES.pdf

Erica Croce, G. P. (2017). Food and Wine Tourism (2nd ed.). CABI.

Getz, D. (1998). Wine tourism: Global overview and perspectives on its development. In R. a. Dowling (Ed.), *Wine Tourism-Perfect Partners, Proceedings of the First Australian Wine Tourism Conference*. Canberra: Bureau of Tourism Research.

Kaddi, A. S. (2013). Understanding the motivations of wine festival visitors in Maharashtra. *ATNA Journal of Tourism Studies*, *8*(2). doi:10.12727/ajts.10.1

Michael Hall, C. L. S. (2009). Wine Tourism Around the World. Routledge.

Mitchell, R. H. (2000). Wine tourism and consumer behaviour. In L. S. C.M. Hall (Ed.), Wine Tourism Around the World: Development, management and markets (pp. 115 - 135). Elsevier.

Morley, M. (n.d.). *Insight - India's growing thirst for wine*. Retrieved from https://www.austrade.gov.au/news/insights/insight-indias-growing-thirst-for-wine

ADDITIONAL READING

Carlsen, J., & Charters, S. (2006). Introduction. In J. Carlsen (Ed.), *Global Wine Tourism: Research Management and Marketing*. London: CABI Publishing.

Croce, E., & Perri, G. (2017). *Food and wine tourism: Integrating food, travel and territory* (2nd ed.). CABI. doi:10.1079/9781786391278.0000

Dodd, T. (2000). Influences on cellar door sales and determinants of wine tourism success: Results for Texas wineries. In C. M. Hall, L. Sharples, B. Cambourne, & N. Macionis (Eds.), *Wine Tourism Around the World* (pp. 136–149). Boston: Butterworth-Heinemann; doi:10.1016/S0261- 5177(02)00105-X

Dodd, T. H., Yuan, J., Adams, C., & Kolesnikova, N. (2006). Motivations of Young People for Visiting Wine Festivals. *Published in the Event Management.*, *10*(1), 23–33. doi:10.3727/152599506779364660

Fraser, R. A., & Alonso, A. (2006). Do tourism and wine always fit together? A consideration of business motivation. In J. Carlsen & S. Charters (Eds.), *Global wine tourism: Marketing, management & research* (pp. 19–26). CAB International. doi:10.1079/9781845931704.0019

Getz, D., Dowling, R., Carlsen, J., & Anderson, D. (1999). Critical success factors for wine tourism. *International Journal of Wine Marketing.*, *11*(Iss: 3), 20–43. doi:10.1108/eb008698

Hall, C. M., & Page, S. (2006). *The geography of tourism and recreation: Environment, place and space*. Routledge. doi:10.4324/9780203420249

Hall, C. M., & Sharples, L. (2003). The Consumption of experiences or the experience of consumption: An introduction to the tourism of taste. In C. M. Hall, L. Sharples, R. Mitchell, N. Macionis, & B. Cambourne (Eds.), *Food tourism around the world: Development, management and markets* (pp. 1–25). London: Butterworth-Heinemann. doi:10.1016/B978-0-7506-5503-3.50004-X

Hall, C. M., & Sharples, L. (2008). *Food and Wine Festivals and Events Around the World (Google eBook)*. Routledge. doi:10.4324/9780080887951

Kirkman, A. (2010). The role of wine tourism in the marketing of wineries in the Stellenbosch wine route of South Africa. (Master's thesis for University of South Africa). Retrieved from http://uir.unisa.ac.za/bitstream/handle/10500/4928/thesis_kirkman_a.pdf?sequence=1

Mitchell, R., Hall, M., & And Mcintosh, A. (2000). Wine tourism and consumer behaviour. In C. M. Hall, L. Sharples, B. Cambourne, & N. Macionis (Eds.), *Wine Tourism Around the World: Development, management and markets* (pp. 115–135). Oxford: Elsevier Science.

Prasenza, A., Minguzzi, A., & Petrillo, C. (2010). Managing wine tourism in Italy. *Journal Tourism Consumption and Practice*, *2*(1), 46–61. Retrieved from http://www.academia.edu/2657497/Managing_Wine_Tourism_in_Italy

Chapter 10
Finance in the Hospitality and Tourism Sector

Adenike A. Adesanmi
Oxford College of Canada, Canada

ABSTRACT

This chapter is set to shed light on how the hospitality and tourism sector is to shape their assets and liquidity to either begin a new venture or expand an existing one. The first part of the chapter will give an elaborate discussion about raising financial capital in the hospitality and tourism sector. This will strengthen the points that are made under capital structure formation. Financial knowledge of budgeting is an area that deserves its place in these sectors; this is the third major highlight of the chapter. The issue of understanding financial statements, especially its use in making predictions through ratio analysis, require a thorough explanation. This is therefore the next point. The limitations and usefulness of ratio analysis will be touched upon. Finally, in this chapter, determining demand in the hospitality and tourism sector is a contemporary issue, and the review of this will give a better viewpoint.

FINANCE IN THE HOSPITALITY AND TOURISM SECTOR

Capital Structure

Most of the areas of hospitality and tourism sector of the economy fall within the SME in the economy. One of the major challenges faced by these sectors is how to finance their activity, being largely dependent on the financial institutions particularly the banking sector. However, since the Basel III regulations where the banking sector is expected to scrutinize their lending activity in order to ensure reduction

DOI: 10.4018/978-1-7998-2204-2.ch010

Copyright © 2020, IGI Global. Copying or distributing in print or electronic forms without written permission of IGI Global is prohibited.

in loan defects, it has greatly impacted the ability of SMEs to access loans both for start – ups and existing businesses.

Capital structure is an important topic in financing businesses across the globe. It started with the Modigliani and Miller (1958) theorem under specific assumptions that the capital structure of a business does not affect the value and the cost of capital. This theory is centred on an assumption of no taxes, no bankruptcy costs and no transaction costs in the economy (Correia, et al., 2015). Corporate capital structure, according to the argument of Myers (1993), is a puzzle; this is because of its inability to provide an answer to a classic question of “how firms should choose their capital structure”. The planning of capital structure involves the consideration of stakeholders' interest. This means businesses in the hospitality and Tourism industry are expected to plan their capital structure from its inception. Capital structure is a vital management decision that influences both owner's equity return and market value of shares. It is therefore important for firms to develop an ideal capital structure (Salawu & Agboola, 2008).

The value of a business venture depends on how well its investment and financial decisions are made. Management's target should be to choose the capital structure that maximises the value of the firm for owners or shareholders. The main aim of management's capital structure decision is to determine how to allocate its operating cash flow at every period between shareholders and debt holders. Both returns to shareholders and debt holders are costs to the firm. The cost of and the access to finance represent an important dimension in firms and the decisions about capital structure choice, which is essential for firm's value as well as the stimulation of shareholders' benefits. The capital structure of a company is said to reflect the debt to equity ratio in the choice of finance. There has been the classification of factors that affect the capital structure of firms which are (a) internal factors that are specific to the firm and (b) external factors that reflect the macroeconomic condition of a specific country.

Developed countries derive knowledge about capital structure formation from data, and different countries have different institutional arrangement especially in the areas of existing market for corporate control, bankruptcy, and tax code as well as the roles of security markets and banks which make it almost impossible to infer that, what determines capital structure in the developed economies can be used to explain what is obtainable in developing countries. This connotes that the vast empirical research of the determinants of capital structure in advanced economies could be limited applicability for financial decision making in developing economies (Pacheca and Tavares, 2017).

A good number of people conducted research on capital structure of tourism and hospitality sector, including Giuseppe (2012) who found that trade credit and trade debt are not relevant to the sector, but loans and mortgages are important medium and long-term financial instruments. He identified the bank as the main provider of adequate source of funds for the sector and suggested it has its shortcomings by penalizing growth opportunities. There are firm stands on the order of preferred financial structure which are as follows: Internal equity/financing, debt and external equity financing. However, only profitable firms can generate the necessary funds to use internal equity or finance. Rapidly growing firms may want to use debt, but lenders are aware of the suboptimal investment effort of shareholders and try to extract wealth from them by increasing interest paid on loans forcing fast growing firms not to use debt. This type of financing however is specific to hotel firms, while restaurant firms exhibit different behaviour regarding capital structure.

The restaurant industry is a diverse one. Restaurant firms have a reputation of excessive risk. Eating and drinking establishments report a very high number of business failures. Firms that suffer from lack of cashflow are forced to find sources of funding outside the firm preferably debt. According to Upneja and Dalbor (2012), restaurant firms on average, strike a balance between short - term and long-term debt. Although short-term debt is considered a necessity in the industry, obtaining this type of financing can be difficult, given the risky nature of the restaurant business. The research found that older firms use more of long-term debt. The findings were specifically for publicly listed restaurant firms in a developed country. The difference between short-term and long-term debt is that the former comprises any debt due within one accounting year, while the latter is a financial obligation that lasts more than one year.

With the in-depth discussion about capital structure, it is certain that the hospitality and tourism sector does not follow a specific theory, which means they vary in their capital structure strategies. It has been discovered that most of the businesses in the hospitality and tourism industry depend on debt financing. This is largely because of perceived high risk, it is therefore a big challenge for businesses in the sector to secure both short and long-term financing.

The whole idea about finance is to determine what to invest in, how to get the capital to invest, and how to manage the investment. Finance is therefore identifying necessary resources, determining how to get funding and managing the assets that are bought with the funds.

What to invest?

There are two main types of investments -- long-term and short-term investments. Long-term investments involve investing in infrastructure such as land, building, machines, equipment etc. while short-term investments are the use of funds to buy inventories, pay staff wages, funds for advertising and marketing activities.

Where to get money?

The decision about where to source for funds could be to borrow from creditors such as banks, to ask shareholders for more funds or to use internally generated profits.

How to manage the money borrowed?

This is an issue of timing, budgets, interfacing with suppliers and staff.

Budgeting

A budget is a plan for the near future, where companies try to estimate their costs and revenues. A budget is future-oriented and it serves as a tool organisation use to steer the wheels of the business. A budget could be short or long-term depending on business needs. A budget helps the management to set a limit on the maximum cost and minimum revenue generation using both micro and macro factors to formulate this. Budgets are usually produced from historical data and since it is only estimating using assumptions, the complete information is therefore missing. The budget helps distribute responsibility to each department to ensure they stick to the overall objective of the business. A budget identifies and allocates necessary resources to effectively and efficiently carry out the objectives of the organisation. Successful budgeting is critical to a successful business or service.

The budget helps to clearly establish a plan so that performance in relation to a goal can be carefully monitored. Thus, budgeting has a two – fold purpose. The first is to allow companies develop a plan to meet specified goal, while the second is to allow ongoing comparison between results and the plan in order to have a better control of operations or activities.

Budgeting is an important activity to top management of most companies to coordinate and participate in the process. There are however certain factors that determine how successful a budgeting process will be. First, the process must be supported by top management, and secondly by employees as well, as managers are more motivated when they participate in the design and preparation of a budget. Lastly, variations or deviations from a budget must be addressed by managers in a constructive manner.

The purpose of budgeting also includes providing a base for measuring, comparing and controlling performance. It is used for planning, coordinating and controlling purposes. It may be in terms of time, money, units or otherwise. It is generally a planning and control technique.

Some firms have the culture of preparing a budget and distributing it across major segments of the company which further spreads out to the lower level of the organisational hierarchy structure. This is an example of a top-down approach, sometimes referred to authoritative budgeting style. The other type of budgeting style is the participative budgeting or bottom-up approach. In this case, each unit manager prepares a budget for his/her division. These requests are combined and reviewed by top managers in the organisational hierarchy with adjustments made to align with goals of individual units within the overall organisation.

The two budgeting styles discussed above are legitimate, therefore most organisations use the combination of the two. The blend of the budgeting styles will vary among organisations. A smaller firm with a typical flat organisational structure relies more on a top-down approach than a large organisation. Budgeting is a complex subject and can get very complicated.

Service sectors especially hospitality and tourism sectors perform budgeting in a way that is different from organisations that deal in products. The examples in this textbook will give an idea of some budgeting plans in various divisions of the hospitality industry. In service-oriented businesses specifically in the hospitality and tourism industry, employees are the primary assets, therefore efficient use of staff strength is vital. They budget staff, sales and administration, capacity utilisation, administrative costs in comparison to the unconsolidated sales.

A front office budget may include forecasting room revenue and estimating related expenses. The front office department of any hotel is responsible for sale of rooms and this account for around 70% of the total earning for a typical hotel. This makes budgeting an important activity in a hotel. The front office department could have a number of sub-units such as reservations, receptions, lobby, information and business centres depending on the size of the hotel.

Front office head prepares a budget to account for labour, materials, sales, cost, capital etc. These budget items are based on previous figures in consultation with the controller to achieve organisational goals. Once approved, it is implemented, and observations are recovered and matched with the set standards to identify deviations and corrections would be made. The front office head produces forecasts of revenue and estimated expenses which must have some of the following information: number of expected rooms walk-ins, number of expected room stayovers, number of expected room arrivals, number of expected room cancellations, number of expected room under stays, number of expected room no shows, number of expected room overstays and number of expected room check-outs.

The department head will have to present some ratios to buttress the validity of the budget. These are known as occupancy ratios. They measure the success of front office in comparison to benchmarks or last period ratios. They are computed by auditors and communicated to the manager or related departments, some of these ratios are shown in Table 1.

The information above, helps in the budget planning process.

Table 1.

Ratios	Calculations
Occupancy Percentage	$\frac{\text{Number of rooms occupied}}{\text{Total number of rooms available for sale}}$ .x 100
Single occupancy percentage	$\frac{\text{Number of single rooms occupied}}{\text{Total number of single rooms available for sale}}$ .x 100
Double occupancy percentage	$\frac{\text{Number of double rooms occupied}}{\text{Total number of double rooms available for sale}}$ .x 100
Multiple occupancy percentage	$\frac{\text{Number of rooms occupied by more than one guest}}{\text{Total number of rooms occupied}}$ .x 100
Average guest per room sold	$\frac{\text{Total number of guest}}{\text{Total number of rooms sold}}$.
Average daily rate	$\frac{\text{Actual room revenue}}{\text{Total number of rooms sold}}$.
Average rate per guest	$\frac{\text{Total room revenue}}{\text{Total number of guests}}$.

Budgeting Process

There are steps to budget planning to ensure the effective implementation of the process. This chapter discusses 9 steps.

- Collection of relevant data
- Forecasting the activities
- Establishing organisation chart, budget committees etc.
- Preparing accounting records
- Framing guidelines
- Awareness of task
- Preparation of budget manual
- Submission of budgets prepared for discussion
- Implementation of budgets

Budget formulation commences with **collection of** relevant **data;** this is done by gathering past and analysing immediate information to study trends. Capital movement, profit, and growth provide a strong base for the preparation of budgets. Each functional division should be asked to submit **forecasts of** its **activities** and assess their resources. This helps in preparing functional budgets. An **organisational chart** should be **designed** to define the functional responsibilities of each member of the management team associated with the preparation of budgets. Fixing the budget period and establishment of budget committees and budget centres should be taken care of at this stage. Budget formulation requires several **accounting records** -- a chart showing each functional accounting records should be prepared. This helps in facilitating the analysis and interpretation of the accounting information required for the preparation of budgets.

Guidelines should be **framed** and should be related to production, stock levels, general choices, product/service promotion and general investment policies. For smooth preparation of budgets, everyone concerned should be known as **task assigned** to them. **Budget manual** assigns responsibilities to each person engaged in the preparation of budget. Every department involved is expected to **present** its **budget** as required by the guideline to the budget committee for top **management's approval**. Approved budgets should be sent to concerned department for **implementation** (Radovic and Radojevic, 2014).

Classification of Types of Budgets

Figure 1 shows the classification of budgets. A budget can also be looked at according to its functions. The purchase budget guides the management in making necessary purchases to be made during the budget period. Purchase budget is mainly concerned with the raw materials in the case of manufacturing. Sales budget is the basis of budgetary control. It is an estimate of expected sales during a budget period. It can be expressed either in physical units or in monetary terms. Production budget is a forecast of the production for the budget period. It determines the quantity of the products to be manufactured. Production cost budget comes after the determination of number of units to be manufactured. The units are converted to monetary terms which become the production cost. Material budget is concerned with determining the quantity of raw materials required for production. Research and Development budget is the amount of time or money set aside for research to improve the position of the organisation by binging new initiatives in the field. The cash budget shows the cash requirement for a future period. Administrative budget covers the expenses of all administrative offices and of management salaries. The selling and distribution budget is an estimate of the expenses involved in selling and distributing products and

Figure 1.

Hotel Revenue Projection Template

Hotel		**Rooms**	**Days open**	**Room Nights**		
Hotel information		25	300	7,500		
		Year 1	**Year 2**	**Year 3**	**Year 4**	**Year 5**
Occupancy						
Occupancy rate		45.0%	50.0%	55.0%	60.0%	70.0%
Room nights occupied		3,375	3,750	4,125	4,500	5,250
Revenue						
Average daily room rate		90.00	93.00	95.00	98.00	100.00
Total room revenue		**303,750**	**348,750**	**391,875**	**441,000**	**525,000**
Other						
Food & beverage	15%	45,563	52,313	58,781	66,150	78,750
Other		5,000	5,200	5,900	6,600	7,800
Total other revenue		**50,563**	**57,513**	**64,681**	**72,750**	**86,550**

services. The capital budget is the process by which funds are allocated to various investment projects designed to ensure profitability and growth in the organisation.

Budget according to nature of expenditure: A fixed budget is also referred to as a static budget. It is a type of budget that is expected to remain unchanged irrespective of changes in activities within an organisation. This type of budget is usually fixed over a given period of time and remains unchanged irrespective of volume of production. This budget does not provide room for changes in expenditure which may arise as a result of changes in activity or capacity levels. A fixed budget functions well when actual level of activity corresponds to the budgeted level of activity. However, if these two differs considerably, variances will arise, and budgetary control becomes ineffective. A flexible budget on the hand is designed to change with the activity level. Flexible budget distinctively differentiates the behaviour between fixed and variable costs in relation to fluctuations in turnover, output level or other variable factors. Some of these factors include the number of employees. In effect, the budget changes appropriately with fluctuations in the variable. This budget can be constructed as a series of fixed budgets for different levels of activity.

Budget according to time: Short-term budget is a budget designed to estimate the forecast of a firm within a short period of time usually less than 5 years. Long -term budget is designed for a long period of time usually above 5 years. Such as budget is usually prepared in physical units for the planning of the operation. Current budget

Figure 2.

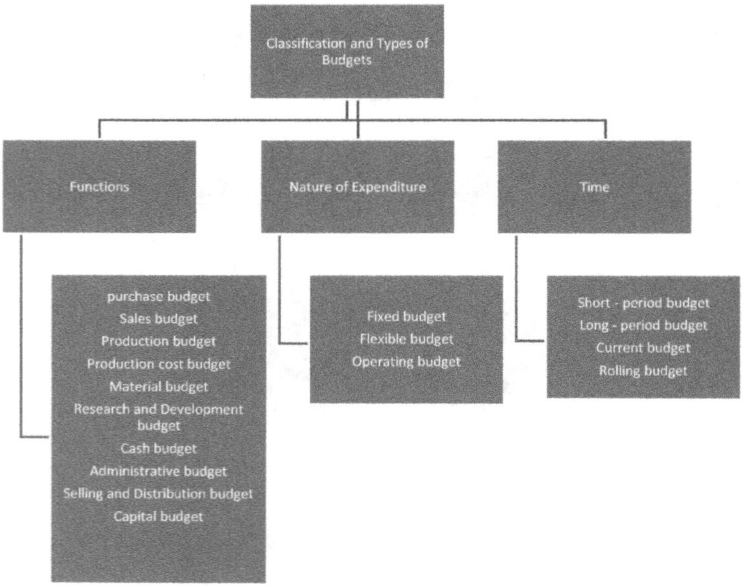

covers a short period of time (i.e. a month or quarter). These budgets are prepared for short period in accordance to prevailing situation of the company. Rolling budget is a progressive budget -- firms which use this have a whole year plan ahead.

Benefits of Budgeting

Budget helps organisations to achieve their objectives and long-term goals. All these are translated into specific plans and tasks, which provide clear guidelines to managers regarding current operational activities. Budget assists management in making comparison selection between alternative courses of action and re-evaluation. Budget provides a means of communicating organisation plans to all members of the organisation. Preparing budgets provides an opportunity to review operations and revise if necessary. Performance at all levels of the organisation can be measured and evaluated against an acceptable yardstick of the budgeted plan.

Shortcomings of Budget Preparation

Budget can be viewed as a competitive bidding tool rather than a planning process. It can cause impossibility to adjust to changes in business environment. Variations require explanation and this may take up managerial time ineffectively if these explanations do not help future performance. Control through budget can only be exercised by an after the event comparison of actuals with budgets and this may be of little help as a guide to current operation.

Financial Statement as a Data Source

The financial statement provides some raw data that is used in making financial decisions. There are three primary types of financial statements most businesses will report.

The first is the Balance Sheet, which is represented in Figure 3 -- it is a listing of a company assets, liabilities and equities. A balance sheet shows the general source that companies' source for money to busy assets, whether borrowed, sourced from private savings or retained profit. Risk, liquidity and financial viability of a business can be determined by looking into the balance sheet. This makes it very useful to creditors and investors. It can be expressed as a simple mathematical equation;

Assets = Liabilities + Equity.

Figure 3.

XYZ Ltd Balance Sheet for the year ending:	Opening	31-Dec-14 Jan-14
Fixed Assets		
Tangible Assets	7,148,660	7,103,899
Current Assets		
Stock	0	0
Trade Debtors	108,111	58,767
VAT	634	18,829
Cash at hand and in Bank	123,822	10,516
	232,568	**88,112**
Current Liabilities		
Trade Creditors	94,904	20,877
Other creditors	35,745	99,838
PAYE / PRSI	7,000	7,250
Overdraft	0	0
Corporation Tax	0	0
VAT	0	0
Bank Loan	50,000	50,000
Loan Obligations	128,865	129,601
Finance Lease Obligations	0	0
	316,514	**307,566**
Net Current Assets / (Liabilities)	(83,947)	(219,453)
Long Term Liabilities		
Bank Loan	8,333	4,167
Loan Obligations	11,180	70
	19,513	**4,237**
Net Assets / (Liabilities)	**7,045,200**	**6,880,209**
Capital and reserves		
Capital a/c	(37,500)	(37,500)
Profit and loss account	0	(158,741)
Drawings	0	(6,250)
Reserves	7,082,700	7,082,700
Shareholders Funds	**7,045,200**	**6,880,209**

The second primary financial statement in Figure 4 is the income statement, which is also referred to as profit and loss statement. This statement tells how much a company makes over a particular period (i.e. monthly, quarterly or yearly). It reveals a company's profitability by summarising all revenues and expenses to determine the company's net income which is a company's bottom line. It is represented as:

Revenue – Expenses = Net Income

The third primary financial statement is the cashflow statement, represented in Figure 5. This is a statement of a company's cash flows as the name implies. It provides a summary of receipts and payments, that is, where its money comes from and where it goes. It shows whether a company generates enough cash to operate and pay its debt.

Figure 4.

XYZ Ltd Profit & Loss Account for the year ending: P&L	31-Dec-14 Jan-14
Sales	**73,724**
Cost of Sales	(22,630)
Gross Profit	**51,093**
Overheads	
Administration	30,830
Marketing	6,625
Operations	31,075
Property-related	32,500
Rooms / Rest. / Events	28,612
Utilities	34,167
Total Overheads	**163,809**
EBITDA	(112,716)
Depreciation	44,761
Earnings Before Interest and Tax	(157,476)
Lease interest	0
Loan interest	1,264
Bank interest	0
Total interest	1,264
Profit Before Tax	(158,741)
Taxation	0
Profit After Tax	(158,741)
Net Income	(206,041)

Figure 5.

XYZ Ltd Cashflow for the year ending:		31-Dec-14 Jan-14
Inflows		
Sales Receipts		134,336
VAT		634
Bank Debt		0
Loans		0
Lease Receipts		0
Equity		0
Total Inflows		**134,970**
Outflows		
Fixed Asset Additions		0
Creditor Payments - COS		101,863
Creditor Payments - Overheads		69,024
Payroll		48,333
PAYE / PRSI		7,000
Drawings		6,250
Corporation Tax		0
VAT		0
Bank Loan - Interest		389
Bank Loan - Repayment		4,167
Loan - Repayment		11,250
Finance Leases		0
Total Outflows		**248,276**
Net Cash Inflow / (Outflow)		(113,306)
Cash Reconciliation		
Opening Balance		123,822
Net Cash Inflow / (Outflow)		(113,306)
Overdraft Interest		0
Closing Balance		10,516

Cashflows are in three categories; the first is operating activities, which are those things that a company does on a daily basis. This includes cash from customers, payment of rent, wages, utilities and payments made to suppliers etc. The second is investing activities, this is investing in the productive capacity of the business which are done occasionally. Examples are payments relating to mergers & acquisition, buying new buildings, machines, sale of asset or loan received etc. The last is financing activities, which are activities needed to get money necessary to buy assets or maintain operations. These include stock repurchases, loans, cash raised from capital and cash paid out to shareholders as dividends.

Most people who have keen interest in economics of tourism and hospitality are usually fascinated by forecasting. Estimation of future demand are equally important in hospitality and tourism especially in management, planning and investment decision making. The World Trade Organization established a long-term forecast for the tourism sector by making assessment of its development until year 2020. This type of forecast, which is purely quantitative covers 6 different travel destinations, which are Americas, East Asia & Pacific, South Asia, Middle East, Africa and Europe. Despite the irregularities of tourism development, UNWTO maintains the long-term vision based on past experience of strong growth, which is usually followed by slow growth with a generally stable trend.

Technology has played a key role in determining the budget of the hospitality and tourism sector. In fact, operational and communication costs are reduced while efficiency, interactivity, productivity and competitiveness are enhanced in the sector. Information Technology have been responsible for the shift from product – oriented to responsive market – oriented service operation, where success is measured by the rapid response to changes in consumer needs. A significant proportion of travellers in the Americas make their bookings online ranging from airline tickets, car rentals, and hotel reservations to package tour. 70% of people who make reservations online travel for pleasure, vacation or personal purposes, while 30% made reservations for convention or business purposes (Merla and Chirita, 2010).

Ratio Analysis

Ratio analysis has been used to evaluate financial conditions of a firms since the inception of finance as a discipline (Lawder, 1989). It has been described as a fundamental tool for evaluating the financial health of a company, and many financial metrics have been developed and used by practitioners. Even though ratio analysis has been a widely used technique, its application in the hospitality industry has received a slight attention. Financial ratios are useful analytical tools that can reveal financial strengths and weaknesses of a firm to help identify potential investment opportunities for investors interested in the Tourism and Hospitality Sector.

Financial ratio expresses a value of a financial variable in relation to another. It helps quantify the degree of change in relationship between variable as well as identify absolute value of a relationship. Managers use the information provided by the figures calculated in ratios to identify any missed information that is relevant in the process of decision making or improving operations. There are two major sources of financial variables that can be used in ratio calculation which are income statement and balance sheet, these has been discussed earlier in the chapter. Almost all business firms develop financial statements. This makes the use of ratio to be found in a variety of industries.

Financial publishing firms and rating agencies collect data on publicly traded firms and make the information available to various interested entities. Banks and other lenders use the information when granting loans, suppliers use this to evaluate credit worthiness of their debtors, investors use the information to decide on alternative investment choices. Financial statements provide numerous amounts of information; it is therefore possible to come up with endless number of ratios.

However, various items in the financial statements are highly correlated which makes ratios to have high correlation, as a result, analysts have classified the number of ratios into subunits. In case there is significant changes in key ratios, more detailed analysis can be carried out.

The Hospitality and Tourism industry needs a high amount of working capital and has a lot of short-term financial obligations to cover, making liquidity ratio an integral part. The liquidity ratio measures the ability of a firm to maintain sufficient liquidity to meet its short – term obligations as they arise. There are two traditional ratios used for this purpose which are current ratio and quick ratio. The current ratio concentrates on current assets and current liabilities while quick ratio focuses on more liquid assets which makes it exclude inventory in its calculation.

Profitability ratio measures the profitability level of a firm at various levels. They include gross profit, operating profit and net profit. It shows the ability of a firm to use its assets and equity to generate return. The net profit is vital as it measures a company's profitability of sales after taking into account all expenses and income taxes. It reveals a company's net income per dollar sale.

Capital structure ratio is also referred to as financial leverage ratio. It is the ratio that gives stakeholders an understanding of the long-term solvency of a firm. It measures a firm's ability to meet its long – term obligations. The Tourism and Hospitality industry have huge long-term liabilities which could be in the form of debts. These debts are used to fund properties, buy fleets of buses etc. The most commonly used ratio is the debt to total assets which reveals the importance of debt financing to the company. It shows the percentage of the company's assets that are financed using debts. Debt to equity ratio can be used to tell the percentage of finance provided by creditors for each one dollar by shareholders. Times interest earned is another ratio, it measures the ability of the company to meet its interest payments to avoid bankruptcy. It can be used to determine the capacity of a company to take on new debt (Kim and Ayoun, 2005).

Asset management ratio and market value ratios: The asset management ratio measures how well or how poorly a company is operating by showing how efficient a firm is using its assets. This ratio is more prevalent in manufacturing industries. It calculates average collection period, inventory turnover and total asset turnover. To determine a number of factors such as profitability, quality of management, risk, the stock or security prices, the market value ratio can be used. The market value ratio indicates the markets assessment of the value of company's stock. The price per earnings ratio and the price to book ratio shows whether investors are optimistic about the market value of company's assets, its intangible assets and ability of its managers. Table 2 below shows the formula to calculate each of the explained ratio.

Table 2.

Ratios		Calculations
Liquidity Ratios	Current ratio	$\frac{\text{current assets}}{\text{current liabilities}}$
	Quick ratio	$\frac{\text{current assets} - \text{inventory}}{\text{current liabilities}}$
Profitability Ratio	Gross Profit Margin	$\frac{\text{Gross profit}}{\text{Sales}} \text{ x } 100$
	Operating Profit Margin	$\frac{\text{Operating profit}}{\text{Sales}} \text{ x } 100$
	Net Profit Margin	$\frac{\text{Earnings available for common shareholders}}{\text{Sales}} \text{ x } 100$
Financial Leverage Ratio	Debt to Total assets	$\frac{\text{Total liabilities}}{\text{Total assets}}$
	Debt to Equity	$\frac{\text{Total liabilities}}{\text{common stock equity}}$
	Times Interest Earned	$\frac{\text{Earnings before interest and taxes}}{\text{Interest expense}}$
Asset Management Ratio	Inventory Turnover	$\frac{\text{Cost of goods sold}}{\text{Inventory}}$
	Average Collection Period	$\frac{\text{Accounts receivable}}{\text{Average sales per day}}$
	Total Asset Turnover	$\frac{\text{Sales}}{\text{Total Assets}}$
Market Value Ratio	Price/Earnings Ratio	$\frac{\text{Market price per share of common stock}}{\text{Earnings per share}}$
	Price to Book Ratio	$\frac{\text{Market price per share of common stock}}{\text{Book value per share of common stock}}$

Determinants of Demand in the Tourism and Hospitality Sector

The global hospitality and tourism industry is one of the largest contributors to the world GDP. The tourism industry alone contributes to almost 10% of world GDP. Depending on the importance countries give to tourism, it is estimated to be around 2 – 10% of its GDP (WTTC, 2017). Apart from this, it creates a large number of jobs. The financial value of the hospitality and tourism creates trillions of dollars annually.

Demand is the desire of consumers for a particular commodity or service, therefore, demand in the tourism and hospitality sector can be defined as the number of customers who use tourism or hospitality facilities in a given timescale. There is a long list of factors that affect demand in the hospitality and tourism sector; some of which are outside of the industry's control. There are factors such as costs, competition, disposable income, advertising, exchange rates, tax policy and government regulations. Some of these factors are discussed in this chapter.

Geopolitical Factors

This has a huge influence on demand for services in the tourism and hospitality industry. A stable geopolitical situation increases demand for tourism and hospitality while instability on the other hand can have a negative effect on the industry. Tourism in the US was impacted greatly as a result of the 9/11 attack. It resulted in increase in surveillance in public areas which made tourists feel insecure. Arrival of tourists from Islamic countries also decreased significantly. Terrorism in the Middle East has played a role in driving down demand in the sector. A country like Egypt with a number of attractive tourist destinations has been deserted. The interventions of governments could further lead to lower tourist activities. People tend to travel to places where safety is certain to an extent and where they can enjoy their vacation without having to look over their shoulders, however, in a time where there are terrorism disruptions, in the polity and local economy, such environment is not encouraging for tourists. Relationships between nations also play a vital role, it can result in a negative effect on demand for tourism and hospitality.

Economic Factors

Fluctuations in local and global economies can affect the level of demand in the tourism and hospitality industry. In local areas and globally, during recessions, the demand for tourism and hospitality is affected at a global scale. Economic boom leads to favourable demand in the sector globally. When employment and economic activity are high, consumers have sufficient disposable income to spend on leisure.

This leads to increase in demand and on the other hand, unemployment and lower economic activity leads to lower consumption of tourism and hospitality services and less spending.

Technological Factors

Technological factors also have a similar influence on the demand for services in the tourism and hospitality sector. In countries where technological advancement is the order of the day, several places, despite not naturally beautiful or geographically attractive attract a large number of tourists because of technology. A beautifully lit metropolitan city with easy access to cars, trains, huge malls and entertainment centres is an example of how technology has led to entirely new rage of tourist activities. Technology has made it easier to connect people and destinations. Technology has also reduced the cost of marketing which has increased competition among airline brands, which has invariably led to reduction in prices of tickets. In addition, lodging has taken a new turn with the increase in the number of Air BnB online booking arrangements, which reduces prices of oversea stays. Websites, blogs and social media also publicize tourist destinations making it easier for people to choose and plan their trips from the comfort of the homes. Technology has also made travel more secure by making sure tourists remain connected to family and friends through the internet. Examples are the use of rating agencies to capture feedback from customers and to reveal customer experiences in the sector.

CONCLUSION

Finance is an essential part of the hospitality and tourism sector, it ensures highlights issues faced by the industry in resource gathering (source of financing the business), efficient resource allocation, resource management, resource control and decision-making process. Management could use this information as a pointer to what is required to start a new business in the sector or to improve on an existing business in the sector.

REFERENCES

Claveria, O., Monte, E., & Torra, S. (2015). A new forecasting approach for the hospitality industry. *International Journal of Contemporary Hospitality Management*, *27*(7), 1520–1538. doi:10.1108/IJCHM-06-2014-0286

Correia, A. M., Cerqueira, A., & Brandao, E. (2015). *Determinants of corporate capital structure: evidence from non-financial listed French firms*. FEP Working Papers.

Kim, W. G., & Ayoun, B. (2005). Ratio Analysis for the Hospitality Industry: A cross Sector Comparison of Financial Trends in the Lodging, Restaurant, Airline and Amusement Sectors. *The Journal of Hospitality Financial Management*, *13*(1), 26. doi:10.1080/10913211.2005.10653800

Lawder, K. (1989). Ratio 101: Back to the basics of financial analysis. *Business Credit*, *91*(6), 28–30.

Mawanza, W., & Mugumisi, N. (2013). Capital Structure and Corporate Performance: A Case for Tourism and Hospitality Sector of Zimbabwe. *Global Journal of Commerce and Management Perspective, 2*, 85-90.

Merla, V. A., & Chirita, S. (2010). Forecasting in Tourism – Important component of the planning process. *Romanian Economic Business Review*, *5*(1), 182–188.

Modigliani, F., & Miller, M. H. (1958). The cost of capital, corporation finance and the theory of investment. *The American Economic Review*, 261–297.

Myers, S. (2001). Capital structure. *The Journal of Economic Perspectives*, *15*(2), 81–102. doi:10.1257/jep.15.2.81

Pacheco, L., & Tavares, F. (2017). Capital structure determinants of hospitality sector SMEs. *Tourism Economics*, *23*(1), 113–132. doi:10.5367/te.2015.0501

Radovic, N., & Radojević, T. (2014). *Operational budgeting in hospitality*. . doi:10.15308/finiz-2014-43-44

Salawu, R. F., & Agboola, A. A. (2008). The determinants of capital structure of large non-financial listed firms in Nigeria. *The International Journal of Business and Finance Research*, *2*(2), 75–84.

Torluccio, G. (2012, Autumn). Financials Menu at European Restaurants, Tourism. *An International Multidisciplinary Journal of Tourism*, *7*(2), 323–342.

Upneja, A., & Dalbor, M. (2001). An Examination of Capital Structure in the Restaurant Industry. *International Journal of Contemporary Hospitality Management*, *13*(2), 54–59. doi:10.1108/09596110110381825

Chapter 11
Finance in the Hospitality Industry

Mudassar Mehmood
Nelson College London, UK

ABSTRACT

By the end of this chapter, it is expected that one will be able to 1) establish various sources of funding that are available to a business in the hospitality industry in the international market, 2) evaluate the advantages and disadvantages of these sources of finance, 3) establish the sources that are available or unavailable for the hospitality business as compared to other industries, 4) evaluate an investment in hospitality industry using various capital budgeting techniques, 5) develop financial statement for businesses in hospitality industry, and 6) evaluate the financial performance of companies in hospitality industry using ratio analysis.

A company is an entity that is an encapsulation of an investment made to cater for needs in the market. It is created to achieve goals and objectives set by the shareholders (Dopson & Hayes, 2009) by its management and employees. Companies starts up with a certain vision and mission which is a summary of the goals and objectives as well as interaction of major parties such as employees, shareholders, suppliers, and purchasing customers. Overtime, companies need to evaluate if they have been able to achieve their visions and missions. One of most relevant way to evaluate this is by conducting an analysis of financial performance of a company. Since the finance is lifeblood of every company, it needs to be carefully sourced, used and controlled, and success reflected in financial evaluation ultimately means overall success of a company.

DOI: 10.4018/978-1-7998-2204-2.ch011

Copyright © 2020, IGI Global. Copying or distributing in print or electronic forms without written permission of IGI Global is prohibited.

The nature of financial management in hospitality industry is quite unique; This is because hospitality industry is mainly service based industry which sometime is coupled with product offers. Nevertheless, procedurally most of the finance related activities are similar as other industries; these activities range from the recording of transactions to the creation of financial reports. Although some of the businesses have been simplified by user friendly systems, they provide ways through which managers can monitor and control at the department level. Subsequent reports are sent to the finance department that oversees the entire operations. This chapter looks into all aspects of finance from financing hospitality start up, time value of money, tools for appraisal of projects as well as components of financial statements of a hospitality business, and their appraisal.

By the end of this section, it is expected that one will be able to:

1. Establish various sources of funding that are available to a business in the hospitality industry in the international market.
2. Evaluate the advantages and disadvantages of these sources of finance.
3. Establish the sources that are available or unavailable for the hospitality business as compared to other industries.
4. Evaluate an investment in hospitality industry using various capital budgeting techniques
5. Develop financial statement for businesses in hospitality industry
6. Evaluate the financial performance of companies in hospitality industry using ratio anlaysis

SOURCES OF FINANCE IN THE HOSPITALITY INDUSTRY

Hospitality industry remains one of the significant contributors to economies around the world. According to the United States Department of Labour, the sector employs about 16.716 million people in the U.S. (Bureau of Labour Statistics, 2019). Compared to other sectors, it may be one of the few that record the highest growth rates and comprises bars and nightclubs, restaurants, food and service management, gambling, events, visitor and tourist attractions (Ogbeide, 2014). It also includes self-catering and holiday parks.

In consideration of businesses at multiple levels, finances are needed. The guiding question for investors or finance personnel is:

- Why do need finance for our business?
- What are the channels where we can get the funding?
- What risks are associated with acquiring finance?

Business Finance Needs

Finance is a standard prerequisite when considering a business, regardless of the sector (Gray, 1996). Even in hospitality, the company require finance for:

I. Initial investment and or expansion
II. Acquiring assets
III. Maintaining cash flow and liquidity
IV. Restructuring of the company
V. Acquiring other businesses and mergers

Once a business is established, it is the intent of the investor for the entity to become a going concern or to achieve its intended goal. In all instances, finances are required to meet needs in the organization such as payment of suppliers, salaries and allowances, levies and permits not forgetting utilities and bills. As such, without finances, operations in the business will be restricted and strained, and it will not be in a position to exploit opportunities (growth and new ventures), as well as actualize its mission and vision. A business with a sound financial backbone will have the flexibility needed to perform at an optimal level (Chibili, 2016).

It is prudent, therefore, to ensure that managers put available finances into proper use and align them with the interests of the shareholders. Managers need to understand what the returns will be for each investment and other alternatives that need to be considered before deciding to embark on an investment. Equally of importance is the assessment of risks that come from such an investment. Some present good potential for returns, but have more risk exposure. Others have a considerably lower risk, but returns are equally lower (Brigham & Houston, 2019). The challenge for a manager is to find an investment for which the risks can be managed, and exposure of the company limited.

Sources of Finance

There are many ways of looking into finance sources for a business. There are internal and external sources of finance as well as short term, and long term sources of finance.

Internal sources are those obtained from the stakeholders of a business. They can form part of either short term or long term financing (Woodhall &Stuttard, 1999). Short term financing involve borrowing money for up to 30 days, whereas, the long term finance involve borrowing from 30 days to up to 5 years. Some of the strategies to raise money for new investment within the confines of a company include:

a) ***Sale of assets.*** Redundant equipment and or properties can be leveraged for better prospects identified that will generate enough revenue to buy such assets in the future. Companies in hospitality industry may also sell out the assets which are least in use and do not contribute significantly to the growth of the companies. For example, automatic vending machines within a hotel which are not much used by customers can be sold out to raise finance. Moreover, if a hotel has extra parking spaces in its parking lot, these spaces can be rented out to other companies.

b) ***Retained profits.*** This is the portion of a profit which is left over after the profit has been distributed among the shareholders. If the business chooses not to give all or any dividend to its shareholders, the retained earnings can be used as funds for new projects or expansion such as opening a new branch of a hotel.

c) ***Cost savings***. For some projects, the foregone choice may be making the company spend more (Ramirez, 2017). If for example, a hotel was using incandescent bulbs and changes them to LED, the cost of electricity will go down, and accumulated saved cost at the end of the year can be used for new projects such as room refurbishment

Following are some of the external long term sources of finance (Kumar, 2017).

a). **Banks Loan:** A hotel may approach banks for a loan to meet its finance needs. Banks offer secured and unsecured loan for amount of interest in return depending upon the type of loan; the interest rate for a secured loan is generally low as such a company has to pledge an assets with the bank for such loan. Such loan involves a lower risk from bank's perspective, and therefore, a low interest rate is charged.

An unsecured loan is offered at a higher interest rate as compared to secured loan due to prevalence of a relatively higher level of risk. An unsecured loan is offered based on a company's financial credibility mainly without pledging any asset.

Be it a secured or unsecured loan, banks run a credit checks of a company and its directors prior to making a loan offer. Generally, companies with poor credit rating are offered loan at higher interest rate and vice versa.

b) **Venture capitalists:** Venture capitalists are individual who are financial sound and are looking for investment opportunities. A hotel may approach venture capitalists to raise finance. However, the venture capitalists require a share of hotel's profit and/or a share in ownership in return of their investments.

c) **Shareholders:** Besides its current shareholders, a company can put its share on offer in stock exchange. This is a relatively easy and quicker method to raise finance. However a company with a poor reputation may find it difficult to raise funds using this method.

d) **Factoring debt:** This is an option available to all and especially to those companies who are financial difficulties or are finding it's difficult to recover debts from account receivables. Factoring involve selling out account receivable to a third party who buy the account receivable for certain percentage of cumulative value of account receivables. For instance, if the cumulative value of account receivables is £10,000, a factoring company might buy them for 90% of the value i.e., £9,000. However, the business in hospitality industry generally do not offer credit to its customers, and therefore, this might not be a viable option for them.

e) **Debentures:** A debentures is a certificate of an unsecured debt. These are offered to external investor(creditors) in return for the their funding. It's a source of long term secured loan which require a payment of fixed interest to the creditor.

f) **Hire purchase agreements:** Hire purchase a useful tool of financing when a company need to buy an asset without paying the full prices upfront. In a hire purchase, a borrower get the right to use the assets for a certain period of time in return of deposit and fixed monthly payments which include principle amount plus interest. So for example, a hotel need to purchase automatic coffee maker of £2000, it may be able to get it on hire purchase for 3 years at an interest of 15% and pay a specific monthly installments e.g. £70.

Following are some of the short term sources of finance available to businesses in hospitality industry.

a) **Trade credits:** Trade credit is general used by manufacturing or trading organizations. This involve buy now and pay later, generally after a month, option. The payment is made free of interest within a specified period of time. However, if a business is unable to pay within the specified time, it is charged a certain percentage of interest is charged after the deadline.

b) **Bank overdrafts:** This is facility provided by a bank to its account holder. Under an overdraft facility a customer/business can withdraw a certain amount from its bank even if the account balance is zero. The overdrawn amount is free of interest for a period of 30 days and over 30 days, the bank charge a certain percentage of interest on the amount overdrawn.

Managers and founders should note that this type of financing has an effect of decreasing equity for the founding owners. In giving up ownership, it may get to a level where the debtors become shareholders and therefore reduces the level of control the founders have on the business (Breitner& Anthony, 2013). Circumstances within a working environment should be a guideline for the selection of a good source of finance for the company. In addition to being blinded by the money on face value, good managers will evaluate the **benefits of taking the funds versus the cost** that they have on the business. Costs, in this case, do not just include the interest rate for the money lent but also the administration charges, valuation fees for the collateral provided, adjustment for inflation, and currency conversion fees in the case of international transactions among others. If the benefits outweigh the costs, then it makes a good source. If the cost of finance is too high, then it is prudent for the manager to look into other means of getting funds (Goodman, 2010).

In addition to the cost, there is another essential aspect that needs consideration. What will you give to get the funds? The **terms of the financing agreement** can be exposing the company in terms of how much equity and or collateral it can provide. Depending on the lender, some may ask for equity in favour of a lower cost of finance, or in case of forfeiture. Others will ask for collateral of too much value to the company increasing the risk. A manager or founder should consider that at times, investments do not pay off, instead end up as a partial or total loss. A partial loss situation means that it will take longer to recoup the investment that was injected into a project (Breitner& Anthony, 2013).

The book mentions that there those financing methods that are debt and those that involve giving up equity. We shall then proceed to look into the pros and cons of the two types. Managers should always have this in mind when making an initial decision on which path to take.

Financing through debt is one of the quickest methods through which a hospitality company can raise funds. Some of the advantages it presents include:

1) Relatively faster processing depending on the market and relationship with the lender.
2) Once the debt is repaid the founder or shareholder will retain the equity held in the business.
3) The capability of debt financing to spur growth means that the net worth of the business will go up. The value of the shares also goes up, increasing wealth portfolio for the shareholder or founder.

Debt also has disadvantages for a hospitality business (Breitner& Anthony, 2013): Such as

1) It tends to decrease profitability because the first responsibility is to pay liabilities before profits can be calculated.
2) It affects the liquidity ratio of the business. When the debt is financed by banks, the strict rules for repayment and engagement terms. For the hospitality industry, this may be a huge risk considering the seasonality of some ventures as well as inconsistencies in generating revenue.
3) When this avenue is exhausted, the company has no other room other than giving up equity for finances.

Financing through equity is another approach that a founder and manager can consider in hospitality. Some of the pros include:

1) Risk is transferred from the business to the investor. It presents a means to reduce the exposure the company will have on a project.
2) Unlike debt, which is paid before the determination of profit, any dividends given to the shareholder is decided by the directors and is pegged on whether the company made a profit or not for that particular period.

It also has some cons associated with taking this route. Such include:

1) There is no repayment to be done to release the company from any agreement. Once the financier has acquired equity, the only way for them to leave is if they wish to sell the stake.
2) When the amount of equity given up is high, the casting vote may not be with the owner. He or she, therefore, relinquish control on future decisions about the company. For some, it may be a bad thing since they may steer the company away from the original vision to another. In other instances, it may help refine the methods used by the founding members, adding subject expertise and networks to open up supply chain issues. It is therefore vital to have a background and understand what additional value the potential investor will add to the company before taking money in exchange for equity.

The choice for a financing method is dependent on the specific business in the hospitality industry. Managers, founders, and proprietors are advised to consider their turnover and nature of work when selecting a source of finance (Fields, 2016). For seasonal businesses, flexibility is needed for long term financing and or short term financing that can be paid during peak time is desired. This can be an example of a seasonal tourist attraction or service (Kotler, Bowen, James &Baloglu 2016). Where the risks are high, and the value of the property to be used as collateral is high, care should be taken so that what was once an income-generating activity is not seized (Hayes, Ninemeier& Miller 2011). For equity type of financing, the potential investor should understand the selling point for the business (Milano Robnett& Milano, 2010). The manager or founder should vet the interests of the investor in the company to avoid future conflicts of interest. Some of the hospitality industries most significant selling points is the different culture and differentiation. Changing this may mean losing clientele. For instance is the Holiday Inn thrives due to the serene environment and rustic looks with no modern upgrades, bringing in modern items as a facelift may work against the company.

TIME VALUE OF MONEY

In so long as money can earn interest, and some uses can increase the value of money, money that is available right now has more value than the same amount at a later date. The earning capacity means that the amount of money at present can generate some amount of money in futre.

Assume someone offered to take a sum of £10,000 right now or £11000 after 5 years. The prudent decision will be to take £10,000 right now as it has higher value than £11,000 in future. Another way of looking at this concept is to focus on is the goods and services that can be bought with a certain amount of money. For instance, £0.90 was average price of soft drink in the UK. However, the same soft drink cost on average £1.10 today which implies a decrease in value of money. The reasons are that:

- Present consumption is preferred over future use. To give up present consumption, one needs an incentive to be added to the amount that will be offered.
- Opportunity costs exist in getting the money now. It can be invested and turn a profit in two years or even earns interest from savings in a bank.
- Considering inflation, currency value decreases in the future when inflation is on the rise. Here it is inversely proportional, the higher the inflation, the lower the value goes.
- If there is a cash flow problem in the future or risk of that happening, the cash flow will have lesser value (Irena and Mariana, 2017).

There are several techniques with which we can compare and calculate the future value of money. The methods include:

a) Compounding
b) Discounting

c) Capitalization
d) Indexing

Although they are closely related, Irena and Mariana (2017) indicate that they can be classified under different conditions and linked to see their relationships. We shall look into the two conventional commonly used methods.

Compounding

This method entails taking a current amount of money (today/present value) and converting it to a future value with the use of a predetermined compounding factor or interest factor (Reilly, Brown & Leeds, 2019).Where

FV- Future value of money
PV- Present value of money
i- Interest rate
n- Number of compounding periods per year
t- Number of years

Time value of money (TVM) will be given by the formula,

$$FV = PV \times \left[1 + \left(\frac{i}{n}\right)\right]^{(n \times t)}$$

The number of times that money is compounded is as important as the time span for which the future value is to be calculated.

Let Us Use an Example

James is, a curio proprietor who owns a hotel in London, learnt that that a consignment of wine is available at a bargain price. It is an abrupt decision he has to make as the shipment has been sold at a price lower than the market price for a larger minimum order quantity. He has to raise £10,000 within one week to buy the consignment which he expects a 45% mark up in 12 months. He has two options for finance. He can take a loan from the bank at 10% interest compounded yearly, or he can use the mobile bank loan from the same bank with 10% interest but compounded monthly. Following is how we assess the cost of both finances and justify which one he should take since he has qualified for both.

Bank loan 10% interest compounded yearly

Using the formula,

$$FV = 10{,}000 \times \left[1 + \left(\frac{10\%}{1}\right)\right]^{(1)}$$

$$FV = £11{,}000$$

Mobile loan 10% interest compounded monthly
Using the formula,

$$FV = 10{,}000 \times \left[1 + \left(\frac{10\%}{12}\right)\right]^{(12\times1)}$$

$$FV = £11{,}047$$

The mobile loan compounded monthly is **more expensive as it will cost £47 more**. He should, therefore, take the bank loan compounded yearly for use in buying the curio that he needed.

Discounting

It is a method of determining the present value of a future sum of money. In discounting we will determine the discounted or present value of the money to be received using an interest rate or profitability rate and the time interval (Brigham & Daves, 2018).Where

FV- Future value of money
PV- Present value of money
i- Interest rate
n- The time interval from present moment to the future moment for which future value has been provided

The discounted or present value will be given by the formula

$$PV = FV \times \frac{1}{(1+i)^n}$$

For example

Winston runs a tour van business in the famous Maasai Mara game reserve in Kenya. He hires out his van for £250 per day if he will fuel and provide a driver or £200 when he provides just the car and fueling and driving are at the discretion of the client. His friend Winnie has started a lodge in the game reserve, and she has created an all inclusive package for tourists who visit her lodge. She will provide a free morning or evening game drive for every purchase of the deluxe package. Since she does not have the capital, she has offered to lease Winston's vehicle, and she will provide fuel and a driver for her lodge. She has offered to pay the £200 per day after the lapse of a year to give her room to stabilize her business. Assume an interest rate of 10% per annum.

Following is the method to evaluates the proposal made and make a counteroffer using time value of money principle.

From information provided,

One year of £200 daily payments is £73,000 for a year (365 days)

To get the present value of that money we use the formula,

$$PV = 73,000 \times \frac{1}{(1+10\%)^1}$$

$$PV = £66,363.64$$

Converting it into a **daily rate, £66,363.63/365 it becomes £181.82**

Compared to **the going rate of £200 per day**, the current value of £181.82 is **£18.18** less indicating a 9.09% decrease in the revenue.

This shows the discount Winston would have given to Winnie if she was to pay me today. Given that she will provide you with the guaranteed business for the year, a discount of 5% can be acceptable from the current rate of £200, which gives £190 as the daily discounted price, and **a year's revenue at £69,350.**

APPRAISAL OF NEW PROJECTS

Investments in hospitality industry like any other sector needs vetting of projects. Potential investors need to establish minimum performance requirements necessary for an investment to be considered financially sound or feasible. There are various techniques to appraise new projects; they include:

a. Net present value (NPV)
b. Benefit-Cost Ratio (BCR)
c. Internal Rate of Return (IRR)
d. Simple payback period

Net Present Value (NPV)

This method entails getting the present value of cash flows for a project or investment less the investment cost. As a formula, it will be

$$NPV = \sum Cash\ flows - Investment\ cost$$

The underlying concept behind the NPV methods is that as we make investments in today's terms and we received benefits in future, it wouldn't be objective to compare current costs with future benefits due to time value of money phenomenon. Therefore, under NPV method, values of all the future cash flows need to be converted into present cash flow and sum of these values is compared with the total investment in order assess feasibility of the project. When the current aggregate value future cash flow is higher than the capital investment (a positive value after working out, using the above formula) it indicates a good project or investment. The higher the net value of NPV the higher is the feasibility of a project. Note that the calculation under NPV methods discounting of future cash flow into present values.

Example:

Kimberly is aspiring entrepreneur in hospitality industry who owns a chain of hotels called Leisure Inn. Due to increased popularity of her hotel, she is planning to start new branch of her hotel in Cape Town. She has conducted her research and have received following information.

- Initial investment required = £150,000
- The ongoing interest is 10%

Table 1.

Revenue	Year 1	Year 2	Year 3	Year 4	Year 5	Year 6
	10,000	30,000	50,000	50,000	40,000	40,000

Required: Being a financial analyst, advise Kimberly if the project is feasible using NPV method

Solution:

Step 1: Identify discount rates for each year using the given interest rate

Step 2: Multiply the discount rates with the corresponding cash flow in order to get present values of all the future revenues

Step 3: Sum up all the present values of revenue.

Step 4: Deduct the value of initial investment from sum of all the present value of revenue calculated in step 3.

As given above, the NPV for the project is £68738.5, which is significantly higher than 0. Therefore it is inferred that the project is highly feasible.

Benefit-Cost Ratio (BCR)

BCR is the sum of all present value of future cash flows divided by initial investment (capital cost). As a formula, it will be

$$BCR = \frac{(P_c + N_c)}{CC}$$

Where:

Pc- Summation of positive cash flows
Nc-Summation of negative cash flows

Table 2.

			Step 1	Step 2	Step 3	Step 4
		Cash flows	**Discount rate**	**Multiply each revenue with discount rate**	**Sum of all the present value of revenues**	**Sum of all the present value of revenues - Cost**
Cost	Year 0	150,000	1	150,000		NPV =68738.5
Revenue	Year 1	10,000.00	0.9091	9,090.91	218,738.49	
	Year 2	30,000.00	0.9901	29,702.97		
	Year 3	50,000.00	0.9990	49,950.05		
	Year 4	50,000.00	0.9999	49,995.00		
	Year 5	40,000.00	1.0000	39,999.60		
	Year 6	40,000.00	1.0000	39,999.96		

CC- Capital cost (Cost of acquiring and installing new machinery) or the total initial investment.

It should be noted that the feasibility criteria using this method is for BCR to be greater than 1. That is, $BCR > 1$

Question: Find feasibly of Kimberly's project (given above) using BCR method.

Solution: We require sum of present value of revenues as well as the investment. The informed is already given in Table 2.

$$\text{BCR} = \frac{Present\ values\ of\ Revenues}{Present\ value\ of\ investment}$$

$$\text{BCR} = \frac{218,738.49}{150,000}$$

$$\text{BCR} = 1.46$$

As the value of BCR is significantly higher than 1, it is inferred that the project is feasible.

Internal Rate of Return (IRR)

It can be described as a discount rate at which the project breaks even. It is closely linked to NPV since this method yield a discount rate at which NPV=0. A higher IRR indicates a more feasible project. It is the discount rate where the sum of all cash outflows in a project equals the NPV of all cash inflows. The outflows, in this case, emanate from the capital, maintenance, and utility costs, among others. Inflows are in terms of the revenues, savings on utilities, and maintenance plus labor costs in the project. It is worthy to note that investors do not require comparing the projects to others to determine whether it is viable, but one can consider other possible returns (Briston, 2018).

The formula for calculating IRR is

$$0 = P_0 + \frac{P_1}{(1+IRR)} + \frac{P_2}{(1+IRR)^2} + \frac{P_3}{(1+IRR)^3} + \ldots \frac{P_n}{(1+IRR)^n}$$

Where

$P_0, P_1, P_2, P_3, \ldots P_n$ are the cash flows for period 1, 2, 3,...n, respectively; and IRR represents the projects internal rate of return.

An example

Rose is thinking of buying touring overland trucks for African safaris. A friend running a travel agency has indicated that they are having an influx of tourists preferring the mode of travel and the available vehicles do not meet the standards they need. She has determined that she will require £300,000 to buy the trucks and get the project running. She would like to use the vehicles for three years and then evaluate whether to continue. She expects to generate about £150,000 of annual profit in the course of the project. After the project, she thinks of selling the trucks at about £10,000. She has another project that can make returns of about 10%.

Using IRR to evaluate whether the project is feasible,

$$0 = -£300,000 + \frac{£150,000}{(1+IRR)} + \frac{£150,000}{(1+IRR)^2} + \frac{£150,000}{(1+IRR)^3} + \frac{£10,000}{(1+IRR)^4}$$

Using IRR entries for calculations (trials), a rate will determine when the project will breakeven. One can use different rates on the formula. In this case, the trial that developed a breakeven is about 24.31%.

$$0 = -£300,000 + \frac{£150,000}{(1+0.2431)} + \frac{£150,000}{(1+0.2431)^2} + \frac{£150,000}{(1+0.2431)^3} + \frac{£10,000}{(1+0.2431)^4}$$

From the financial analysis, the project will generate a 24.31% return on the investment for Rose. It is much better than the 10% possible from the other investment. Therefore she should invest.

Simple Payback Period

This method looks into how much time it will take to earn back the amount that had been invested in a project. The net cash flows used shows how much risk is involved. Getting money back in a short time is better since the invested about has a shorter exposure time. It is expressed in term of years or fractions of years for the shortest periods (Reilly, Brown & Leeds, 2019).

$$Simple\ Payback\ Period\,(SPBP) = \frac{Investment\ cost}{Net\ positive\ annual\ cash\ flow}$$

An example

Matt is contemplating buying a service van to increase the outreach of his hotel to make outdoor catering services easier. He expects to buy a van at £30,000 and plans to save about £10,000 in costs for hire vans.

$$Simple\ Payback\ Period\left(SPBP\right)=\frac{30,000}{10,000}$$

He will recoup his investment after 3.0 years.

COMPONENTS OF FINANCIAL STATEMENTS

There are three primary financial statements that are important in understanding and evaluating business performance. The financial statements describe, indicate, or measure different aspects of the business (Brigham & Daves, 2018). In this section, we will look into the components of two key financial statements, and we will draw the reports from the sample trial balance. Also, we shall look into the appraisal of the financial statements with an example.

Income Statement

The statement is useful in the hospitality and business in general as it measures profitability and the operational well being of the company. Some of the key characteristics include:

i. It reports financial results for a business for a specific time period.
ii. It covers a time period ranging from monthly, quarterly or annually.
iii. It compares performance to the budget and other aspects from the previous periods.
iv. It summaries revenue and expenses for each department.
v. For each department, the Income Statements have more details in terms of expenses, revenue and profit.
vi. The Income Statement is made each month or period and contains information for the month or year-to-date (YTD).
vii. Investors and managers analyse the P&L Statement monthly and also annually to see the positive or negative variations from the budget.

Managers and investors in the hospitality industry must review the Income Statement, even daily. Daily activities and operational decision affect the Income Statement and are only useful when what is entered is accurate, and no information is omitted (Brigham &Daves, 2018).

Balance Sheet

It is also known as the Asset and Liability (A&L) Statement. It measures and indicates the value of a business. This is one of the important documents that one needs to understand and review to know the worth of a company (Brigham &Daves, 2018). The key characteristics include:

i. It measures the value of a company at a specific point in time. If a balance sheet is indicated in December 2018, it shows the status then.
ii. The fundamental contents are the assets (what the company owns), liability (what it owes others), and equity (who owns the company and what shares they have). The equation for the statement is $Assets = Liabilities + Owner\ equity$
iii. The A&L Statement consists of accounts organized by assets, liabilities, and owner equity. They are divided into current account or working capital (which has under a year obligation) and the long term account or capitalization (which has over one-year commitments).
iv. Accounting managers in the hospitality industry balance the accounts of the balance sheet monthly. It is not expected that the other department managers critique the A&L statement.

In the hospitality sector, the manager uses the working capital (current assets and liability accounts) for daily operations in the establishments. They use the A&L statement to know the extent to which a company is capitalized. That way, they can see the long term debt that the company has to be paid in capital or both. The aim is for managers to use the assets that the company has to operate the business and turn a profit for the shareholders.

Note that starting point for any financial statement is the balance sheet. A balance sheet is statement of all the balances of companies accounts.

Example:

The following trial balance was obtained from Lux Inn for the period ending December 2014. Closing Inventory as at December 31, 2019 was valued at £4500. You are required to generate an income statement for the year ended 31 December 2019 and a balance sheet as at the same date.

Solution: (See Table 4)

Table 3.

Trial Balance Lux Inn 31 December 2019		
	Debit £	**Credit £**
Account Payable		6000
Account Receivable	14000	
Lindsey Ley, Capital		123000
Cash	18000	
Lindsey Ley, Drawing	4000	
Equipment	10000	
Vending Revenue		6000
Inventory (Food & Beverages)	9000	
General Expenses	1000	
Rent Expense	5000	
Salaries Expense	8000	
Supplies	6000	
Room Revenue		20000
Land and Building	80000	
	155000	**155000**

Table 4.

Income Statement Lux Inn For the year ending 2019			
			£
Room Revenue			**20000**
Add **Vendig Revenue**			**6000**
Minus Cost of Goods Sold			
	Opening Inventory	9000	
	add Purchases	0	
	Minus Closing Inventory	4500	4500
Gross Profit			**21500**
Minus Expenses	Rent Expense	5000	
	add Salaries Expense	8000	
	add General Expense	1000	14000
Net Profit			**7500**

Table 5.

Balance Sheet **Lux Inn** **As on 31 December 2019**	
Assets	
Fixed Assets	
Equipment	10000
Add Land Building	80000
Total Fixed Assets	90000
Current Assets	
Cash	18000
Account Receivable	14000
Add Closing Inventory	4500
Add Supplies	6000
Add Total current Assets	42500
Total Assets (Total Fixed assets + Total Current Assets)	132500
Minus Liabilities	
Total Long term Liabilities	
Short Term Liabilities	
Account Payable	6000
Total liabilities (short term + Long Term)	6000
Net Assets (Total assets - Total Liabilities)	**126500**
Owner's Equity	
Capita	123000
Add Net Income	7500
Minus Drawing	4000
Total Owner Equity	**126500**

APPRAISING THE COMPANY'S FINANCIAL POSITION

Preparing financial statement isn't the ultimate goal of accountants and finance managers of an organization. The main reason behind preparing the financial statement is the assessment of financial performance of the company. The figures in financial statement provide useful information and insight into the performance of an organization, however, analysis that is based on the use of these figures alone and in isolation tend to be limited and in some cases inaccurate. For example a company X earned of revenue of £100,000 and made of net income of £15,000, and company Z earned a of revenue of £10,000 and made of net income of £2,000. The comparison of figures of net income shows that company X made a higher net income than company Z, but that is not the true assessment of companies' profitability. Company X made a net income of £15000 out of a revenue of £100,000 which is 15% of the revenue. Whereas, the company Z made a net income of £2000 out of a revenue of £10,000 which is 20% of the revenue. Therefore the company Z is more profitable than the company X as it is earning higher net income per pound of revenue than the company X.

Financial ratios can be divided in into three main categories: 1) Profitability ratios, 2) Liquidity ratios, 3) leverage ratio. For the calculation and interpretation of the ratios, financial statements of Arena Group plc (which have been presented below) for the year 2016 and 2017 have been used as example. Arena group plc is an event management company that operates in a service industry similar to the companies in the hospitality industry.

1) Liquidity Ratios

Liquidity ratios measure the ability of a company to repay its short obligations i.e., loans or debts. Liquidity ratio can be divided into current ratios and quick ratios.

a) The Current Ratio

It is an indicator of the company's ability to meet its short term liabilities. It is obtained from current assets divided by the current liabilities. The current assets are those assets which are liquid i.e., cash form or which can be converted into cash immediately.

$$Current\ Ratio = \frac{Current\ Assets}{Current\ Liabilities}$$

Table 6. Consolidated Income Statement (Year ended 31 December 2017)

	2017 £m	2016 £m
REVENUE	109.6	93.2
Cost of sales	(74.0)	(63.9)
GROSS PROFIT	35.6	29.3
Administrative expenses	(35.3)	(28.3)
Share of profit from joint venture	–	0.2
OPERATING PROFIT	0.3	1.2
Earnings before interest, taxation, depreciation, exceptional items, share option costs and intangible amortisation	10.6	8.5
Depreciation	(5.2)	(5.7)
Exceptional administrative expenses	(4.9)	(1.6)
Share option costs	(0.1)	–
Intangible amortisation	(0.1)	–
	0.3	1.2
Finance costs	(3.2)	(4.8)
LOSS BEFORE TAXATION	**(2.9)**	**(3.6)**
Tax on loss on ordinary activities	(0.2)	(0.2)
LOSS AFTER TAXATION	**(3.1)**	**(3.8)**

Generally, companies tries to achieve and maintain a current ratio of 2 and above as a low current ratio indicates impending insolvency. Nevertheless, a value too high indicates the company may be holding too much cash or inventory and hasn't been utilizing these resource optimally. However, the benchmark for current ratio also depends on the type of industry a company operates in. For example, Facebook Inc is a service based company and it doesn't need to hold or maintain any inventory. Therefore, it's current ratio tends to lower than the current ratio of Tesco plc.

For the Arena Group, the calculation for the current ratio has been determined to be 1.86 for the year 2017 and 0.87 for the year 2016. It shows the current assets are considerably high, mostly held in cash or equivalents in 2016 than the 2017's. Company is in a safer position in 2017 as the ratio is closer to 2. However, the 2016 ratio i.e., 0.86 may not signify any threat as the company operates in a service industry.

b) Quick Ratio

Quick ratio makes use of only those current assets which are in cash form already in order to analyses liquidity of a company. These assets are called quick assets.

Table 7. Consolidated Balance Sheet (As on 31 December 2017)

	2017 £m	2016 £m
NON-CURRENT ASSETS		
Goodwill and other intangibles	34.8	33.8
Property, plant and equipment	34.0	32.2
Interests in joint ventures	-	0.4
Trade and other receivables due after one year	0.4	1.1
CURRENT ASSETS	69.2	67.5
Inventories	4.3	2.7
Trade and other receivables	13.8	12.5
Cash and cash equivalents	4.3	1.6
CURRENT LIABILITIES	22.4	16.8
Trade and other payables	(11.4)	(9.9)
Current tax liabilities	-	(0.2)
Obligations under finance leases and hire purchase contracts	(0.7)	(0.4)
Borrowings	-	(1.5)
Accruals, deferred revenue and deferred consideration	(8.6)	(7.4)
	(20.7)	(19.4)
NET CURRENT ASSETS / (LIABILITIES)	1.7	(2.6)
TOTAL ASSETS LESS CURRENT LIABILITIES	70.9	64.9
NON-CURRENT LIABILITIES		
Borrowings	(15.2)	(29.2)
Loan note and interest	-	(33.3)
Net obligations under finance leases and hire purchase contracts	(0.8)	(0.8)
Deferred tax liabilities	(0.4)	(0.3)
	(16.4)	(63.6)
NET ASSETS	**54.5**	**1.3**
EQUITY		
Share capital	1.1	**1.1**
Share premium account	57.3	**57.3**
Merger reserve	10.9	**(47.2)**
Share option reserve	0.1	**-**
Retranslation reserve	(1.5)	**(0.4)**
Retained earnings	(13.4)	**(9.7)**
EQUITY ATTRIBUTABLE TO THE OWNERS OF THE COMPANY	54.5	**1.1**
Non-controlling interest	-	**0.2**
TOTAL EQUITY	**54.5**	**1.3**

Among all the current assets, inventory is considered as an assets which cannot be converted into cash immediately as it takes time to sell or dispose of. Therefore, the quick ratios is calculate using following equation. Generally, a quick ratio of 1 or greater indicates that a company is in a safe financial position.

$$Quick\ Ratio = \frac{(Current\ Assets - Inventoy)}{Current\ Liabilities}$$

Quick ratio of Arena group is 0.87 for 2017 and 0.73 for 2016. There gap between the quick ratio for the year 2016 and year 2017 is less as compared to the gap between current ratios for year 2017 and 2016. This is due to the fact that the company had accumulated a significantly larger inventory in 2017 than in 2016.

The ratios are less than but closer to one, and as company operates in service industry, it indicate that the company is in sound financial position to pay off its quick obligations.

2) Profitability Ratio

Profitability ratios are comparison of a company's profits/incomes and revenue/ sales. It measures ability a company's to generate income relative its revenue.

The profitability ratios include Gross Profit margin, Net Profit margin and Operating Expense ratio.

a) Gross Profit Margin

Gross profit is achieved by deducting costs of sale (revenue) from sales (revenue) margin is a comparison of gross profit and revenue. It measures the efficiency of a company's core operations and profit information about setting price for its product and service and direct controlling costs. Generally, a higher gross profit margin depict a highly efficient management of a company's core operations.

$$Gross\ Profit\ Margin = \frac{Gross\ Profit \times 100}{Net\ Revenue}$$

The gross profit margin of Arena groups is 32% for the year 2017 and 31% for the year 2016. The company has been showing a consistent performance in terms of maintain is level of profitability.

b) Operating Profit Margin

Operating profit is reached at by subtracting operating expense from gross profit. Operating profit margin is measure of company's ability to meet all core expenses. A company with a higher operating expense tend to easily survive any financial crisis. It also shows that a company is well equip to pay its fixed costs(depreciation etc) and interests.

$$Operaing\ Profit\ Margin = \frac{Operating\ Profit \times 100}{Net\ Revenue}$$

Arena group operating profit margin is 0.27% for 2017 and 1.29% for 2017. Both the ratios are at the very border level, and as they are significantly low, they show that company won't be able to pay its other financial and non-financial costs, and it might eventually end up making a net loss.

c) Net Profit Margin

Net profit is determined by subtract all the indirect costs from gross profit. Net profit margin shows the efficient of management in terms of controlling indirect expenses such as rent, utilities and interest etc. It shows a company's ability to generate profit after paying for operating expense, financial expense and taxes.

$$Net\ Profit\ Margin = \frac{Net\ Profit \times 100}{Net\ Revenue}$$

Net profit margin of Arena Group for 2017 is -3% and for 2016 it is -4%. The negative figures shows that the company was in loss during both the years. However, its relative loss has reduced by 1% in 2017 as compared to its loss in 2016.

d) Return on Equity

Return on equity is a comparison of net profit/income and stockholders' investment. It depicts the attractiveness of a company to stockholders and investors. A company with high return on equity can easily raise finance for any feasible project.

$$Return on\ Equity = \frac{Net\ Profit \times 100}{Total\ Equity}$$

The return on equity of Arena group is -292% for the year 2016. This is an extremely high amount of loss which deter investors from investing in the company. However, the company somehow manage to acquire further funding as well as it has been able to reduce its loss in 2017; this resulted in improvement of return on equity which as -6% in 2017. Although it representa loss on stockholder's investment, yet it also shows an improving trend in profitability which may attract investors in future.

3) Leverage Ratios

Business requires equity as well as debt finance to start up, maintain and grow. The decision to use equity or debt financing should be well thought out as well excess or dearth of any one of the type of finance may be serious implications for the businesses. Businesses attempt to achieve an optimal mix of debt and equity finance to maximize benefits. Leverage ratios in this regard provide relevant information as it a comparison of equity and debt financing use by a business. Two commonly use leverage ratios are debt to equity ratio and debt to total assets ratio.

a) Debt to Equity Ratio

This ratio is compare the level of debt a company has injected as compared to the total shareholders' equity.

$$Debt\,to\,Equity\,ratio = \frac{(Current\,liabilities + Long\,term\,Liabilities)}{Total\,Equity}$$

The debt to equity ratio for 2017 is 0.41 and 13.78 in 2016. The ratio for 2016 suggests a serious risk to company's survival as the company has acquired approximately 16 times higher debt financing than equity. However, in 2017, the ratio is 0.41 which suggest that the company has increased the percentage of equity financing in its capital. In 2017, for every £1 of equity financing the company had acquired £0.41 debt financings.

b) Debt to Total Assets ratio

Debt to Total Assets ratio is a comparison of company's total liabilities and total assets. It measures a company's ability to pay off its liabilities in short as well as in long term. A higher amount of total liabilities than the total assets signals the risk of insolvency as the company wouldn't be able to pay off all the liabilities using all its assets.

$$Debt\ to\ Total\ Assets\ ratio = \frac{(Current\ liabilities + Long\ term\ Liabilities)}{(Current\ Assets + Fixed\ Assets)}$$

For Arena Group, the debt to total assets ratio for 2017 is 0.61 and for 2016 it is 0.22; it represents that for every £1 of total asset, the company has employed £ 0.61 of debt financing in 2017 and £0.22 debt financing in 2016. The ratio shows that the company has acquired more debt financing during the year 2017. Nevertheless, the company seems in a sound position to pay off all the liabilities using its assets in both the year.

CONCLUSION

The hospitality is an integral part of the economy and a viable investment area. It is crucial that also managers and personnel understand how the companies operate to make good decisions on their operations. In this chapter, we have looked into the methods of raising finance for a business in hospitality industry, methods of appraising new project for feasibility and how to evaluate the statements of existing companies to see their financial health. It is noteworthy that the pros and cons of all methods used should be understood thoroughly to avoid making wrong decisions. Especially when making evaluations for projects one would like to engage in, it is necessary to take into account that most items on anticipated cash flows are based on assumptions. Therefore, there is an element of uncertainty, even when the calculations have been done in the right way.

REFERENCES

Andrew, W. P., Damitio, J. W., & Schmidgall, R. S. (2007). *Financial management for the hospitality industry*. Upper Saddle River, NJ: Pearson Prentice Hall.

Arena Hospitality Group. (2017). *Annual Report and Accounts 2017*. Retrieved August 8, 2019 from https://www.arenahospitalitygroup.com/datastore/filestore/42/Annual_Report_and_Accounts_2017_kons.pdf

Breitner, L. K., & Anthony, R. N. (2013). *Essentials of accounting*. Boston: Prentice Hall.

Brigham, E. F., & Daves, P. R. (2018). *Intermediate Financial Management* (13th ed.). Boston, MA: Cengage Learning.

Brigham, E. F., & Houston, J. F. (2019). *Fundamentals of financial management*. Boston, MA: USA Cengage.

Briston, R. J. (2018). *The Stock Exchange and investment analysis*. London: Routledge.

Bureau of Labor Statistics. (2019). *Industries at a glance: Leisure and Hospitality*. Retrieved August 9, 2019 from https://www.bls.gov/iag/tgs/iag70.htm

Chartered Institute of Management Accountants. (2014). *Financial management*. London: BPP Learning Media Ltd.

Chibili, M. (2016). Basic Management Accounting for the Hospitality Industry. Noordhoff Uitgevers bv, Groningen.

DeFranco, A. L., & Lattin, T. W. (2009). *Hospitality financial management*. Hoboken, NJ: Wiley.

Dopson, L. R., & Hayes, D. K. (2009). *Managerial accounting for the hospitality industry*. Hoboken, NJ: John Wiley & Sons.

Fields, E. (2016). *The Essentials of Finance and Accounting for Nonfinancial Managers* (3rd ed.). AMACOM.

Financialaccountancy.org. (2015). *Trial balance and Income statement examples*. Accessed August 9, 2019 from http://www.financialaccountancy.org/financial-statements-an-introduction/sol-sheet-and-income-statement-solved-examples/

Goodman, P. B. (2010). *Accounting savvy for business owners: A guide to the bare essentials*. Philadelphia, PA: CPA911 Pub.

Gray, W. S. (1996). *Hospitality accounting*. Upper Saddle River, NJ: Prentice Hall.

Guilding, C. (2009). *Accounting essentials for hospitality managers*. Oxford, UK: Elsevier.

Hales, J., & Hubert, V. B. (2010). *Accounting and Financial Analysis in the Hospitality Industry (Hospitality Management Essentials Series)*. New York, NY: Pearson.

Hayes, D., Ninemeier, J. D., & Miller, A. A. (2011). *Foundations of Lodging Management* (2nd ed.). New York, NY: Pearson.

Iyengar, A. (2008). *Hotel finance*. New Delhi: Oxford University Press.

Jagels, M., & Ralston, C. E. (2010). *Hospitality management accounting*. Hoboken, NJ: Wiley.

Kotler, P. T., Bowen, J. T., James, M., & Baloglu, S. (2016). *Marketing for Hospitality and Tourism* (7th ed.). New York, NY: Pearson.

Kumar, R. (2017). *Strategic financial management casebook*. Amsterdam: Academic Press/Elsevier.

Milano, D. R., Robnett, C. S., & Milano, D. R. (2010). *The essentials of accounting I*. Piscataway, NJ: Research and Education Association.

Ninemeier, J. D. (2015). *Management of Food and Beverage Operations*. Educational Institute of the American Hotel Motel Assoc.

Ogbeide, G.-C. (2014). *Revenue management, cost control, and financial analysis in the hospitality industry*. San Diego, CA: Cognella.

Ramirez, E. (2017). *Financial management: Methods, outcomes and challenges*. Hauppauge, NY: Nova Science Publishers, Inc.

Reilly, F. K., Brown, K. C., & Leeds, S. J. (2019). *Investment analysis & portfolio management*. Boston, MA: Cengage.

Schmidgall, R. S. (2016). *Hospitality industry managerial accounting*. Lansing, MI: AHLEI American Hotel & Lodging Educational Institute.

Tainer, E. M. (2006). *Using economic indicators to improve investment analysis*. Hoboken, NJ: J. Wiley & Sons.

Woodhall, G., & Stuttard, A. (1999). *Financial Management*. London: Macmillan Education UK Imprint.

Compilation of References

About Jammu and Kashmir: Information on Tourism, Industries, Economy & Geography. (2017). Retrieved from http://www.ibef.org/download/Jammu-Kashmir-August-2017.pdf

About Jammu and Kashmir: Information on Tourism, Industries, Economy & Geography. (2018). Retrieved from http://www.ibef.org/download/Jammu-Kashmir-January-2018.pdf

Abtahi, M. S., Behboudi, L., & Hasanabad, H. M. (2017). Factors Affecting Internet Advertising Adoption in Ad Agencies. *International Journal of Innovation in the Digital Economy*, *8*(4), 18–29. doi:10.4018/IJIDE.2017100102

Agrawal, S. (2017). The Impact of Emerging Technologies and Social Media on Different Business(es): Marketing and Management. In O. Rishi & A. Sharma (Eds.), *Maximizing Business Performance and Efficiency Through Intelligent Systems* (pp. 37–49). Hershey, PA: IGI Global. doi:10.4018/978-1-5225-2234-8.ch002

Agwu, E. M. (2013, April-June). Cyber criminals on the internet super highways: A technical investigation of different shades and colours within the Nigerian cyber space. *International Journal of Online Marketing*, *3*(2), 56–74. doi:10.4018/ijom.2013040104

Agwu, M. E. (2016). ICT Diffusion, Adoption and Strategic importance in Nigerian SMEs. *International Journal of Research in Management. Science & Technology*, *4*(3), 64–75.

Ajmal, M., Tuomi, V., Helo, P., & Sandhu, M. (2016). TQM Practices in Public Sector. *International Journal of Information Systems in the Service Sector*, *8*(1), 34–44. doi:10.4018/IJISSS.2016010103

Allison, P. B. (2009). *Mystery shopper motivations and the presence of motivation crowding*. University of Central Florida.

Allison, P., Severt, D., & Dickson, D. (2010). A conceptual model for mystery shopping motivations. *Journal of Hospitality Marketing & Management*, *19*(6), 629–657. doi:10.1080/19368623.2010.493077

Alnoukari, M., Razouk, R., & Hanano, A. (2016). BSC-SI, A Framework for Integrating Strategic Intelligence in Corporate Strategic Management. *International Journal of Strategic Information Technology and Applications*, *7*(1), 32–44. doi:10.4018/IJSITA.2016010103

Alnoukari, M., Razouk, R., & Hanano, A. (2016). BSC-SI: A Framework for Integrating Strategic Intelligence in Corporate Strategic Management. *International Journal of Social and Organizational Dynamics in IT*, *5*(2), 1–14. doi:10.4018/IJSODIT.2016070101

Alonso, A. D. (2005). *Wine Tourism Experience in New Zealand: An Exploratory Study*. Lincoln University. Retrieved from https://core.ac.uk/download/pdf/35460457.pdf

Altinay, A., Mercan, N., Aksanyar, Y., & Sert, S. (2012). Işletme körlüğü, silo sendromu ve çözüm önerisi olarak örgütsel zekâ. *Organizasyon ve Yönetim Bilimleri Dergisi, 4*(1).

Altındağ, E. (2016). Current Approaches in Change Management. In A. Goksoy (Ed.), *Organizational Change Management Strategies in Modern Business* (pp. 24–51). Hershey, PA: IGI Global. doi:10.4018/978-1-4666-9533-7.ch002

Alvarez-Dionisi, L. E., Turner, R., & Mittra, M. (2016). Global Project Management Trends. *International Journal of Information Technology Project Management*, *7*(3), 54–73. doi:10.4018/IJITPM.2016070104

Amandanoventa. (2015). Mulheres que viajam sozinhas são mais autoconfiantes. Retrieved October 20, 2015, from http://viagem.estadao.com.br/blogs/amanda-viaja/mulheres-que-viajam-sozinhas-sao-mais-autoconfiantes/

Anantharaman, R. N., Rajeswari, K. S., Angusamy, A., & Kuppusamy, J. (2017). Role of Self-Efficacy and Collective Efficacy as Moderators of Occupational Stress Among Software Development Professionals. *International Journal of Human Capital and Information Technology Professionals*, *8*(2), 45–58. doi:10.4018/IJHCITP.2017040103

Andrew, W. P., Damitio, J. W., & Schmidgall, R. S. (2007). *Financial management for the hospitality industry*. Upper Saddle River, NJ: Pearson Prentice Hall.

Aninze, F., El-Gohary, H., & Hussain, J. (2018). The Role of Microfinance to Empower Women: The Case of Developing Countries. *International Journal of Customer Relationship Marketing and Management*, *9*(1), 54–78. doi:10.4018/IJCRMM.2018010104

Annual Report 2017-18. (n.d.). Ministry of Tourism Government of India. Retrieved from http://tourism.gov.in/sites/default/files/annualreports/MoT%20Annual%20Report%20201617_English.pdf

Antunes, L. (2015). 7 Relatos de mulheres para te inspirar a viajar sozinha. Retrieved October 21, 2015, from http://www.360meridianos.com/2015/01/relatos-de-mulheres-que-vao-te-inspirar-a-viajar-sozinha.html

APEDA. (2018). *Grapes*. Retrieved from www.agriexchange.apeda.gov.in: http://agriexchange.apeda.gov.in/Market%20Profile/MOA/Product/GRAPES.pdf

Aramendia-Muneta, M.E. & Ollo-Lopez, A. (2015). ICT impact on tourism industry. Retrieved from https://www.researchgate.net/publication/268563002_ICT_impact_on_tourism_industry

Arana, J. E., & León, C. J. (2008). The impact of terrorism on tourism demand. *Annals of Tourism Research*, *35*(2), 299–315. doi:10.1016/j.annals.2007.08.003

Arena Hospitality Group. (2017). *Annual Report and Accounts 2017*. Retrieved August 8, 2019 from https://www.arenahospitalitygroup.com/datastore/filestore/42/Annual_Report_and_Accounts_2017_kons.pdf

Armano, D. (2009). *Five Challenges Social Media Will Bring to Business*. Harvard Business Review. Retrieved from https://hbr.org/2009/08/a-recent-survey-conducted-by

Armstrong, J. S., & Overton, T. S. (1977). Estimating nonresponse bias in mail surveys. *JMR, Journal of Marketing Research*, *14*(3), 396–402. doi:10.1177/002224377701400320

Arsenijević, O. M., Orčić, D., & Kastratović, E. (2017). Development of an Optimization Tool for Intangibles in SMEs: A Case Study from Serbia with a Pilot Research in the Prestige by Milka Company. In M. Vemić (Ed.), *Optimal Management Strategies in Small and Medium Enterprises* (pp. 320–347). Hershey, PA: IGI Global. doi:10.4018/978-1-5225-1949-2.ch015

Aryanto, V. D., Wismantoro, Y., & Widyatmoko, K. (2018). Implementing Eco-Innovation by Utilizing the Internet to Enhance Firm's Marketing Performance: Study of Green Batik Small and Medium Enterprises in Indonesia. *International Journal of E-Business Research*, *14*(1), 21–36. doi:10.4018/IJEBR.2018010102

Athanasopoulos, G., & Hyndman, R. J. (2008). Modelling and forecasting Australian domestic tourism. *Tourism Management*, *29*(1), 19–31. doi:10.1016/j.tourman.2007.04.009

Atiku, S. O., & Fields, Z. (2017). Multicultural Orientations for 21st Century Global Leadership. In N. Baporikar (Ed.), *Management Education for Global Leadership* (pp. 28–51). Hershey, PA: IGI Global. doi:10.4018/978-1-5225-1013-0.ch002

Atiku, S. O., & Fields, Z. (2018). Organisational Learning Dimensions and Talent Retention Strategies for the Service Industries. In N. Baporikar (Ed.), *Global Practices in Knowledge Management for Societal and Organizational Development* (pp. 358–381). Hershey, PA: IGI Global. doi:10.4018/978-1-5225-3009-1.ch017

Atkinson, H., & Brander Brown, J. (2001). Rethinking performance measures: Assessing progress in UK hotels. *International Journal of Contemporary Hospitality Management*, *13*(3), 128–136. doi:10.1108/09596110110388918

auMushtaq, A. L., Ahmad Fayyaz, S., & Tanveer, A. (2013). Organizational Culture in Hotel Industry: Perceptions and Preferences among Staff. *Advances In Management*, *6*(5).

Ávila, L., & Teixeira, L. (2018). The Main Concepts Behind the Dematerialization of Business Processes. In M. Khosrow-Pour, D.B.A. (Ed.), Encyclopedia of Information Science and Technology, Fourth Edition (pp. 888-898). Hershey, PA: IGI Global. doi:10.4018/978-1-5225-2255-3.ch076

Bagozzi, R. P., Verbeke, W., & Gavino, J. C. Jr. (2003). Culture moderates the self-regulation of shame and its effects on performance: The case of salespersons in The Netherlands and the Philippines. *The Journal of Applied Psychology*, *88*(2), 219–233. doi:10.1037/0021-9010.88.2.219 PMID:12731706

Baker, D. A., & Crompton, J. L. (2000). Quality, Satisfaction and Behavioural Intentions. *Annals of Tourism Research*, *27*(3), 785–80. doi:10.1016/S0160-7383(99)00108-5

Baker, D. M. A. (2014). The effects of terrorism on the travel and tourism industry. *International Journal of Religious Tourism and Pilgrimage*, *2*(1), 9.

Bartens, Y., Chunpir, H. I., Schulte, F., & Voß, S. (2017). Business/IT Alignment in Two-Sided Markets: A COBIT 5 Analysis for Media Streaming Business Models. In S. De Haes & W. Van Grembergen (Eds.), *Strategic IT Governance and Alignment in Business Settings* (pp. 82–111). Hershey, PA: IGI Global. doi:10.4018/978-1-5225-0861-8.ch004

Bashayreh, A. M. (2018). Organizational Culture and Organizational Performance. In W. Lee & F. Sabetzadeh (Eds.), *Contemporary Knowledge and Systems Science* (pp. 50–69). Hershey, PA: IGI Global. doi:10.4018/978-1-5225-5655-8.ch003

Beck, J., Lalopa, J., & Hall, J. (2004). Insuring quality service: Training mystery shoppers. *Journal of Human Resources in Hospitality & Tourism*, *2*(2), 41–56. doi:10.1300/J171v02n02_03

Beck, J., & Miao, L. (2003). Mystery shopping in lodging properties as a measurement of service quality. *Journal of Quality Assurance in Hospitality & Tourism*, *4*(1-2), 1–21. doi:10.1300/J162v04n01_01

Bedford, D. A. (2018). Sustainable Knowledge Management Strategies: Aligning Business Capabilities and Knowledge Management Goals. In N. Baporikar (Ed.), *Global Practices in Knowledge Management for Societal and Organizational Development* (pp. 46–73). Hershey, PA: IGI Global. doi:10.4018/978-1-5225-3009-1.ch003

Benmoussa, F., Nakara, W. A., & Jaouen, A. (2016). The Use of Social Media by SMEs in the Tourism Industry. In I. Lee (Ed.), *Encyclopedia of E-Commerce Development, Implementation, and Management* (pp. 2159–2170). Hershey, PA: IGI Global. doi:10.4018/978-1-4666-9787-4.ch155

Berger, R. (2016). Indigenous Management and Bottom of Pyramid Countries: The Role of National Institutions. In U. Aung & P. Ordoñez de Pablos (Eds.), *Managerial Strategies and Practice in the Asian Business Sector* (pp. 107–123). Hershey, PA: IGI Global. doi:10.4018/978-1-4666-9758-4.ch007

Bharwani, S., & Musunuri, D. (2018). Reflection as a Process From Theory to Practice. In M. Khosrow-Pour, D.B.A. (Ed.), Encyclopedia of Information Science and Technology, Fourth Edition (pp. 1529-1539). Hershey, PA: IGI Global. doi:10.4018/978-1-5225-2255-3.ch132

Bhatt, G. D., Wang, Z., & Rodger, J. A. (2017). Information Systems Capabilities and Their Effects on Competitive Advantages: A Study of Chinese Companies. *Information Resources Management Journal*, *30*(3), 41–57. doi:10.4018/IRMJ.2017070103

Bhushan, M., & Yadav, A. (2017). Concept of Cloud Computing in ESB. In R. Bhadoria, N. Chaudhari, G. Tomar, & S. Singh (Eds.), *Exploring Enterprise Service Bus in the Service-Oriented Architecture Paradigm* (pp. 116–127). Hershey, PA: IGI Global. doi:10.4018/978-1-5225-2157-0.ch008

Bhushan, S. (2017). System Dynamics Base-Model of Humanitarian Supply Chain (HSCM) in Disaster Prone Eco-Communities of India: A Discussion on Simulation and Scenario Results. *International Journal of System Dynamics Applications*, *6*(3), 20–37. doi:10.4018/IJSDA.2017070102

Biswas, A., & De, A. K. (2017). On Development of a Fuzzy Stochastic Programming Model with Its Application to Business Management. In S. Trivedi, S. Dey, A. Kumar, & T. Panda (Eds.), *Handbook of Research on Advanced Data Mining Techniques and Applications for Business Intelligence* (pp. 353–378). Hershey, PA: IGI Global. doi:10.4018/978-1-5225-2031-3.ch021

Blake, A., & Sinclair, M. T. (2003). Tourism crisis management - US response to September 11. *Annals of Tourism Research*, *30*(4), 813–832. doi:10.1016/S0160-7383(03)00056-2

Blanke, J., Chiesa, T., & Herrera, E. T. (2009). The travel and tourism competitiveness index 2009: measuring sectoral drivers in a downturn. In J. Blanke, & T. Chiesa (Eds.), *The travel and tourism competitive report 2009* (pp. 3-38). Geneva, Switzerland: World Economic Forum.

Bloom, J. Z. Market Segmentation. (. (2005). A Neural Network Application. *Annals of Tourism Research*, *32*(1), 93–111. doi:10.1016/j.annals.2004.05.001

Bornhorst, T., Brent, R. J. R., & Sheehan, L. (2010). Determinants of tourism success for DMOs & destinations: An empirical examination of stakeholders' perspectives. *Tourism Management*, *31*(5), 572–589. doi:10.1016/j.tourman.2009.06.008

Brander Brown, J., & McDonnell, B. (1995). The balanced score-card: Short-term guest or long-term resident? *International Journal of Contemporary Hospitality Management*, *7*(2/3), 7–11. doi:10.1108/09596119510146751

Breitner, L. K., & Anthony, R. N. (2013). *Essentials of accounting*. Boston: Prentice Hall.

Brigham, E. F., & Daves, P. R. (2018). *Intermediate Financial Management* (13th ed.). Boston, MA: Cengage Learning.

Brigham, E. F., & Houston, J. F. (2019). *Fundamentals of financial management*. Boston, MA: USA Cengage.

Briston, R. J. (2018). *The Stock Exchange and investment analysis*. London: Routledge.

Bücker, J., & Ernste, K. (2018). Use of Brand Heroes in Strategic Reputation Management: The Case of Bacardi, Adidas, and Daimler. In A. Erdemir (Ed.), *Reputation Management Techniques in Public Relations* (pp. 126–150). Hershey, PA: IGI Global. doi:10.4018/978-1-5225-3619-2.ch007

Buhalis, D. (1998). Strategic use of information technologies in the tourism industry. [online]. *Tourism Management*, *19*(5), 409–421. doi:10.1016/S0261-5177(98)00038-7

Buhalis, D. (2000). Marketing the Competitive Destination of the Future. *Tourism Management, 21*(1), 97–116. doi:10.1016/S0261-5177(99)00095-3

Buhalis, D., & Law, R. (2008). Progress in information technology and tourism management: 20 years on and 10 years after the Internet—The state of eTourism research. *Tourism Management, 29*(4), 609–623. doi:10.1016/j.tourman.2008.01.005

Buhalis, D., & Licata, C. (2002). The future eTourism intermediaries. *Tourism Management, 23*(3), 207–220. doi:10.1016/S0261-5177(01)00085-1

Bureau of Labor Statistics. (2019). *Industries at a glance: Leisure and Hospitality*. Retrieved August 9, 2019 from https://www.bls.gov/iag/tgs/iag70.htm

Bureš, V. (2018). Industry 4.0 From the Systems Engineering Perspective: Alternative Holistic Framework Development. In R. Brunet-Thornton & F. Martinez (Eds.), *Analyzing the Impacts of Industry 4.0 in Modern Business Environments* (pp. 199–223). Hershey, PA: IGI Global. doi:10.4018/978-1-5225-3468-6.ch011

Buzady, Z. (2017). Resolving the Magic Cube of Effective Case Teaching: Benchmarking Case Teaching Practices in Emerging Markets – Insights from the Central European University Business School, Hungary. In D. Latusek (Ed.), *Case Studies as a Teaching Tool in Management Education* (pp. 79–103). Hershey, PA: IGI Global. doi:10.4018/978-1-5225-0770-3.ch005

Calder, J., & Edward, C. (2005). Managing Media and Advertising Change with Integrated Marketing. *Journal of Advertising Research*, *45*(4), 1–6.

Calder, J., Edward, C., & Ute, S. (2009). An Experimental Study of the Relationship Between Online Engagement and Advertising Effectiveness. *Journal of Interactive Marketing*, *23*(November), 321–331. doi:10.1016/j.intmar.2009.07.002

Calori, R., & Sarnin, P. (1991). Corporate culture and economic performance: A French study. *Organization studies, 12*(1), 049-74.

Calvert, P. (2005). It's a mystery: Mystery shopping in New Zealand's public libraries. *Library Review*, *54*(1), 24–35. doi:10.1108/00242530510574138

Cameron, K. S., & Freeman, S. J. (1991). Cultural congruence, strength, and type: Relationships to effectiveness. *Research in Organizational Change and Development*, *5*, 23–58.

Cameron, K. S., & Quinn, R. E. (1999). *Diagnosing and changing organisational culture*. Reading: Addison-Wesley.

Campatelli, G., Richter, A., & Stocker, A. (2016). Participative Knowledge Management to Empower Manufacturing Workers. *International Journal of Knowledge Management*, *12*(4), 37–50. doi:10.4018/IJKM.2016100103

Campbell, D. J., Bommer, W., & Yeo, E. (1993). Perceptions of appropriate leadership style: Participation versus consultation across two cultures. *Asia Pacific Journal of Management*, *10*(1), 1–19. doi:10.1007/BF01732221

Căpusneanu, S., & Topor, D. I. (2018). Business Ethics and Cost Management in SMEs: Theories of Business Ethics and Cost Management Ethos. In I. Oncioiu (Ed.), *Ethics and Decision-Making for Sustainable Business Practices* (pp. 109–127). Hershey, PA: IGI Global. doi:10.4018/978-1-5225-3773-1.ch007

Carneiro, A. (2016). Maturity in Health Organization Information Systems: Metrics and Privacy Perspectives. *International Journal of Privacy and Health Information Management*, *4*(2), 1–18. doi:10.4018/IJPHIM.2016070101

Carr, N. (2000). An exploratory study of young women's use of leisure spaces and times: Constrained, negotiated, or unconstrained behaviour? *World Leisure Journal*, *42*(3), 25–32. doi:10.1080/04419057.2000.9674193

Carvalho, G., Baptista, M. M., & Costa, C. (2015). Brazilian women's perception of risk when travelling alone. In Risk in travel and tourism: Geographies, behaviours and strategies (pp. 22–25). Lisbon: ATLAS: Association for Tourism and Leisure Education and Research.

Chandan, H. C. (2016). Motivations and Challenges of Female Entrepreneurship in Developed and Developing Economies. In N. Baporikar (Ed.), *Handbook of Research on Entrepreneurship in the Contemporary Knowledge-Based Global Economy* (pp. 260–286). Hershey, PA: IGI Global. doi:10.4018/978-1-4666-8798-1.ch012

Chan, R. L., Mo, P. L., & Moon, K. K. (2018). Strategic and Tactical Measures in Managing Enterprise Risks: A Study of the Textile and Apparel Industry. In K. Strang, M. Korstanje, & N. Vajjhala (Eds.), *Research, Practices, and Innovations in Global Risk and Contingency Management* (pp. 1–19). Hershey, PA: IGI Global. doi:10.4018/978-1-5225-4754-9.ch001

Charlier, S. D., Burke-Smalley, L. A., & Fisher, S. L. (2018). Undergraduate Programs in the U.S: A Contextual and Content-Based Analysis. In J. Mendy (Ed.), *Teaching Human Resources and Organizational Behavior at the College Level* (pp. 26–57). Hershey, PA: IGI Global. doi:10.4018/978-1-5225-2820-3.ch002

Chartered Institute of Management Accountants. (2014). *Financial management*. London: BPP Learning Media Ltd.

Chatman, J. A., & Jehn, K. A. (1994). Assessing the relationship between industry characteristics and organizational culture: How different can you be? *Academy of Management Journal*, *37*(3), 522–553. doi:10.5465/256699

Chaudhuri, S. (2016). Application of Web-Based Geographical Information System (GIS) in E-Business. In U. Panwar, R. Kumar, & N. Ray (Eds.), *Handbook of Research on Promotional Strategies and Consumer Influence in the Service Sector* (pp. 389–405). Hershey, PA: IGI Global. doi:10.4018/978-1-5225-0143-5.ch023

Chen, Y., Scott Fay, S., & Wang, Q. (2011). The Role of Marketing in Social Media: How Online Consumer Reviews Evolve. *Journal of Interactive Marketing*, *25*(2), 85–94. doi:10.1016/j.intmar.2011.01.003

Chiang, C.-Y., & Jogaratnam, G. (2006). Why do women travel solo for purposes of leisure? *Journal of Vacation Marketing*, *12*(1), 59–70. doi:10.1177/1356766706059041

Chibili, M. (2016). Basic Management Accounting for the Hospitality Industry. Noordhoff Uitgevers bv, Groningen.

Choudhuri, P. S. (2016). An Empirical Study on the Quality of Services Offered by the Private Life Insurers in Burdwan. In U. Panwar, R. Kumar, & N. Ray (Eds.), *Handbook of Research on Promotional Strategies and Consumer Influence in the Service Sector* (pp. 31–55). Hershey, PA: IGI Global. doi:10.4018/978-1-5225-0143-5.ch002

Chu, F. L. (2008). A fractionally integrated autoregressive moving average approach to forecasting tourism demand. *Tourism Management*, *29*(1), 79–88. doi:10.1016/j.tourman.2007.04.003

Claveria, O., Monte, E., & Torra, S. (2015). A new forecasting approach for the hospitality industry. *International Journal of Contemporary Hospitality Management*, *27*(7), 1520–1538. doi:10.1108/IJCHM-06-2014-0286

Collins, D., & Tisdell, C. (2002). Gender and differences in travel life cycles. *Journal of Travel Research*, *41*(2), 133–143. doi:10.1177/004728702237413

Comptoir Libanais. (2019). *Overview*. Retrieved from https://investors.comptoirlibanais.com/

Coombs, W. T. (2012). *Ongoing crisis communication: planning, managing, and responding* (3rd ed.). Thousand Oaks, CA: Sage.

Corbetta, P. (2003). Social research: Theory, methods and techniques. London: SAGE Publications; doi:10.4135/9781849209922.

Cordeiro, I. (2008). *Instrumentos de avaliação da sustentabilidade do turismo: Uma análise crítica*. Dissertação de Mestrado, Universidade Nova de Lisboa.

Correia, A. M., Cerqueira, A., & Brandao, E. (2015). *Determinants of corporate capital structure: evidence from non-financial listed French firms*. FEP Working Papers.

Crosby, P. (1967). Cutting the cost of quality. Industrial Education Institute.

Cui, X., & Hu, J. (2012). A literature review on organization culture and corporate performance. *International Journal of Business Administration*, *3*(2), 28. doi:10.5430/ijba.v3n2p28

Dahlberg, T., Kivijärvi, H., & Saarinen, T. (2017). IT Investment Consistency and Other Factors Influencing the Success of IT Performance. In S. De Haes & W. Van Grembergen (Eds.), *Strategic IT Governance and Alignment in Business Settings* (pp. 176–208). Hershey, PA: IGI Global. doi:10.4018/978-1-5225-0861-8.ch007

Damnjanović, A. M. (2017). Knowledge Management Optimization through IT and E-Business Utilization: A Qualitative Study on Serbian SMEs. In M. Vemić (Ed.), *Optimal Management Strategies in Small and Medium Enterprises* (pp. 249–267). Hershey, PA: IGI Global. doi:10.4018/978-1-5225-1949-2.ch012

Daneshpour, H. (2017). Integrating Sustainable Development into Project Portfolio Management through Application of Open Innovation. In M. Vemić (Ed.), *Optimal Management Strategies in Small and Medium Enterprises* (pp. 370–387). Hershey, PA: IGI Global. doi:10.4018/978-1-5225-1949-2.ch017

Daniel, A. D., & Reis de Castro, V. (2018). Entrepreneurship Education: How to Measure the Impact on Nascent Entrepreneurs. In A. Carrizo Moreira, J. Guilherme Leitão Dantas, & F. Manuel Valente (Eds.), *Nascent Entrepreneurship and Successful New Venture Creation* (pp. 85–110). Hershey, PA: IGI Global. doi:10.4018/978-1-5225-2936-1.ch004

David, F., van der Sijde, P., & van den Besselaar, P. (2016). Enterpreneurial Incentives, Obstacles, and Management in University-Business Co-Operation: The Case of Indonesia. In J. Saiz-Álvarez (Ed.), *Handbook of Research on Social Entrepreneurship and Solidarity Economics* (pp. 499–518). Hershey, PA: IGI Global. doi:10.4018/978-1-5225-0097-1.ch024

David, R., Swami, B. N., & Tangirala, S. (2018). Ethics Impact on Knowledge Management in Organizational Development: A Case Study. In N. Baporikar (Ed.), *Global Practices in Knowledge Management for Societal and Organizational Development* (pp. 19–45). Hershey, PA: IGI Global. doi:10.4018/978-1-5225-3009-1.ch002

Dawson, J., & Hillier, J. (1995). Competitor mystery shopping: Methodological considerations and implications for the MRS code of conduct. *Journal of the Market Research Society*, *37*(4), 417–428. doi:10.1177/147078539503700406

Dayananda, K. (2014). Tourism and Employment: Opportunities and Challenges in Karnataka - Special Reference to Kodagu District. *IOSR Journal of Humanities and Social Science,* 19, 11.

DeFranco, A. L., & Lattin, T. W. (2009). *Hospitality financial management.* Hoboken, NJ: Wiley.

Delias, P., & Lakiotaki, K. (2018). Discovering Process Horizontal Boundaries to Facilitate Process Comprehension. *International Journal of Operations Research and Information Systems*, *9*(2), 1–31. doi:10.4018/IJORIS.2018040101

Deming, W. E. (1982). *Quality, Productivity and Competitive Position.* Cambridge: MIT Press.

Denholm, J., & Lee-Davies, L. (2018). Success Factors for Games in Business and Project Management. In *Enhancing Education and Training Initiatives Through Serious Games* (pp. 34–68). Hershey, PA: IGI Global. doi:10.4018/978-1-5225-3689-5.ch002

Deshpande, M. (2017). Best Practices in Management Institutions for Global Leadership: Policy Aspects. In N. Baporikar (Ed.), *Management Education for Global Leadership* (pp. 1–27). Hershey, PA: IGI Global. doi:10.4018/978-1-5225-1013-0.ch001

Deshpande, M. (2018). Policy Perspectives for SMEs Knowledge Management. In N. Baporikar (Ed.), *Knowledge Integration Strategies for Entrepreneurship and Sustainability* (pp. 23–46). Hershey, PA: IGI Global. doi:10.4018/978-1-5225-5115-7.ch002

Deshpandé, R., Farley, J. U., & Webster, F. E. Jr. (1993). Corporate culture, customer orientation, and innovativeness in Japanese firms: A quadrad analysis. *Journal of Marketing*, *57*(1), 23–37. doi:10.1177/002224299305700102

Dezdar, S. (2017). ERP Implementation Projects in Asian Countries: A Comparative Study on Iran and China. *International Journal of Information Technology Project Management*, *8*(3), 52–68. doi:10.4018/IJITPM.2017070104

Dias, J. (2016). Environmental sustainability measurement in the Travel & Tourism Competitiveness Index: An empirical analysis of its reliability. *Ecological Indicators*, *73*, 589–596. doi:10.1016/j.ecolind.2016.10.008

Domestic Tourist Arrival in Kashmir. (n.d.) Retrieved from http://www.Jammuandkashmirstat.com/tourism/29/stats.aspx

Domingos, D., Martinho, R., & Varajão, J. (2016). Controlled Flexibility in Healthcare Processes: A BPMN-Extension Approach. In M. Cruz-Cunha, I. Miranda, R. Martinho, & R. Rijo (Eds.), *Encyclopedia of E-Health and Telemedicine* (pp. 521–535). Hershey, PA: IGI Global. doi:10.4018/978-1-4666-9978-6.ch040

Domingos, D., Respício, A., & Martinho, R. (2017). Reliability of IoT-Aware BPMN Healthcare Processes. In C. Reis & M. Maximiano (Eds.), *Internet of Things and Advanced Application in Healthcare* (pp. 214–248). Hershey, PA: IGI Global. doi:10.4018/978-1-5225-1820-4.ch008

Dopson, L. R., & Hayes, D. K. (2009). *Managerial accounting for the hospitality industry*. Hoboken, NJ: John Wiley & Sons.

Doran, M., Haddad, K., & Chow, C. (2003). The Relationship between Corporate Culture and Performance in Bahrain Hotels. *International Journal of Hospitality & Tourism Administration*, *4*(3), 3. doi:10.1300/J149v04n03_04

Dosumu, O., Hussain, J., & El-Gohary, H. (2017). An Exploratory Study of the Impact of Government Policies on the Development of Small and Medium Enterprises in Developing Countries: The Case of Nigeria. *International Journal of Customer Relationship Marketing and Management*, *8*(4), 51–62. doi:10.4018/IJCRMM.2017100104

Durst, S., Bruns, G., & Edvardsson, I. R. (2017). Retaining Knowledge in Smaller Building and Construction Firms. *International Journal of Knowledge and Systems Science*, *8*(3), 1–12. doi:10.4018/IJKSS.2017070101

Edvardsson, I. R., & Durst, S. (2017). Outsourcing, Knowledge, and Learning: A Critical Review. *International Journal of Knowledge-Based Organizations*, *7*(2), 13–26. doi:10.4018/IJKBO.2017040102

Edwards, J. S. (2018). Integrating Knowledge Management and Business Processes. In M. Khosrow-Pour, D.B.A. (Ed.), Encyclopedia of Information Science and Technology, Fourth Edition (pp. 5046-5055). Hershey, PA: IGI Global. doi:10.4018/978-1-5225-2255-3.ch437

Ejiogu, A. O. (2018). Economics of Farm Management. In *Agricultural Finance and Opportunities for Investment and Expansion* (pp. 56–72). Hershey, PA: IGI Global. doi:10.4018/978-1-5225-3059-6.ch003

Ekanem, I., & Abiade, G. E. (2018). Factors Influencing the Use of E-Commerce by Small Enterprises in Nigeria. *International Journal of ICT Research in Africa and the Middle East*, *7*(1), 37–53. doi:10.4018/IJICTRAME.2018010103

Ekanem, I., & Alrossais, L. A. (2017). Succession Challenges Facing Family Businesses in Saudi Arabia. In P. Zgheib (Ed.), *Entrepreneurship and Business Innovation in the Middle East* (pp. 122–146). Hershey, PA: IGI Global. doi:10.4018/978-1-5225-2066-5.ch007

El Faquih, L., & Fredj, M. (2017). Ontology-Based Framework for Quality in Configurable Process Models. *Journal of Electronic Commerce in Organizations*, *15*(2), 48–60. doi:10.4018/JECO.2017040104

Eleren, A., & Kılıç, B. (2007). Turizm sektöründe SERVQUAL analizi ile hizmet kalitesinin ölçülmesi ve bir termal otelde uygulama. *Afyon Kocatepe Üniversitesi, İİBF Dergisi*, *IX-1*, 235–263.

El-Gohary, H., & El-Gohary, Z. (2016). An Attempt to Explore Electronic Marketing Adoption and Implementation Aspects in Developing Countries: The Case of Egypt. *International Journal of Customer Relationship Marketing and Management*, *7*(4), 1–26. doi:10.4018/IJCRMM.2016100101

Enders, W. & Sandler, T. (1991). Causality between Transnational Terrorism and Tourism: The Case of Spain. *Terrorism*, *14*(January), 49–58.

Enders, W., Sandler, T., & Parise, G. (1992). An Econometric Analysis of the Impact of Terrorism on Tourism. *Kylos*, *45*(4), 531–554. doi:10.1111/j.1467-6435.1992.tb02758.x

Entico, G. J. (2016). Knowledge Management and the Medical Health Librarians: A Perception Study. In J. Yap, M. Perez, M. Ayson, & G. Entico (Eds.), *Special Library Administration, Standardization and Technological Integration* (pp. 52–77). Hershey, PA: IGI Global. doi:10.4018/978-1-4666-9542-9.ch003

Erica Croce, G. P. (2017). Food and Wine Tourism (2nd ed.). CABI.

Erstad, M. (1998). Mystery shopping programmes and human resource management. *International Journal of Contemporary Hospitality Management*, *10*(1), 34–38. doi:10.1108/09596119810199318

Faisal, M. N., & Talib, F. (2017). Building Ambidextrous Supply Chains in SMEs: How to Tackle the Barriers? *International Journal of Information Systems and Supply Chain Management*, *10*(4), 80–100. doi:10.4018/IJISSCM.2017100105

Fernandes, T. M., Gomes, J., & Romão, M. (2017). Investments in E-Government: A Benefit Management Case Study. *International Journal of Electronic Government Research*, *13*(3), 1–17. doi:10.4018/IJEGR.2017070101

Fields, E. (2016). *The Essentials of Finance and Accounting for Nonfinancial Managers* (3rd ed.). AMACOM.

Financialaccountancy.org. (2015). *Trial balance and Income statement examples.* Accessed August 9, 2019 from http://www.financialaccountancy.org/financial-statements-an-introduction/sol-sheet-and-income-statement-solved-examples/

Flick, U. (2007). Designing qualitative research. London: SAGE Publications; doi:10.4135/9781849208826.

Food Standards Agency (2019). *Food Hygiene Rating Scheme.* Retrieved from https://www.food.gov.uk/safety-hygiene/food-hygiene-rating-scheme

Fouda, F. A. (2016). A Suggested Curriculum in Career Education to Develop Business Secondary Schools Students' Career Knowledge Management Domains and Professional Thinking. *International Journal of Technology Diffusion*, *7*(2), 42–62. doi:10.4018/IJTD.2016040103

Frost & Sullivan. (2016). Social media customer engagement. Retrieved from http://frostftp.com/JE/Events/CC/Sitel/Social_Media_Customer_Engagement.pdf

Gallardo-Vázquez, D., & Pajuelo-Moreno, M. L. (2016). How Spanish Universities are Promoting Entrepreneurship through Your Own Lines of Teaching and Research? In L. Carvalho (Ed.), *Handbook of Research on Entrepreneurial Success and its Impact on Regional Development* (pp. 431–454). Hershey, PA: IGI Global. doi:10.4018/978-1-4666-9567-2.ch019

Gallaugher, J., & Ransbotham, S. (2010). Social media and customer dialog management at Starbucks. *MIS Quarterly Executive*, *9*, 1389–1404.

Gao, S. S., Oreal, S., & Zhang, J. (2018). Contemporary Financial Risk Management Perceptions and Practices of Small-Sized Chinese Businesses. In I. Management Association (Ed.), Global Business Expansion: Concepts, Methodologies, Tools, and Applications (pp. 917-931). Hershey, PA: IGI Global. doi:10.4018/978-1-5225-5481-3.ch041

Garg, R., & Berning, S. C. (2017). Indigenous Chinese Management Philosophies: Key Concepts and Relevance for Modern Chinese Firms. In B. Christiansen & G. Koc (Eds.), *Transcontinental Strategies for Industrial Development and Economic Growth* (pp. 43–57). Hershey, PA: IGI Global. doi:10.4018/978-1-5225-2160-0.ch003

Gencer, Y. G. (2017). Supply Chain Management in Retailing Business. In U. Akkucuk (Ed.), *Ethics and Sustainability in Global Supply Chain Management* (pp. 197–210). Hershey, PA: IGI Global. doi:10.4018/978-1-5225-2036-8.ch011

Gentles, S. J., Charles, C., & Ploeg, J. (2015). Sampling in qualitative research. The SAGE Encyclopedia of Social Science Research Methods, 20(11), 1772–1789. doi:10.4135/9781412950589.n885

Getz, D. (1998). Wine tourism: Global overview and perspectives on its development. In R. a. Dowling (Ed.), *Wine Tourism-Perfect Partners, Proceedings of the First Australian Wine Tourism Conference*. Canberra: Bureau of Tourism Research.

GhulamRabbany, M., Afrin, S., Rahman, A., Islam, F., & Hoque, F., (2013). Environmental effects of tourism. *American Journal of Environment, Energy and Power Research, 1*(7), 117-130

Giacosa, E. (2016). Innovation in Luxury Fashion Businesses as a Means for the Regional Development. In L. Carvalho (Ed.), *Handbook of Research on Entrepreneurial Success and its Impact on Regional Development* (pp. 206–222). Hershey, PA: IGI Global. doi:10.4018/978-1-4666-9567-2.ch010

Giacosa, E. (2018). The Increasing of the Regional Development Thanks to the Luxury Business Innovation. In L. Carvalho (Ed.), *Handbook of Research on Entrepreneurial Ecosystems and Social Dynamics in a Globalized World* (pp. 260–273). Hershey, PA: IGI Global. doi:10.4018/978-1-5225-3525-6.ch011

Gianni, M., & Gotzamani, K. (2016). Integrated Management Systems and Information Management Systems: Common Threads. In P. Papajorgji, F. Pinet, A. Guimarães, & J. Papathanasiou (Eds.), *Automated Enterprise Systems for Maximizing Business Performance* (pp. 195–214). Hershey, PA: IGI Global. doi:10.4018/978-1-4666-8841-4.ch011

Gianni, M., Gotzamani, K., & Linden, I. (2016). How a BI-wise Responsible Integrated Management System May Support Food Traceability. *International Journal of Decision Support System Technology*, *8*(2), 1–17. doi:10.4018/IJDSST.2016040101

Glykas, M., & George, J. (2017). Quality and Process Management Systems in the UAE Maritime Industry. *International Journal of Productivity Management and Assessment Technologies*, *5*(1), 20–39. doi:10.4018/IJPMAT.2017010102

Glykas, M., Valiris, G., Kokkinaki, A., & Koutsoukou, Z. (2018). Banking Business Process Management Implementation. *International Journal of Productivity Management and Assessment Technologies*, *6*(1), 50–69. doi:10.4018/IJPMAT.2018010104

Goetsch, D. L., & Davis, S. B. (2014). *Quality Management for Organisational Excellence* (7th ed.). USA: Pearson.

Goetzl, D., & Healy, B. (2000). Turkey lures visitors with historical appeal. *Advertising Age*, *71*(26), 50–51.

Gomes, J., & Romão, M. (2017). Aligning Information Systems and Technology with Benefit Management and Balanced Scorecard. In S. De Haes & W. Van Grembergen (Eds.), *Strategic IT Governance and Alignment in Business Settings* (pp. 112–131). Hershey, PA: IGI Global. doi:10.4018/978-1-5225-0861-8.ch005

Gomes, J., & Romão, M. (2017). The Balanced Scorecard: Keeping Updated and Aligned with Today's Business Trends. *International Journal of Productivity Management and Assessment Technologies*, *5*(2), 1–15. doi:10.4018/IJPMAT.2017070101

Goodman, P. B. (2010). *Accounting savvy for business owners: A guide to the bare essentials.* Philadelphia, PA: CPA911 Pub.

Goodrich, J. N. (2001). September 11, 2001 attack on America: A record of the immediate impacts and reactions in the USA travel and tourism industry. *Tourism Management, 23*(6), 573–580. doi:10.1016/S0261-5177(02)00029-8

Gordon, G., & Christensen, E. (1993). Industry influences on the relationships between management culture and performance. In *annual meeting of the Academy of Management, Atlanta, GA*.

Gordon, G. G., & DiTomaso, N. (1992). Predicting corporate performance from organizational culture. *Journal of Management Studies, 29*(6), 783–798. doi:10.1111/j.1467-6486.1992.tb00689.x

Gössling, S., Scott, D., & Hall, C. (2013). Challenges of tourism in a low-carbon economy. *WIREs Clim Change, 4*(6), 525–538. doi:10.1002/wcc.243

Gray, W. S. (1996). *Hospitality accounting*. Upper Saddle River, NJ: Prentice Hall.

Grefen, P., & Turetken, O. (2017). Advanced Business Process Management in Networked E-Business Scenarios. *International Journal of E-Business Research, 13*(4), 70–104. doi:10.4018/IJEBR.2017100105

Guest, G., Bunce, A., & Johnson, L. (2006). How many interviews are enough? An experiment with data saturation and variability. *Field Methods, 18*(1), 59–82. doi:10.1177/1525822X05279903

Guilding, C. (2009). *Accounting essentials for hospitality managers*. Oxford, UK: Elsevier.

Hai. A.M, Chik.R.A (2011) Political stability: country image for tourism industry in Bangladesh.

Haider, A., & Saetang, S. (2017). Strategic IT Alignment in Service Sector. In S. Rozenes & Y. Cohen (Eds.), *Handbook of Research on Strategic Alliances and Value Co-Creation in the Service Industry* (pp. 231–258). Hershey, PA: IGI Global. doi:10.4018/978-1-5225-2084-9.ch012

Haider, A., & Tang, S. S. (2016). Maximising Value Through IT and Business Alignment: A Case of IT Governance Institutionalisation at a Thai Bank. *International Journal of Technology Diffusion, 7*(3), 33–58. doi:10.4018/IJTD.2016070104

Hair, J. F. Jr, Hult, G. T. M., Ringle, C., & Sarstedt, M. (2016). *A primer on partial least squares structural equation modeling (PLS-SEM)*. Sage Publications.

Hair, J. F., Ringle, C. M., & Sarstedt, M. (2011). PLS-SEM: Indeed a silver bullet. *Journal of Marketing Theory and Practice, 19*(2), 139–152. doi:10.2753/MTP1069-6679190202

Hajilari, A. B., Ghadaksaz, M., & Fasghandis, G. S. (2017). Assessing Organizational Readiness for Implementing ERP System Using Fuzzy Expert System Approach. *International Journal of Enterprise Information Systems, 13*(1), 67–85. doi:10.4018/IJEIS.2017010105

Haldorai, A., Ramu, A., & Murugan, S. (2018). Social Aware Cognitive Radio Networks: Effectiveness of Social Networks as a Strategic Tool for Organizational Business Management. In H. Bansal, G. Shrivastava, G. Nguyen, & L. Stanciu (Eds.), *Social Network Analytics for Contemporary Business Organizations* (pp. 188–202). Hershey, PA: IGI Global. doi:10.4018/978-1-5225-5097-6.ch010

Hales, J., & Hubert, V. B. (2010). *Accounting and Financial Analysis in the Hospitality Industry (Hospitality Management Essentials Series)*. New York, NY: Pearson.

Hall, O. P. Jr. (2017). Social Media Driven Management Education. *International Journal of Knowledge-Based Organizations, 7*(2), 43–59. doi:10.4018/IJKBO.2017040104

Han, H., & Verma, R. (2012). The Effect of Corporate Culture and Strategic Orientation on Financial Performance: An analysis of the South Korean Upscale and Luxury Hotels. *Cornell Hospitality Report, 12*(4), 6–14.

Hanifah, H., Halim, H. A., Ahmad, N. H., & Vafaei-Zadeh, A. (2017). Innovation Culture as a Mediator Between Specific Human Capital and Innovation Performance Among Bumiputera SMEs in Malaysia. In N. Ahmad, T. Ramayah, H. Halim, & S. Rahman (Eds.), *Handbook of Research on Small and Medium Enterprises in Developing Countries* (pp. 261–279). Hershey, PA: IGI Global. doi:10.4018/978-1-5225-2165-5.ch012

Harris, P. J., & Mongiello, M. (2001). Key performance indicators in European hotel properties: General managers' choices and company profiles. *International Journal of Contemporary Hospitality Management, 13*(3), 120–128. doi:10.1108/09596110110388909

Hartlieb, S., & Silvius, G. (2017). Handling Uncertainty in Project Management and Business Development: Similarities and Differences. In Y. Raydugin (Ed.), *Handbook of Research on Leveraging Risk and Uncertainties for Effective Project Management* (pp. 337–362). Hershey, PA: IGI Global. doi:10.4018/978-1-5225-1790-0.ch016

Hassan, A., & Privitera, D. S. (2016). Google AdSense as a Mobile Technology in Education. In J. Holland (Ed.), *Wearable Technology and Mobile Innovations for Next-Generation Education* (pp. 200–223). Hershey, PA: IGI Global. doi:10.4018/978-1-5225-0069-8.ch011

Hassan, A., & Rahimi, R. (2016). Consuming "Innovation" in Tourism: Augmented Reality as an Innovation Tool in Digital Tourism Marketing. In N. Pappas & I. Bregoli (Eds.), *Global Dynamics in Travel, Tourism, and Hospitality* (pp. 130–147). Hershey, PA: IGI Global. doi:10.4018/978-1-5225-0201-2.ch008

Hass, K. B. (2017). Living on the Edge: Managing Project Complexity. In Y. Raydugin (Ed.), *Handbook of Research on Leveraging Risk and Uncertainties for Effective Project Management* (pp. 177–201). Hershey, PA: IGI Global. doi:10.4018/978-1-5225-1790-0.ch009

Haven, B. (2007). Marketing's New Key Metric: Engagement. *Forrester Research.*

Hawking, P., & Carmine Sellitto, C. (2017). Developing an Effective Strategy for Organizational Business Intelligence. In M. Tavana (Ed.), *Enterprise Information Systems and the Digitalization of Business Functions* (pp. 222–237). Hershey, PA: IGI Global. doi:10.4018/978-1-5225-2382-6.ch010

Hawking, P., & Sellitto, C. (2017). A Fast-Moving Consumer Goods Company and Business Intelligence Strategy Development. *International Journal of Enterprise Information Systems, 13*(2), 22–33. doi:10.4018/IJEIS.2017040102

Hawking, P., & Sellitto, C. (2017). Business Intelligence Strategy: Two Case Studies. *International Journal of Business Intelligence Research*, *8*(2), 17–30. doi:10.4018/IJBIR.2017070102

Hayes, D. K., Ninemeier, J. D., & Miller, A. A. (2012). *Foundations of Lodging Management* (2nd ed.). Pearson.

Haynes, J. D., Arockiasamy, S., Al Rashdi, M., & Al Rashdi, S. (2016). Business and E Business Strategies for Coopetition and Thematic Management as a Sustained Basis for Ethics and Social Responsibility in Emerging Markets. In M. Al-Shammari & H. Masri (Eds.), *Ethical and Social Perspectives on Global Business Interaction in Emerging Markets* (pp. 25–39). Hershey, PA: IGI Global. doi:10.4018/978-1-4666-9864-2.ch002

Hee, W. J., Jalleh, G., Lai, H., & Lin, C. (2017). E-Commerce and IT Projects: Evaluation and Management Issues in Australian and Taiwanese Hospitals. *International Journal of Public Health Management and Ethics*, *2*(1), 69–90. doi:10.4018/IJPHME.2017010104

Heimtun, B. (2012). The friend, the loner and the independent traveller: Norwegian midlife single women's social identities when on holiday. *Gender, Place and Culture*, *19*(1), 83–101. doi:10.1080/0966369X.2011.617881

Hermalin, B. E., & Weisbach, M. S. (1991). The effects of board composition and direct incentives on firm performance. *Financial Management*, *20*(4), 101–112. doi:10.2307/3665716

Hernandez, A. A. (2018). Exploring the Factors to Green IT Adoption of SMEs in the Philippines. *Journal of Cases on Information Technology*, *20*(2), 49–66. doi:10.4018/JCIT.2018040104

Hernandez, A. A., & Ona, S. E. (2016). Green IT Adoption: Lessons from the Philippines Business Process Outsourcing Industry. *International Journal of Social Ecology and Sustainable Development*, *7*(1), 1–34. doi:10.4018/IJSESD.2016010101

Hesselink, M., van der Wiele, T., & Shopping, M. (2003). *In-Depth Measurement of Shopper Satisfaction*. ERIM Report Series Reference No. ERS-2003-020-ORG. Available at SSRN: https://ssrn.com/abstract=411653

Hesselink, M., van Iwaarden, J., & van der Wiele, T. (2004). Mystery shopping: A tool to develop insight into shopper service provision. *ERIM Report Series Research in Management, 9*(3).

Hollman, A., Bickford, S., & Hollman, T. (2017). Cyber InSecurity: A Post-Mortem Attempt to Assess Cyber Problems from IT and Business Management Perspectives. *Journal of Cases on Information Technology*, *19*(3), 42–70. doi:10.4018/JCIT.2017070104

Hotelstars Union. (2019). *The System of the Hotelstars Union.* Retrieved from https://www.hotelstars.eu/system/description/

Huang, J. H., & Min, J. C. H. (2002). Earthquake devastation and recovery in tourism: The Taiwan case. *Tourism Management*, *23*(2), 145–154. doi:10.1016/S0261-5177(01)00051-6

Hudrea, A. (2006). Organizational Culture. *Transylvanian Review of Administrative Sciences*, *2*(16), 47–56.

Hudson, S., Snaith, T., Miller, G. A., & Hudson, P. (2001). Distribution channels in the travel industry: Using mystery shoppers to understand the influence of travel agency recommendations. *Journal of Travel Research, 40*(2), 148–154. doi:10.1177/004728750104000205

Hu, N., Liu, L., & Zhang, J. (2008). Do online reviews affect product sales? The role of reviewer characteristics and temporal effects. *Information Technology Management, 9*(3), 201–214. doi:10.100710799-008-0041-2

IBGE – Instituto Brasileiro de Geografia e Estatística. (2015). *Estatísticas – população*. Available at: https://www.ibge.gov.br/estatisticas-novoportal/sociais/populacao.html

Igbinakhase, I. (2017). Responsible and Sustainable Management Practices in Developing and Developed Business Environments. In Z. Fields (Ed.), *Collective Creativity for Responsible and Sustainable Business Practice* (pp. 180–207). Hershey, PA: IGI Global. doi:10.4018/978-1-5225-1823-5.ch010

Ilahi, L., Ghannouchi, S. A., & Martinho, R. (2016). A Business Process Management Approach to Home Healthcare Processes: On the Gap between Intention and Reality. In M. Cruz-Cunha, I. Miranda, R. Martinho, & R. Rijo (Eds.), *Encyclopedia of E-Health and Telemedicine* (pp. 439–457). Hershey, PA: IGI Global. doi:10.4018/978-1-4666-9978-6.ch035

India Tourism Statistics. (2015). Retrieved from http://tourism.gov.in/market-research-and-statistics

India Tourism Statistics. (2017). Retrieved from http://tourism.gov.in/market-research-and-statistics

India Tourism Statistics. (2018). Retrieved from http://tourism.gov.in/market-research-and-statistics

International labour organization. (2010). *Development and Challenges in Tourism and Hospitality Sector.*

International Organisation for Standardisation. (2019). *Standards.* Retrieved from https://www.iso.org/standards.html

Itoo, M.A. (2013). Tourism industry of Kashmir (1947-1989). *International journal of management and sustainability, 2*(4), 63-71.

Iwata, J. J., & Hoskins, R. G. (2017). Managing Indigenous Knowledge in Tanzania: A Business Perspective. In P. Jain & N. Mnjama (Eds.), *Managing Knowledge Resources and Records in Modern Organizations* (pp. 198–214). Hershey, PA: IGI Global. doi:10.4018/978-1-5225-1965-2.ch012

Iyengar, A. (2008). *Hotel finance*. New Delhi: Oxford University Press.

Jabeen, F., Ahmad, S. Z., & Alkaabi, S. (2016). The Internationalization Decision-Making of United Arab Emirates Family Businesses. In N. Zakaria, A. Abdul-Talib, & N. Osman (Eds.), *Handbook of Research on Impacts of International Business and Political Affairs on the Global Economy* (pp. 1–22). Hershey, PA: IGI Global. doi:10.4018/978-1-4666-9806-2.ch001

Jagels, M., & Ralston, C. E. (2010). *Hospitality management accounting*. Hoboken, NJ: Wiley.

Jain, P. (2017). Ethical and Legal Issues in Knowledge Management Life-Cycle in Business. In P. Jain & N. Mnjama (Eds.), *Managing Knowledge Resources and Records in Modern Organizations* (pp. 82–101). Hershey, PA: IGI Global. doi:10.4018/978-1-5225-1965-2.ch006

Jamali, D., Abdallah, H., & Matar, F. (2016). Opportunities and Challenges for CSR Mainstreaming in Business Schools. *International Journal of Technology and Educational Marketing*, *6*(2), 1–29. doi:10.4018/IJTEM.2016070101

James, P. (1996). *Total Quality Management. An Introductory Text*. Prentice Hall.

James, S., & Hauli, E. (2017). Holistic Management Education at Tanzanian Rural Development Planning Institute. In N. Baporikar (Ed.), *Management Education for Global Leadership* (pp. 112–136). Hershey, PA: IGI Global. doi:10.4018/978-1-5225-1013-0.ch006

Jammu and Kashmir State Economic survey. (2016). Retrieved from https://openbudgetsindia.org/dataset/jk-economic-survey-2016-2017-18/resource/7f67ef5f-222c-4bd3-80e8-fba10e61578d

Janošková, M., Csikósová, A., & Čulková, K. (2018). Measurement of Company Performance as Part of Its Strategic Management. In R. Leon (Ed.), *Managerial Strategies for Business Sustainability During Turbulent Times* (pp. 309–335). Hershey, PA: IGI Global. doi:10.4018/978-1-5225-2716-9.ch017

Jean-Vasile, A., & Alecu, A. (2017). Theoretical and Practical Approaches in Understanding the Influences of Cost-Productivity-Profit Trinomial in Contemporary Enterprises. In A. Jean Vasile & D. Nicolò (Eds.), *Sustainable Entrepreneurship and Investments in the Green Economy* (pp. 28–62). Hershey, PA: IGI Global. doi:10.4018/978-1-5225-2075-7.ch002

Jha, D. G. (2016). Preparing for Information Technology Driven Changes. In S. Tiwari & L. Nafees (Eds.), *Innovative Management Education Pedagogies for Preparing Next-Generation Leaders* (pp. 258–274). Hershey, PA: IGI Global. doi:10.4018/978-1-4666-9691-4.ch015

Jogaratnam, G. (2017). How organizational culture influences market orientation and business performance in the restaurant industry. *Journal of Hospitality and Tourism Management*, *31*, 211–219. doi:10.1016/j.jhtm.2017.03.002

Joia, L. A., & Correia, J. C. (2018). CIO Competencies From the IT Professional Perspective: Insights From Brazil. *Journal of Global Information Management*, *26*(2), 74–103. doi:10.4018/JGIM.2018040104

Joseph, O. O., & Francis, K. (2015). The influence of organizational culture and market orientation on performance of microfinance institutions in Kenya. *International Journal of Business and Management*, *10*(8), 204. doi:10.5539/ijbm.v10n8p204

Jucan, M. S., & Jucan, C. N. (2013). Gender trends in tourism destination. *Procedia: Social and Behavioral Sciences*, *92*, 437–444. doi:10.1016/j.sbspro.2013.08.698

Juma, A., & Mzera, N. (2017). Knowledge Management and Records Management and Competitive Advantage in Business. In P. Jain & N. Mnjama (Eds.), *Managing Knowledge Resources and Records in Modern Organizations* (pp. 15–28). Hershey, PA: IGI Global. doi:10.4018/978-1-5225-1965-2.ch002

Jumeirah Group. (2019). *Philosophy.* Retrieved from https://www.jumeirah.com/en/jumeirah-group/about-jumeirah-group/philosophy/

Jupp, V. (2006). The SAGE Dictionary of social research methods. London: SAGE Publications; doi:10.4135/9780857020116.

Juran, J. M., & Godfrey, A. B. (1998). *Juran's Quality Handbook* (5th ed.). USA: McGraw-Hill.

K., I., & A, V. (2018). Monitoring and Auditing in the Cloud. In K. Munir (Ed.), *Cloud Computing Technologies for Green Enterprises* (pp. 318-350). Hershey, PA: IGI Global. doi:10.4018/978-1-5225-3038-1.ch013

Kabra, G., Ghosh, V., & Ramesh, A. (2018). Enterprise Integrated Business Process Management and Business Intelligence Framework for Business Process Sustainability. In A. Paul, D. Bhattacharyya, & S. Anand (Eds.), *Green Initiatives for Business Sustainability and Value Creation* (pp. 228–238). Hershey, PA: IGI Global. doi:10.4018/978-1-5225-2662-9.ch010

Kaddi, A. S. (2013). Understanding the motivations of wine festival visitors in Maharashtra. *ATNA Journal of Tourism Studies*, *8*(2). doi:10.12727/ajts.10.1

Kaoud, M. (2017). Investigation of Customer Knowledge Management: A Case Study Research. *International Journal of Service Science, Management, Engineering, and Technology*, *8*(2), 12–22. doi:10.4018/IJSSMET.2017040102

Kapiki, S. T. (2012). *Quality management in tourism and hospitality: An exploratory study among tourism stakeholders*.

Kaplan, A., & Haenlein, M. (2010). Users of the world, unite! The challenges and opportunities of Social Media. *Business Horizons*, *53*(1), 59–68. doi:10.1016/j.bushor.2009.09.003

Kaplan, R. S., & Norton, D. P. (2007). Using the balanced scorecard as a strategic management system. *Harvard Business Review*, *85*(7/8), 150.

Kara, M. E., & Fırat, S. Ü. (2016). Sustainability, Risk, and Business Intelligence in Supply Chains. In M. Erdoğdu, T. Arun, & I. Ahmad (Eds.), *Handbook of Research on Green Economic Development Initiatives and Strategies* (pp. 501–538). Hershey, PA: IGI Global. doi:10.4018/978-1-5225-0440-5.ch022

Katuu, S. (2018). A Comparative Assessment of Enterprise Content Management Maturity Models. In N. Gwangwava & M. Mutingi (Eds.), *E-Manufacturing and E-Service Strategies in Contemporary Organizations* (pp. 93–118). Hershey, PA: IGI Global. doi:10.4018/978-1-5225-3628-4.ch005

Kayode-Adedeji, T. K. & Agwu, M.E. (2015). Application of ICT to agriculture as a panacea to unemployment in Nigeria. *International Journals of Multidisciplinary Research Academy, 3*(4), 26-48.

Kelly, K. J., Redfern, P., & Munaita, P. (2002). How Western security failure led to bombing. The East African weekly. Retrieved from http://www.nationaudio.com

Khan, M. A. (2016). MNEs Management Strategies in Developing Countries: Establishing the Context. In M. Khan (Ed.), *Multinational Enterprise Management Strategies in Developing Countries* (pp. 1–33). Hershey, PA: IGI Global. doi:10.4018/978-1-5225-0276-0.ch001

Khan, M. A. (2016). Operational Approaches in Organizational Structure: A Case for MNEs in Developing Countries. In M. Khan (Ed.), *Multinational Enterprise Management Strategies in Developing Countries* (pp. 129–151). Hershey, PA: IGI Global. doi:10.4018/978-1-5225-0276-0.ch007

Khrisna, R. (2015). Effects of terrorism in tourism industry. A case study of 9/11 terrorist attacks in world trade centre. Unpublished Bachelor's thesis, Centria University of Applied Sciences. Retrieved from https://www.theseus.fi/bitstream/handle/10024/103202/krishna.pdf?sequence=1

Kim Jean Lee, S., & Yu, K. (2004). Corporate culture and organizational performance. *Journal of Managerial Psychology, 19*(4), 340–359. doi:10.1108/02683940410537927

Kim, S., & Mukhopadhyay, T. (2011). Determining Optimal CRM Implementation Strategies. *Information Systems Research, 22*(3), 624–639. doi:10.1287/isre.1100.0309

Kim, W. G., & Ayoun, B. (2005). Ratio Analysis for the Hospitality Industry: A cross Sector Comparison of Financial Trends in the Lodging, Restaurant, Airline and Amusement Sectors. *The Journal of Hospitality Financial Management, 13*(1), 26. doi:10.1080/10913211.2005.10653800

Kinnunen, S., Ylä-Kujala, A., Marttonen-Arola, S., Kärri, T., & Baglee, D. (2018). Internet of Things in Asset Management: Insights from Industrial Professionals and Academia. *International Journal of Service Science, Management, Engineering, and Technology, 9*(2), 104–119. doi:10.4018/IJSSMET.2018040105

Klein, A. Z., Sabino de Freitas, A., Machado, L., Freitas, J. C. Jr, Graziola, P. G. Jr, & Schlemmer, E. (2017). Virtual Worlds Applications for Management Education. In L. Tomei (Ed.), *Exploring the New Era of Technology-Infused Education* (pp. 279–299). Hershey, PA: IGI Global. doi:10.4018/978-1-5225-1709-2.ch017

Kotler, P. (2000). *Pazarlama Yöntemi*. İstanbul: Beta Pub.

Kotler, P. T., Bowen, J. T., James, M., & Baloglu, S. (2016). *Marketing for Hospitality and Tourism* (7th ed.). New York, NY: Pearson.

Kożuch, B., & Jabłoński, A. (2017). Adopting the Concept of Business Models in Public Management. In M. Lewandowski & B. Kożuch (Eds.), *Public Sector Entrepreneurship and the Integration of Innovative Business Models* (pp. 10–46). Hershey, PA: IGI Global. doi:10.4018/978-1-5225-2215-7.ch002

Krejcie, R. V., & Morgan, D. W. (1970). Determining sample size for research activities. *Educational and Psychological Measurement, 30*(3), 607–610. doi:10.1177/001316447003000308

Kroller, E.-M. (1990). First impressions: Rhetorical strategies in travel writing Victorian Women. A Review of International English Literature, 21(4), 87–99.

Kumar, J., Adhikary, A., & Jha, A. (2017). Small Active Investors' Perceptions and Preferences Towards Tax Saving Mutual Fund Schemes in Eastern India: An Empirical Note. *International Journal of Asian Business and Information Management, 8*(2), 35–45. doi:10.4018/IJABIM.2017040103

Kumar, R. (2017). *Strategic financial management casebook*. Amsterdam: Academic Press/Elsevier.

Kumar, V., Lerzan, A., Bas, D., Rajkumar, V., Thorsten, W., & Sebastian, T. (2010). Undervalued or Overvalued Customers: Capturing Total Customer Engagement Value. *Journal of Service Research, 13*(3), 297–310. doi:10.1177/1094670510375602

Laesser, C., Beritelli, P., & Bieger, T. (2009). Solo travel: Explorative insights from a mature market (Switzerland). *Journal of Vacation Marketing, 15*(3), 217–227. doi:10.1177/1356766709104268

Lassoued, Y., Bouzguenda, L., & Mahmoud, T. (2016). Context-Aware Business Process Versions Management. *International Journal of e-Collaboration, 12*(3), 7–33. doi:10.4018/IJeC.2016070102

Lavassani, K. M., & Movahedi, B. (2017). Applications Driven Information Systems: Beyond Networks toward Business Ecosystems. *International Journal of Innovation in the Digital Economy, 8*(1), 61–75. doi:10.4018/IJIDE.2017010104

Lawder, K. (1989). Ratio 101: Back to the basics of financial analysis. *Business Credit, 91*(6), 28–30.

Lazzareschi, V. H., & Brito, M. S. (2017). Strategic Information Management: Proposal of Business Project Model. In G. Jamil, A. Soares, & C. Pessoa (Eds.), *Handbook of Research on Information Management for Effective Logistics and Supply Chains* (pp. 59–88). Hershey, PA: IGI Global. doi:10.4018/978-1-5225-0973-8.ch004

Lederer, M., Kurz, M., & Lazarov, P. (2017). Usage and Suitability of Methods for Strategic Business Process Initiatives: A Multi Case Study Research. *International Journal of Productivity Management and Assessment Technologies, 5*(1), 40–51. doi:10.4018/IJPMAT.2017010103

Leeds, B. (1995). Mystery shopping: From novelty to necessity. *Bank Marketing, 27*, 17–17.

Lee, I. (2017). A Social Enterprise Business Model and a Case Study of Pacific Community Ventures (PCV). In V. Potocan, M. Üngan, & Z. Nedelko (Eds.), *Handbook of Research on Managerial Solutions in Non-Profit Organizations* (pp. 182–204). Hershey, PA: IGI Global. doi:10.4018/978-1-5225-0731-4.ch009

Lee, L. J., & Leu, J. (2016). Exploring the Effectiveness of IT Application and Value Method in the Innovation Performance of Enterprise. *International Journal of Enterprise Information Systems, 12*(2), 47–65. doi:10.4018/IJEIS.2016040104

Lee, Y. (2016). Alignment Effect of Entrepreneurial Orientation and Marketing Orientation on Firm Performance. *International Journal of Customer Relationship Marketing and Management*, *7*(4), 58–69. doi:10.4018/IJCRMM.2016100104

Leon, L. A., Seal, K. C., Przasnyski, Z. H., & Wiedenman, I. (2017). Skills and Competencies Required for Jobs in Business Analytics: A Content Analysis of Job Advertisements Using Text Mining. *International Journal of Business Intelligence Research*, *8*(1), 1–25. doi:10.4018/IJBIR.2017010101

Leu, J., Lee, L. J., & Krischke, A. (2016). Value Engineering-Based Method for Implementing the ISO14001 System in the Green Supply Chains. *International Journal of Strategic Decision Sciences*, *7*(4), 1–20. doi:10.4018/IJSDS.2016100101

Levy, C. L., & Elias, N. I. (2017). SOHO Users' Perceptions of Reliability and Continuity of Cloud-Based Services. In M. Moore (Ed.), *Cybersecurity Breaches and Issues Surrounding Online Threat Protection* (pp. 248–287). Hershey, PA: IGI Global. doi:10.4018/978-1-5225-1941-6.ch011

Levy, M. (2018). Change Management Serving Knowledge Management and Organizational Development: Reflections and Review. In N. Baporikar (Ed.), *Global Practices in Knowledge Management for Societal and Organizational Development* (pp. 256–270). Hershey, PA: IGI Global. doi:10.4018/978-1-5225-3009-1.ch012

Lew, A. A. (1987). A framework of tourist attraction research. *Annals of Tourism Research*, *14*(4), 553–557. doi:10.1016/0160-7383(87)90071-5

Lewandowski, M. (2017). Public Organizations and Business Model Innovation: The Role of Public Service Design. In M. Lewandowski & B. Kożuch (Eds.), *Public Sector Entrepreneurship and the Integration of Innovative Business Models* (pp. 47–72). Hershey, PA: IGI Global. doi:10.4018/978-1-5225-2215-7.ch003

Lhannaoui, H., Kabbaj, M. I., & Bakkoury, Z. (2017). A Survey of Risk-Aware Business Process Modelling. *International Journal of Risk and Contingency Management*, *6*(3), 14–26. doi:10.4018/IJRCM.2017070102

Li, J., Sun, W., Jiang, W., Yang, H., & Zhang, L. (2017). How the Nature of Exogenous Shocks and Crises Impact Company Performance?: The Effects of Industry Characteristics. *International Journal of Risk and Contingency Management*, *6*(4), 40–55. doi:10.4018/IJRCM.2017100103

Lu, C., & Liu, S. (2016). Cultural Tourism O2O Business Model Innovation-A Case Study of CTrip. *Journal of Electronic Commerce in Organizations*, *14*(2), 16–31. doi:10.4018/JECO.2016040102

Lund, D. B. (2003). Organizational culture and job satisfaction. *Journal of Business and Industrial Marketing*, *18*(3), 219–236. doi:10.1108/0885862031047313

Lutz, J. M., & Lutz, B. J. (2008). *Global Terrorism*. Oxford: Oxford University Press. doi:10.4324/9780203895030

Machen, B., Hosseini, M. R., Wood, A., & Bakhshi, J. (2016). An Investigation into using SAP-PS as a Multidimensional Project Control System (MPCS). *International Journal of Enterprise Information Systems, 12*(2), 66–81. doi:10.4018/IJEIS.2016040105

Malega, P. (2017). Small and Medium Enterprises in the Slovak Republic: Status and Competitiveness of SMEs in the Global Markets and Possibilities of Optimization. In M. Vemić (Ed.), *Optimal Management Strategies in Small and Medium Enterprises* (pp. 102–124). Hershey, PA: IGI Global. doi:10.4018/978-1-5225-1949-2.ch006

Malewska, K. M. (2017). Intuition in Decision-Making on the Example of a Non-Profit Organization. In V. Potocan, M. Üngan, & Z. Nedelko (Eds.), *Handbook of Research on Managerial Solutions in Non-Profit Organizations* (pp. 378–399). Hershey, PA: IGI Global. doi:10.4018/978-1-5225-0731-4.ch018

Mallett, M. (2008). Pair training with mystery shopping. *Restaurant Hospitality, 92*(4), 20.

Manolică, A., & Roman, T. (2012). Globalisation–advantages and disadvantages from the perspective of the manufacturer. Editorial Board, 747.

Mansfeld, Y., & Pizam, A. (2006). *Tourism, Security, and Safety: From Theory to Practice.* Burlington, MA: Elsevier Butterworth-Heinemann.

Maroofi, F. (2017). Entrepreneurial Orientation and Organizational Learning Ability Analysis for Innovation and Firm Performance. In N. Baporikar (Ed.), *Innovation and Shifting Perspectives in Management Education* (pp. 144–165). Hershey, PA: IGI Global. doi:10.4018/978-1-5225-1019-2.ch007

Marriott. (n.d.). *Core Values.* Retrieved from www.marriott.com/culture-and-values/core-values.mi#

Martinez Lucio, M., & Kirkpatrick, I. (1995). The Politics of Quality in the British Public Sector. In *The Politics of Quality and the Management of Change in the Public Sector.* Routledge.

Martins, P. V., & Zacarias, M. (2017). A Web-based Tool for Business Process Improvement. *International Journal of Web Portals, 9*(2), 68–84. doi:10.4018/IJWP.2017070104

Marzuki, A., Chin, T. L., & Razak, A. A. (2012). What women want: Hotel characteristics preferences of women travellers. In M. Kasimoglu (Ed.), Strategies for tourism industry: Micro and macro perspectives (pp. 143–164). Rijeka: InTech; doi:10.5772/37101.

Mason, D., & Milne, S. (2002). E-Commerce and Community Tourism. In P. C. Palvia, S. C. Palvia & E. M. Roche (Eds.), Global Information Technology and Electronic Commerce: issues for the New Millennium (pp. 294–310). Marietta, Gerogia: Ivy League Publishing Ltd.

Mason, R. O., & Mitroff, I. I. (1973). A program for research on management information systems. *Management Science, 19*(5), 475–487. doi:10.1287/mnsc.19.5.475

Matthies, B., & Coners, A. (2017). Exploring the Conceptual Nature of e-Business Projects. *Journal of Electronic Commerce in Organizations, 15*(3), 33–63. doi:10.4018/JECO.2017070103

Mawanza, W., & Mugumisi, N. (2013). Capital Structure and Corporate Performance: A Case for Tourism and Hospitality Sector of Zimbabwe. *Global Journal of Commerce and Management Perspective, 2*, 85-90.

McCulley, K. (2015). Adventurous Kate's solo female travel blog. Retrieved October 21, 2015, from http://www.adventurouskate.com/blog/

McKee, J. (2018). Architecture as a Tool to Solve Business Planning Problems. In M. Khosrow-Pour, D.B.A. (Ed.), Encyclopedia of Information Science and Technology, Fourth Edition (pp. 573-586). Hershey, PA: IGI Global. doi:10.4018/978-1-5225-2255-3.ch050

Mcmullen, R., & Åkesson, E. (2011). *Mystery Shopping: En mätning av kvaliteten på Connect Hotels* (Master's thesis). Örebro Universistet Restaurang- och Hotellhögskolan Grythytte Academy.

McMurray, A. J., Cross, J., & Caponecchia, C. (2018). The Risk Management Profession in Australia: Business Continuity Plan Practices. In N. Bajgoric (Ed.), *Always-On Enterprise Information Systems for Modern Organizations* (pp. 112–129). Hershey, PA: IGI Global. doi:10.4018/978-1-5225-3704-5.ch006

McNamara, K. E., & Prideaux, B. (2010). A typology of solo independent women travellers. *International Journal of Tourism Research, 12*(3), 253–264. doi:10.1002/jtr.751

Meddah, I. H., & Belkadi, K. (2018). Mining Patterns Using Business Process Management. In R. Hamou (Ed.), *Handbook of Research on Biomimicry in Information Retrieval and Knowledge Management* (pp. 78–89). Hershey, PA: IGI Global. doi:10.4018/978-1-5225-3004-6.ch005

Mendes, L. (2017). TQM and Knowledge Management: An Integrated Approach Towards Tacit Knowledge Management. In D. Jaziri-Bouagina & G. Jamil (Eds.), *Handbook of Research on Tacit Knowledge Management for Organizational Success* (pp. 236–263). Hershey, PA: IGI Global. doi:10.4018/978-1-5225-2394-9.ch009

Meng, F., & Uysal, M. (2008). Effects of gender differences on perceptions of destination attributes, motivations, and travel values: An examination of a nature-based resort destination. *Journal of Sustainable Tourism, 16*(4), 445–466. doi:10.1080/09669580802154231

Merla, V. A., & Chirita, S. (2010). Forecasting in Tourism – Important component of the planning process. *Romanian Economic Business Review, 5*(1), 182–188.

Michael Hall, C. L. S. (2009). Wine Tourism Around the World. Routledge.

Michael, H. C. (2010). Crisis events in tourism: Subjects of crisis in tourism. *Current Issues in Tourism, 13*(5), 401–417. doi:10.1080/13683500.2010.491900

Middleton, V. T. C., & Clark, J. (2004). *Marketing in Travel and Tourism* (3rd ed.). Cornwall: Elsevier: Butterworth-Heinemann.

Mikhalkina, T. (2013). Netflix Business Model. Retrieved from http://www.cass.city.ac.uk/__data/assets/pdf_file/0017/220517/Netflix.pdf

Milano, D. R., Robnett, C. S., & Milano, D. R. (2010). *The essentials of accounting I*. Piscataway, NJ: Research and Education Association.

Min, J. C. H. (2008). Forecasting Japanese tourism demand in Taiwan using an intervention analysis. *International Journal of Culture, Tourism and Hospitality Research*, *2*(3), 197–216. doi:10.1108/17506180810891582

Mitchell, R. H. (2000). Wine tourism and consumer behaviour. In L. S. C.M. Hall (Ed.), Wine Tourism Around the World: Development, management and markets (pp. 115 - 135). Elsevier.

Mnjama, N. M. (2017). Preservation of Recorded Information in Public and Private Sector Organizations. In P. Jain & N. Mnjama (Eds.), *Managing Knowledge Resources and Records in Modern Organizations* (pp. 149–167). Hershey, PA: IGI Global. doi:10.4018/978-1-5225-1965-2.ch009

Modigliani, F., & Miller, M. H. (1958). The cost of capital, corporation finance and the theory of investment. *The American Economic Review*, 261–297.

Mokoqama, M., & Fields, Z. (2017). Principles of Responsible Management Education (PRME): Call for Responsible Management Education. In Z. Fields (Ed.), *Collective Creativity for Responsible and Sustainable Business Practice* (pp. 229–241). Hershey, PA: IGI Global. doi:10.4018/978-1-5225-1823-5.ch012

Mollen, A., & Hugh, W. (2010). Engagement, Telepresence, and Interactivity in Online Consumer Experience: Reconciling Scholastic and Managerial Perspectives. *Journal of Business Research*, *63*(9/10), 919–925. doi:10.1016/j.jbusres.2009.05.014

Morley, M. (n.d.). *Insight - India's growing thirst for wine*. Retrieved from https://www.austrade.gov.au/news/insights/insight-indias-growing-thirst-for-wine

Morrison, L. J., Colman, A. M., & Preston, C. C. (1997). Mystery shopper research: Cognitive processes affecting accuracy. *Journal of the Market Research Society*, *39*(2), 349–361. doi:10.1177/147078539703900203

Mota, I., Pinto, M., Sá, J., Marques, V., & Ribeiro, J. (2005). *Estratégia Nacional para o Desenvolvimento Sustentável ENDS 2005-2015*. Available at: https://infoeuropa.eurocid.pt/files/database/000015001-000020000/000019537.pdf

Mota, K., & Almeida, J. (2016). Educação superior em turismo, hospitalidade e lazer no Brasil: Análise do panorama de cursos ofertados frente ao contexto contemporâneo. *Revista Turismo & Desenvolvimento*, *26*, 65–77.

Muniapan, B. (2017). Philosophy and Management: The Relevance of Vedanta in Management. In P. Ordóñez de Pablos (Ed.), *Managerial Strategies and Solutions for Business Success in Asia* (pp. 124–139). Hershey, PA: IGI Global. doi:10.4018/978-1-5225-1886-0.ch007

Muniapan, B., Gregory, M. L., & Ling, L. A. (2016). Marketing Education in Sarawak: Looking at It from the Employers' Viewpoint. In B. Smith & A. Porath (Eds.), *Global Perspectives on Contemporary Marketing Education* (pp. 112–130). Hershey, PA: IGI Global. doi:10.4018/978-1-4666-9784-3.ch008

Murad, S. E., & Dowaji, S. (2017). Using Value-Based Approach for Managing Cloud-Based Services. In A. Turuk, B. Sahoo, & S. Addya (Eds.), *Resource Management and Efficiency in Cloud Computing Environments* (pp. 33–60). Hershey, PA: IGI Global. doi:10.4018/978-1-5225-1721-4.ch002

Mutahar, A. M., Daud, N. M., Thurasamy, R., Isaac, O., & Abdulsalam, R. (2018). The Mediating of Perceived Usefulness and Perceived Ease of Use: The Case of Mobile Banking in Yemen. *International Journal of Technology Diffusion*, *9*(2), 21–40. doi:10.4018/IJTD.2018040102

Myers, S. (2001). Capital structure. *The Journal of Economic Perspectives*, *15*(2), 81–102. doi:10.1257/jep.15.2.81

Mystery Shopping Providers Web Site. (n.d.). Retrieved from http://www.mysteryshop.org/

Naidoo, V. (2017). E-Learning and Management Education at African Universities. In N. Baporikar (Ed.), *Management Education for Global Leadership* (pp. 181–201). Hershey, PA: IGI Global. doi:10.4018/978-1-5225-1013-0.ch009

Naidoo, V., & Igbinakhase, I. (2018). Opportunities and Challenges of Knowledge Retention in SMEs. In N. Baporikar (Ed.), *Knowledge Integration Strategies for Entrepreneurship and Sustainability* (pp. 70–94). Hershey, PA: IGI Global. doi:10.4018/978-1-5225-5115-7.ch004

Nayak, S., & Prabhu, N. (2017). Paradigm Shift in Management Education: Need for a Cross Functional Perspective. In N. Baporikar (Ed.), *Management Education for Global Leadership* (pp. 241–255). Hershey, PA: IGI Global. doi:10.4018/978-1-5225-1013-0.ch012

Nazarian, A., Atkinson, P., & Foroudi, P. (2017). Influence of national culture and balanced organizational culture on the hotel industry's performance. *International Journal of Hospitality Management*, *63*, 22–32. doi:10.1016/j.ijhm.2017.01.003

Ndanusa, M. M., Harada, Y., & Islam, M. (2014). Challenges to Growth in Tourism Industry of a Developing Country: The Case of Nigeria. *Asian Social Science*, *10*(19), 282–290. doi:10.5539/ass.v10n19p282

Ndede-Amadi, A. A. (2016). Student Interest in the IS Specialization as Predictor of the Success Potential of New Information Systems Programmes within the Schools of Business in Kenyan Public Universities. *International Journal of Information Systems and Social Change*, *7*(2), 63–79. doi:10.4018/IJISSC.2016040104

Nedelko, Z., & Potocan, V. (2016). Management Practices for Processes Optimization: Case of Slovenia. In G. Alor-Hernández, C. Sánchez-Ramírez, & J. García-Alcaraz (Eds.), *Handbook of Research on Managerial Strategies for Achieving Optimal Performance in Industrial Processes* (pp. 545–561). Hershey, PA: IGI Global. doi:10.4018/978-1-5225-0130-5.ch025

Nedelko, Z., & Potocan, V. (2017). Management Solutions in Non-Profit Organizations: Case of Slovenia. In V. Potocan, M. Üngan, & Z. Nedelko (Eds.), *Handbook of Research on Managerial Solutions in Non-Profit Organizations* (pp. 1–22). Hershey, PA: IGI Global. doi:10.4018/978-1-5225-0731-4.ch001

Nedelko, Z., & Potocan, V. (2017). Priority of Management Tools Utilization among Managers: International Comparison. In V. Wang (Ed.), *Encyclopedia of Strategic Leadership and Management* (pp. 1083–1094). Hershey, PA: IGI Global. doi:10.4018/978-1-5225-1049-9.ch075

Nedelko, Z., Raudeliūnienė, J., & Črešnar, R. (2018). Knowledge Dynamics in Supply Chain Management. In N. Baporikar (Ed.), *Knowledge Integration Strategies for Entrepreneurship and Sustainability* (pp. 150–166). Hershey, PA: IGI Global. doi:10.4018/978-1-5225-5115-7.ch008

Ng Kwet Shing, M., & Spence, L. J. (2002). Investigating the limits of competitive intelligence gathering: Is mystery shopping ethical? *Business Ethics*, *11*(4), 343–353. doi:10.1111/1467-8608.00294

Nguyen, H. T., & Hipsher, S. A. (2018). Innovation and Creativity Used by Private Sector Firms in a Resources-Constrained Environment. In S. Hipsher (Ed.), *Examining the Private Sector's Role in Wealth Creation and Poverty Reduction* (pp. 219–238). Hershey, PA: IGI Global. doi:10.4018/978-1-5225-3117-3.ch010

Nikpour, A. (2017). The impact of organizational culture on organizational performance: The mediating role of employee's organizational commitment. *International Journal of Organizational Leadership*, *6*(1), 65–72. doi:10.33844/ijol.2017.60432

Ninemeier, J. D. (2015). *Management of Food and Beverage Operations*. Educational Institute of the American Hotel Motel Assoc.

Nycz, M., & Pólkowski, Z. (2016). Business Intelligence as a Modern IT Supporting Management of Local Government Units in Poland. *International Journal of Knowledge and Systems Science*, *7*(4), 1–18. doi:10.4018/IJKSS.2016100101

O'Connor, P., & Frew, A. J. (2002). The future of hotel electronic distribution: Expert and industry perspectives. *The Cornell Hotel and Restaurant Administration Quarterly*, *43*(3), 33–45. doi:10.1016/S0010-8804(02)80016-7

Obaji, N. O., Senin, A. A., & Olugu, M. U. (2016). Supportive Government Policy as a Mechanism for Business Incubation Performance in Nigeria. *International Journal of Information Systems and Social Change*, *7*(4), 52–66. doi:10.4018/IJISSC.2016100103

Obicci, P. A. (2017). Risk Sharing in a Partnership. In *Risk Management Strategies in Public-Private Partnerships* (pp. 115–152). Hershey, PA: IGI Global. doi:10.4018/978-1-5225-2503-5.ch004

Obidallah, W. J., & Raahemi, B. (2017). Managing Changes in Service Oriented Virtual Organizations: A Structural and Procedural Framework to Facilitate the Process of Change. *Journal of Electronic Commerce in Organizations*, *15*(1), 59–83. doi:10.4018/JECO.2017010104

Office for National Statistics. (2018). Population estimates by marital status and living arrangements, England and Wales: 2002 to 2017. Retrieved on July 23, 2019 from https://www.ons.gov.uk/peoplepopulationandcommunity/populationandmigration/populationestimates/bulletins/populationestimatesbymaritalstatusandlivingarrangements/2002to2017#an-increasing-proportion-of-50-to-64-year-olds-are-single-never-married-and-cohabitation-for-this-group-is-becoming-more-common

Ogbeide, G.-C. (2014). *Revenue management, cost control, and financial analysis in the hospitality industry*. San Diego, CA: Cognella.

Ojasalo, J., & Ojasalo, K. (2016). Service Logic Business Model Canvas for Lean Development of SMEs and Start-Ups. In N. Baporikar (Ed.), *Handbook of Research on Entrepreneurship in the Contemporary Knowledge-Based Global Economy* (pp. 217–243). Hershey, PA: IGI Global. doi:10.4018/978-1-4666-8798-1.ch010

Ojo, O. (2017). Impact of Innovation on the Entrepreneurial Success in Selected Business Enterprises in South-West Nigeria. *International Journal of Innovation in the Digital Economy*, *8*(2), 29–38. doi:10.4018/IJIDE.2017040103

Okdinawati, L., Simatupang, T. M., & Sunitiyoso, Y. (2017). Multi-Agent Reinforcement Learning for Value Co-Creation of Collaborative Transportation Management (CTM). *International Journal of Information Systems and Supply Chain Management*, *10*(3), 84–95. doi:10.4018/IJISSCM.2017070105

Olding, A., & Turner, P. (2007). Cyber vulnerabilities and the tourism industry: developing a conceptual framework. In *ACIS 2007 Proceedings*. Academic Press.

Orgaad, T., Marnburg, E., & Larsen, S. (2008). Perception of organizational structure in the hospitality industry: Consequences for commitment, job satisfaction and perceived performance. *Tourism Management*, *29*(4), 661–671. doi:10.1016/j.tourman.2007.07.006

Ortner, E., Mevius, M., Wiedmann, P., & Kurz, F. (2016). Design of Interactional Decision Support Applications for E-Participation in Smart Cities. *International Journal of Electronic Government Research*, *12*(2), 18–38. doi:10.4018/IJEGR.2016040102

Öter, Z., Ayaz Olay, N., & Kömürcü, S. (2015). *Gizli Müşteri Uygulamaları. In Turizm Pazarlamasında Güncel Yaklaşımlar*. İstanbul: Beta Yayıncılık.

Ouchi, W. G., & Wilkins, A. L. (1985). Organizational culture. *Annual Review of Sociology*, *11*(1), 457–483. doi:10.1146/annurev.so.11.080185.002325

Pacheco, L., & Tavares, F. (2017). Capital structure determinants of hospitality sector SMEs. *Tourism Economics*, *23*(1), 113–132. doi:10.5367/te.2015.0501

Pal, K. (2018). Building High Quality Big Data-Based Applications in Supply Chains. In A. Kumar & S. Saurav (Eds.), *Supply Chain Management Strategies and Risk Assessment in Retail Environments* (pp. 1–24). Hershey, PA: IGI Global. doi:10.4018/978-1-5225-3056-5.ch001

Palmatier, R., Rajiv, P., Dhruv, G., & Kenneth, R. (2006). Factors Influencing the Effectiveness of Relationship Marketing: A Meta-Analysis. *Journal of Marketing*, *70*(October), 136–153. doi:10.1509/jmkg.70.4.136

Palos-Sanchez, P. R., & Correia, M. B. (2018). Perspectives of the Adoption of Cloud Computing in the Tourism Sector. In J. Rodrigues, C. Ramos, P. Cardoso, & C. Henriques (Eds.), *Handbook of Research on Technological Developments for Cultural Heritage and eTourism Applications* (pp. 377–400). Hershey, PA: IGI Global. doi:10.4018/978-1-5225-2927-9.ch018

PamlnCa. (2009). The Essential Guide to Mystery Shopping. Silicon Valley. *Happy About*, *2009*, 119.

Pantiyasa, I. W., & Michelle, M. (2017). Organization culture impact to performance of hotel employees (case study: Hotel Legian Resort–Bali). *Journal of Business on Hospitality and Tourism*, *2*(1), 330–346. doi:10.22334/jbhost.v2i1.68

Parent, M., Kirk, P., & Anjali, B. (2011). The New WTP: Willingness to Participate. *Business Horizons*, *54*(3), 219–229. doi:10.1016/j.bushor.2011.01.003

Parikshat, S. M. (2012). Sustainable and responsible tourism: Trends practices and cases. PHI learning.

Parry, V. K., & Lind, M. L. (2016). Alignment of Business Strategy and Information Technology Considering Information Technology Governance, Project Portfolio Control, and Risk Management. *International Journal of Information Technology Project Management*, *7*(4), 21–37. doi:10.4018/IJITPM.2016100102

Pashkova, N., Trujillo-Barrera, A., Apostolakis, G., Van Dijk, G., Drakos, P. D., & Baourakis, G. (2016). Business Management Models of Microfinance Institutions (MFIs) in Africa: A Study into Their Enabling Environments. *International Journal of Food and Beverage Manufacturing and Business Models*, *1*(2), 63–82. doi:10.4018/IJFBMBM.2016070105

Patiño, B. E. (2017). New Generation Management by Convergence and Individual Identity: A Systemic and Human-Oriented Approach. In N. Baporikar (Ed.), *Innovation and Shifting Perspectives in Management Education* (pp. 119–143). Hershey, PA: IGI Global. doi:10.4018/978-1-5225-1019-2.ch006

Pauchant, T., & Mitroff, I. (1992). *Transforming the Crisis Prone Organization*. San Francisco, CA: Jossey-Bass Publishers.

Pawliczek, A., & Rössler, M. (2017). Knowledge of Management Tools and Systems in SMEs: Knowledge Transfer in Management. In A. Bencsik (Ed.), *Knowledge Management Initiatives and Strategies in Small and Medium Enterprises* (pp. 180–203). Hershey, PA: IGI Global. doi:10.4018/978-1-5225-1642-2.ch009

Pejic-Bach, M., Omazic, M. A., Aleksic, A., & Zoroja, J. (2018). Knowledge-Based Decision Making: A Multi-Case Analysis. In R. Leon (Ed.), *Managerial Strategies for Business Sustainability During Turbulent Times* (pp. 160–184). Hershey, PA: IGI Global. doi:10.4018/978-1-5225-2716-9.ch009

Pennington-Gray, L. A., & Kerstetter, D. L. (2001). What do university-educated women want from their pleasure travel experiences? *Journal of Travel Research*, *40*(1), 49–56. doi:10.1177/004728750104000107

PENT - Plano Estratégico Nacional do Turismo. (2015). *Ministério da Economia e do Emprego.* Available at: https://www.portugal.gov.pt/media/820185/20130111%20consulta%20publica%20pent.pdf

Perano, M., Hysa, X., & Calabrese, M. (2018). Strategic Planning, Cultural Context, and Business Continuity Management: Business Cases in the City of Shkoder. In A. Presenza & L. Sheehan (Eds.), *Geopolitics and Strategic Management in the Global Economy* (pp. 57–77). Hershey, PA: IGI Global. doi:10.4018/978-1-5225-2673-5.ch004

Pereira, R., Mira da Silva, M., & Lapão, L. V. (2017). IT Governance Maturity Patterns in Portuguese Healthcare. In S. De Haes & W. Van Grembergen (Eds.), *Strategic IT Governance and Alignment in Business Settings* (pp. 24–52). Hershey, PA: IGI Global. doi:10.4018/978-1-5225-0861-8.ch002

Pérez-Uribe, R. I., Torres, D. A., Jurado, S. P., & Prada, D. M. (2018). Cloud Tools for the Development of Project Management in SMEs. In R. Perez-Uribe, C. Salcedo-Perez, & D. Ocampo-Guzman (Eds.), *Handbook of Research on Intrapreneurship and Organizational Sustainability in SMEs* (pp. 95–120). Hershey, PA: IGI Global. doi:10.4018/978-1-5225-3543-0.ch005

Perez-Uribe, R., & Ocampo-Guzman, D. (2016). Conflict within Colombian Family Owned SMEs: An Explosive Blend between Feelings and Business. In J. Saiz-Álvarez (Ed.), *Handbook of Research on Social Entrepreneurship and Solidarity Economics* (pp. 329–354). Hershey, PA: IGI Global. doi:10.4018/978-1-5225-0097-1.ch017

Petrisor, I., & Cozmiuc, D. (2017). Global Supply Chain Management Organization at Siemens in the Advent of Industry 4.0. In L. Saglietto & C. Cezanne (Eds.), *Global Intermediation and Logistics Service Providers* (pp. 123–142). Hershey, PA: IGI Global. doi:10.4018/978-1-5225-2133-4.ch007

Pew Research. (2012). *Pew Internet: Social Networking*. Retrieved from http://www.pewinternet.org/Commentary/2012/March/Pew-Internet-Social-Networking-less-detail.aspx

Pierce, J. M., Velliaris, D. M., & Edwards, J. (2017). A Living Case Study: A Journey Not a Destination. In N. Silton (Ed.), *Exploring the Benefits of Creativity in Education, Media, and the Arts* (pp. 158–178). Hershey, PA: IGI Global. doi:10.4018/978-1-5225-0504-4.ch008

Pizam, A., & Fleischer, A. (2002). Severity Versus Frequency of Acts of Terrorism: Which Has a Larger Impact on Tourism Demand? *Journal of Travel Research*, *40*(3), 337–339. doi:10.1177/0047287502040003011

Pritchard, A., Morgan, N., Ateljevic, I., & Harris, C. (Eds.). (2007). Tourism and gender: Embodiment, sensuality and experience. Oxfordshire, UK: CABI; doi:10.1079/9781845932718.0000.

Quinn, R. E. (1988). *Beyond rational management: Mastering the paradoxes and competing demands of high performance*. Jossey-Bass.

Radford, G. S. (1922). *The Control of Quality in Manufacturing*. New York: The Ronald Press Company. Retrieved from https://archive.org/details/controlofquality00radfrich/page/n5

Radosavljevic, M., & Andjelkovic, A. (2017). Multi-Criteria Decision Making Approach for Choosing Business Process for the Improvement: Upgrading of the Six Sigma Methodology. In J. Stanković, P. Delias, S. Marinković, & S. Rochhia (Eds.), *Tools and Techniques for Economic Decision Analysis* (pp. 225–247). Hershey, PA: IGI Global. doi:10.4018/978-1-5225-0959-2.ch011

Radovic, N., & Radojević, T. (2014). *Operational budgeting in hospitality*. . doi:10.15308/finiz-2014-43-44

Radovic, V. M. (2017). Corporate Sustainability and Responsibility and Disaster Risk Reduction: A Serbian Overview. In M. Camilleri (Ed.), *CSR 2.0 and the New Era of Corporate Citizenship* (pp. 147–164). Hershey, PA: IGI Global. doi:10.4018/978-1-5225-1842-6.ch008

Raghunath, K. M., Devi, S. L., & Patro, C. S. (2018). Impact of Risk Assessment Models on Risk Factors: A Holistic Outlook. In K. Strang, M. Korstanje, & N. Vajjhala (Eds.), *Research, Practices, and Innovations in Global Risk and Contingency Management* (pp. 134–153). Hershey, PA: IGI Global. doi:10.4018/978-1-5225-4754-9.ch008

Raman, A., & Goyal, D. P. (2017). Extending IMPLEMENT Framework for Enterprise Information Systems Implementation to Information System Innovation. In M. Tavana (Ed.), *Enterprise Information Systems and the Digitalization of Business Functions* (pp. 137–177). Hershey, PA: IGI Global. doi:10.4018/978-1-5225-2382-6.ch007

Ramirez, E. (2017). *Financial management: Methods, outcomes and challenges*. Hauppauge, NY: Nova Science Publishers, Inc.

Rao, Y., & Zhang, Y. (2017). The Construction and Development of Academic Library Digital Special Subject Databases. In L. Ruan, Q. Zhu, & Y. Ye (Eds.), *Academic Library Development and Administration in China* (pp. 163–183). Hershey, PA: IGI Global. doi:10.4018/978-1-5225-0550-1.ch010

Ravasan, A. Z., Mohammadi, M. M., & Hamidi, H. (2018). An Investigation Into the Critical Success Factors of Implementing Information Technology Service Management Frameworks. In K. Jakobs (Ed.), *Corporate and Global Standardization Initiatives in Contemporary Society* (pp. 200–218). Hershey, PA: IGI Global. doi:10.4018/978-1-5225-5320-5.ch009

Reilly, F. K., Brown, K. C., & Leeds, S. J. (2019). *Investment analysis & portfolio management*. Boston, MA: Cengage.

Renna, P., Izzo, C., & Romaniello, T. (2016). The Business Process Management Systems to Support Continuous Improvements. In W. Nuninger & J. Châtelet (Eds.), *Handbook of Research on Quality Assurance and Value Management in Higher Education* (pp. 237–256). Hershey, PA: IGI Global. doi:10.4018/978-1-5225-0024-7.ch009

Rezaie, S., Mirabedini, S. J., & Abtahi, A. (2018). Designing a Model for Implementation of Business Intelligence in the Banking Industry. *International Journal of Enterprise Information Systems, 14*(1), 77–103. doi:10.4018/IJEIS.2018010105

Rhodes Plaza Hotel. (n.d.). *Quality Policy.* Retrieved from https://www.rhodesplazahotel.com/quality-policy/

Riccò, R. (2016). Diversity Management: Bringing Equality, Equity, and Inclusion in the Workplace. In J. Prescott (Ed.), *Handbook of Research on Race, Gender, and the Fight for Equality* (pp. 335–359). Hershey, PA: IGI Global. doi:10.4018/978-1-5225-0047-6.ch015

Ritchie, B.W., Dorrell, H., Miller, D., & Miller, G. (2002). Crisis Communication and recovery for the tourism industry: Lessons from the 2001 Foot and Mouth Disease Outbreak in the United Kingdom.

Ritchie, B. W. (2009). *Crisis and disaster management for tourism.* Bristol, UK: Channel View. doi:10.21832/9781845411077

Romano, L., Grimaldi, R., & Colasuonno, F. S. (2017). Demand Management as a Success Factor in Project Portfolio Management. In L. Romano (Ed.), *Project Portfolio Management Strategies for Effective Organizational Operations* (pp. 202–219). Hershey, PA: IGI Global. doi:10.4018/978-1-5225-2151-8.ch008

Rood, A. S., & Dziadkowiec, J. (2010). Why use importance performance analysis in mystery shopping? A USA–Poland comparative answer. *Journal of Quality Assurance in Hospitality & Tourism, 11*(1), 1–16. doi:10.1080/15280080903520592

Ross, A. (2015). Why every woman should travel alone. Retrieved October 20, 2015, from http://time.com/3708374/women-travel-alone/

Ross, G. F. (2005). Tourism industry employee workstress – a present and future crisis. *Journal of Travel & Tourism Marketing, 19*(2/3), 133–147. doi:10.1300/J073v19n02_11

Rostek, K. B. (2016). Risk Management: Role and Importance in Business Organization. In D. Jakóbczak (Ed.), *Analyzing Risk through Probabilistic Modeling in Operations Research* (pp. 149–178). Hershey, PA: IGI Global. doi:10.4018/978-1-4666-9458-3.ch007

Rouhani, S., & Savoji, S. R. (2016). A Success Assessment Model for BI Tools Implementation: An Empirical Study of Banking Industry. *International Journal of Business Intelligence Research, 7*(1), 25–44. doi:10.4018/IJBIR.2016010103

Ruan, Z. (2016). A Corpus-Based Functional Analysis of Complex Nominal Groups in Written Business Discourse: The Case of "Business". *International Journal of Computer-Assisted Language Learning and Teaching, 6*(2), 74–90. doi:10.4018/IJCALLT.2016040105

Rudas, I. J., & Fodor, J. (2008). Intelligent systems. *International Journal of Computers, Communications & Control, III*(Suppl.), 132–138.

Ruhi, U. (2018). Towards an Interdisciplinary Socio-Technical Definition of Virtual Communities. In M. Khosrow-Pour, D.B.A. (Ed.), Encyclopedia of Information Science and Technology, Fourth Edition (pp. 4278-4295). Hershey, PA: IGI Global. doi:10.4018/978-1-5225-2255-3.ch371

Ryan, J., Doster, B., Daily, S., & Lewis, C. (2016). A Case Study Perspective for Balanced Perioperative Workflow Achievement through Data-Driven Process Improvement. *International Journal of Healthcare Information Systems and Informatics, 11*(3), 19–41. doi:10.4018/IJHISI.2016070102

Safari, M. R., & Jiang, Q. (2018). The Theory and Practice of IT Governance Maturity and Strategies Alignment: Evidence From Banking Industry. *Journal of Global Information Management, 26*(2), 127–146. doi:10.4018/JGIM.2018040106

Sahoo, J., Pati, B., & Mohanty, B. (2017). Knowledge Management as an Academic Discipline: An Assessment. In B. Gunjal (Ed.), *Managing Knowledge and Scholarly Assets in Academic Libraries* (pp. 99–126). Hershey, PA: IGI Global. doi:10.4018/978-1-5225-1741-2.ch005

Saini, D. (2017). Relevance of Teaching Values and Ethics in Management Education. In N. Baporikar (Ed.), *Management Education for Global Leadership* (pp. 90–111). Hershey, PA: IGI Global. doi:10.4018/978-1-5225-1013-0.ch005

Salawu, R. F., & Agboola, A. A. (2008). The determinants of capital structure of large non-financial listed firms in Nigeria. *The International Journal of Business and Finance Research, 2*(2), 75–84.

Sambhanthan, A. (2017). Assessing and Benchmarking Sustainability in Organisations: An Integrated Conceptual Model. *International Journal of Systems and Service-Oriented Engineering, 7*(4), 22–43. doi:10.4018/IJSSOE.2017100102

Sambhanthan, A., & Potdar, V. (2017). A Study of the Parameters Impacting Sustainability in Information Technology Organizations. *International Journal of Knowledge-Based Organizations, 7*(3), 27–39. doi:10.4018/IJKBO.2017070103

Sánchez-Fernández, M. D., & Manríquez, M. R. (2018). The Entrepreneurial Spirit Based on Social Values: The Digital Generation. In P. Isaias & L. Carvalho (Eds.), *User Innovation and the Entrepreneurship Phenomenon in the Digital Economy* (pp. 173–193). Hershey, PA: IGI Global. doi:10.4018/978-1-5225-2826-5.ch009

Sanchez-Ruiz, L., & Blanco, B. (2017). Process Management for SMEs: Barriers, Enablers, and Benefits. In M. Vemić (Ed.), *Optimal Management Strategies in Small and Medium Enterprises* (pp. 293–319). Hershey, PA: IGI Global. doi:10.4018/978-1-5225-1949-2.ch014

Sanz, L. F., Gómez-Pérez, J., & Castillo-Martinez, A. (2018). Analysis of the European ICT Competence Frameworks. In V. Ahuja & S. Rathore (Eds.), *Multidisciplinary Perspectives on Human Capital and Information Technology Professionals* (pp. 225–245). Hershey, PA: IGI Global. doi:10.4018/978-1-5225-5297-0.ch012

Sarason, S. B. (1974). *The psychological sense of community: Prospects for the community*. San Francisco: Jossey-Bass.

Sarvepalli, A., & Godin, J. (2017). Business Process Management in the Classroom. *Journal of Cases on Information Technology*, *19*(2), 17–28. doi:10.4018/JCIT.2017040102

Satpathy, B., & Muniapan, B. (2016). Ancient Wisdom for Transformational Leadership and Its Insights from the Bhagavad-Gita. In U. Aung & P. Ordoñez de Pablos (Eds.), *Managerial Strategies and Practice in the Asian Business Sector* (pp. 1–10). Hershey, PA: IGI Global. doi:10.4018/978-1-4666-9758-4.ch001

Saygili, E. E., Ozturkoglu, Y., & Kocakulah, M. C. (2017). End Users' Perceptions of Critical Success Factors in ERP Applications. *International Journal of Enterprise Information Systems*, *13*(4), 58–75. doi:10.4018/IJEIS.2017100104

Saygili, E. E., & Saygili, A. T. (2017). Contemporary Issues in Enterprise Information Systems: A Critical Review of CSFs in ERP Implementations. In M. Tavana (Ed.), *Enterprise Information Systems and the Digitalization of Business Functions* (pp. 120–136). Hershey, PA: IGI Global. doi:10.4018/978-1-5225-2382-6.ch006

Schmidgall, R. S. (2016). *Hospitality industry managerial accounting*. Lansing, MI: AHLEI American Hotel & Lodging Educational Institute.

Seidenstricker, S., & Antonino, A. (2018). Business Model Innovation-Oriented Technology Management for Emergent Technologies. In M. Khosrow-Pour, D.B.A. (Ed.), Encyclopedia of Information Science and Technology, Fourth Edition (pp. 4560-4569). Hershey, PA: IGI Global. doi:10.4018/978-1-5225-2255-3.ch396

Senaratne, S., & Gunarathne, A. D. (2017). Excellence Perspective for Management Education from a Global Accountants' Hub in Asia. In N. Baporikar (Ed.), *Management Education for Global Leadership* (pp. 158–180). Hershey, PA: IGI Global. doi:10.4018/978-1-5225-1013-0.ch008

Sensuse, D. I., & Cahyaningsih, E. (2018). Knowledge Management Models: A Summative Review. *International Journal of Information Systems in the Service Sector*, *10*(1), 71–100. doi:10.4018/IJISSS.2018010105

Sensuse, D. I., Wibowo, W. C., & Cahyaningsih, E. (2016). Indonesian Government Knowledge Management Model: A Theoretical Model. *Information Resources Management Journal*, *29*(1), 91–108. doi:10.4018/irmj.2016010106

Seth, M., Goyal, D., & Kiran, R. (2017). Diminution of Impediments in Implementation of Supply Chain Management Information System for Enhancing its Effectiveness in Indian Automobile Industry. *Journal of Global Information Management*, *25*(3), 1–20. doi:10.4018/JGIM.2017070101

Seyal, A. H., & Rahman, M. N. (2017). Investigating Impact of Inter-Organizational Factors in Measuring ERP Systems Success: Bruneian Perspectives. In M. Tavana (Ed.), *Enterprise Information Systems and the Digitalization of Business Functions* (pp. 178–204). Hershey, PA: IGI Global. doi:10.4018/978-1-5225-2382-6.ch008

Shahzad, F., Luqman, R. A., Khan, A. R., & Shabbir, L. (2012). Impact of organizational culture on organizational performance: An overview. *Interdisciplinary Journal of Contemporary Research in Business*, *3*(9), 975–985.

Shaikh, A. A., & Karjaluoto, H. (2016). On Some Misconceptions Concerning Digital Banking and Alternative Delivery Channels. *International Journal of E-Business Research*, *12*(3), 1–16. doi:10.4018/IJEBR.2016070101

Shams, S. M. (2016). Stakeholder Relationship Management in Online Business and Competitive Value Propositions: Evidence from the Sports Industry. *International Journal of Online Marketing*, *6*(2), 1–17. doi:10.4018/IJOM.2016040101

Shamsuzzoha, A. (2016). Management of Risk and Resilience within Collaborative Business Network. In R. Addo-Tenkorang, J. Kantola, P. Helo, & A. Shamsuzzoha (Eds.), *Supply Chain Strategies and the Engineer-to-Order Approach* (pp. 143–159). Hershey, PA: IGI Global. doi:10.4018/978-1-5225-0021-6.ch008

Shankar, J., Jeffrey I., Murali M., Eileen K., & Ross, R. (2011). Innovations in Shopper Marketing: Current Insights and Future Research Issues. *Journal of Retailing*, *87*(1), 29-42.

Shanker, D. (2008). ICT and tourism: Challenges and opportunities. *Paper presented at Conference on Tourism in India – Challenges Ahead*. Academic Press.

Shaqrah, A. A. (2018). Analyzing Business Intelligence Systems Based on 7s Model of McKinsey. *International Journal of Business Intelligence Research*, *9*(1), 53–63. doi:10.4018/IJBIR.2018010104

Sharma, A. J. (2017). Enhancing Sustainability through Experiential Learning in Management Education. In N. Baporikar (Ed.), *Management Education for Global Leadership* (pp. 256–274). Hershey, PA: IGI Global. doi:10.4018/978-1-5225-1013-0.ch013

Shetty, K. P. (2017). Responsible Global Leadership: Ethical Challenges in Management Education. In N. Baporikar (Ed.), *Innovation and Shifting Perspectives in Management Education* (pp. 194–223). Hershey, PA: IGI Global. doi:10.4018/978-1-5225-1019-2.ch009

Shewhart, W. A. (1930). Economic Quality Control of Manufactured Product. *The Bell System Technical Journal*, *9*(2), 2. doi:10.1002/j.1538-7305.1930.tb00373.x

Sigala, M., & Chalkiti, K. (2014). Investigating the exploitation of web 2.0 for knowledge management in the Greek tourism industry: An utilisation–importance analysis. *Computers in Human Behavior*, *30*, 800–812. doi:10.1016/j.chb.2013.05.032

Simão, J., & Partidário, M. (2012). How does tourism planning contribute to sustainable development? *Sustainable Development*, *20*(6), 372–385. doi:10.1002d.495

Sinthupundaja, J., & Kohda, Y. (2017). Effects of Corporate Social Responsibility and Creating Shared Value on Sustainability. *International Journal of Sustainable Entrepreneurship and Corporate Social Responsibility*, *2*(1), 27–38. doi:10.4018/IJSECSR.2017010103

Škarica, I., & Hrgović, A. V. (2018). Implementation of Total Quality Management Principles in Public Health Institutes in the Republic of Croatia. *International Journal of Productivity Management and Assessment Technologies*, *6*(1), 1–16. doi:10.4018/IJPMAT.2018010101

Small, J. (1999). Memory-work: A method for researching women's tourist experiences. *Tourism Management*, *20*(1), 25–35. doi:10.1016/S0261-5177(98)00091-0

Smircich, L. (1983). Concepts of culture and organizational analysis. *Administrative Science Quarterly*, *28*(3), 339–358. doi:10.2307/2392246

Smuts, H., Kotzé, P., Van der Merwe, A., & Loock, M. (2017). Framework for Managing Shared Knowledge in an Information Systems Outsourcing Context. *International Journal of Knowledge Management*, *13*(4), 1–30. doi:10.4018/IJKM.2017100101

Soares, E. R., & Zaidan, F. H. (2016). Information Architecture and Business Modeling in Modern Organizations of Information Technology: Professional Career Plan in Organizations IT. In G. Jamil, J. Poças Rascão, F. Ribeiro, & A. Malheiro da Silva (Eds.), *Handbook of Research on Information Architecture and Management in Modern Organizations* (pp. 439–457). Hershey, PA: IGI Global. doi:10.4018/978-1-4666-8637-3.ch020

Sonmez, S. F., Apostolopoulos, Y., & Peter, E. T. (1999). Tourism in crisis: Managing the effects of terrorism. *Journal of Travel Research*, *38*(1), 13–21. doi:10.1177/004728759903800104

Sonmez, S. F., Yiorgos, A., & Tarlow, P. (1999). Tourism in crisis: Managing the effects of terrorism. *Journal of Travel Research*, *38*(6), 3.

Sørensen, J. B. (2002). The strength of corporate culture and the reliability of firm performance. *Administrative Science Quarterly*, *47*(1), 70–91. doi:10.2307/3094891

Sousa, M. J., Cruz, R., Dias, I., & Caracol, C. (2017). Information Management Systems in the Supply Chain. In G. Jamil, A. Soares, & C. Pessoa (Eds.), *Handbook of Research on Information Management for Effective Logistics and Supply Chains* (pp. 469–485). Hershey, PA: IGI Global. doi:10.4018/978-1-5225-0973-8.ch025

Spender, J. C. (1989). Industry recipes: The nature and sources of managerial judgment. *Oxford, UK: Basic Blackwell.(1994)," Knowing, Managing and Learning. Management Learning*, *25*(3), 387–412. doi:10.1177/135050769402500302

Spremic, M., Turulja, L., & Bajgoric, N. (2018). Two Approaches in Assessing Business Continuity Management Attitudes in the Organizational Context. In N. Bajgoric (Ed.), *Always-On Enterprise Information Systems for Modern Organizations* (pp. 159–183). Hershey, PA: IGI Global. doi:10.4018/978-1-5225-3704-5.ch008

State-wise Number of Domestic Tourist Visits in India. (n.d.). India stat. Retrieved from http://www.indiastat.com/tourism/29/stats.aspx

Stblaw.com. (2013). *Social Media and Regulation FD: SEC Uses Netflix Episode to Clarify Policy, Not Liberalize It*. Retrieved from http://www.stblaw.com/docs/default-source/cold-fusion-existing-content/publications/pub1605.pdf?sfvrsn=2

Steenkamp, A. L. (2018). Some Insights in Computer Science and Information Technology. In *Examining the Changing Role of Supervision in Doctoral Research Projects: Emerging Research and Opportunities* (pp. 113–133). Hershey, PA: IGI Global. doi:10.4018/978-1-5225-2610-0.ch005

Stefanelli, J. M. (1994). Using mystery shoppers to maintain hospitality company service standards. *Hospitality & Tourism Educator*, *6*(1), 17–18. doi:10.1080/23298758.1994.10685540

Stilwell, D. (2011). *Indicadores de sustentabilidade aplicados ao contexto do desenvolvimento turístico português. Dissertação de Mestrado*. Faculty of Sciences, University of Lisbon.

Stone, G. J., & Nichol, S. (1999). Older, single female holidaymakers in the United Kingdom: Who needs them? *Journal of Vacation Marketing*, *5*(1), 7–17. doi:10.1177/135676679900500102

Studdard, N., Dawson, M., Burton, S. L., Jackson, N., Leonard, B., Quisenberry, W., & Rahim, E. (2016). Nurturing Social Entrepreneurship and Building Social Entrepreneurial Self-Efficacy: Focusing on Primary and Secondary Schooling to Develop Future Social Entrepreneurs. In Z. Fields (Ed.), *Incorporating Business Models and Strategies into Social Entrepreneurship* (pp. 154–175). Hershey, PA: IGI Global. doi:10.4018/978-1-4666-8748-6.ch010

Sun, Z. (2016). A Framework for Developing Management Intelligent Systems. *International Journal of Systems and Service-Oriented Engineering*, *6*(1), 37–53. doi:10.4018/IJSSOE.2016010103

Survey on Domestic Tourism. (n.d.). Retrieved from http://www.jammuandkashmirstat.com/tourism/29/stats.aspx

Sustainability Index, G. D. S. (2017). *Sustainable destination management trends and insights: A path to a brighter future*. Available at: http://www.100carbonneutral.com/assets/sustainable-destination-management-trends-and-insights--a-path-to-a-brighter-future.pdf

Swami, B., & Mphele, G. T. (2016). Problems Preventing Growth of Small Entrepreneurs: A Case Study of a Few Small Entrepreneurs in Botswana Sub-Urban Areas. In N. Baporikar (Ed.), *Handbook of Research on Entrepreneurship in the Contemporary Knowledge-Based Global Economy* (pp. 479–508). Hershey, PA: IGI Global. doi:10.4018/978-1-4666-8798-1.ch020

Tabach, A., & Croteau, A. (2017). Configurations of Information Technology Governance Practices and Business Unit Performance. *International Journal of IT/Business Alignment and Governance*, *8*(2), 1–27. doi:10.4018/IJITBAG.2017070101

Tainer, E. M. (2006). *Using economic indicators to improve investment analysis*. Hoboken, NJ: J. Wiley & Sons.

Talaue, G. M., & Iqbal, T. (2017). Assessment of e-Business Mode of Selected Private Universities in the Philippines and Pakistan. *International Journal of Online Marketing*, *7*(4), 63–77. doi:10.4018/IJOM.2017100105

Tambo, T. (2018). Fashion Retail Innovation: About Context, Antecedents, and Outcome in Technological Change Projects. In I. Management Association (Ed.), Fashion and Textiles: Breakthroughs in Research and Practice (pp. 233-260). Hershey, PA: IGI Global. doi:10.4018/978-1-5225-3432-7.ch010

Tambo, T., & Mikkelsen, O. E. (2016). Fashion Supply Chain Optimization: Linking Make-to-Order Purchasing and B2B E-Commerce. In S. Joshi & R. Joshi (Eds.), *Designing and Implementing Global Supply Chain Management* (pp. 1–21). Hershey, PA: IGI Global. doi:10.4018/978-1-4666-9720-1.ch001

Tam, G. C. (2017). Project Manager Sustainability Competence. In *Managerial Strategies and Green Solutions for Project Sustainability* (pp. 178–207). Hershey, PA: IGI Global. doi:10.4018/978-1-5225-2371-0.ch008

Tandon, K. (2016). Innovative Andragogy: The Paradigm Shift to Heutagogy. In S. Tiwari & L. Nafees (Eds.), *Innovative Management Education Pedagogies for Preparing Next-Generation Leaders* (pp. 238–257). Hershey, PA: IGI Global. doi:10.4018/978-1-4666-9691-4.ch014

Tantau, A. D., & Frăţilă, L. C. (2018). Information and Management System for Renewable Energy Business. In *Entrepreneurship and Business Development in the Renewable Energy Sector* (pp. 200–244). Hershey, PA: IGI Global. doi:10.4018/978-1-5225-3625-3.ch006

Tavmergen, İ. P. (2002). *Turizm Sektöründe Kalite Yönetimi.* Seçkin Pub.

Taylor, F. W. (1911). *Principles of Scientific Management.* New York: Harper The Automobile Association (2019). *Ratings and Awards.* Retrieved from http://www.theaa.com/hotel-services/ratings-and-awards

Teixeira, N., Pardal, P. N., & Rafael, B. G. (2018). Internationalization, Financial Performance, and Organizational Challenges: A Success Case in Portugal. In L. Carvalho (Ed.), *Handbook of Research on Entrepreneurial Ecosystems and Social Dynamics in a Globalized World* (pp. 379–423). Hershey, PA: IGI Global. doi:10.4018/978-1-5225-3525-6.ch017

The Walt Disney Company. (2019). *About.* Retrieved from https://www.thewaltdisneycompany.com/about/

Torluccio, G. (2012, Autumn). Financials Menu at European Restaurants, Tourism. *An International Multidisciplinary Journal of Tourism*, *7*(2), 323–342.

Torres, E. N. (2012). *Hotel general managers' use of consumer, expert, and internal feedback to improve service quality*(Doctoral dissertation). Purdue University.

Trad, A., & Kalpić, D. (2018). The Business Transformation Framework, Agile Project and Change Management. In M. Khosrow-Pour, D.B.A. (Ed.), Encyclopedia of Information Science and Technology, Fourth Edition (pp. 620-635). Hershey, PA: IGI Global. doi:10.4018/978-1-5225-2255-3.ch054

Trad, A., & Kalpić, D. (2016). The E-Business Transformation Framework for E-Commerce Architecture-Modeling Projects. In I. Lee (Ed.), *Encyclopedia of E-Commerce Development, Implementation, and Management* (pp. 733–753). Hershey, PA: IGI Global. doi:10.4018/978-1-4666-9787-4.ch052

Trad, A., & Kalpić, D. (2016). The E-Business Transformation Framework for E-Commerce Control and Monitoring Pattern. In I. Lee (Ed.), *Encyclopedia of E-Commerce Development, Implementation, and Management* (pp. 754–777). Hershey, PA: IGI Global. doi:10.4018/978-1-4666-9787-4.ch053

Trad, A., & Kalpić, D. (2018). The Business Transformation and Enterprise Architecture Framework: The Financial Engineering E-Risk Management and E-Law Integration. In B. Sergi, F. Fidanoski, M. Ziolo, & V. Naumovski (Eds.), *Regaining Global Stability After the Financial Crisis* (pp. 46–65). Hershey, PA: IGI Global. doi:10.4018/978-1-5225-4026-7.ch003

Tükeltürk Aydın, Ş. (2008). *Hizmet İşletmelerinde Gizli Müşteri Uygulamalarının İnsan Kaynakları Yönetimi Açısından Değerlendirilmesi*. Ekim-Kasım-Aralık.

Turulja, L., & Bajgoric, N. (2018). Business Continuity and Information Systems: A Systematic Literature Review. In N. Bajgoric (Ed.), *Always-On Enterprise Information Systems for Modern Organizations* (pp. 60–87). Hershey, PA: IGI Global. doi:10.4018/978-1-5225-3704-5.ch004

UNTWO. (2016, June 28). *Quality Management Key Competitiveness Tourism Destinations*. [Press release]. Retrieved from www.media.unwto.org/press-release/2016-06-28/quality-management-key-competitiveness-tourism-destinations

Upneja, A., & Dalbor, M. (2001). An Examination of Capital Structure in the Restaurant Industry. *International Journal of Contemporary Hospitality Management*, *13*(2), 54–59. doi:10.1108/09596110110381825

USAID. (2006). Information Communication Technologies (ICT) and Tourism. Presentation hold in Arusha, Tanzania. Retrieved from www.usaid.gov/our_work/agriculture/landmanagement/tourism/sidebar/ict.pdf

Van Hooft, S.J.C. (2010). Towards an ICT framework for sustainable tourism (Masters Dissertation). Retrieved from https://webcache.googleusercontent.com/search?q=cache:crsritxHRTUJ:https://www.ru.n/publish/pages/769526/towards_an_ict_framework_for_sustainable_tourism__sander_van_hooft.pdf+&cd=1&hl=en&ct=clnk&gl=ng

van Wessel, R. M., de Vries, H. J., & Ribbers, P. M. (2016). Business Benefits through Company IT Standardization. In K. Jakobs (Ed.), *Effective Standardization Management in Corporate Settings* (pp. 34–53). Hershey, PA: IGI Global. doi:10.4018/978-1-4666-9737-9.ch003

Vargas-Hernández, J. G. (2017). Professional Integrity in Business Management Education. In N. Baporikar (Ed.), *Management Education for Global Leadership* (pp. 70–89). Hershey, PA: IGI Global. doi:10.4018/978-1-5225-1013-0.ch004

Vasista, T. G., & AlAbdullatif, A. M. (2017). Role of Electronic Customer Relationship Management in Demand Chain Management: A Predictive Analytic Approach. *International Journal of Information Systems and Supply Chain Management*, *10*(1), 53–67. doi:10.4018/IJISSCM.2017010104

Vergidis, K. (2016). Rediscovering Business Processes: Definitions, Patterns, and Modelling Approaches. In P. Papajorgji, F. Pinet, A. Guimarães, & J. Papathanasiou (Eds.), *Automated Enterprise Systems for Maximizing Business Performance* (pp. 97–122). Hershey, PA: IGI Global. doi:10.4018/978-1-4666-8841-4.ch007

Vieru, D., & Bourdeau, S. (2017). Survival in the Digital Era: A Digital Competence-Based Multi-Case Study in the Canadian SME Clothing Industry. *International Journal of Social and Organizational Dynamics in IT*, *6*(1), 17–34. doi:10.4018/IJSODIT.2017010102

Vijayan, G., & Kamarulzaman, N. H. (2017). An Introduction to Sustainable Supply Chain Management and Business Implications. In M. Khan, M. Hussain, & M. Ajmal (Eds.), *Green Supply Chain Management for Sustainable Business Practice* (pp. 27–50). Hershey, PA: IGI Global. doi:10.4018/978-1-5225-0635-5.ch002

VisitBritain. (2017). *VisitEngland announces contract with the AA to run the VisitEngland Quality Assessment Schemes*. Retrieved from https://www.visitbritain.org/visitengland-announces-contract-aa-run-visitengland-quality-assessment-schemes

Vlachvei, A., & Notta, O. (2017). Firm Competitiveness: Theories, Evidence, and Measurement. In A. Vlachvei, O. Notta, K. Karantininis, & N. Tsounis (Eds.), *Factors Affecting Firm Competitiveness and Performance in the Modern Business World* (pp. 1–42). Hershey, PA: IGI Global. doi:10.4018/978-1-5225-0843-4.ch001

von Rosing, M., Fullington, N., & Walker, J. (2016). Using the Business Ontology and Enterprise Standards to Transform Three Leading Organizations. *International Journal of Conceptual Structures and Smart Applications*, *4*(1), 71–99. doi:10.4018/IJCSSA.2016010104

von Rosing, M., & von Scheel, H. (2016). Using the Business Ontology to Develop Enterprise Standards. *International Journal of Conceptual Structures and Smart Applications*, *4*(1), 48–70. doi:10.4018/IJCSSA.2016010103

Wadongo, B., Odhuno, E., Kambona, O., & Othuon, L. (2010). Key performance indicators in the Kenyan hospitality industry: A managerial perspective. *Benchmarking. International Journal (Toronto, Ont.)*, *17*(6), 858–875.

Waghmode, M. L., & Jamsandekar, P. P. (2013). Role of ICT in tourism. *International E-journal of ongoing research in management and IT.*

Walczak, S. (2016). Artificial Neural Networks and other AI Applications for Business Management Decision Support. *International Journal of Sociotechnology and Knowledge Development*, *8*(4), 1–20. doi:10.4018/IJSKD.2016100101

Walters, G. A., Mair, J. A., & Ritchie, B. (2012). *The Australian Tourism Market's Response to the 2011 Queensland Floods*. Australia: University of Queensland.

Wamba, S. F., Akter, S., Kang, H., Bhattacharya, M., & Upal, M. (2016). The Primer of Social Media Analytics. *Journal of Organizational and End User Computing*, *28*(2), 1–12. doi:10.4018/JOEUC.2016040101

Wang, C., Schofield, M., Li, X., & Ou, X. (2017). Do Chinese Students in Public and Private Higher Education Institutes Perform at Different Level in One of the Leadership Skills: Critical Thinking?: An Exploratory Comparison. In V. Wang (Ed.), *Encyclopedia of Strategic Leadership and Management* (pp. 160–181). Hershey, PA: IGI Global. doi:10.4018/978-1-5225-1049-9.ch013

Wang, F., Raisinghani, M. S., Mora, M., & Wang, X. (2016). Strategic E-Business Management through a Balanced Scored Card Approach. In I. Lee (Ed.), *Encyclopedia of E-Commerce Development, Implementation, and Management* (pp. 361–386). Hershey, PA: IGI Global. doi:10.4018/978-1-4666-9787-4.ch027

Wang, J. (2017). Multi-Agent based Production Management Decision System Modelling for the Textile Enterprise. *Journal of Global Information Management*, *25*(4), 1–15. doi:10.4018/JGIM.2017100101

Wang, Y. S. (2009). The impact of crisis events and macroeconomic activity on Taiwan's international inbound tourism demand. *Tourism Management*, *30*(1), 75–82. doi:10.1016/j.tourman.2008.04.010

Warner-Smith, P. (2013). Travel, young women and "The Weekly", 1959-1968. *Annals of Leisure Research*, *3*(1), 33–46. doi:10.1080/11745398.2000.10600884

Washburn, D., Sindhu, U., Balaouras, S., Dines, R. A., Hayes, N., & Nelson, L. E. (2010). Helping CIOs Understand "Smart City" Initiatives. UWForum. Retrieved from http://www.uwforum.org/upload/board/forrester_help_cios_smart_city.pdf

Werthner, H. (2003). Intelligent Systems in Travel and Tourism. In *Proceedings of International Joint Conference on Artificial Intelligence (IJCAI 2003)* (pp. 1620-1625). Retrieved from http://ijcai.org/Past%20Proceedings/IJCAI-2003/PDF/286.pdf

Westwood, S., Pritchard, A., & Morgan, N. J. (2000). Gender-blind marketing: Businesswomen's perceptions of airline services. *Tourism Management*, *21*(4), 353–362. doi:10.1016/S0261-5177(99)00069-2

Wiedemann, A., & Gewald, H. (2017). Examining Cross-Domain Alignment: The Correlation of Business Strategy, IT Management, and IT Business Value. *International Journal of IT/Business Alignment and Governance*, *8*(1), 17–31. doi:10.4018/IJITBAG.2017010102

Wiele, T. V. D., Hesselink, M., & Iwaarden, J. V. (2005). Mystery shopping: A tool to develop insight into shopper service provision. *Total Quality Management & Business Excellence*, *16*(4), 529–541. doi:10.1080/14783360500078433

Wilkins, A. L., & Ouchi, W. G. (1983). Efficient cultures: Exploring the relationship between culture and organizational performance. *Administrative Science Quarterly*, *28*(3), 468–481. doi:10.2307/2392253

Wilson, E. (2004). A "Journey of her own"? The impact of constraints on women's solo travel (PhD Thesis). Griffith University.

Wilson, A. M. (1998). The use of mystery shopping in the measurement of service delivery. *Service Industries Journal, 18*(3), 148–163. doi:10.1080/02642069800000037

Wilson, A. M. (2001). Mystery shopping: Using deception to measure service performance. *Psychology and Marketing, 18*(7), 721–734. doi:10.1002/mar.1027

Wilson, E., & Little, D. E. (2005). A "relative escape"? The impact of constraints on women who travel solo. *Tourism Review International, 9*(2), 155–175. doi:10.3727/154427205774791672

Wilson, E., & Little, D. E. (2008). The solo female travel experience: Exploring the "geography of women's fear". *Current Issues in Tourism, 11*(2), 167–186. doi:10.2167/cit342.0

Wöber, K. W. (2003). Information supply in tourism management by marketing decision support systems. *Tourism Management, 24*(3), 241–255. doi:10.1016/S0261-5177(02)00071-7

Wolf, R., & Thiel, M. (2018). Advancing Global Business Ethics in China: Reducing Poverty Through Human and Social Welfare. In S. Hipsher (Ed.), *Examining the Private Sector's Role in Wealth Creation and Poverty Reduction* (pp. 67–84). Hershey, PA: IGI Global. doi:10.4018/978-1-5225-3117-3.ch004

Woodhall, G., & Stuttard, A. (1999). *Financial Management.* London: Macmillan Education UK Imprint.

World Trade and Tourism Council Report. (2018). Travel & Tourism Economic Impact 2018. Retrieved from Https://Www.Wttc.Org//Media/Files/Reports/Economic%20impact%20research/Regions%202016/World2018.Pdf

WTO - World Tourism Organisation (2013). *Sustainable Tourism for Development.* Author.

WTO - World Tourism Organisation. (2004). Indicators of sustainable development for tourism destinations. A guidebook. Author.

WTTC. (2014). *Travel and Tourism Economic Impact.*

Wu, J., Ding, F., Xu, M., Mo, Z., & Jin, A. (2016). Investigating the Determinants of Decision-Making on Adoption of Public Cloud Computing in E-government. *Journal of Global Information Management, 24*(3), 71–89. doi:10.4018/JGIM.2016070104

Xu, L., & de Vrieze, P. (2016). Building Situational Applications for Virtual Enterprises. In I. Lee (Ed.), *Encyclopedia of E-Commerce Development, Implementation, and Management* (pp. 715–724). Hershey, PA: IGI Global. doi:10.4018/978-1-4666-9787-4.ch050

Yablonsky, S. (2018). Innovation Platforms: Data and Analytics Platforms. In *Multi-Sided Platforms (MSPs) and Sharing Strategies in the Digital Economy: Emerging Research and Opportunities* (pp. 72–95). Hershey, PA: IGI Global. doi:10.4018/978-1-5225-5457-8.ch003

Yaprak, A., Tasoluk, B., & Kocas, C. (2015). Market orientation, managerial perceptions, and corporate culture in an emerging market: Evidence from Turkey. *International Business Review, 24*(3), 443–456. doi:10.1016/j.ibusrev.2014.10.003

Yıldırgan, Ö. G. R., Met, Ö. L., & Batman, O. (2016). Müşteri İlişkileri Yönetimi Kapsamında Gizli Müşteri Alışverişi: Zincir Otel Örneği. *Journal of Travel and Hospitality Management, 13*(3), 56–67.

Yusoff, A., Ahmad, N. H., & Halim, H. A. (2017). Agropreneurship among Gen Y in Malaysia: The Role of Academic Institutions. In N. Ahmad, T. Ramayah, H. Halim, & S. Rahman (Eds.), *Handbook of Research on Small and Medium Enterprises in Developing Countries* (pp. 23–47). Hershey, PA: IGI Global. doi:10.4018/978-1-5225-2165-5.ch002

Zanin, F., Comuzzi, E., & Costantini, A. (2018). The Effect of Business Strategy and Stock Market Listing on the Use of Risk Assessment Tools. In *Management Control Systems in Complex Settings: Emerging Research and Opportunities* (pp. 145–168). Hershey, PA: IGI Global. doi:10.4018/978-1-5225-3987-2.ch007

Zgheib, P. W. (2017). Corporate Innovation and Intrapreneurship in the Middle East. In P. Zgheib (Ed.), *Entrepreneurship and Business Innovation in the Middle East* (pp. 37–56). Hershey, PA: IGI Global. doi:10.4018/978-1-5225-2066-5.ch003

Zhou, Z., Zhang, Q., Chenting, S., & Zhou, N. (2011). How do brand communities generate brand relationships? Intermediate mechanisms. *Journal of Business Research*, 890–895.

Zikmund, W. G., Babin, B. J., Carr, J. C., & Griffin, M. (2013). *Business research methods*. Cengage Learning. Retrieved from http://bdrc-continental.com/solutions/mystery-shopping/

Zulkiffli, S. N. A., & Perera, N. (2011). A Literature Analysis on Business Performance For SMEs: Subjective or Objective Measures?

Related References

To continue our tradition of advancing information science and technology research, we have compiled a list of recommended IGI Global readings. These references will provide additional information and guidance to further enrich your knowledge and assist you with your own research and future publications.

Abtahi, M. S., Behboudi, L., & Hasanabad, H. M. (2017). Factors Affecting Internet Advertising Adoption in Ad Agencies. *International Journal of Innovation in the Digital Economy*, *8*(4), 18–29. doi:10.4018/IJIDE.2017100102

Agrawal, S. (2017). The Impact of Emerging Technologies and Social Media on Different Business(es): Marketing and Management. In O. Rishi & A. Sharma (Eds.), *Maximizing Business Performance and Efficiency Through Intelligent Systems* (pp. 37–49). Hershey, PA: IGI Global. doi:10.4018/978-1-5225-2234-8.ch002

Alnoukari, M., Razouk, R., & Hanano, A. (2016). BSC-SI: A Framework for Integrating Strategic Intelligence in Corporate Strategic Management. *International Journal of Social and Organizational Dynamics in IT*, *5*(2), 1–14. doi:10.4018/IJSODIT.2016070101

Alnoukari, M., Razouk, R., & Hanano, A. (2016). BSC-SI, A Framework for Integrating Strategic Intelligence in Corporate Strategic Management. *International Journal of Strategic Information Technology and Applications*, *7*(1), 32–44. doi:10.4018/IJSITA.2016010103

Altındağ, E. (2016). Current Approaches in Change Management. In A. Goksoy (Ed.), *Organizational Change Management Strategies in Modern Business* (pp. 24–51). Hershey, PA: IGI Global. doi:10.4018/978-1-4666-9533-7.ch002

Related References

Alvarez-Dionisi, L. E., Turner, R., & Mittra, M. (2016). Global Project Management Trends. *International Journal of Information Technology Project Management, 7*(3), 54–73. doi:10.4018/IJITPM.2016070104

Anantharaman, R. N., Rajeswari, K. S., Angusamy, A., & Kuppusamy, J. (2017). Role of Self-Efficacy and Collective Efficacy as Moderators of Occupational Stress Among Software Development Professionals. *International Journal of Human Capital and Information Technology Professionals, 8*(2), 45–58. doi:10.4018/IJHCITP.2017040103

Aninze, F., El-Gohary, H., & Hussain, J. (2018). The Role of Microfinance to Empower Women: The Case of Developing Countries. *International Journal of Customer Relationship Marketing and Management, 9*(1), 54–78. doi:10.4018/IJCRMM.2018010104

Arsenijević, O. M., Orčić, D., & Kastratović, E. (2017). Development of an Optimization Tool for Intangibles in SMEs: A Case Study from Serbia with a Pilot Research in the Prestige by Milka Company. In M. Vemić (Ed.), *Optimal Management Strategies in Small and Medium Enterprises* (pp. 320–347). Hershey, PA: IGI Global. doi:10.4018/978-1-5225-1949-2.ch015

Aryanto, V. D., Wismantoro, Y., & Widyatmoko, K. (2018). Implementing Eco-Innovation by Utilizing the Internet to Enhance Firm's Marketing Performance: Study of Green Batik Small and Medium Enterprises in Indonesia. *International Journal of E-Business Research, 14*(1), 21–36. doi:10.4018/IJEBR.2018010102

Atiku, S. O., & Fields, Z. (2017). Multicultural Orientations for 21st Century Global Leadership. In N. Baporikar (Ed.), *Management Education for Global Leadership* (pp. 28–51). Hershey, PA: IGI Global. doi:10.4018/978-1-5225-1013-0.ch002

Atiku, S. O., & Fields, Z. (2018). Organisational Learning Dimensions and Talent Retention Strategies for the Service Industries. In N. Baporikar (Ed.), *Global Practices in Knowledge Management for Societal and Organizational Development* (pp. 358–381). Hershey, PA: IGI Global. doi:10.4018/978-1-5225-3009-1.ch017

Ávila, L., & Teixeira, L. (2018). The Main Concepts Behind the Dematerialization of Business Processes. In M. Khosrow-Pour, D.B.A. (Ed.), Encyclopedia of Information Science and Technology, Fourth Edition (pp. 888-898). Hershey, PA: IGI Global. doi:10.4018/978-1-5225-2255-3.ch076

Bartens, Y., Chunpir, H. I., Schulte, F., & Voß, S. (2017). Business/IT Alignment in Two-Sided Markets: A COBIT 5 Analysis for Media Streaming Business Models. In S. De Haes & W. Van Grembergen (Eds.), *Strategic IT Governance and Alignment in Business Settings* (pp. 82–111). Hershey, PA: IGI Global. doi:10.4018/978-1-5225-0861-8.ch004

Bashayreh, A. M. (2018). Organizational Culture and Organizational Performance. In W. Lee & F. Sabetzadeh (Eds.), *Contemporary Knowledge and Systems Science* (pp. 50–69). Hershey, PA: IGI Global. doi:10.4018/978-1-5225-5655-8.ch003

Bedford, D. A. (2018). Sustainable Knowledge Management Strategies: Aligning Business Capabilities and Knowledge Management Goals. In N. Baporikar (Ed.), *Global Practices in Knowledge Management for Societal and Organizational Development* (pp. 46–73). Hershey, PA: IGI Global. doi:10.4018/978-1-5225-3009-1.ch003

Benmoussa, F., Nakara, W. A., & Jaouen, A. (2016). The Use of Social Media by SMEs in the Tourism Industry. In I. Lee (Ed.), *Encyclopedia of E-Commerce Development, Implementation, and Management* (pp. 2159–2170). Hershey, PA: IGI Global. doi:10.4018/978-1-4666-9787-4.ch155

Berger, R. (2016). Indigenous Management and Bottom of Pyramid Countries: The Role of National Institutions. In U. Aung & P. Ordoñez de Pablos (Eds.), *Managerial Strategies and Practice in the Asian Business Sector* (pp. 107–123). Hershey, PA: IGI Global. doi:10.4018/978-1-4666-9758-4.ch007

Bharwani, S., & Musunuri, D. (2018). Reflection as a Process From Theory to Practice. In M. Khosrow-Pour, D.B.A. (Ed.), Encyclopedia of Information Science and Technology, Fourth Edition (pp. 1529-1539). Hershey, PA: IGI Global. doi:10.4018/978-1-5225-2255-3.ch132

Bhatt, G. D., Wang, Z., & Rodger, J. A. (2017). Information Systems Capabilities and Their Effects on Competitive Advantages: A Study of Chinese Companies. *Information Resources Management Journal, 30*(3), 41–57. doi:10.4018/IRMJ.2017070103

Bhushan, M., & Yadav, A. (2017). Concept of Cloud Computing in ESB. In R. Bhadoria, N. Chaudhari, G. Tomar, & S. Singh (Eds.), *Exploring Enterprise Service Bus in the Service-Oriented Architecture Paradigm* (pp. 116–127). Hershey, PA: IGI Global. doi:10.4018/978-1-5225-2157-0.ch008

Bhushan, S. (2017). System Dynamics Base-Model of Humanitarian Supply Chain (HSCM) in Disaster Prone Eco-Communities of India: A Discussion on Simulation and Scenario Results. *International Journal of System Dynamics Applications, 6*(3), 20–37. doi:10.4018/IJSDA.2017070102

Biswas, A., & De, A. K. (2017). On Development of a Fuzzy Stochastic Programming Model with Its Application to Business Management. In S. Trivedi, S. Dey, A. Kumar, & T. Panda (Eds.), *Handbook of Research on Advanced Data Mining Techniques and Applications for Business Intelligence* (pp. 353–378). Hershey, PA: IGI Global. doi:10.4018/978-1-5225-2031-3.ch021

Bücker, J., & Ernste, K. (2018). Use of Brand Heroes in Strategic Reputation Management: The Case of Bacardi, Adidas, and Daimler. In A. Erdemir (Ed.), *Reputation Management Techniques in Public Relations* (pp. 126–150). Hershey, PA: IGI Global. doi:10.4018/978-1-5225-3619-2.ch007

Bureš, V. (2018). Industry 4.0 From the Systems Engineering Perspective: Alternative Holistic Framework Development. In R. Brunet-Thornton & F. Martinez (Eds.), *Analyzing the Impacts of Industry 4.0 in Modern Business Environments* (pp. 199–223). Hershey, PA: IGI Global. doi:10.4018/978-1-5225-3468-6.ch011

Buzady, Z. (2017). Resolving the Magic Cube of Effective Case Teaching: Benchmarking Case Teaching Practices in Emerging Markets – Insights from the Central European University Business School, Hungary. In D. Latusek (Ed.), *Case Studies as a Teaching Tool in Management Education* (pp. 79–103). Hershey, PA: IGI Global. doi:10.4018/978-1-5225-0770-3.ch005

Campatelli, G., Richter, A., & Stocker, A. (2016). Participative Knowledge Management to Empower Manufacturing Workers. *International Journal of Knowledge Management*, *12*(4), 37–50. doi:10.4018/IJKM.2016100103

Căpusneanu, S., & Topor, D. I. (2018). Business Ethics and Cost Management in SMEs: Theories of Business Ethics and Cost Management Ethos. In I. Oncioiu (Ed.), *Ethics and Decision-Making for Sustainable Business Practices* (pp. 109–127). Hershey, PA: IGI Global. doi:10.4018/978-1-5225-3773-1.ch007

Carneiro, A. (2016). Maturity in Health Organization Information Systems: Metrics and Privacy Perspectives. *International Journal of Privacy and Health Information Management*, *4*(2), 1–18. doi:10.4018/IJPHIM.2016070101

Chan, R. L., Mo, P. L., & Moon, K. K. (2018). Strategic and Tactical Measures in Managing Enterprise Risks: A Study of the Textile and Apparel Industry. In K. Strang, M. Korstanje, & N. Vajjhala (Eds.), *Research, Practices, and Innovations in Global Risk and Contingency Management* (pp. 1–19). Hershey, PA: IGI Global. doi:10.4018/978-1-5225-4754-9.ch001

Chandan, H. C. (2016). Motivations and Challenges of Female Entrepreneurship in Developed and Developing Economies. In N. Baporikar (Ed.), *Handbook of Research on Entrepreneurship in the Contemporary Knowledge-Based Global Economy* (pp. 260–286). Hershey, PA: IGI Global. doi:10.4018/978-1-4666-8798-1.ch012

Charlier, S. D., Burke-Smalley, L. A., & Fisher, S. L. (2018). Undergraduate Programs in the U.S: A Contextual and Content-Based Analysis. In J. Mendy (Ed.), *Teaching Human Resources and Organizational Behavior at the College Level* (pp. 26–57). Hershey, PA: IGI Global. doi:10.4018/978-1-5225-2820-3.ch002

Chaudhuri, S. (2016). Application of Web-Based Geographical Information System (GIS) in E-Business. In U. Panwar, R. Kumar, & N. Ray (Eds.), *Handbook of Research on Promotional Strategies and Consumer Influence in the Service Sector* (pp. 389–405). Hershey, PA: IGI Global. doi:10.4018/978-1-5225-0143-5.ch023

Choudhuri, P. S. (2016). An Empirical Study on the Quality of Services Offered by the Private Life Insurers in Burdwan. In U. Panwar, R. Kumar, & N. Ray (Eds.), *Handbook of Research on Promotional Strategies and Consumer Influence in the Service Sector* (pp. 31–55). Hershey, PA: IGI Global. doi:10.4018/978-1-5225-0143-5.ch002

Dahlberg, T., Kivijärvi, H., & Saarinen, T. (2017). IT Investment Consistency and Other Factors Influencing the Success of IT Performance. In S. De Haes & W. Van Grembergen (Eds.), *Strategic IT Governance and Alignment in Business Settings* (pp. 176–208). Hershey, PA: IGI Global. doi:10.4018/978-1-5225-0861-8.ch007

Damnjanović, A. M. (2017). Knowledge Management Optimization through IT and E-Business Utilization: A Qualitative Study on Serbian SMEs. In M. Vemić (Ed.), *Optimal Management Strategies in Small and Medium Enterprises* (pp. 249–267). Hershey, PA: IGI Global. doi:10.4018/978-1-5225-1949-2.ch012

Daneshpour, H. (2017). Integrating Sustainable Development into Project Portfolio Management through Application of Open Innovation. In M. Vemić (Ed.), *Optimal Management Strategies in Small and Medium Enterprises* (pp. 370–387). Hershey, PA: IGI Global. doi:10.4018/978-1-5225-1949-2.ch017

Daniel, A. D., & Reis de Castro, V. (2018). Entrepreneurship Education: How to Measure the Impact on Nascent Entrepreneurs. In A. Carrizo Moreira, J. Guilherme Leitão Dantas, & F. Manuel Valente (Eds.), *Nascent Entrepreneurship and Successful New Venture Creation* (pp. 85–110). Hershey, PA: IGI Global. doi:10.4018/978-1-5225-2936-1.ch004

David, F., van der Sijde, P., & van den Besselaar, P. (2016). Enterpreneurial Incentives, Obstacles, and Management in University-Business Co-Operation: The Case of Indonesia. In J. Saiz-Álvarez (Ed.), *Handbook of Research on Social Entrepreneurship and Solidarity Economics* (pp. 499–518). Hershey, PA: IGI Global. doi:10.4018/978-1-5225-0097-1.ch024

David, R., Swami, B. N., & Tangirala, S. (2018). Ethics Impact on Knowledge Management in Organizational Development: A Case Study. In N. Baporikar (Ed.), *Global Practices in Knowledge Management for Societal and Organizational Development* (pp. 19–45). Hershey, PA: IGI Global. doi:10.4018/978-1-5225-3009-1.ch002

Delias, P., & Lakiotaki, K. (2018). Discovering Process Horizontal Boundaries to Facilitate Process Comprehension. *International Journal of Operations Research and Information Systems*, *9*(2), 1–31. doi:10.4018/IJORIS.2018040101

Denholm, J., & Lee-Davies, L. (2018). Success Factors for Games in Business and Project Management. In *Enhancing Education and Training Initiatives Through Serious Games* (pp. 34–68). Hershey, PA: IGI Global. doi:10.4018/978-1-5225-3689-5.ch002

Deshpande, M. (2017). Best Practices in Management Institutions for Global Leadership: Policy Aspects. In N. Baporikar (Ed.), *Management Education for Global Leadership* (pp. 1–27). Hershey, PA: IGI Global. doi:10.4018/978-1-5225-1013-0.ch001

Deshpande, M. (2018). Policy Perspectives for SMEs Knowledge Management. In N. Baporikar (Ed.), *Knowledge Integration Strategies for Entrepreneurship and Sustainability* (pp. 23–46). Hershey, PA: IGI Global. doi:10.4018/978-1-5225-5115-7.ch002

Dezdar, S. (2017). ERP Implementation Projects in Asian Countries: A Comparative Study on Iran and China. *International Journal of Information Technology Project Management*, *8*(3), 52–68. doi:10.4018/IJITPM.2017070104

Domingos, D., Martinho, R., & Varajão, J. (2016). Controlled Flexibility in Healthcare Processes: A BPMN-Extension Approach. In M. Cruz-Cunha, I. Miranda, R. Martinho, & R. Rijo (Eds.), *Encyclopedia of E-Health and Telemedicine* (pp. 521–535). Hershey, PA: IGI Global. doi:10.4018/978-1-4666-9978-6.ch040

Domingos, D., Respício, A., & Martinho, R. (2017). Reliability of IoT-Aware BPMN Healthcare Processes. In C. Reis & M. Maximiano (Eds.), *Internet of Things and Advanced Application in Healthcare* (pp. 214–248). Hershey, PA: IGI Global. doi:10.4018/978-1-5225-1820-4.ch008

Dosumu, O., Hussain, J., & El-Gohary, H. (2017). An Exploratory Study of the Impact of Government Policies on the Development of Small and Medium Enterprises in Developing Countries: The Case of Nigeria. *International Journal of Customer Relationship Marketing and Management, 8*(4), 51–62. doi:10.4018/IJCRMM.2017100104

Durst, S., Bruns, G., & Edvardsson, I. R. (2017). Retaining Knowledge in Smaller Building and Construction Firms. *International Journal of Knowledge and Systems Science, 8*(3), 1–12. doi:10.4018/IJKSS.2017070101

Edvardsson, I. R., & Durst, S. (2017). Outsourcing, Knowledge, and Learning: A Critical Review. *International Journal of Knowledge-Based Organizations, 7*(2), 13–26. doi:10.4018/IJKBO.2017040102

Edwards, J. S. (2018). Integrating Knowledge Management and Business Processes. In M. Khosrow-Pour, D.B.A. (Ed.), Encyclopedia of Information Science and Technology, Fourth Edition (pp. 5046-5055). Hershey, PA: IGI Global. doi:10.4018/978-1-5225-2255-3.ch437

Ejiogu, A. O. (2018). Economics of Farm Management. In *Agricultural Finance and Opportunities for Investment and Expansion* (pp. 56–72). Hershey, PA: IGI Global. doi:10.4018/978-1-5225-3059-6.ch003

Ekanem, I., & Abiade, G. E. (2018). Factors Influencing the Use of E-Commerce by Small Enterprises in Nigeria. *International Journal of ICT Research in Africa and the Middle East, 7*(1), 37–53. doi:10.4018/IJICTRAME.2018010103

Ekanem, I., & Alrossais, L. A. (2017). Succession Challenges Facing Family Businesses in Saudi Arabia. In P. Zgheib (Ed.), *Entrepreneurship and Business Innovation in the Middle East* (pp. 122–146). Hershey, PA: IGI Global. doi:10.4018/978-1-5225-2066-5.ch007

El Faquih, L., & Fredj, M. (2017). Ontology-Based Framework for Quality in Configurable Process Models. *Journal of Electronic Commerce in Organizations, 15*(2), 48–60. doi:10.4018/JECO.2017040104

El-Gohary, H., & El-Gohary, Z. (2016). An Attempt to Explore Electronic Marketing Adoption and Implementation Aspects in Developing Countries: The Case of Egypt. *International Journal of Customer Relationship Marketing and Management, 7*(4), 1–26. doi:10.4018/IJCRMM.2016100101

Entico, G. J. (2016). Knowledge Management and the Medical Health Librarians: A Perception Study. In J. Yap, M. Perez, M. Ayson, & G. Entico (Eds.), *Special Library Administration, Standardization and Technological Integration* (pp. 52–77). Hershey, PA: IGI Global. doi:10.4018/978-1-4666-9542-9.ch003

Faisal, M. N., & Talib, F. (2017). Building Ambidextrous Supply Chains in SMEs: How to Tackle the Barriers? *International Journal of Information Systems and Supply Chain Management, 10*(4), 80–100. doi:10.4018/IJISSCM.2017100105

Fernandes, T. M., Gomes, J., & Romão, M. (2017). Investments in E-Government: A Benefit Management Case Study. *International Journal of Electronic Government Research, 13*(3), 1–17. doi:10.4018/IJEGR.2017070101

Fouda, F. A. (2016). A Suggested Curriculum in Career Education to Develop Business Secondary Schools Students' Career Knowledge Management Domains and Professional Thinking. *International Journal of Technology Diffusion, 7*(2), 42–62. doi:10.4018/IJTD.2016040103

Gallardo-Vázquez, D., & Pajuelo-Moreno, M. L. (2016). How Spanish Universities are Promoting Entrepreneurship through Your Own Lines of Teaching and Research? In L. Carvalho (Ed.), *Handbook of Research on Entrepreneurial Success and its Impact on Regional Development* (pp. 431–454). Hershey, PA: IGI Global. doi:10.4018/978-1-4666-9567-2.ch019

Gao, S. S., Oreal, S., & Zhang, J. (2018). Contemporary Financial Risk Management Perceptions and Practices of Small-Sized Chinese Businesses. In I. Management Association (Ed.), Global Business Expansion: Concepts, Methodologies, Tools, and Applications (pp. 917-931). Hershey, PA: IGI Global. doi:10.4018/978-1-5225-5481-3.ch041

Garg, R., & Berning, S. C. (2017). Indigenous Chinese Management Philosophies: Key Concepts and Relevance for Modern Chinese Firms. In B. Christiansen & G. Koc (Eds.), *Transcontinental Strategies for Industrial Development and Economic Growth* (pp. 43–57). Hershey, PA: IGI Global. doi:10.4018/978-1-5225-2160-0.ch003

Gencer, Y. G. (2017). Supply Chain Management in Retailing Business. In U. Akkucuk (Ed.), *Ethics and Sustainability in Global Supply Chain Management* (pp. 197–210). Hershey, PA: IGI Global. doi:10.4018/978-1-5225-2036-8.ch011

Giacosa, E. (2016). Innovation in Luxury Fashion Businesses as a Means for the Regional Development. In L. Carvalho (Ed.), *Handbook of Research on Entrepreneurial Success and its Impact on Regional Development* (pp. 206–222). Hershey, PA: IGI Global. doi:10.4018/978-1-4666-9567-2.ch010

Giacosa, E. (2018). The Increasing of the Regional Development Thanks to the Luxury Business Innovation. In L. Carvalho (Ed.), *Handbook of Research on Entrepreneurial Ecosystems and Social Dynamics in a Globalized World* (pp. 260–273). Hershey, PA: IGI Global. doi:10.4018/978-1-5225-3525-6.ch011

Gianni, M., & Gotzamani, K. (2016). Integrated Management Systems and Information Management Systems: Common Threads. In P. Papajorgji, F. Pinet, A. Guimarães, & J. Papathanasiou (Eds.), *Automated Enterprise Systems for Maximizing Business Performance* (pp. 195–214). Hershey, PA: IGI Global. doi:10.4018/978-1-4666-8841-4.ch011

Gianni, M., Gotzamani, K., & Linden, I. (2016). How a BI-wise Responsible Integrated Management System May Support Food Traceability. *International Journal of Decision Support System Technology*, *8*(2), 1–17. doi:10.4018/IJDSST.2016040101

Glykas, M., & George, J. (2017). Quality and Process Management Systems in the UAE Maritime Industry. *International Journal of Productivity Management and Assessment Technologies*, *5*(1), 20–39. doi:10.4018/IJPMAT.2017010102

Glykas, M., Valiris, G., Kokkinaki, A., & Koutsoukou, Z. (2018). Banking Business Process Management Implementation. *International Journal of Productivity Management and Assessment Technologies*, *6*(1), 50–69. doi:10.4018/IJPMAT.2018010104

Gomes, J., & Romão, M. (2017). The Balanced Scorecard: Keeping Updated and Aligned with Today's Business Trends. *International Journal of Productivity Management and Assessment Technologies*, *5*(2), 1–15. doi:10.4018/IJPMAT.2017070101

Gomes, J., & Romão, M. (2017). Aligning Information Systems and Technology with Benefit Management and Balanced Scorecard. In S. De Haes & W. Van Grembergen (Eds.), *Strategic IT Governance and Alignment in Business Settings* (pp. 112–131). Hershey, PA: IGI Global. doi:10.4018/978-1-5225-0861-8.ch005

Grefen, P., & Turetken, O. (2017). Advanced Business Process Management in Networked E-Business Scenarios. *International Journal of E-Business Research*, *13*(4), 70–104. doi:10.4018/IJEBR.2017100105

Haider, A., & Saetang, S. (2017). Strategic IT Alignment in Service Sector. In S. Rozenes & Y. Cohen (Eds.), *Handbook of Research on Strategic Alliances and Value Co-Creation in the Service Industry* (pp. 231–258). Hershey, PA: IGI Global. doi:10.4018/978-1-5225-2084-9.ch012

Haider, A., & Tang, S. S. (2016). Maximising Value Through IT and Business Alignment: A Case of IT Governance Institutionalisation at a Thai Bank. *International Journal of Technology Diffusion*, *7*(3), 33–58. doi:10.4018/IJTD.2016070104

Hajilari, A. B., Ghadaksaz, M., & Fasghandis, G. S. (2017). Assessing Organizational Readiness for Implementing ERP System Using Fuzzy Expert System Approach. *International Journal of Enterprise Information Systems*, *13*(1), 67–85. doi:10.4018/IJEIS.2017010105

Haldorai, A., Ramu, A., & Murugan, S. (2018). Social Aware Cognitive Radio Networks: Effectiveness of Social Networks as a Strategic Tool for Organizational Business Management. In H. Bansal, G. Shrivastava, G. Nguyen, & L. Stanciu (Eds.), *Social Network Analytics for Contemporary Business Organizations* (pp. 188–202). Hershey, PA: IGI Global. doi:10.4018/978-1-5225-5097-6.ch010

Hall, O. P. Jr. (2017). Social Media Driven Management Education. *International Journal of Knowledge-Based Organizations*, *7*(2), 43–59. doi:10.4018/IJKBO.2017040104

Hanifah, H., Halim, H. A., Ahmad, N. H., & Vafaei-Zadeh, A. (2017). Innovation Culture as a Mediator Between Specific Human Capital and Innovation Performance Among Bumiputera SMEs in Malaysia. In N. Ahmad, T. Ramayah, H. Halim, & S. Rahman (Eds.), *Handbook of Research on Small and Medium Enterprises in Developing Countries* (pp. 261–279). Hershey, PA: IGI Global. doi:10.4018/978-1-5225-2165-5.ch012

Hartlieb, S., & Silvius, G. (2017). Handling Uncertainty in Project Management and Business Development: Similarities and Differences. In Y. Raydugin (Ed.), *Handbook of Research on Leveraging Risk and Uncertainties for Effective Project Management* (pp. 337–362). Hershey, PA: IGI Global. doi:10.4018/978-1-5225-1790-0.ch016

Hass, K. B. (2017). Living on the Edge: Managing Project Complexity. In Y. Raydugin (Ed.), *Handbook of Research on Leveraging Risk and Uncertainties for Effective Project Management* (pp. 177–201). Hershey, PA: IGI Global. doi:10.4018/978-1-5225-1790-0.ch009

Hassan, A., & Privitera, D. S. (2016). Google AdSense as a Mobile Technology in Education. In J. Holland (Ed.), *Wearable Technology and Mobile Innovations for Next-Generation Education* (pp. 200–223). Hershey, PA: IGI Global. doi:10.4018/978-1-5225-0069-8.ch011

Hassan, A., & Rahimi, R. (2016). Consuming "Innovation" in Tourism: Augmented Reality as an Innovation Tool in Digital Tourism Marketing. In N. Pappas & I. Bregoli (Eds.), *Global Dynamics in Travel, Tourism, and Hospitality* (pp. 130–147). Hershey, PA: IGI Global. doi:10.4018/978-1-5225-0201-2.ch008

Hawking, P., & Carmine Sellitto, C. (2017). Developing an Effective Strategy for Organizational Business Intelligence. In M. Tavana (Ed.), *Enterprise Information Systems and the Digitalization of Business Functions* (pp. 222–237). Hershey, PA: IGI Global. doi:10.4018/978-1-5225-2382-6.ch010

Hawking, P., & Sellitto, C. (2017). A Fast-Moving Consumer Goods Company and Business Intelligence Strategy Development. *International Journal of Enterprise Information Systems*, *13*(2), 22–33. doi:10.4018/IJEIS.2017040102

Hawking, P., & Sellitto, C. (2017). Business Intelligence Strategy: Two Case Studies. *International Journal of Business Intelligence Research*, *8*(2), 17–30. doi:10.4018/IJBIR.2017070102

Haynes, J. D., Arockiasamy, S., Al Rashdi, M., & Al Rashdi, S. (2016). Business and E Business Strategies for Coopetition and Thematic Management as a Sustained Basis for Ethics and Social Responsibility in Emerging Markets. In M. Al-Shammari & H. Masri (Eds.), *Ethical and Social Perspectives on Global Business Interaction in Emerging Markets* (pp. 25–39). Hershey, PA: IGI Global. doi:10.4018/978-1-4666-9864-2.ch002

Hee, W. J., Jalleh, G., Lai, H., & Lin, C. (2017). E-Commerce and IT Projects: Evaluation and Management Issues in Australian and Taiwanese Hospitals. *International Journal of Public Health Management and Ethics*, *2*(1), 69–90. doi:10.4018/IJPHME.2017010104

Hernandez, A. A. (2018). Exploring the Factors to Green IT Adoption of SMEs in the Philippines. *Journal of Cases on Information Technology*, *20*(2), 49–66. doi:10.4018/JCIT.2018040104

Hernandez, A. A., & Ona, S. E. (2016). Green IT Adoption: Lessons from the Philippines Business Process Outsourcing Industry. *International Journal of Social Ecology and Sustainable Development*, *7*(1), 1–34. doi:10.4018/IJSESD.2016010101

Hollman, A., Bickford, S., & Hollman, T. (2017). Cyber InSecurity: A Post-Mortem Attempt to Assess Cyber Problems from IT and Business Management Perspectives. *Journal of Cases on Information Technology*, *19*(3), 42–70. doi:10.4018/JCIT.2017070104

Igbinakhase, I. (2017). Responsible and Sustainable Management Practices in Developing and Developed Business Environments. In Z. Fields (Ed.), *Collective Creativity for Responsible and Sustainable Business Practice* (pp. 180–207). Hershey, PA: IGI Global. doi:10.4018/978-1-5225-1823-5.ch010

Ilahi, L., Ghannouchi, S. A., & Martinho, R. (2016). A Business Process Management Approach to Home Healthcare Processes: On the Gap between Intention and Reality. In M. Cruz-Cunha, I. Miranda, R. Martinho, & R. Rijo (Eds.), *Encyclopedia of E-Health and Telemedicine* (pp. 439–457). Hershey, PA: IGI Global. doi:10.4018/978-1-4666-9978-6.ch035

Iwata, J. J., & Hoskins, R. G. (2017). Managing Indigenous Knowledge in Tanzania: A Business Perspective. In P. Jain & N. Mnjama (Eds.), *Managing Knowledge Resources and Records in Modern Organizations* (pp. 198–214). Hershey, PA: IGI Global. doi:10.4018/978-1-5225-1965-2.ch012

Jabeen, F., Ahmad, S. Z., & Alkaabi, S. (2016). The Internationalization Decision-Making of United Arab Emirates Family Businesses. In N. Zakaria, A. Abdul-Talib, & N. Osman (Eds.), *Handbook of Research on Impacts of International Business and Political Affairs on the Global Economy* (pp. 1–22). Hershey, PA: IGI Global. doi:10.4018/978-1-4666-9806-2.ch001

Jain, P. (2017). Ethical and Legal Issues in Knowledge Management Life-Cycle in Business. In P. Jain & N. Mnjama (Eds.), *Managing Knowledge Resources and Records in Modern Organizations* (pp. 82–101). Hershey, PA: IGI Global. doi:10.4018/978-1-5225-1965-2.ch006

Jamali, D., Abdallah, H., & Matar, F. (2016). Opportunities and Challenges for CSR Mainstreaming in Business Schools. *International Journal of Technology and Educational Marketing*, *6*(2), 1–29. doi:10.4018/IJTEM.2016070101

James, S., & Hauli, E. (2017). Holistic Management Education at Tanzanian Rural Development Planning Institute. In N. Baporikar (Ed.), *Management Education for Global Leadership* (pp. 112–136). Hershey, PA: IGI Global. doi:10.4018/978-1-5225-1013-0.ch006

Janošková, M., Csikósová, A., & Čulková, K. (2018). Measurement of Company Performance as Part of Its Strategic Management. In R. Leon (Ed.), *Managerial Strategies for Business Sustainability During Turbulent Times* (pp. 309–335). Hershey, PA: IGI Global. doi:10.4018/978-1-5225-2716-9.ch017

Jean-Vasile, A., & Alecu, A. (2017). Theoretical and Practical Approaches in Understanding the Influences of Cost-Productivity-Profit Trinomial in Contemporary Enterprises. In A. Jean Vasile & D. Nicolò (Eds.), *Sustainable Entrepreneurship and Investments in the Green Economy* (pp. 28–62). Hershey, PA: IGI Global. doi:10.4018/978-1-5225-2075-7.ch002

Jha, D. G. (2016). Preparing for Information Technology Driven Changes. In S. Tiwari & L. Nafees (Eds.), *Innovative Management Education Pedagogies for Preparing Next-Generation Leaders* (pp. 258–274). Hershey, PA: IGI Global. doi:10.4018/978-1-4666-9691-4.ch015

Joia, L. A., & Correia, J. C. (2018). CIO Competencies From the IT Professional Perspective: Insights From Brazil. *Journal of Global Information Management, 26*(2), 74–103. doi:10.4018/JGIM.2018040104

Juma, A., & Mzera, N. (2017). Knowledge Management and Records Management and Competitive Advantage in Business. In P. Jain & N. Mnjama (Eds.), *Managing Knowledge Resources and Records in Modern Organizations* (pp. 15–28). Hershey, PA: IGI Global. doi:10.4018/978-1-5225-1965-2.ch002

K., I., & A, V. (2018). Monitoring and Auditing in the Cloud. In K. Munir (Ed.), *Cloud Computing Technologies for Green Enterprises* (pp. 318-350). Hershey, PA: IGI Global. doi:10.4018/978-1-5225-3038-1.ch013

Kabra, G., Ghosh, V., & Ramesh, A. (2018). Enterprise Integrated Business Process Management and Business Intelligence Framework for Business Process Sustainability. In A. Paul, D. Bhattacharyya, & S. Anand (Eds.), *Green Initiatives for Business Sustainability and Value Creation* (pp. 228–238). Hershey, PA: IGI Global. doi:10.4018/978-1-5225-2662-9.ch010

Kaoud, M. (2017). Investigation of Customer Knowledge Management: A Case Study Research. *International Journal of Service Science, Management, Engineering, and Technology, 8*(2), 12–22. doi:10.4018/IJSSMET.2017040102

Kara, M. E., & Fırat, S. Ü. (2016). Sustainability, Risk, and Business Intelligence in Supply Chains. In M. Erdoğdu, T. Arun, & I. Ahmad (Eds.), *Handbook of Research on Green Economic Development Initiatives and Strategies* (pp. 501–538). Hershey, PA: IGI Global. doi:10.4018/978-1-5225-0440-5.ch022

Katuu, S. (2018). A Comparative Assessment of Enterprise Content Management Maturity Models. In N. Gwangwava & M. Mutingi (Eds.), *E-Manufacturing and E-Service Strategies in Contemporary Organizations* (pp. 93–118). Hershey, PA: IGI Global. doi:10.4018/978-1-5225-3628-4.ch005

Khan, M. A. (2016). MNEs Management Strategies in Developing Countries: Establishing the Context. In M. Khan (Ed.), *Multinational Enterprise Management Strategies in Developing Countries* (pp. 1–33). Hershey, PA: IGI Global. doi:10.4018/978-1-5225-0276-0.ch001

Khan, M. A. (2016). Operational Approaches in Organizational Structure: A Case for MNEs in Developing Countries. In M. Khan (Ed.), *Multinational Enterprise Management Strategies in Developing Countries* (pp. 129–151). Hershey, PA: IGI Global. doi:10.4018/978-1-5225-0276-0.ch007

Kinnunen, S., Ylä-Kujala, A., Marttonen-Arola, S., Kärri, T., & Baglee, D. (2018). Internet of Things in Asset Management: Insights from Industrial Professionals and Academia. *International Journal of Service Science, Management, Engineering, and Technology*, *9*(2), 104–119. doi:10.4018/IJSSMET.2018040105

Klein, A. Z., Sabino de Freitas, A., Machado, L., Freitas, J. C. Jr, Graziola, P. G. Jr, & Schlemmer, E. (2017). Virtual Worlds Applications for Management Education. In L. Tomei (Ed.), *Exploring the New Era of Technology-Infused Education* (pp. 279–299). Hershey, PA: IGI Global. doi:10.4018/978-1-5225-1709-2.ch017

Kożuch, B., & Jabłoński, A. (2017). Adopting the Concept of Business Models in Public Management. In M. Lewandowski & B. Kożuch (Eds.), *Public Sector Entrepreneurship and the Integration of Innovative Business Models* (pp. 10–46). Hershey, PA: IGI Global. doi:10.4018/978-1-5225-2215-7.ch002

Kumar, J., Adhikary, A., & Jha, A. (2017). Small Active Investors' Perceptions and Preferences Towards Tax Saving Mutual Fund Schemes in Eastern India: An Empirical Note. *International Journal of Asian Business and Information Management*, *8*(2), 35–45. doi:10.4018/IJABIM.2017040103

Lassoued, Y., Bouzguenda, L., & Mahmoud, T. (2016). Context-Aware Business Process Versions Management. *International Journal of e-Collaboration*, *12*(3), 7–33. doi:10.4018/IJeC.2016070102

Lavassani, K. M., & Movahedi, B. (2017). Applications Driven Information Systems: Beyond Networks toward Business Ecosystems. *International Journal of Innovation in the Digital Economy*, *8*(1), 61–75. doi:10.4018/IJIDE.2017010104

Lazzareschi, V. H., & Brito, M. S. (2017). Strategic Information Management: Proposal of Business Project Model. In G. Jamil, A. Soares, & C. Pessoa (Eds.), *Handbook of Research on Information Management for Effective Logistics and Supply Chains* (pp. 59–88). Hershey, PA: IGI Global. doi:10.4018/978-1-5225-0973-8.ch004

Lederer, M., Kurz, M., & Lazarov, P. (2017). Usage and Suitability of Methods for Strategic Business Process Initiatives: A Multi Case Study Research. *International Journal of Productivity Management and Assessment Technologies*, *5*(1), 40–51. doi:10.4018/IJPMAT.2017010103

Lee, I. (2017). A Social Enterprise Business Model and a Case Study of Pacific Community Ventures (PCV). In V. Potocan, M. Ünğan, & Z. Nedelko (Eds.), *Handbook of Research on Managerial Solutions in Non-Profit Organizations* (pp. 182–204). Hershey, PA: IGI Global. doi:10.4018/978-1-5225-0731-4.ch009

Lee, L. J., & Leu, J. (2016). Exploring the Effectiveness of IT Application and Value Method in the Innovation Performance of Enterprise. *International Journal of Enterprise Information Systems*, *12*(2), 47–65. doi:10.4018/IJEIS.2016040104

Lee, Y. (2016). Alignment Effect of Entrepreneurial Orientation and Marketing Orientation on Firm Performance. *International Journal of Customer Relationship Marketing and Management*, *7*(4), 58–69. doi:10.4018/IJCRMM.2016100104

Leon, L. A., Seal, K. C., Przasnyski, Z. H., & Wiedenman, I. (2017). Skills and Competencies Required for Jobs in Business Analytics: A Content Analysis of Job Advertisements Using Text Mining. *International Journal of Business Intelligence Research*, *8*(1), 1–25. doi:10.4018/IJBIR.2017010101

Leu, J., Lee, L. J., & Krischke, A. (2016). Value Engineering-Based Method for Implementing the ISO14001 System in the Green Supply Chains. *International Journal of Strategic Decision Sciences*, *7*(4), 1–20. doi:10.4018/IJSDS.2016100101

Levy, C. L., & Elias, N. I. (2017). SOHO Users' Perceptions of Reliability and Continuity of Cloud-Based Services. In M. Moore (Ed.), *Cybersecurity Breaches and Issues Surrounding Online Threat Protection* (pp. 248–287). Hershey, PA: IGI Global. doi:10.4018/978-1-5225-1941-6.ch011

Levy, M. (2018). Change Management Serving Knowledge Management and Organizational Development: Reflections and Review. In N. Baporikar (Ed.), *Global Practices in Knowledge Management for Societal and Organizational Development* (pp. 256–270). Hershey, PA: IGI Global. doi:10.4018/978-1-5225-3009-1.ch012

Lewandowski, M. (2017). Public Organizations and Business Model Innovation: The Role of Public Service Design. In M. Lewandowski & B. Kożuch (Eds.), *Public Sector Entrepreneurship and the Integration of Innovative Business Models* (pp. 47–72). Hershey, PA: IGI Global. doi:10.4018/978-1-5225-2215-7.ch003

Lhannaoui, H., Kabbaj, M. I., & Bakkoury, Z. (2017). A Survey of Risk-Aware Business Process Modelling. *International Journal of Risk and Contingency Management*, *6*(3), 14–26. doi:10.4018/IJRCM.2017070102

Li, J., Sun, W., Jiang, W., Yang, H., & Zhang, L. (2017). How the Nature of Exogenous Shocks and Crises Impact Company Performance?: The Effects of Industry Characteristics. *International Journal of Risk and Contingency Management*, *6*(4), 40–55. doi:10.4018/IJRCM.2017100103

Lu, C., & Liu, S. (2016). Cultural Tourism O2O Business Model Innovation-A Case Study of CTrip. *Journal of Electronic Commerce in Organizations*, *14*(2), 16–31. doi:10.4018/JECO.2016040102

Machen, B., Hosseini, M. R., Wood, A., & Bakhshi, J. (2016). An Investigation into using SAP-PS as a Multidimensional Project Control System (MPCS). *International Journal of Enterprise Information Systems*, *12*(2), 66–81. doi:10.4018/IJEIS.2016040105

Malega, P. (2017). Small and Medium Enterprises in the Slovak Republic: Status and Competitiveness of SMEs in the Global Markets and Possibilities of Optimization. In M. Vemić (Ed.), *Optimal Management Strategies in Small and Medium Enterprises* (pp. 102–124). Hershey, PA: IGI Global. doi:10.4018/978-1-5225-1949-2.ch006

Malewska, K. M. (2017). Intuition in Decision-Making on the Example of a Non-Profit Organization. In V. Potocan, M. Üngan, & Z. Nedelko (Eds.), *Handbook of Research on Managerial Solutions in Non-Profit Organizations* (pp. 378–399). Hershey, PA: IGI Global. doi:10.4018/978-1-5225-0731-4.ch018

Maroofi, F. (2017). Entrepreneurial Orientation and Organizational Learning Ability Analysis for Innovation and Firm Performance. In N. Baporikar (Ed.), *Innovation and Shifting Perspectives in Management Education* (pp. 144–165). Hershey, PA: IGI Global. doi:10.4018/978-1-5225-1019-2.ch007

Martins, P. V., & Zacarias, M. (2017). A Web-based Tool for Business Process Improvement. *International Journal of Web Portals*, *9*(2), 68–84. doi:10.4018/IJWP.2017070104

Matthies, B., & Coners, A. (2017). Exploring the Conceptual Nature of e-Business Projects. *Journal of Electronic Commerce in Organizations*, *15*(3), 33–63. doi:10.4018/JECO.2017070103

McKee, J. (2018). Architecture as a Tool to Solve Business Planning Problems. In M. Khosrow-Pour, D.B.A. (Ed.), Encyclopedia of Information Science and Technology, Fourth Edition (pp. 573-586). Hershey, PA: IGI Global. doi:10.4018/978-1-5225-2255-3.ch050

McMurray, A. J., Cross, J., & Caponecchia, C. (2018). The Risk Management Profession in Australia: Business Continuity Plan Practices. In N. Bajgoric (Ed.), *Always-On Enterprise Information Systems for Modern Organizations* (pp. 112–129). Hershey, PA: IGI Global. doi:10.4018/978-1-5225-3704-5.ch006

Meddah, I. H., & Belkadi, K. (2018). Mining Patterns Using Business Process Management. In R. Hamou (Ed.), *Handbook of Research on Biomimicry in Information Retrieval and Knowledge Management* (pp. 78–89). Hershey, PA: IGI Global. doi:10.4018/978-1-5225-3004-6.ch005

Mendes, L. (2017). TQM and Knowledge Management: An Integrated Approach Towards Tacit Knowledge Management. In D. Jaziri-Bouagina & G. Jamil (Eds.), *Handbook of Research on Tacit Knowledge Management for Organizational Success* (pp. 236–263). Hershey, PA: IGI Global. doi:10.4018/978-1-5225-2394-9.ch009

Mnjama, N. M. (2017). Preservation of Recorded Information in Public and Private Sector Organizations. In P. Jain & N. Mnjama (Eds.), *Managing Knowledge Resources and Records in Modern Organizations* (pp. 149–167). Hershey, PA: IGI Global. doi:10.4018/978-1-5225-1965-2.ch009

Mokoqama, M., & Fields, Z. (2017). Principles of Responsible Management Education (PRME): Call for Responsible Management Education. In Z. Fields (Ed.), *Collective Creativity for Responsible and Sustainable Business Practice* (pp. 229–241). Hershey, PA: IGI Global. doi:10.4018/978-1-5225-1823-5.ch012

Muniapan, B. (2017). Philosophy and Management: The Relevance of Vedanta in Management. In P. Ordóñez de Pablos (Ed.), *Managerial Strategies and Solutions for Business Success in Asia* (pp. 124–139). Hershey, PA: IGI Global. doi:10.4018/978-1-5225-1886-0.ch007

Muniapan, B., Gregory, M. L., & Ling, L. A. (2016). Marketing Education in Sarawak: Looking at It from the Employers' Viewpoint. In B. Smith & A. Porath (Eds.), *Global Perspectives on Contemporary Marketing Education* (pp. 112–130). Hershey, PA: IGI Global. doi:10.4018/978-1-4666-9784-3.ch008

Murad, S. E., & Dowaji, S. (2017). Using Value-Based Approach for Managing Cloud-Based Services. In A. Turuk, B. Sahoo, & S. Addya (Eds.), *Resource Management and Efficiency in Cloud Computing Environments* (pp. 33–60). Hershey, PA: IGI Global. doi:10.4018/978-1-5225-1721-4.ch002

Mutahar, A. M., Daud, N. M., Thurasamy, R., Isaac, O., & Abdulsalam, R. (2018). The Mediating of Perceived Usefulness and Perceived Ease of Use: The Case of Mobile Banking in Yemen. *International Journal of Technology Diffusion*, *9*(2), 21–40. doi:10.4018/IJTD.2018040102

Naidoo, V. (2017). E-Learning and Management Education at African Universities. In N. Baporikar (Ed.), *Management Education for Global Leadership* (pp. 181–201). Hershey, PA: IGI Global. doi:10.4018/978-1-5225-1013-0.ch009

Naidoo, V., & Igbinakhase, I. (2018). Opportunities and Challenges of Knowledge Retention in SMEs. In N. Baporikar (Ed.), *Knowledge Integration Strategies for Entrepreneurship and Sustainability* (pp. 70–94). Hershey, PA: IGI Global. doi:10.4018/978-1-5225-5115-7.ch004

Nayak, S., & Prabhu, N. (2017). Paradigm Shift in Management Education: Need for a Cross Functional Perspective. In N. Baporikar (Ed.), *Management Education for Global Leadership* (pp. 241–255). Hershey, PA: IGI Global. doi:10.4018/978-1-5225-1013-0.ch012

Ndede-Amadi, A. A. (2016). Student Interest in the IS Specialization as Predictor of the Success Potential of New Information Systems Programmes within the Schools of Business in Kenyan Public Universities. *International Journal of Information Systems and Social Change*, *7*(2), 63–79. doi:10.4018/IJISSC.2016040104

Nedelko, Z., & Potocan, V. (2016). Management Practices for Processes Optimization: Case of Slovenia. In G. Alor-Hernández, C. Sánchez-Ramírez, & J. García-Alcaraz (Eds.), *Handbook of Research on Managerial Strategies for Achieving Optimal Performance in Industrial Processes* (pp. 545–561). Hershey, PA: IGI Global. doi:10.4018/978-1-5225-0130-5.ch025

Nedelko, Z., & Potocan, V. (2017). Management Solutions in Non-Profit Organizations: Case of Slovenia. In V. Potocan, M. Üngan, & Z. Nedelko (Eds.), *Handbook of Research on Managerial Solutions in Non-Profit Organizations* (pp. 1–22). Hershey, PA: IGI Global. doi:10.4018/978-1-5225-0731-4.ch001

Nedelko, Z., & Potocan, V. (2017). Priority of Management Tools Utilization among Managers: International Comparison. In V. Wang (Ed.), *Encyclopedia of Strategic Leadership and Management* (pp. 1083–1094). Hershey, PA: IGI Global. doi:10.4018/978-1-5225-1049-9.ch075

Nedelko, Z., Raudeliūnienė, J., & Črešnar, R. (2018). Knowledge Dynamics in Supply Chain Management. In N. Baporikar (Ed.), *Knowledge Integration Strategies for Entrepreneurship and Sustainability* (pp. 150–166). Hershey, PA: IGI Global. doi:10.4018/978-1-5225-5115-7.ch008

Nguyen, H. T., & Hipsher, S. A. (2018). Innovation and Creativity Used by Private Sector Firms in a Resources-Constrained Environment. In S. Hipsher (Ed.), *Examining the Private Sector's Role in Wealth Creation and Poverty Reduction* (pp. 219–238). Hershey, PA: IGI Global. doi:10.4018/978-1-5225-3117-3.ch010

Nycz, M., & Pólkowski, Z. (2016). Business Intelligence as a Modern IT Supporting Management of Local Government Units in Poland. *International Journal of Knowledge and Systems Science*, *7*(4), 1–18. doi:10.4018/IJKSS.2016100101

Obaji, N. O., Senin, A. A., & Olugu, M. U. (2016). Supportive Government Policy as a Mechanism for Business Incubation Performance in Nigeria. *International Journal of Information Systems and Social Change*, *7*(4), 52–66. doi:10.4018/IJISSC.2016100103

Obicci, P. A. (2017). Risk Sharing in a Partnership. In *Risk Management Strategies in Public-Private Partnerships* (pp. 115–152). Hershey, PA: IGI Global. doi:10.4018/978-1-5225-2503-5.ch004

Obidallah, W. J., & Raahemi, B. (2017). Managing Changes in Service Oriented Virtual Organizations: A Structural and Procedural Framework to Facilitate the Process of Change. *Journal of Electronic Commerce in Organizations*, *15*(1), 59–83. doi:10.4018/JECO.2017010104

Ojasalo, J., & Ojasalo, K. (2016). Service Logic Business Model Canvas for Lean Development of SMEs and Start-Ups. In N. Baporikar (Ed.), *Handbook of Research on Entrepreneurship in the Contemporary Knowledge-Based Global Economy* (pp. 217–243). Hershey, PA: IGI Global. doi:10.4018/978-1-4666-8798-1.ch010

Ojo, O. (2017). Impact of Innovation on the Entrepreneurial Success in Selected Business Enterprises in South-West Nigeria. *International Journal of Innovation in the Digital Economy*, *8*(2), 29–38. doi:10.4018/IJIDE.2017040103

Okdinawati, L., Simatupang, T. M., & Sunitiyoso, Y. (2017). Multi-Agent Reinforcement Learning for Value Co-Creation of Collaborative Transportation Management (CTM). *International Journal of Information Systems and Supply Chain Management*, *10*(3), 84–95. doi:10.4018/IJISSCM.2017070105

Ortner, E., Mevius, M., Wiedmann, P., & Kurz, F. (2016). Design of Interactional Decision Support Applications for E-Participation in Smart Cities. *International Journal of Electronic Government Research*, *12*(2), 18–38. doi:10.4018/IJEGR.2016040102

Pal, K. (2018). Building High Quality Big Data-Based Applications in Supply Chains. In A. Kumar & S. Saurav (Eds.), *Supply Chain Management Strategies and Risk Assessment in Retail Environments* (pp. 1–24). Hershey, PA: IGI Global. doi:10.4018/978-1-5225-3056-5.ch001

Palos-Sanchez, P. R., & Correia, M. B. (2018). Perspectives of the Adoption of Cloud Computing in the Tourism Sector. In J. Rodrigues, C. Ramos, P. Cardoso, & C. Henriques (Eds.), *Handbook of Research on Technological Developments for Cultural Heritage and eTourism Applications* (pp. 377–400). Hershey, PA: IGI Global. doi:10.4018/978-1-5225-2927-9.ch018

Parry, V. K., & Lind, M. L. (2016). Alignment of Business Strategy and Information Technology Considering Information Technology Governance, Project Portfolio Control, and Risk Management. *International Journal of Information Technology Project Management, 7*(4), 21–37. doi:10.4018/IJITPM.2016100102

Pashkova, N., Trujillo-Barrera, A., Apostolakis, G., Van Dijk, G., Drakos, P. D., & Baourakis, G. (2016). Business Management Models of Microfinance Institutions (MFIs) in Africa: A Study into Their Enabling Environments. *International Journal of Food and Beverage Manufacturing and Business Models, 1*(2), 63–82. doi:10.4018/IJFBMBM.2016070105

Patiño, B. E. (2017). New Generation Management by Convergence and Individual Identity: A Systemic and Human-Oriented Approach. In N. Baporikar (Ed.), *Innovation and Shifting Perspectives in Management Education* (pp. 119–143). Hershey, PA: IGI Global. doi:10.4018/978-1-5225-1019-2.ch006

Pawliczek, A., & Rössler, M. (2017). Knowledge of Management Tools and Systems in SMEs: Knowledge Transfer in Management. In A. Bencsik (Ed.), *Knowledge Management Initiatives and Strategies in Small and Medium Enterprises* (pp. 180–203). Hershey, PA: IGI Global. doi:10.4018/978-1-5225-1642-2.ch009

Pejic-Bach, M., Omazic, M. A., Aleksic, A., & Zoroja, J. (2018). Knowledge-Based Decision Making: A Multi-Case Analysis. In R. Leon (Ed.), *Managerial Strategies for Business Sustainability During Turbulent Times* (pp. 160–184). Hershey, PA: IGI Global. doi:10.4018/978-1-5225-2716-9.ch009

Perano, M., Hysa, X., & Calabrese, M. (2018). Strategic Planning, Cultural Context, and Business Continuity Management: Business Cases in the City of Shkoder. In A. Presenza & L. Sheehan (Eds.), *Geopolitics and Strategic Management in the Global Economy* (pp. 57–77). Hershey, PA: IGI Global. doi:10.4018/978-1-5225-2673-5.ch004

Pereira, R., Mira da Silva, M., & Lapão, L. V. (2017). IT Governance Maturity Patterns in Portuguese Healthcare. In S. De Haes & W. Van Grembergen (Eds.), *Strategic IT Governance and Alignment in Business Settings* (pp. 24–52). Hershey, PA: IGI Global. doi:10.4018/978-1-5225-0861-8.ch002

Perez-Uribe, R., & Ocampo-Guzman, D. (2016). Conflict within Colombian Family Owned SMEs: An Explosive Blend between Feelings and Business. In J. Saiz-Álvarez (Ed.), *Handbook of Research on Social Entrepreneurship and Solidarity Economics* (pp. 329–354). Hershey, PA: IGI Global. doi:10.4018/978-1-5225-0097-1.ch017

Pérez-Uribe, R. I., Torres, D. A., Jurado, S. P., & Prada, D. M. (2018). Cloud Tools for the Development of Project Management in SMEs. In R. Perez-Uribe, C. Salcedo-Perez, & D. Ocampo-Guzman (Eds.), *Handbook of Research on Intrapreneurship and Organizational Sustainability in SMEs* (pp. 95–120). Hershey, PA: IGI Global. doi:10.4018/978-1-5225-3543-0.ch005

Petrisor, I., & Cozmiuc, D. (2017). Global Supply Chain Management Organization at Siemens in the Advent of Industry 4.0. In L. Saglietto & C. Cezanne (Eds.), *Global Intermediation and Logistics Service Providers* (pp. 123–142). Hershey, PA: IGI Global. doi:10.4018/978-1-5225-2133-4.ch007

Pierce, J. M., Velliaris, D. M., & Edwards, J. (2017). A Living Case Study: A Journey Not a Destination. In N. Silton (Ed.), *Exploring the Benefits of Creativity in Education, Media, and the Arts* (pp. 158–178). Hershey, PA: IGI Global. doi:10.4018/978-1-5225-0504-4.ch008

Radosavljevic, M., & Andjelkovic, A. (2017). Multi-Criteria Decision Making Approach for Choosing Business Process for the Improvement: Upgrading of the Six Sigma Methodology. In J. Stanković, P. Delias, S. Marinković, & S. Rochhia (Eds.), *Tools and Techniques for Economic Decision Analysis* (pp. 225–247). Hershey, PA: IGI Global. doi:10.4018/978-1-5225-0959-2.ch011

Radovic, V. M. (2017). Corporate Sustainability and Responsibility and Disaster Risk Reduction: A Serbian Overview. In M. Camilleri (Ed.), *CSR 2.0 and the New Era of Corporate Citizenship* (pp. 147–164). Hershey, PA: IGI Global. doi:10.4018/978-1-5225-1842-6.ch008

Raghunath, K. M., Devi, S. L., & Patro, C. S. (2018). Impact of Risk Assessment Models on Risk Factors: A Holistic Outlook. In K. Strang, M. Korstanje, & N. Vajjhala (Eds.), *Research, Practices, and Innovations in Global Risk and Contingency Management* (pp. 134–153). Hershey, PA: IGI Global. doi:10.4018/978-1-5225-4754-9.ch008

Raman, A., & Goyal, D. P. (2017). Extending IMPLEMENT Framework for Enterprise Information Systems Implementation to Information System Innovation. In M. Tavana (Ed.), *Enterprise Information Systems and the Digitalization of Business Functions* (pp. 137–177). Hershey, PA: IGI Global. doi:10.4018/978-1-5225-2382-6.ch007

Rao, Y., & Zhang, Y. (2017). The Construction and Development of Academic Library Digital Special Subject Databases. In L. Ruan, Q. Zhu, & Y. Ye (Eds.), *Academic Library Development and Administration in China* (pp. 163–183). Hershey, PA: IGI Global. doi:10.4018/978-1-5225-0550-1.ch010

Ravasan, A. Z., Mohammadi, M. M., & Hamidi, H. (2018). An Investigation Into the Critical Success Factors of Implementing Information Technology Service Management Frameworks. In K. Jakobs (Ed.), *Corporate and Global Standardization Initiatives in Contemporary Society* (pp. 200–218). Hershey, PA: IGI Global. doi:10.4018/978-1-5225-5320-5.ch009

Renna, P., Izzo, C., & Romaniello, T. (2016). The Business Process Management Systems to Support Continuous Improvements. In W. Nuninger & J. Châtelet (Eds.), *Handbook of Research on Quality Assurance and Value Management in Higher Education* (pp. 237–256). Hershey, PA: IGI Global. doi:10.4018/978-1-5225-0024-7.ch009

Rezaie, S., Mirabedini, S. J., & Abtahi, A. (2018). Designing a Model for Implementation of Business Intelligence in the Banking Industry. *International Journal of Enterprise Information Systems, 14*(1), 77–103. doi:10.4018/IJEIS.2018010105

Riccò, R. (2016). Diversity Management: Bringing Equality, Equity, and Inclusion in the Workplace. In J. Prescott (Ed.), *Handbook of Research on Race, Gender, and the Fight for Equality* (pp. 335–359). Hershey, PA: IGI Global. doi:10.4018/978-1-5225-0047-6.ch015

Romano, L., Grimaldi, R., & Colasuonno, F. S. (2017). Demand Management as a Success Factor in Project Portfolio Management. In L. Romano (Ed.), *Project Portfolio Management Strategies for Effective Organizational Operations* (pp. 202–219). Hershey, PA: IGI Global. doi:10.4018/978-1-5225-2151-8.ch008

Rostek, K. B. (2016). Risk Management: Role and Importance in Business Organization. In D. Jakóbczak (Ed.), *Analyzing Risk through Probabilistic Modeling in Operations Research* (pp. 149–178). Hershey, PA: IGI Global. doi:10.4018/978-1-4666-9458-3.ch007

Rouhani, S., & Savoji, S. R. (2016). A Success Assessment Model for BI Tools Implementation: An Empirical Study of Banking Industry. *International Journal of Business Intelligence Research, 7*(1), 25–44. doi:10.4018/IJBIR.2016010103

Ruan, Z. (2016). A Corpus-Based Functional Analysis of Complex Nominal Groups in Written Business Discourse: The Case of "Business". *International Journal of Computer-Assisted Language Learning and Teaching*, *6*(2), 74–90. doi:10.4018/IJCALLT.2016040105

Ruhi, U. (2018). Towards an Interdisciplinary Socio-Technical Definition of Virtual Communities. In M. Khosrow-Pour, D.B.A. (Ed.), Encyclopedia of Information Science and Technology, Fourth Edition (pp. 4278-4295). Hershey, PA: IGI Global. doi:10.4018/978-1-5225-2255-3.ch371

Ryan, J., Doster, B., Daily, S., & Lewis, C. (2016). A Case Study Perspective for Balanced Perioperative Workflow Achievement through Data-Driven Process Improvement. *International Journal of Healthcare Information Systems and Informatics*, *11*(3), 19–41. doi:10.4018/IJHISI.2016070102

Safari, M. R., & Jiang, Q. (2018). The Theory and Practice of IT Governance Maturity and Strategies Alignment: Evidence From Banking Industry. *Journal of Global Information Management*, *26*(2), 127–146. doi:10.4018/JGIM.2018040106

Sahoo, J., Pati, B., & Mohanty, B. (2017). Knowledge Management as an Academic Discipline: An Assessment. In B. Gunjal (Ed.), *Managing Knowledge and Scholarly Assets in Academic Libraries* (pp. 99–126). Hershey, PA: IGI Global. doi:10.4018/978-1-5225-1741-2.ch005

Saini, D. (2017). Relevance of Teaching Values and Ethics in Management Education. In N. Baporikar (Ed.), *Management Education for Global Leadership* (pp. 90–111). Hershey, PA: IGI Global. doi:10.4018/978-1-5225-1013-0.ch005

Sambhanthan, A. (2017). Assessing and Benchmarking Sustainability in Organisations: An Integrated Conceptual Model. *International Journal of Systems and Service-Oriented Engineering*, *7*(4), 22–43. doi:10.4018/IJSSOE.2017100102

Sambhanthan, A., & Potdar, V. (2017). A Study of the Parameters Impacting Sustainability in Information Technology Organizations. *International Journal of Knowledge-Based Organizations*, *7*(3), 27–39. doi:10.4018/IJKBO.2017070103

Sánchez-Fernández, M. D., & Manríquez, M. R. (2018). The Entrepreneurial Spirit Based on Social Values: The Digital Generation. In P. Isaias & L. Carvalho (Eds.), *User Innovation and the Entrepreneurship Phenomenon in the Digital Economy* (pp. 173–193). Hershey, PA: IGI Global. doi:10.4018/978-1-5225-2826-5.ch009

Sanchez-Ruiz, L., & Blanco, B. (2017). Process Management for SMEs: Barriers, Enablers, and Benefits. In M. Vemić (Ed.), *Optimal Management Strategies in Small and Medium Enterprises* (pp. 293–319). Hershey, PA: IGI Global. doi:10.4018/978-1-5225-1949-2.ch014

Sanz, L. F., Gómez-Pérez, J., & Castillo-Martinez, A. (2018). Analysis of the European ICT Competence Frameworks. In V. Ahuja & S. Rathore (Eds.), *Multidisciplinary Perspectives on Human Capital and Information Technology Professionals* (pp. 225–245). Hershey, PA: IGI Global. doi:10.4018/978-1-5225-5297-0.ch012

Sarvepalli, A., & Godin, J. (2017). Business Process Management in the Classroom. *Journal of Cases on Information Technology, 19*(2), 17–28. doi:10.4018/JCIT.2017040102

Satpathy, B., & Muniapan, B. (2016). Ancient Wisdom for Transformational Leadership and Its Insights from the Bhagavad-Gita. In U. Aung & P. Ordoñez de Pablos (Eds.), *Managerial Strategies and Practice in the Asian Business Sector* (pp. 1–10). Hershey, PA: IGI Global. doi:10.4018/978-1-4666-9758-4.ch001

Saygili, E. E., Ozturkoglu, Y., & Kocakulah, M. C. (2017). End Users' Perceptions of Critical Success Factors in ERP Applications. *International Journal of Enterprise Information Systems, 13*(4), 58–75. doi:10.4018/IJEIS.2017100104

Saygili, E. E., & Saygili, A. T. (2017). Contemporary Issues in Enterprise Information Systems: A Critical Review of CSFs in ERP Implementations. In M. Tavana (Ed.), *Enterprise Information Systems and the Digitalization of Business Functions* (pp. 120–136). Hershey, PA: IGI Global. doi:10.4018/978-1-5225-2382-6.ch006

Seidenstricker, S., & Antonino, A. (2018). Business Model Innovation-Oriented Technology Management for Emergent Technologies. In M. Khosrow-Pour, D.B.A. (Ed.), Encyclopedia of Information Science and Technology, Fourth Edition (pp. 4560-4569). Hershey, PA: IGI Global. doi:10.4018/978-1-5225-2255-3.ch396

Senaratne, S., & Gunarathne, A. D. (2017). Excellence Perspective for Management Education from a Global Accountants' Hub in Asia. In N. Baporikar (Ed.), *Management Education for Global Leadership* (pp. 158–180). Hershey, PA: IGI Global. doi:10.4018/978-1-5225-1013-0.ch008

Sensuse, D. I., & Cahyaningsih, E. (2018). Knowledge Management Models: A Summative Review. *International Journal of Information Systems in the Service Sector, 10*(1), 71–100. doi:10.4018/IJISSS.2018010105

Sensuse, D. I., Wibowo, W. C., & Cahyaningsih, E. (2016). Indonesian Government Knowledge Management Model: A Theoretical Model. *Information Resources Management Journal, 29*(1), 91–108. doi:10.4018/irmj.2016010106

Seth, M., Goyal, D., & Kiran, R. (2017). Diminution of Impediments in Implementation of Supply Chain Management Information System for Enhancing its Effectiveness in Indian Automobile Industry. *Journal of Global Information Management, 25*(3), 1–20. doi:10.4018/JGIM.2017070101

Seyal, A. H., & Rahman, M. N. (2017). Investigating Impact of Inter-Organizational Factors in Measuring ERP Systems Success: Bruneian Perspectives. In M. Tavana (Ed.), *Enterprise Information Systems and the Digitalization of Business Functions* (pp. 178–204). Hershey, PA: IGI Global. doi:10.4018/978-1-5225-2382-6.ch008

Shaikh, A. A., & Karjaluoto, H. (2016). On Some Misconceptions Concerning Digital Banking and Alternative Delivery Channels. *International Journal of E-Business Research, 12*(3), 1–16. doi:10.4018/IJEBR.2016070101

Shams, S. M. (2016). Stakeholder Relationship Management in Online Business and Competitive Value Propositions: Evidence from the Sports Industry. *International Journal of Online Marketing, 6*(2), 1–17. doi:10.4018/IJOM.2016040101

Shamsuzzoha, A. (2016). Management of Risk and Resilience within Collaborative Business Network. In R. Addo-Tenkorang, J. Kantola, P. Helo, & A. Shamsuzzoha (Eds.), *Supply Chain Strategies and the Engineer-to-Order Approach* (pp. 143–159). Hershey, PA: IGI Global. doi:10.4018/978-1-5225-0021-6.ch008

Shaqrah, A. A. (2018). Analyzing Business Intelligence Systems Based on 7s Model of McKinsey. *International Journal of Business Intelligence Research, 9*(1), 53–63. doi:10.4018/IJBIR.2018010104

Sharma, A. J. (2017). Enhancing Sustainability through Experiential Learning in Management Education. In N. Baporikar (Ed.), *Management Education for Global Leadership* (pp. 256–274). Hershey, PA: IGI Global. doi:10.4018/978-1-5225-1013-0.ch013

Shetty, K. P. (2017). Responsible Global Leadership: Ethical Challenges in Management Education. In N. Baporikar (Ed.), *Innovation and Shifting Perspectives in Management Education* (pp. 194–223). Hershey, PA: IGI Global. doi:10.4018/978-1-5225-1019-2.ch009

Sinthupundaja, J., & Kohda, Y. (2017). Effects of Corporate Social Responsibility and Creating Shared Value on Sustainability. *International Journal of Sustainable Entrepreneurship and Corporate Social Responsibility*, *2*(1), 27–38. doi:10.4018/IJSECSR.2017010103

Škarica, I., & Hrgović, A. V. (2018). Implementation of Total Quality Management Principles in Public Health Institutes in the Republic of Croatia. *International Journal of Productivity Management and Assessment Technologies*, *6*(1), 1–16. doi:10.4018/IJPMAT.2018010101

Smuts, H., Kotzé, P., Van der Merwe, A., & Loock, M. (2017). Framework for Managing Shared Knowledge in an Information Systems Outsourcing Context. *International Journal of Knowledge Management*, *13*(4), 1–30. doi:10.4018/IJKM.2017100101

Soares, E. R., & Zaidan, F. H. (2016). Information Architecture and Business Modeling in Modern Organizations of Information Technology: Professional Career Plan in Organizations IT. In G. Jamil, J. Poças Rascão, F. Ribeiro, & A. Malheiro da Silva (Eds.), *Handbook of Research on Information Architecture and Management in Modern Organizations* (pp. 439–457). Hershey, PA: IGI Global. doi:10.4018/978-1-4666-8637-3.ch020

Sousa, M. J., Cruz, R., Dias, I., & Caracol, C. (2017). Information Management Systems in the Supply Chain. In G. Jamil, A. Soares, & C. Pessoa (Eds.), *Handbook of Research on Information Management for Effective Logistics and Supply Chains* (pp. 469–485). Hershey, PA: IGI Global. doi:10.4018/978-1-5225-0973-8.ch025

Spremic, M., Turulja, L., & Bajgoric, N. (2018). Two Approaches in Assessing Business Continuity Management Attitudes in the Organizational Context. In N. Bajgoric (Ed.), *Always-On Enterprise Information Systems for Modern Organizations* (pp. 159–183). Hershey, PA: IGI Global. doi:10.4018/978-1-5225-3704-5.ch008

Steenkamp, A. L. (2018). Some Insights in Computer Science and Information Technology. In *Examining the Changing Role of Supervision in Doctoral Research Projects: Emerging Research and Opportunities* (pp. 113–133). Hershey, PA: IGI Global. doi:10.4018/978-1-5225-2610-0.ch005

Studdard, N., Dawson, M., Burton, S. L., Jackson, N., Leonard, B., Quisenberry, W., & Rahim, E. (2016). Nurturing Social Entrepreneurship and Building Social Entrepreneurial Self-Efficacy: Focusing on Primary and Secondary Schooling to Develop Future Social Entrepreneurs. In Z. Fields (Ed.), *Incorporating Business Models and Strategies into Social Entrepreneurship* (pp. 154–175). Hershey, PA: IGI Global. doi:10.4018/978-1-4666-8748-6.ch010

Sun, Z. (2016). A Framework for Developing Management Intelligent Systems. *International Journal of Systems and Service-Oriented Engineering*, *6*(1), 37–53. doi:10.4018/IJSSOE.2016010103

Swami, B., & Mphele, G. T. (2016). Problems Preventing Growth of Small Entrepreneurs: A Case Study of a Few Small Entrepreneurs in Botswana Sub-Urban Areas. In N. Baporikar (Ed.), *Handbook of Research on Entrepreneurship in the Contemporary Knowledge-Based Global Economy* (pp. 479–508). Hershey, PA: IGI Global. doi:10.4018/978-1-4666-8798-1.ch020

Tabach, A., & Croteau, A. (2017). Configurations of Information Technology Governance Practices and Business Unit Performance. *International Journal of IT/Business Alignment and Governance*, *8*(2), 1–27. doi:10.4018/IJITBAG.2017070101

Talaue, G. M., & Iqbal, T. (2017). Assessment of e-Business Mode of Selected Private Universities in the Philippines and Pakistan. *International Journal of Online Marketing*, *7*(4), 63–77. doi:10.4018/IJOM.2017100105

Tam, G. C. (2017). Project Manager Sustainability Competence. In *Managerial Strategies and Green Solutions for Project Sustainability* (pp. 178–207). Hershey, PA: IGI Global. doi:10.4018/978-1-5225-2371-0.ch008

Tambo, T. (2018). Fashion Retail Innovation: About Context, Antecedents, and Outcome in Technological Change Projects. In I. Management Association (Ed.), Fashion and Textiles: Breakthroughs in Research and Practice (pp. 233-260). Hershey, PA: IGI Global. doi:10.4018/978-1-5225-3432-7.ch010

Tambo, T., & Mikkelsen, O. E. (2016). Fashion Supply Chain Optimization: Linking Make-to-Order Purchasing and B2B E-Commerce. In S. Joshi & R. Joshi (Eds.), *Designing and Implementing Global Supply Chain Management* (pp. 1–21). Hershey, PA: IGI Global. doi:10.4018/978-1-4666-9720-1.ch001

Tandon, K. (2016). Innovative Andragogy: The Paradigm Shift to Heutagogy. In S. Tiwari & L. Nafees (Eds.), *Innovative Management Education Pedagogies for Preparing Next-Generation Leaders* (pp. 238–257). Hershey, PA: IGI Global. doi:10.4018/978-1-4666-9691-4.ch014

Tantau, A. D., & Frăţilă, L. C. (2018). Information and Management System for Renewable Energy Business. In *Entrepreneurship and Business Development in the Renewable Energy Sector* (pp. 200–244). Hershey, PA: IGI Global. doi:10.4018/978-1-5225-3625-3.ch006

Teixeira, N., Pardal, P. N., & Rafael, B. G. (2018). Internationalization, Financial Performance, and Organizational Challenges: A Success Case in Portugal. In L. Carvalho (Ed.), *Handbook of Research on Entrepreneurial Ecosystems and Social Dynamics in a Globalized World* (pp. 379–423). Hershey, PA: IGI Global. doi:10.4018/978-1-5225-3525-6.ch017

Trad, A., & Kalpić, D. (2016). The E-Business Transformation Framework for E-Commerce Architecture-Modeling Projects. In I. Lee (Ed.), *Encyclopedia of E-Commerce Development, Implementation, and Management* (pp. 733–753). Hershey, PA: IGI Global. doi:10.4018/978-1-4666-9787-4.ch052

Trad, A., & Kalpić, D. (2016). The E-Business Transformation Framework for E-Commerce Control and Monitoring Pattern. In I. Lee (Ed.), *Encyclopedia of E-Commerce Development, Implementation, and Management* (pp. 754–777). Hershey, PA: IGI Global. doi:10.4018/978-1-4666-9787-4.ch053

Trad, A., & Kalpić, D. (2018). The Business Transformation Framework, Agile Project and Change Management. In M. Khosrow-Pour, D.B.A. (Ed.), Encyclopedia of Information Science and Technology, Fourth Edition (pp. 620-635). Hershey, PA: IGI Global. doi:10.4018/978-1-5225-2255-3.ch054

Trad, A., & Kalpić, D. (2018). The Business Transformation and Enterprise Architecture Framework: The Financial Engineering E-Risk Management and E-Law Integration. In B. Sergi, F. Fidanoski, M. Ziolo, & V. Naumovski (Eds.), *Regaining Global Stability After the Financial Crisis* (pp. 46–65). Hershey, PA: IGI Global. doi:10.4018/978-1-5225-4026-7.ch003

Turulja, L., & Bajgoric, N. (2018). Business Continuity and Information Systems: A Systematic Literature Review. In N. Bajgoric (Ed.), *Always-On Enterprise Information Systems for Modern Organizations* (pp. 60–87). Hershey, PA: IGI Global. doi:10.4018/978-1-5225-3704-5.ch004

van Wessel, R. M., de Vries, H. J., & Ribbers, P. M. (2016). Business Benefits through Company IT Standardization. In K. Jakobs (Ed.), *Effective Standardization Management in Corporate Settings* (pp. 34–53). Hershey, PA: IGI Global. doi:10.4018/978-1-4666-9737-9.ch003

Vargas-Hernández, J. G. (2017). Professional Integrity in Business Management Education. In N. Baporikar (Ed.), *Management Education for Global Leadership* (pp. 70–89). Hershey, PA: IGI Global. doi:10.4018/978-1-5225-1013-0.ch004

Vasista, T. G., & AlAbdullatif, A. M. (2017). Role of Electronic Customer Relationship Management in Demand Chain Management: A Predictive Analytic Approach. *International Journal of Information Systems and Supply Chain Management, 10*(1), 53–67. doi:10.4018/IJISSCM.2017010104

Vergidis, K. (2016). Rediscovering Business Processes: Definitions, Patterns, and Modelling Approaches. In P. Papajorgji, F. Pinet, A. Guimarães, & J. Papathanasiou (Eds.), *Automated Enterprise Systems for Maximizing Business Performance* (pp. 97–122). Hershey, PA: IGI Global. doi:10.4018/978-1-4666-8841-4.ch007

Vieru, D., & Bourdeau, S. (2017). Survival in the Digital Era: A Digital Competence-Based Multi-Case Study in the Canadian SME Clothing Industry. *International Journal of Social and Organizational Dynamics in IT, 6*(1), 17–34. doi:10.4018/IJSODIT.2017010102

Vijayan, G., & Kamarulzaman, N. H. (2017). An Introduction to Sustainable Supply Chain Management and Business Implications. In M. Khan, M. Hussain, & M. Ajmal (Eds.), *Green Supply Chain Management for Sustainable Business Practice* (pp. 27–50). Hershey, PA: IGI Global. doi:10.4018/978-1-5225-0635-5.ch002

Vlachvei, A., & Notta, O. (2017). Firm Competitiveness: Theories, Evidence, and Measurement. In A. Vlachvei, O. Notta, K. Karantininis, & N. Tsounis (Eds.), *Factors Affecting Firm Competitiveness and Performance in the Modern Business World* (pp. 1–42). Hershey, PA: IGI Global. doi:10.4018/978-1-5225-0843-4.ch001

von Rosing, M., Fullington, N., & Walker, J. (2016). Using the Business Ontology and Enterprise Standards to Transform Three Leading Organizations. *International Journal of Conceptual Structures and Smart Applications, 4*(1), 71–99. doi:10.4018/IJCSSA.2016010104

von Rosing, M., & von Scheel, H. (2016). Using the Business Ontology to Develop Enterprise Standards. *International Journal of Conceptual Structures and Smart Applications, 4*(1), 48–70. doi:10.4018/IJCSSA.2016010103

Walczak, S. (2016). Artificial Neural Networks and other AI Applications for Business Management Decision Support. *International Journal of Sociotechnology and Knowledge Development, 8*(4), 1–20. doi:10.4018/IJSKD.2016100101

Wamba, S. F., Akter, S., Kang, H., Bhattacharya, M., & Upal, M. (2016). The Primer of Social Media Analytics. *Journal of Organizational and End User Computing, 28*(2), 1–12. doi:10.4018/JOEUC.2016040101

Wang, C., Schofield, M., Li, X., & Ou, X. (2017). Do Chinese Students in Public and Private Higher Education Institutes Perform at Different Level in One of the Leadership Skills: Critical Thinking?: An Exploratory Comparison. In V. Wang (Ed.), *Encyclopedia of Strategic Leadership and Management* (pp. 160–181). Hershey, PA: IGI Global. doi:10.4018/978-1-5225-1049-9.ch013

Wang, F., Raisinghani, M. S., Mora, M., & Wang, X. (2016). Strategic E-Business Management through a Balanced Scored Card Approach. In I. Lee (Ed.), *Encyclopedia of E-Commerce Development, Implementation, and Management* (pp. 361–386). Hershey, PA: IGI Global. doi:10.4018/978-1-4666-9787-4.ch027

Wang, J. (2017). Multi-Agent based Production Management Decision System Modelling for the Textile Enterprise. *Journal of Global Information Management, 25*(4), 1–15. doi:10.4018/JGIM.2017100101

Wiedemann, A., & Gewald, H. (2017). Examining Cross-Domain Alignment: The Correlation of Business Strategy, IT Management, and IT Business Value. *International Journal of IT/Business Alignment and Governance, 8*(1), 17–31. doi:10.4018/IJITBAG.2017010102

Wolf, R., & Thiel, M. (2018). Advancing Global Business Ethics in China: Reducing Poverty Through Human and Social Welfare. In S. Hipsher (Ed.), *Examining the Private Sector's Role in Wealth Creation and Poverty Reduction* (pp. 67–84). Hershey, PA: IGI Global. doi:10.4018/978-1-5225-3117-3.ch004

Wu, J., Ding, F., Xu, M., Mo, Z., & Jin, A. (2016). Investigating the Determinants of Decision-Making on Adoption of Public Cloud Computing in E-government. *Journal of Global Information Management, 24*(3), 71–89. doi:10.4018/JGIM.2016070104

Xu, L., & de Vrieze, P. (2016). Building Situational Applications for Virtual Enterprises. In I. Lee (Ed.), *Encyclopedia of E-Commerce Development, Implementation, and Management* (pp. 715–724). Hershey, PA: IGI Global. doi:10.4018/978-1-4666-9787-4.ch050

Yablonsky, S. (2018). Innovation Platforms: Data and Analytics Platforms. In *Multi-Sided Platforms (MSPs) and Sharing Strategies in the Digital Economy: Emerging Research and Opportunities* (pp. 72–95). Hershey, PA: IGI Global. doi:10.4018/978-1-5225-5457-8.ch003

Yusoff, A., Ahmad, N. H., & Halim, H. A. (2017). Agropreneurship among Gen Y in Malaysia: The Role of Academic Institutions. In N. Ahmad, T. Ramayah, H. Halim, & S. Rahman (Eds.), *Handbook of Research on Small and Medium Enterprises in Developing Countries* (pp. 23–47). Hershey, PA: IGI Global. doi:10.4018/978-1-5225-2165-5.ch002

Zanin, F., Comuzzi, E., & Costantini, A. (2018). The Effect of Business Strategy and Stock Market Listing on the Use of Risk Assessment Tools. In *Management Control Systems in Complex Settings: Emerging Research and Opportunities* (pp. 145–168). Hershey, PA: IGI Global. doi:10.4018/978-1-5225-3987-2.ch007

Zgheib, P. W. (2017). Corporate Innovation and Intrapreneurship in the Middle East. In P. Zgheib (Ed.), *Entrepreneurship and Business Innovation in the Middle East* (pp. 37–56). Hershey, PA: IGI Global. doi:10.4018/978-1-5225-2066-5.ch003

About the Editors

Abraham Pius is a senior academic with extensive experience in teaching, developing and leading academics in professional and executive education programmes in business / hospitality management. Currently, working as a programme leader on business and hospitality management BA (Hons) Top Up programmes, accredited by the University of East London (UEL) for the LCCA. He works with Arden University, as undergraduate and postgraduate senior BL / DL lecturer where he delivers lectures and workshops for the BA (Hons) and Master of Business Administration (Online MBA) students. He has worked for the University International Telematic (UNINETTUNO) Italy, accredited programme in International Tourism, Hospitality and Event Management (MA), as a module leader and dissertation supervisor. He has international exposure having taught students from various nationalities and backgrounds across HNc to Masters' levels, which evidences his adaptability and multi-leveled skills needed to do well in UK contemporary higher education.

Husam H. Alharahsheh is an experienced senior academic with an extensive experience of teaching, supervision and research within higher education context. His higher education qualification at the undergraduate and postgraduate levels were focused on the fields of business management and higher education management. He is an active contributor to the development of process of wide range of higher education courses at the undergraduate and postgraduate levels in the fields of business, hospitality and education management. He has excellent experience in academic management and leadership within UK higher education institutions. He is also a visiting academic across various universities as well as other academic institutions based in the UK and abroad. His academic and professional experience is developed through working across a wide number of UK based higher education institutions within the public, private as well as not for profit sectors. He has developed links with external networks within the industry to maintain understanding of the key trends and challenges that can be proactively and reactively researched and implemented within curriculum. His contributions in UK and abroad are giving him the opportunity to have further global exposure and understanding of key trends within various sectors.

His key research interest are mainly in employability enhancement, internationalization, Globalization, sustainability, Education and enhancement of curriculum at various levels within higher education. His research is communicated nationally and internationally in the form of academic papers and books/book chapters published through highly reputable international academic journals and publishers. He is also actively contributing to enhancement of research quality published through acting as an executive editor of the Global Academic Journal of Economics and Business, associate editor of East African Journal of Economics, Business and Management, and Cross Current International Journal of Economics, Management and Media Studies. Furthermore, He has varied contributions to a wide number of international academic journals as a reviewer including but not limited to the Journal of Media Management and Entrepreneurship (JMME), International Journal of Responsible Leadership and Ethical Decision-Making (IJRLEDM), International Journal of Marketing and Sales Education (IJMSE), Saudi Journal of Business and Management Studies (SJBMS), International Journal of Teacher Education and Professional Development (IJTEPD), International Journal of Sustainable Entrepreneurship and Corporate Social Responsibility (IJSECSR), and International Journal of Tourism and Hospitality Management in the Digital Age (IJTHMDA).

Adenike A. Adesanmi (MSc, PhD Finance) is a finance expert with more than four years of teaching finance and accounting related courses. Adenike has worked in University of Westminster, University of East London (LCCA Top – up) and a couple of colleges. She is currently working as a Business Instructor at Oxford College of Canada in Toronto Ontario.

Index

K

M

N

P

Q

R

S

T

W

Purchase Print, E-Book, or Print + E-Book

IGI Global's reference books can now be purchased from three unique pricing formats: Print Only, E-Book Only, or Print + E-Book.
Shipping fees may apply.

www.igi-global.com

Recommended Reference Books

ISBN: 978-1-5225-6201-6
© 2019; 341 pp.
List Price: $345

ISBN: 978-1-5225-7262-6
© 2019; 360 pp.
List Price: $215

ISBN: 978-1-5225-8003-4
© 2019; 216 pp.
List Price: $205

ISBN: 978-1-5225-5763-0
© 2019; 304 pp.
List Price: $205

ISBN: 978-1-5225-6980-0
© 2019; 325 pp.
List Price: $235

ISBN: 978-1-5225-7808-6
© 2019; 397 pp.
List Price: $215

Looking for free content, product updates, news, and special offers?
Join IGI Global's mailing list today and start enjoying exclusive perks sent only to IGI Global members.
Add your name to the list at **www.igi-global.com/newsletters.**

Publisher of Peer-Reviewed, Timely, and Innovative Academic Research IGI Global DISSEMINATOR OF KNOWLEDGE

www.igi-global.com Sign up at www.igi-global.com/newsletters facebook.com/igiglobal twitter.com/igiglobal

Ensure Quality Research is Introduced to the Academic Community

Become an IGI Global Reviewer for Authored Book Projects

The overall success of an authored book project is dependent on quality and timely reviews.

In this competitive age of scholarly publishing, constructive and timely feedback significantly expedites the turnaround time of manuscripts from submission to acceptance, allowing the publication and discovery of forward-thinking research at a much more expeditious rate. Several IGI Global authored book projects are currently seeking highly-qualified experts in the field to fill vacancies on their respective editorial review boards:

Applications and Inquiries may be sent to:
development@igi-global.com

Applicants must have a doctorate (or an equivalent degree) as well as publishing and reviewing experience. Reviewers are asked to complete the open-ended evaluation questions with as much detail as possible in a timely, collegial, and constructive manner. All reviewers' tenures run for one-year terms on the editorial review boards and are expected to complete at least three reviews per term. Upon successful completion of this term, reviewers can be considered for an additional term.

If you have a colleague that may be interested in this opportunity, we encourage you to share this information with them.

eContent Pro International
PARTNERING
IGI Global

IGI Global Proudly Partners With eContent Pro International

Receive a 25% Discount on all Editorial Services

Editorial Services

IGI Global expects all final manuscripts submitted for publication to be in their final form. This means they must be reviewed, revised, and professionally copy edited prior to their final submission. Not only does this support with accelerating the publication process, but it also ensures that the highest quality scholarly work can be disseminated.

English Language Copy Editing

Let eContent Pro International's expert copy editors perform edits on your manuscript to resolve spelling, punctuaion, grammar, syntax, flow, formatting issues and more.

Scientific and Scholarly Editing

Allow colleagues in your research area to examine the content of your manuscript and provide you with valuable feedback and suggestions before submission.

Figure, Table, Chart & Equation Conversions

Do you have poor quality figures? Do you need visual elements in your manuscript created or converted? A design expert can help!

Translation

Need your documjent translated into English? eContent Pro International's expert translators are fluent in English and more than 40 different languages.

Hear What Your Colleagues are Saying About Editorial Services Supported by IGI Global

"The service was very fast, very thorough, and very helpful in ensuring our chapter meets the criteria and requirements of the book's editors. I was quite impressed and happy with your service."

– Prof. Tom Brinthaupt,
Middle Tennessee State University, USA

"I found the work actually spectacular. The editing, formatting, and other checks were very thorough. The turnaround time was great as well. I will definitely use eContent Pro in the future."

– Nickanor Amwata, Lecturer,
University of Kurdistan Hawler, Iraq

"I was impressed that it was done timely, and wherever the content was not clear for the reader, the paper was improved with better readability for the audience."

– Prof. James Chilembwe,
Mzuzu University, Malawi

Email: customerservice@econtentpro.com

www.igi-global.com/editorial-service-partners

IGI Global
DISSEMINATOR OF KNOWLEDGE
www.igi-global.com

Celebrating Over 30 Years of Scholarly Knowledge Creation & Dissemination

InfoSci®-Books

A Database of Over 5,300+ Reference Books Containing Over 100,000+ Chapters Focusing on Emerging Research

InfoSci®-Books Database

The **InfoSci®-Books** database is a collection of over 5,300+ IGI Global single and multi-volume reference books, handbooks of research, and encyclopedias, encompassing groundbreaking research from prominent experts worldwide that span over 350+ topics in 11 core subject areas including business, computer science, education, science and engineering, social sciences and more.

Open Access Fee Waiver (Offset Model) Initiative

For any library that invests in IGI Global's InfoSci-Journals and/or InfoSci-Books databases, IGI Global will match the library's investment with a fund of equal value to go toward **subsidizing the OA article processing charges (APCs) for their students, faculty, and staff** at that institution when their work is submitted and accepted under OA into an IGI Global journal.*

INFOSCI® PLATFORM FEATURES

- No DRM
- No Set-Up or Maintenance Fees
- A Guarantee of No More Than a 5% Annual Increase
- Full-Text HTML and PDF Viewing Options
- Downloadable MARC Records
- Unlimited Simultaneous Access
- COUNTER 5 Compliant Reports
- Formatted Citations With Ability to Export to RefWorks and EasyBib
- No Embargo of Content (Research is Available Months in Advance of the Print Release)

**The fund will be offered on an annual basis and expire at the end of the subscription period. The fund would renew as the subscription is renewed for each year thereafter. The open access fees will be waived after the student, faculty, or staff's paper has been vetted and accepted into an IGI Global journal and the fund can only be used toward publishing OA in an IGI Global journal. Libraries in developing countries will have the match on their investment doubled.*

To Learn More or To Purchase This Database:
www.igi-global.com/infosci-books
eresources@igi-global.com • Toll Free: 1-866-342-6657 ext. 100 • Phone: 717-533-8845 x100

IGI Global
DISSEMINATOR OF KNOWLEDGE
www.igi-global.com

IGI Global
DISSEMINATOR OF KNOWLEDGE
www.igi-global.com

Publisher of Peer-Reviewed, Timely, and Innovative Academic Research Since 1988

IGI Global's Transformative Open Access (OA) Model: How to Turn Your University Library's Database Acquisitions Into a Source of OA Funding

In response to the OA movement and well in advance of Plan S, IGI Global, early last year, unveiled their OA Fee Waiver (Offset Model) Initiative.

Under this initiative, librarians who invest in IGI Global's InfoSci-Books (5,300+ reference books) and/or InfoSci-Journals (185+ scholarly journals) databases will be able to subsidize their patron's OA article processing charges (APC) when their work is submitted and accepted (after the peer review process) into an IGI Global journal.*

How Does it Work?

1. When a library subscribes or perpetually purchases IGI Global's InfoSci-Databases including InfoSci-Books (5,300+ e-books), InfoSci-Journals (185+ e-journals), and/or their discipline/subject-focused subsets, IGI Global will match the library's investment with a fund of equal value to go toward subsidizing the OA article processing charges (APCs) for their patrons.

   Researchers: Be sure to recommend the InfoSci-Books and InfoSci-Journals to take advantage of this initiative.
2. When a student, faculty, or staff member submits a paper and it is accepted (following the peer review) into one of IGI Global's 185+ scholarly journals, the author will have the option to have their paper published under a traditional publishing model or as OA.
3. When the author chooses to have their paper published under OA, IGI Global will notify them of the OA Fee Waiver (Offset Model) Initiative. If the author decides they would like to take advantage of this initiative, IGI Global will deduct the US$ 1,500 APC from the created fund.
4. This fund will be offered on an annual basis and will renew as the subscription is renewed for each year thereafter. IGI Global will manage the fund and award the APC waivers unless the librarian has a preference as to how the funds should be managed.

Hear From the Experts on This Initiative:

"I'm very happy to have been able to make one of my recent research contributions, 'Visualizing the Social Media Conversations of a National Information Technology Professional Association' featured in the *International Journal of Human Capital and Information Technology Professionals*, freely available along with having access to the valuable resources found within IGI Global's InfoSci-Journals database."

– **Prof. Stuart Palmer,**
Deakin University, Australia

For More Information, Visit: www.igi-global.com/publish/contributor-resources/open-access or contact IGI Global's Database Team at eresources@igi-global.com

ARE YOU READY TO PUBLISH YOUR RESEARCH?

IGI Global
DISSEMINATOR OF KNOWLEDGE

IGI Global offers book authorship and editorship opportunities across 11 subject areas, including business, computer science, education, science and engineering, social sciences, and more!

Benefits of Publishing with IGI Global:

- Free, one-on-one editorial and promotional support.
- Expedited publishing timelines that can take your book from start to finish in less than one (1) year.
- Choose from a variety of formats including: Edited and Authored References, Handbooks of Research, Encyclopedias, and Research Insights.
- Utilize IGI Global's eEditorial Discovery® submission system in support of conducting the submission and blind review process.
- IGI Global maintains a strict adherence to ethical practices due in part to our full membership with the Committee on Publication Ethics (COPE).
- Indexing potential in prestigious indices such as Scopus®, Web of Science™, PsycINFO®, and ERIC – Education Resources Information Center.
- Ability to connect your ORCID iD to your IGI Global publications.
- Earn royalties on your publication as well as receive complimentary copies and exclusive discounts.

Get Started Today by Contacting the Acquisitions Department at:

acquisition@igi-global.com

www.igi-global.com/infosci-ondemand

InfoSci®-OnDemand

Continuously updated with new material on a weekly basis, InfoSci®-OnDemand offers the ability to search through thousands of quality full-text research papers. Users can narrow each search by identifying key topic areas of interest, then display a complete listing of relevant papers, and purchase materials specific to their research needs.

Comprehensive Service

- Over 125,000+ journal articles, book chapters, and case studies.
- All content is downloadable in PDF and HTML format and can be stored locally for future use.

No Subscription Fees

- One time fee of $37.50 per PDF download.

Instant Access

- Receive a download link immediately after order completion!

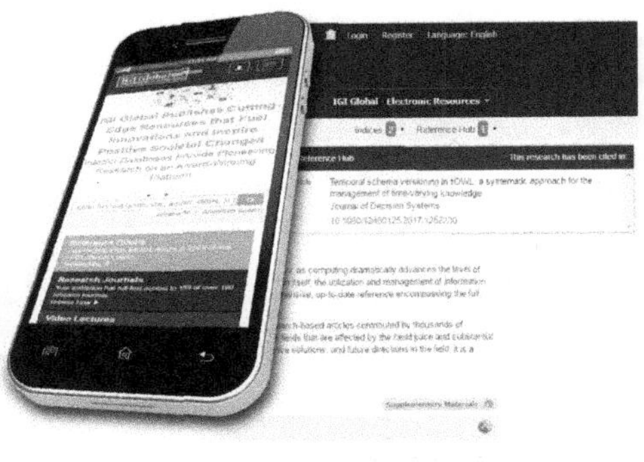

"It really provides an excellent entry into the research literature of the field. It presents a manageable number of highly relevant sources on topics of interest to a wide range of researchers. The sources are scholarly, but also accessible to 'practitioners'."

- Lisa Stimatz, MLS, University of North Carolina at Chapel Hill, USA

"It is an excellent and well designed database which will facilitate research, publication, and teaching. It is a very useful tool to have."

- George Ditsa, PhD, University of Wollongong, Australia

"I have accessed the database and find it to be a valuable tool to the IT/IS community. I found valuable articles meeting my search criteria 95% of the time."

- Prof. Lynda Louis, Xavier University of Louisiana, USA

Recommended for use by researchers who wish to immediately download PDFs of individual chapters or articles.

www.igi-global.com/e-resources/infosci-ondemand

IGI Global
DISSEMINATOR OF KNOWLEDGE
www.igi-global.com

www.ingramcontent.com/pod-product-compliance
Lightning Source LLC
LaVergne TN
LVHW061541290926
849162LV00004B/872